Diversity Consciousness

Opening Our Minds to People, Cultures, and Opportunities

Fourth Edition

Richard D. Bucher
Baltimore City Community College

With contributions from
Patricia L. Bucher

Boston   Columbus   Indianapolis   New York   San Francisco   Upper Saddle River
Amsterdam   Cape Town   Dubai   London   Madrid   Milan   Munich   Paris   Montreal   Toronto
Delhi   Mexico City   Sao Paulo   Sydney   Hong Kong   Seoul   Singapore   Taipei   Tokyo

Editor in Chief: Jodi McPherson
Acquisitions Editor: Katie Mahan
Editorial Assistant: Erin Carreiro
Senior Development Editor: Shannon Steed
Executive Marketing Manager: Amy Judd
Project Manager: Ron Hampton
Production Coordination: Electronic Publishing Services Inc., NYC
Composition: Aptara
Design Coordination: Heather Scott
Cover Design: Heather Scott
Cover Image: Faces of Diversity © Shutterstock

Text and Image Credits: Page 1: Haralduc/Shutterstock   Page 6: Jamille René Graves/Flickr/Getty Images; Westend61/Getty Images; Lianne Milton/Getty Images; Patricia Bucher   Page 8: "Profile in Diversity Consciousness" by Shannon Luders-Manuel from *Teaching Tolerance*. Copyright © 2013 by Teaching Tolerance, a project of the Southern Poverty Law Center. Used by permission of *Teaching Tolerance*, Southern Poverty Law Center.   Page 20: Courtesy of Eunice LaFate/Everyday Democracy   Page 23: By permission of Michael Ramirez and Creators Syndicate, Inc.   Page 44: Pearson Education, Inc.   Page 48: Patricia Bucher   Page 64: Used with permission from Archives of the History of American Psychology/University of Akron   Page 65: Courtesy of Cingular Wireless   Page 87: Patricia Bucher   Page 98: Pearson Education, Inc.   Page 107: From "Underneath We are All the Same" by Amy Maddox from Teaching Tolerance. Copyright © 2013 by Teaching Tolerance, a Project of the Southern Poverty Law Center. Used by permission of Teaching Tolerance, Southern Poverty Law Center.   Page 108: "African Eyes" by Laura Lee Gulledge. Copyright © by Laura Lee Gulledge. Used by permission of Laura Lee Gulledge.   Page 108: Courtesy of Laura Lee Gulledge   Page 111: Pearson Education, Inc.   Page 119: Courtesy of Semester at Sea and Institute for Shipboard Education   Page 127: Patricia Bucher   Page 128: Courtesy of the Office of Public Relations, Gallaudet University, Washington, DC   Page 131: Patricia Bucher   Page 134: Yuriko Nakao/Reuters   Page 143: Pearson Education, Inc.   Page 146: Pearson Education, Inc.   Page 155: From "Informal Social Networks and Career Advancement" from "The Micro-Politics of Gendering in Networking" by Yvonne Benschop from Gender, Work and Organization, 16(2), March 2009, pp. 217–237. Copyright 2009 by Yvonne Benschop. Published by Blackwell Publishing Ltd.   Page 158: tagxedo.com   Page 175: A. M. Ahad/AP Image   Page 181: Courtesy of Leilani Wheeler   Page 192: Mike Garland/Dorling Kindersley, Ltd.   Page 195: Courtesy of Sanjay Puri Architects   Page 198: Richard D. Bucher   Page 200: Courtesy of Office of Communications and Public Affairs, Johns Hopkins Medical Institutions, Baltimore, MD   Page 202: Gerry Gall/Courtesy of Colgate University   Page 204: Pearson Education, Inc.   Page 210: Marcin Balcerzak/Shutterstock   Page 218: iStockphoto/Thinkstock   Page 220: Patricia Bucher   Page 244: Jonathan Smith/Dorling Kindersley, Ltd. Page 249: Courtesy of Office of Communications, Colgate University, Hamilton, NY   Page 250: Courtesy of Pamela Zappardino/Ira and Mary Zepp Center for Nonviolence and Peace Education/Common Ground on the Hill, Ltd.   Page 251: PeacePlayers International Page   Page 251 (in margin): From the transcript of former President Bill Clinton's speech at the dedication ceremony for the William J. Clinton Presidential Library and Museum in Little Rock, Arkansas, on Thursday, November 18, 2004, 2:31 p.m.

Library of Congress Cataloging-in-Publication Data

Bucher, Richard D., Diversity consciousness : opening our minds to people, cultures, and opportunities/Richard D. Bucher. — Fourth edition.

pages cm

Includes bibliographical references and index.

ISBN 978-0-321-91906-9

1. Diversity in the workplace.   2. Multiculturalism.   I. Title.

HF5549.5.M5B83 2015

331.13'3—dc23   2013030234

10 9 8 7 6 5 4 3 2 1—CRK—16 15 14 13

pearsonhighered.com

ISBN-13: 978-0-321-91906-9
ISBN-10:   0-321-91906-8

About the Author

Richard Bucher, Ph.D. is an internationally recognized scholar, teacher, and author on the subject of diversity. He earned his doctorate from Howard University with a specialization in race and ethnic relations. Currently a professor at Baltimore City Community College (BCCC), he was honored as Maryland's Professor of the Year. Dr. Bucher is also the author of *Building Cultural Intelligence (CQ): Nine Megaskills* (Pearson).

Dedication

For my faith, family, friends, and students,
I am truly grateful and blessed.

Brief Contents

Contents

Preface

Diversity Consciousness is an outgrowth of my lifelong personal, educational, and professional experiences. As a student, I found diversity to be a fascinating subject. In college, I remember wrestling, both emotionally and intellectually, with issues involving race, ethnicity, gender, class, and many other dimensions of diversity. I attended Howard University, a historically Black institution, to pursue my doctorate degree in the area of sociology. Howard offered me a wonderful opportunity to specialize in the area of race and ethnic relations. As a white male, this experience radically altered my thinking about diversity.

My experiences as a college professor have also been invaluable. For more than three decades, I have taught students from a rich variety of cultures and socioeconomic backgrounds at Baltimore City Community College (BCCC). More than anything, this experience continues to show me how learning, achievement, and personal growth as well as professional growth, depend on our ability to engage each other and value diversity.

In addition to my teaching, I served as the first director of BCCC's Institute for InterCultural Understanding (IIU). Nationally recognized for its work in diversity education, the IIU nourished an inclusive, international learning community of students, faculty, staff, and community members. My work with the IIU makes me more aware of the difficulty and importance of making students as well as educators more conscious of diversity and its central place in a high-quality education.

Furthermore, my work on two major grants broadened and deepened my knowledge base. The first grant, "Integrating the Scholarship on Women into the Curriculum," allowed me to evaluate critically what I teach and how I teach. Also, as director of the IIU, I created and helped direct a Kellogg/Beacon grant titled, "Promoting Intercultural Understanding Among Maryland Community Colleges." The grant was a collaborative effort on the part of BCCC and a number of other community colleges.

Another extremely important dimension of my own diversity is my family life. I am the father of a son who has autism. My son, as well as the rest of my family, provide me with daily reminders of the joys and challenges of diversity. Jimmy enriches our lives, helps keep us grounded, and brings our family closer together. Because of Jimmy, my family and I see and experience life differently. When she applied to college, my daughter Katie was asked to write about someone who has had a profound influence on her life. She wrote about Jimmy. "Growing up with my autistic brother, I have discovered more and more about myself and other people. He has shown me that not everything wonderful seems wonderful at first sight. When you have someone so different that is so close to you, you develop an uncommon compassion for others."

The aim of this book is two-dimensional. First, it examines the relationship between a person's success and his or her ability to recognize, understand, and value diversity. Success, as defined in this book, means achieving your goals, whatever they may be. A second aim is to explore how people can develop diversity consciousness and specific diversity skills such as teamwork, conflict management, communication, social networking, and leadership.

Diversity Consciousness introduces a perspective that is often absent or marginalized in academic courses and workplace training. In many instances, diversity issues are dealt with superficially or treated as an afterthought. One common assumption is that people will learn about diversity "on the side" or "on their own." Unfortunately, we may interpret this to mean that diversity is not central to our education or our success. This interpretation is not borne out by research. These studies, cited throughout the book, reveal that a wide range of diversity skills can be developed and are absolutely essential to success in college, the workplace, and beyond.

Throughout *Diversity Consciousness*, I use different terminology to refer to certain groups of people. For instance, I use the term Black as well as African-American, and Latino/Latina as well as Hispanic. Using a variety of terms is one way to acknowledge that we do not all agree on the labels we attach to human differences.

Diversity Consciousness possesses seven key features that make it relevant, meaningful, and useful. This book is:

1. *Learner-Oriented.* It is infused with genuine anecdotes and perspectives that represent a broad range of diversity, serving as a sounding board for people from a wide variety of educational, social, and ethnic backgrounds. One distinguishing feature is the integration of real-life "perspectives" throughout each chapter. They provide a wealth of insight that we need to digest, reflect on, and share. As you read this book, you will recognize everyday struggles, stories, and achievements. For example, "running" case studies appear at the end of each chapter. Three individuals are followed throughout the book. After reading about their personal experiences dealing with complex issues and situations involving diversity, you are asked to analyze each specific case study.

2. *Success-Oriented.* More and more employers are realizing that diversity awareness and skills are crucial because they result in greater teamwork, creativity, productivity, and profit. Those who have a solid grounding in the area of diversity have more to offer their employers. Research shows that diversity is not some feel-good issue. Increasingly we realize that diversity consciousness—awareness, understanding, and skills in the area of diversity—relates strongly to individual, group, and organizational success.

3. *Focused on Personal Growth and Empowerment.* The book emphasizes the importance of educating oneself in the area of diversity. The process begins with one's own background and culture and then extends to others. In addition, the book views diversity education as a never-ending process rather than an event—a process that requires self-reflection and evaluation, patience, practice, and a strong commitment. Although education of this nature is hard work, it pays off regardless of who you are or where you come from.

4. *Grounded in Research.* A growing number of studies have examined the impact of education or training in the area of diversity. For example, research indicates that college students who are exposed to diversity issues are more apt to be culturally sensitive, satisfied with college life, and develop an array of cognitive skills. Similarly, a number of companies report that diversity education programs are making a measurable difference in worker creativity and productivity. These kinds of studies are important because they move us beyond anecdotal evidence. Research can help us evaluate the impact of educational strategies and specific diversity skills.

5. *Based on an Inclusive Definition of Diversity.* Rather than limiting diversity to gender, race, and ethnicity, *Diversity Consciousness* examines differences of all kinds, as well as their interrelationships.

6. *Oriented Toward the Value of Diversity.* Throughout our lives, many of us have been taught that diversity is a problem rather than a valuable resource. Traditionally, the focus has been on minimizing or denying differences rather than rethinking how we approach differences. To be successful, we need to develop a new kind of thinking that enables us to appreciate diversity and use it to benefit ourselves and others.

7. *Versatile.* This book is used extensively in both online and classroom courses, in workplace training and professional development programs, and in a variety of other venues both in the United States and abroad.

This work on human diversity integrates personal and organizational perspectives, research, and theories while discussing teamwork, communication, leadership, conflict, social networking, and other issues in the workplace, at school, and in the community. *Diversity Consciousness* empowers students by helping them develop a mindset which will enable them to be more successful in the 21st century.

New to This Edition

- **NEW! Now a 4-color interior design.** More appealing and accessible to readers.

- **NEW! Colorful and engaging infographics, tables, images, and photos throughout.** New visuals aid learning and support diverse learning styles.

Personalized Learning with MyStudentSuccessLab

NEW! MyStudentSuccessLab (www.mystudentsuccesslab.com) is a Learning Outcomes based technology that promotes student engagement through:

- Full Course Pre- and Post-Diagnostic test based on Bloom's Taxonomy linked to key learning objectives in each topic.

- Each individual topic in the Learning Path offers a Pre- and Post-Test dedicated to that topic, an Overview of objectives to build vocabulary and repetition, access to Video interviews to learn about key issues 'by students, for students', Practice exercises to improve class prep and learning, and Graded Activities to build critical thinking skills and develop problem-solving abilities.

- Student Resources include Finish Strong 247 YouTube videos, calculators, and Professionalism/Research & Writing/Student Success tools.

- Three Student Inventories are also available to increase self-awareness, and include Golden Personality (similar to Meyers-Briggs, gives insights on personal style), ACES (Academic Competence Evaluation Scales) (identifies at-risk), and Thinking Styles (shows how they make decisions).

Personal and Professional Relevance

- **NEW! Greater focus on more dimensions of diversity.** For example, there is greater coverage of issues that relate to social class and generational differences.

- **NEW! New examples and stories shared in "Another Perspective" feature.** Brief profiles, personal experiences, and relatable moments that connect students to new and different ways of understanding other perspectives and experiences.

- **NEW! Chapter 6 Social Networking,** including the multiple Learning Outcomes. Examines how social networking interrelates with diversity and diversity consciousness. In addition to looking at the social context of networking, this chapter provides insight into how we can diversify our online networks, and extend their reach and power.

- **REVISED and UPDATED! Chapter 9 Preparing for the Future,** focuses on inclusion and its relationship to diversity, inclusion in the workplace, the values and behaviors of Millennials, future challenges (Demographic shifts, Leveraging technology and global connections, Finding common ground, Continuing potential for divisiveness and hope), and future opportunities.

End-of-Chapter Applications

- **REVISED and UPDATED! End-of-chapter *case studies*.** Follows three individuals throughout the book. Requires students to assess each specific case, and familiarizes them with the complexities and nuances of issues and situations involving diversity.

- **REVISED and UPDATED! End-of-chapter *exercises*.** Includes experiential, online, and research-oriented activities.

References and Research

- **NEW! Fully updated and revised references and research.** Moves beyond anecdotal evidence by seamlessly integrating many research studies derived from real-life organizations and circumstances, as well as new data from the U.S. Census and Pew Research Center.

- **REVISED! Even more grounded in research that directly relates to success in the workplace.** Highlights the positive impact of education/training in the area of diversity, i.e., how students' ability to engage, understand, and discuss diversity issues helps make them more diversity conscious and productive on the job.

As you read the book, remember that it is designed to help you do more than just learn about diversity. Regardless of your feelings about diversity, try to approach the book with an open mind. Rather than simply taking in what you read, get involved and stretch yourself intellectually and emotionally. One way to do this is to respond to journal questions. Whenever you see ▧ or any time you feel a need to record something in writing, place an entry in your journal. Writing in a journal reinforces your learning, records your thoughts, and provides a basis for further reflection.

Try to open your thinking to different points of view. Take time to reflect on what you read and how it relates to you. Imagine how the world might be viewed by people who do not look, think, and act like you. Wrestle with the subject matter. If what you read makes you feel uncomfortable, that is okay. It is an inevitable part of the learning process. Finally, share your thoughts and feelings and learn to listen carefully and respectfully to others—even when it is difficult.

I welcome feedback from students, faculty, employees and employers, or anyone else who might read this book. You may e-mail me at rdbucher@aol.com; write to me at Baltimore City Community College, 2901 Liberty Heights Avenue, Baltimore, MD 21215, and access my Web site at diversityconsciousness.com. Also, you may keep in contact with me through my blog (http://www.diversityconsciousness.com/blog)

or connect through Facebook (https://www.facebook.com/diversityconsciousness) for relevant, current postings.

INSTRUCTOR RESOURCES

Online Instructor's Manual

This thoroughly revised and updated manual provides a framework of ideas and suggestions for online and classroom activities, journal writing, pedagogy, resources, and online implementation including MyStudentSuccessLab recommendations.

Online PowerPoint Presentation

A comprehensive set of PowerPoint slides can be used by instructors for class presentations and also by students for lecture preview or review. The revised PowerPoint presentation includes summary slides with overview information and infographics for each chapter. These slides help students understand and review concepts within each chapter.

ABOUT THE STUDENT EDITOR

My name is Tiana L. Davis. My initial perception of the world was shaped by growing up in a single-parent home in Baltimore, Maryland. As I began to participate in various community actions and volunteer projects, my views of the world started to change. I began to understand that the world should focus more on unity, less on elitism, classism, and hierarchy as it pertains to humanity. My college education involving the liberal arts has also shaped not only how I perceive the world but also how I perceive myself in it. I am currently a student at the University of Baltimore, majoring in Simulation and Digital Entertainment. My goal is to open a design firm that focuses on products geared towards young Black females.

ABOUT THE CONTRIBUTOR

Patricia L. Bucher is a graduate of Skidmore College and received her master's degree in mathematics education at McDaniel College. She has over 60 additional hours of graduate work in the areas of learning differences and behavior management. A former curriculum specialist and staff developer, she recently retired from teaching mathematics and computer science at Montgomery County Public Schools (MCPS). The student population of MCPS, located in suburban Washington, DC, is one of the most racially and ethnically diverse in the nation. MCPS serves more than 150,000 students speaking 138 different languages. Currently, Pat is an adjunct faculty member at Frederick Community College.

Pat is an experienced, highly innovative educator. She regularly presents workshops on diversity and cultural intelligence. She has also received local and national recognition for her teaching excellence. As a diversity consultant for the Maryland State Department of Education, she reviewed and revised an online algebra course in order to make it more inclusive.

After graduating from Skidmore College, Pat had a brief career as a music teacher, which included teaching children with severe developmental and behavioral problems. She soon found out that those years would prove invaluable to her after giving birth to her first child, Jimmy, who has autism and mild cerebral palsy. The next 14 years she spent at home teaching her own son whom many labeled as unteachable. Jimmy can now read, watch over his finances, and hold a job. Pat says, "Those years of trying to reach and teach my son taught me more about flexible thinking and creative pedagogy than any other experience of my life."

During that time, she also became a passionate advocate for children with developmental disabilities. Pat created a camp in Carroll County, Maryland, where none existed for children like her son, started a parent support group, and lobbied locally as well as nationally for better educational opportunities for children with disabilities. She was the recipient of the "Carnation Volunteer of the Year for Central Maryland."

A NOTE ABOUT THE INFOGRAPHICS

My wife, Patricia Bucher, is the creator of the new infographics in this revision. Her computer skills, creativity, and teaching expertise came together to create these visual representations of data. These engaging and relevant infographics serve as learning aids, bringing data "to life" and making it possible to more readily process complex information and see as well as interpret patterns and trends.

IN APPRECIATION

This book has been a true team effort, from its inception to the final product. Indeed, it "takes a village" to write and revise a book such as this. I am deeply indebted to so many people.

First, I want to thank all the students from many different educational institutions who have taught me so much and are such a big part of this book. In particular, I would like to acknowledge the valuable contributions of current and former students of mine at Baltimore City Community College (BCCC). I would be remiss if I did not mention my wonderful student editor, Tiana Davis of Baltimore City Community College and the University of Baltimore. She has "stretched me," and taught me a great deal about diversity by sharing her thoughts and life experiences. Her contributions to the fourth edition are significant.

In addition, the help of colleagues and friends has been invaluable. These people include numerous individuals at BCCC and those with whom I network. Particularly, I am indebted to Jim Lynch and Chikao Tsubaki. Furthermore, two mentors who continue to shape my thinking and fuel my passion are BCCC Professor Emeritus Walter Dean and the late Professor Emeritus of Religious Studies at McDaniel College, Dr. Ira Zepp.

My job is made that much easier by an extremely strong, supportive team at Pearson. Although I cannot name everyone, there are four people to whom I am especially indebted. They are Shannon Steed, Senior Development Editor; Katie Mahan, Acquisitions Editor; Ron Hampton, Project Manager; and Amy Judd, Executive Marketing Manager. Each of these individuals provided me with the encouragement, support, and guidance I needed, but also the freedom to explore and create. Their expertise, probing questions, suggestions, and exceptional listening skills bring out the best in me. Equally important, I enjoy working with each of them, and appreciate their genuine interest and concern for me and my life away from writing. Over the years, I have developed a close working relationship with a diverse team of individuals in Student Success and Career Development at Pearson.

This relationship is based on trust and a strong commitment to promote the value of diversity and inclusion in everything we do.

Alice Barr, Executive Sales Representative and Manuscript Consultant at Pearson, is someone who has been pivotal in my development as a writer. Before I gave serious consideration to writing a book, Alice and I got to know each other and our families, and our friendship has grown over the years. She encouraged me to try my hand at writing and she continues to provide me with advice and support whenever I reach out to her. My relationship with Sande Johnson, a former Executive Editor of mine at Pearson, made me a better writer. Sande has played a pivotal role in the success of *Diversity Consciousness*. I feel very fortunate that both Alice and Sande took such a personal interest in me.

For every edition, I have had the luxury of working with a very diverse and knowledgeable group of reviewers. Their input has been extremely helpful. The reviewers for the fourth edition include LaVonne Fox, University of North Dakota, and Nanci Howard, Coastal Carolina University.

A number of other people have also made significant contributions. As I researched and wrote the chapter on social networking, Tom Hessen and J. D. Douglas, both of whom have a strong background in technology and business, provided valuable insight. Additionally, I continue to correspond with a large number of educators, businesspersons, and leaders throughout the country. I cherish both their support and insight.

I would like to express my deep gratitude to members of my family. Every day they teach me something new and different about diversity. My son, Jimmy, and my daughters, Katie and Suzy, help me laugh at myself and keep my priorities in order. My mother, who is now living in the Ithaca, New York area, and my late father, a teacher as well as a prolific writer, as well as my sisters and brother, provided me with my first lessons in valuing diversity.

Finally, my wife, Pat, has been the person who has supported me the most. While revising this book, I have continually asked questions of her. Somehow she always finds the time to help, whether it is providing another perspective, helping me with a computer question, creating thought-provoking images, or pushing me to probe deeper. Without Pat's help, this book and this revision would never have been written.

Richard D. Bucher

1

Diversity: An Overview

Learning Outcomes

Upon completion of this chapter, you will be able to:

- Analyze significant changes in the cultural landscape of the United States.
- Differentiate among people's reactions to the changing cultural landscape.
- Contrast assimilation and pluralism.
- Elaborate on various dimensions of diversity.
- Give examples of diversity within and among groups.
- Critique the diversity myths.
- Explain diversity consciousness.
- Elaborate on diversity education.

"There never were in the world two opinions alike, no more than two hairs or two grains; the most universal quality is diversity."

—Michel de Montaigne[1]

MyStudentSuccessLab

MyStudentSuccessLab (www.mystudentsuccesslab.com) is an online solution designed to help you 'Start Strong, Finish Stronger' by building skills for ongoing personal and professional development.

In recent years, the term diversity has grown in use. The term regularly appears in the popular media, professional magazines, trade books, and scholarly literature. Nevertheless, there is no single, agreed upon definition of diversity. To some it means tolerance, acceptance, or perhaps an attitude. To others, diversity may mean racial and gender differences. Still others see diversity as a code word for affirmative action or laws designed to ensure representation of minority groups.

Unlike affirmative action, diversity is not a legal concept. Nor does it include only some people. *Diversity* is defined in the dictionary as "a state of unlikeness" or "the condition of being different." Because we are all different, diversity includes everyone. In this book, **diversity** refers to all of the ways in which people are different. This includes individual, group, and cultural differences. Our ability to recognize, understand, and adapt to these differences is a major focus of *Diversity Consciousness*.

OUR CHANGING CULTURAL LANDSCAPE

Traditionally, the concept of diversity is most often used in relation to culture. **Culture** refers to our way of life, including everything that is learned, shared, and transmitted from one generation to the next. Although culture endures over time, it is not static. Language, values, rules, beliefs, and even the material things we create are all part of one's culture.

Culture's influence on us is profound. As we internalize culture throughout our lives, it influences who we are, what we think, how we behave, and how we evaluate our surroundings. For example, culture shapes the way we communicate, view work, interpret conflict, define and solve problems, and resolve dilemmas. Culture, which Hofstede describes as a collective programming of the mind that reveals itself in symbols, values, and rituals, is often so embedded in us that we may be unaware of its influence.[2]

Landscape means a scene or a setting. When we talk about **cultural landscape**, we are referring to the different lifestyles, traditions, and perspectives that can be found in the United States and throughout the world. The cultural landscape that surrounds us is both fluid and complex. Increasing our awareness and understanding of a variety of cultural landscapes enables us to appreciate why interacting with people with different "collective programming" can be such a challenge.

The ancient Greek philosopher Heraclitus said, "You cannot step into the same river twice." If we were to rephrase Heraclitus using modern-day terminology, we might simply say that "change is constant." Certainly, this applies to the cultural landscape that surrounds us. For instance, each time we interact with coworkers, customers, or clients, no matter how familiar the situation, it is never exactly the same. People and their cultures change incessantly, from moment to moment.

As individuals, each day we are more experienced and knowledgeable than we were the day before. Similarly, culture is ever changing. Languages, values, religious beliefs, and customs rub up against each other, dominate and accommodate, blend together, and evolve into new hybrids. Consider just a few of the ways in which the cultural landscape is changing.

- *Languages.* Languages transmit and preserve culture. Of the estimated 7,000 languages spoken throughout the world, one becomes extinct every two weeks. The state of Oklahoma is one of the areas of the world in which languages are disappearing fastest. Many of these languages are spoken by Native American tribes (National Geographic, Living Tongues Institute for Endangered Languages). To Dr. Mary Linn, a linguist from the University of Oklahoma, "Every language is a huge library. And once that disappears, we really cannot get it back."[3]

- *Work/Life Issues.* Work schedules are becoming more flexible as mothers and fathers look to balance their careers with child-raising responsibilities. As employees attach greater importance to flexibility, the traditional career path is being rewritten. Work/life policies, including paid and unpaid time off, dependents' care, flextime, and telecommuting, are becoming increasingly important considerations for working men and women.

- *Surnames.* Data from a new analysis by the Census Bureau show that the most common surnames in the United States have changed in recent times. Six Hispanic surnames are found among the top twenty-five, and four—Garcia, Rodriguez, Martinez, and Hernandez—are among the top fifteen (see Table 1.1). According to several demographers, this is in all likelihood the first time that non-Anglo names are among the most common in the United States.[4]

Top Fifteen Surnames in the United States

Surname	Number of Occurrences
SMITH	2,376,206
JOHNSON	1,857,160
WILLIAMS	1,534,042
BROWN	1,380,145
JONES	1,362,755
MILLER	1,127,803
DAVIS	1,072,335
GARCIA	858,289
RODRIGUEZ	804,240
WILSON	783,051
MARTINEZ	775,072
ANDERSON	762,394
TAYLOR	720,370
THOMAS	710,696
HERNANDEZ	706,372

Table 1.1 Top Fifteen Surnames in the United States.
Source: Population Division, U.S. Census Bureau.

- *Generational Issues.* Different generations, which have been shaped by different life experiences, are characterized as having divergent values, priorities, communication styles, and leadership styles. While differences do exist, such as the reliance of **Millennials** (born from about 1980 to 2000) on technology, they are not absolute and uniform. Generational differences tend to vary depending on one's cultural background and upbringing. For instance, there are subcultural and demographic differences within each generation. As we communicate and interact, we need to take into account possible differences and similarities. One business leader, for example, advocates using different channels of communication to reach multiple generations. In doing this, we recognize that "the same message delivered through four or five or six types of media will reach different parts of your organization and different generations in different ways."[5]

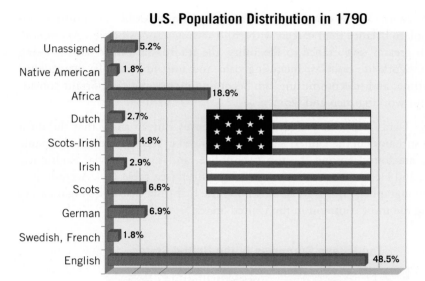

Figure 1.1 U.S. Population Distribution in 1790.
Source: U.S. Bureau of the Census, Historical Statistics of the United States, Part II, Series Z, 20–132, U.S. Government Printing Office, 1976.

Demographic Changes in the United States

Diversity is not a new phenomenon. If we look back at the first U.S. Census in 1790, we see some interesting differences and similarities with today's society. The first U.S. census revealed our rural character. Only 3 percent of the population lived in settlements of 8,000 or more.[6] In 1790, almost one of five residents (about 19 percent) was African-American (see Fig. 1.1). It is interesting to note the cultural diversity among Whites at that time. About 75 percent of the White population was White Anglo-Saxon Protestant (English, Scots, Scots-Irish); 25 percent were mainly Dutch, French, German, Irish, and Swedish.[7] These statistics show that early inhabitants of this country were not monocultural. Rather, their cultural differences were significant.

Since 1790, the cultural landscape of the United States has continued to change. We are no longer a rural society. Slightly more than 80 percent of our population lives in urban areas.[8] Our racial and ethnic mix has a different look as well (see Fig. 1.2).

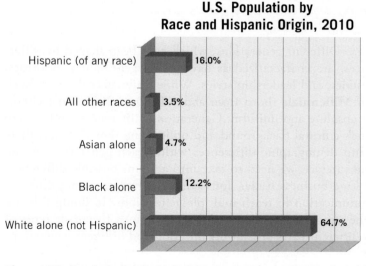

Figure 1.2 Population of the United States, by Race and Hispanic Origin, 2010.
Source: Population Division, U.S. Census Bureau.

The percentage of African-Americans, or Blacks, has declined from approximately 19 percent in 1790 to approximately 13 percent today. Asians have steadily increased in numbers since they were first counted in the 1860 Census. Data from the most recent census show that Asians and Pacific Islanders as well as Hispanics are the two fastest growing minority populations in the United States. Since 2000, Hispanics have accounted for more than half of the total population growth in the United States. Note that the term *Hispanic* or *Latino* refers to a cultural attribute, rather than race or a specific country of origin.

The rapid growth in U.S. minority populations is being fueled by immigration. And for the first time, a majority of babies born in the United States are racial and ethnic minorities. William Frey, a well-known demographer with the Brookings Institution, comments on the changing cultural landscape: "We are pivoting from a white–black dominated American population to one that is multiracial and multicultural."[9] The impact of immigration, according to essayist Richard Rodriguez, can be seen in the number of people who come to this country speaking a language other than English. For example, he observes, "Because of the massive migration of Latin Americans northward, the United States has become the fifth-largest Spanish-speaking country in the world, after Mexico, Spain, Argentina, and Colombia."[10]

In comparison to Asians and Hispanics, the growth rate among non-Hispanic Whites was significantly less in recent years. This continues a trend. Whites made up approximately 90 percent of the U.S. population in 1940. Based on census estimates for the year 2050, the percentage of Whites who are not Hispanic (Hispanics can be of any race) will shrink noticeably to just under 50 percent.

Census data must be interpreted cautiously. Different groupings have been used since the first census. In 1870, for instance, the terms *quadroon* (a fourth Black, or having one Black grandparent) and *octoroon* (an eighth Black, or having one Black great-grandparent) were used to indicate the exact amount of a person's Black heritage.

In recent years, racial categories have been added and an increasing number of people have chosen to identify themselves as "other." Many people do not feel that they belong in a single category, and others do not want to be categorized at all. An employee who refuses to select any category explains, "I'm not White, I'm not Black, and I sure don't want to be an '*other*.'"

A number of authors have written autobiographical accounts describing experiences in which they cope and adjust to fitting no single racial category. Examples include *The Color of Water: A Black Man's Tribute to His White Mother* by James McBride, and *Black, White, and Jewish: Autobiography of a Shifting Self* by Rebecca Walker. In *What Are You? Voices of Mixed-Race Young People*, Pearl Fuyo Gaskins shares poetry, essays, and portions of interviews of some 45 mixed-race youth. She organizes her chapters around a variety of themes such as "The Color of My Skin Is Not the Color of My Heart," "Roots: Random Thoughts on Random Hair," and "Are You Dating Me or My Hair?"

For three years, Kip Fulbeck, an artist, filmmaker, and professor, conducted an artistic survey of Hapas. The term *hapa*, as defined in his book *part asian –100% hapa*, is slang for "mixed racial heritage with partial roots in Asian and/or Pacific Islander ancestry." Traveling the United States, Fulbeck interviewed hundreds of Hapas of varying ages and genders. He asked each of them the same question; a question Fulbeck says he has been asked every day of his life. *What are you?*[11] This question, and others like it, reveal varying levels of discomfort with people who do not seem to conform to our oversimplified and antiquated perceptions of race. Likewise, intrusive questions of this nature can make members of the mixed-race community feel devalued and stigmatized (see Photo 1.2).

Photo 1.2 Have you been asked...?

The racial options of the 2000 Census were modified to accommodate those who want to express their multiracial heritage. For the first time, respondents could identify themselves as members of more than one racial category. Also, a separate question about ethnicity appeared before race. Figure 1.3 shows other major changes.

In the 2010 U.S. Census, 9 million Americans, or roughly 3 percent, identified themselves as members of more than one race. Many demographers expect this figure to increase dramatically by 2050. Evidence for this can be found in the growing number of young people who identify themselves as multiracial. U.S. Census officials maintain that the major reason for this response is the significant increase in the number of interracial couples. According to Paul Taylor of Pew Research Center,

Don't Box Me In

An increasing number of people are resisting the pressure to be boxed in by color. Tiger Woods, for example, has made it known that he objects to being called African-American. Rather he prefers "Cablinasian," a term he made up that combines his Caucasian, Black, Indian, and Asian ancestry. Other well-known people who have affirmed their mixed ancestry are Keanu Reeves (Hawaiian, Chinese, Caucasian), Mariah Carey (Black, Venezuelan, Caucasian), and Johnny Depp (Cherokee, Caucasian). Groups such as the Multiracial and Biracial Student Association at the University of Maryland are becoming more common on college campuses. This trend will likely continue as interracial marriages become more common and society becomes more comfortable with different and new ways of defining one's heritage.

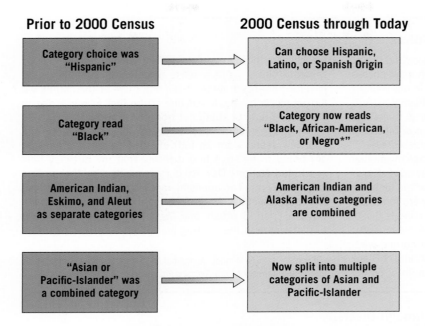

Prior to 2000 Census   **2000 Census through Today**

Category choice was "Hispanic"	→ Can choose Hispanic, Latino, or Spanish Origin
Category read "Black"	→ Category now reads "Black, African-American, or Negro*"
American Indian, Eskimo, and Aleut as separate categories	→ American Indian and Alaska Native categories are combined
"Asian or Pacific-Islander" was a combined category	→ Now split into multiple categories of Asian and Pacific-Islander

Figure 1.3 U.S. Census Changes: Race and Hispanic Origin. *The Census Bureau recently announced it will no longer include the term "Negro" to describe Black/African-Americans in its population surveys.
Source: U.S. Census Bureau. More detailed information concerning the new racial categories is available on the U.S. Census Bureau Web site (http://www.census.gov).

"Interracial marriage has gone from taboo to a rarity, and with each passing year, it's less of a rarity."[12]

Latinos, who can be of any race, often find it difficult to relate to the rigid racial categories found in the census. Clara Rodríguez, author of *Changing Race: Latinos, the Census, and the History of Ethnicity in the United States,* points out analysts often misinterpret what this means. Analysts mistakenly assume Latinos are confused, says the author, when in fact they see themselves as stretching across racial lines.[13]

I was born in 1959 and I was "Black." I did not challenge forms when I was younger, because I did not realize then how important the information those forms requested would become to me. If the form asked me to check "Negro," I did. I don't remember there being racial categories other than Black/Negro or White.

As I grew older and learned through family conversation that there was another culture that was part of me, I began a hesitant journey of uncovering who I am as a complete person. This began with acknowledgment that my Native American heritage is as important to me as being Black. My first acknowledgment of my racial completeness was to check "other." Checking "other" was one of the most difficult things I have ever done. With that act came extreme guilt at the thought of abandoning my given culture and race.

I soon discovered that the guilt came from a sense of having banished myself to neutrality. "Other" meant recognizing no race at all. I went back to checking "Black," which once again made me comfortable but incomplete. I have now settled on checking both "Native American" and "Black."

—Another perspective

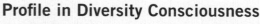

Profile in Diversity Consciousness

"There is often a divide, as we know, between Black and White. For those of us in the middle, we often feel we must choose one side of this divide or the other, especially in our younger years. For me, growing up identifying predominantly as African-American in a White family gave me a sense that I was interminably an outsider. My family loved me unconditionally, but it was hard to love myself with the same unbiased eyes.

I felt this most acutely during sixth grade when my mother and I moved to a more diverse, and more racially divided, part of town. African-American eighth graders teased me for being so light-skinned, while my best friend and I were forbidden to continue our friendship because her white parents disapproved of my dark skin and of my cousins' Japanese ancestry.

A few years ago I was standing at a street corner, waiting for the walk signal, when a White woman and a Black man came up beside me with their young daughter on her bicycle. In those moments before we continued on our separate paths, I felt a sense of completeness like I had never experienced before. Standing there at the corner, we looked like a family. It was one of the first moments in my life when I did not stand out from the crowd.

My struggle for identity has pretty well ceased within the past few years. I am an individual of complex origin and am proud to be so. I find it fitting that my birthday falls on United Nations Day. By default of identity, those of us who incorporate two opposing races do much to bring those two races together. As an American with African, German, English, Irish, Scottish, and Mexican heritage, I am proud to participate in the melting pot that is America."

—Shannon Luders-Manuel, as quoted in *Teaching Tolerance* magazine (permission to reprint from *Teaching Tolerance*, http://www.tolerance.org).

Thinking Through Diversity

Would you describe yourself as multiracial, or do you see yourself as belonging to a single race? Why?

It is clear that our nation's schools and workforce will feel the effects of growing diversity for some time. Demographic data indicate that:

- Women, minorities, and older people will continue to account for the vast majority of new entries in the workforce (see Fig. 1.4). Sociologically speaking, the term **minorities** refers to categories of people whose members are singled out and denied equal power and opportunity in the larger society. This definition places the emphasis on power rather than numbers. For instance, even though women constitute a numeric majority in the United States, they lack political, economic, and social power relative to men and therefore constitute a minority. With regard to minorities, immigration and population changes will alter workforce demographics for years to come. As more women are added to the labor force, their share will approach that of men. Employment projections for 2050 show that women will comprise nearly half of the U.S. labor force. The new elders, as they become even healthier and better educated, are more likely to continue working rather than fully retiring. Finally, the percentage of workers with disabilities is expected to increase because of a number of factors. The workplace is becoming more accessible due to the protection afforded by the Americans with Disabilities Act and the removal of both attitudinal and physical barriers. Recent census data point to future growth in the number of employed people with physical and mental disabilities.

- Students at all levels of education will continue to grow increasingly diverse. One indication of this trend is the dramatic upsurge in the number of K–12 public school students who are members of racial and ethnic minorities. Likewise, the number of ELL (English Language Learner) students has increased dramatically, accounting for more than 10 percent of students enrolled in U.S. public schools.[14] Data from the U.S. Department of Education reveal a similar pattern among college students, who have become increasingly diversified in terms of their race, ethnicity, gender, and age.[15]

- The international student population in the United States is growing. The Institute of International Education estimates that there are now more than 700,000 international students in the United States.[16] Most of these students come from

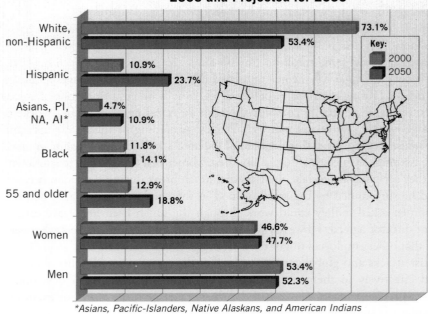

**U.S. Workforce Demographics:
2000 and Projected for 2050**

White, non-Hispanic: 73.1%, 53.4%
Hispanic: 10.9%, 23.7%
Asians, PI, NA, AI*: 4.7%, 10.9%
Black: 11.8%, 14.1%
55 and older: 12.9%, 18.8%
Women: 46.6%, 47.7%
Men: 53.4%, 52.3%

Key: 2000, 2050

Asians, Pacific-Islanders, Native Alaskans, and American Indians

Figure 1.4 U.S. Workforce Demographics: 2000 and Projected for 2050.
*Sources: Bureau of Labor Statistics, Current Population Survey Annual Averages.
Projections: M. Toossi, "A New Look at Long-Term Labor Force Projections to 2050,"
Monthly Labor Review, November 2006, 19–39.*

Asian and Latin American countries. In addition, more U.S. students than ever are now studying abroad.

Technological and Social Changes

A number of social and technological changes have also altered the cultural landscape in recent years.

Globalization and Technology

In *The World Is Flat*, Thomas Friedman emphasizes how **globalization**, the growing interdependence of people and cultures, has accelerated in the twenty-first century. Globalization is impacting individuals of every conceivable color and culture. To use Friedman's terminology, the world is being flattened in all kinds of ways. For example, there is no such thing as an "American job" in a flat world. Factors such as immigration, the speed and ease of modern transportation, outsourcing, environmental changes, and the globalization of markets and technology contribute to this trend.

Technological advances have transformed our social world into what Marshall McLuhan termed a *global village*.[17] In other words, increasingly we need to think of the entire world when we talk about our social environment. Computers, satellites, and communication technology have brought the world closer together and made cross-cultural encounters an everyday occurrence.

The emergence of the global economy, immigration, and the growing diversity of the U.S. population are transforming the business arena. For example, U.S. companies are creating more multilingual Web sites to expand their market, improve sales, and remain competitive. Dress codes are being revised to include headwear and other articles of clothing required by various religions. Companies are providing consumers with a greater array of products that reflect their diverse lifestyles and tastes. With an increase in white-collar service jobs, companies are paying more attention to cross-cultural interaction among workers and between workers and customers.

The impact of globalization has been particularly noticeable in the hotel and restaurant business. A case in point is a Hilton hotel in Washington, D.C., where workers speak 36 languages and some speak no English at all. To communicate with his staff, the hotel's general manager has memos translated into five different languages and read aloud to workers. During meetings, supervisors rely heavily on gesturing, tone of voice, and the written word to clarify complex thoughts to non-English-speaking workers. And language is only one of the many challenges. According to the hotel's assistant director of housekeeping, a growing segment of the hotel's workforce is Muslim women. During the Islamic holy month of Ramadan, these women fast from sunup to sundown. However, they are reluctant to take their normal lunch break during Ramadan because they would be surrounded by the smell of food in the employee cafeteria. When the Muslim women asked if they could work through the lunch hour and leave earlier, the assistant director agreed. However, she later heard from fellow managers who were concerned that other employees might take advantage of the situation.

Terrorist attacks and global conflict, as well as the economic and political efforts to respond effectively to them, underscore the growing importance of developing a **global perspective**, meaning a view of the world and our place in it. For example, the government is stepping up its efforts to address current and projected shortages of employees with foreign language skills. Agencies such as the U.S. Army, the FBI, the State Department, and the Commerce Department are in dire need of language specialists with expertise in Arabic, Mandarin and Cantonese Chinese, Indonesian, Japanese, Korean, Farsi, Russian, Turkish, and other languages.

For each of us, developing a clearer, more encompassing view of the world around us is absolutely necessary. By doing so, we:

1. *Develop greater insight into our interconnectedness.* Technology, commerce across national borders, as well as immigration and emigration have linked the United States with the rest of the world like never before. The loss of human life on 9/11 was not just an American tragedy; it was felt worldwide (see Fig. 1.5). People from more than 60 countries were victims of the World Trade Center disaster. Figures provided by individual governments, or the U.S. Department of State, show the number of victims from countries such as Pakistan (200), India (250), Australia (55), El Salvador (71), Austria (15), and Nigeria (94 reported missing by Nigerian press; no official number).[18]

2. *Expand our awareness of different perspectives.* Without a global perspective, we are more likely to assume that our way of doing things is universal. This is particularly true of those aspects of our culture that are not readily visible to us. Consider how we view time. Do we view time as a precious resource that should not be wasted? What do we assume about someone who is late to an appointment to finish a conversation with a friend? Perhaps we have always lived in a culture where being on time and meeting deadlines are extremely important. Consequently, we make all sorts of judgments about people on the basis of their promptness. However, what if we find ourselves in a culture that does not share our time orientation? For example, different time perspectives can be viewed along a continuum, extending from a monochronic to a polychronic time orientation.[19] *Polychronic* time means people engage in multiple activities within a certain time frame and plans are subject to change, especially if they interfere with personal commitments. This cultural preference is at odds with *monochronic* time, in which people follow a strict schedule and focus on one activity or project at a time. Whereas the United States, Canada, and many

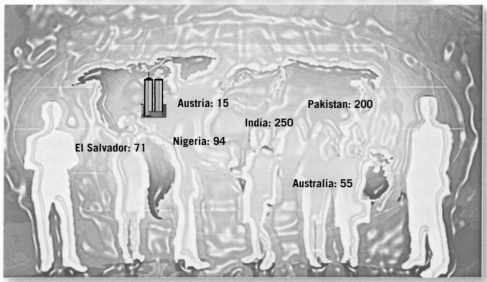

Figure 1.5 World Trade Center Tragedy: Victims Worldwide.

Western cultures tend to be predominantly monochronic, countries in the Middle East and Latin America are more polychronic.

3. *Enhance our self-awareness.* When we visit another country, we may complain about a wide variety of things such as the food, odors, standards of cleanliness, dress, and the way people converse. Uncomfortable experiences in strange lands can teach us about ourselves. By examining how we react and adjust to these experiences, we learn more about the ways in which cultural experiences shape our thinking and behavior. Furthermore, we become more aware of just how difficult it is to change culturally ingrained habits, no matter how insignificant they may seem.

Expanding our global perspective is not easy. Keeping up with world news each day does not begin to fill the void. A college president recently told the story of a visiting professor from Australia who spent a semester in the United States. During that time, he did not see a single news story or commentary about *his* country, except for a shootout with a madman.[20]

Heightened Awareness of Diversity

Stories about diversity appear in the news each day. These stories deal with such issues as discrimination in the workplace, cultural conflict, global education, and religious as well as language differences. On 9/11, many of these issues captured the public's attention in an instant. People in the United States suddenly became much more aware of their own vulnerability and cultural isolation, as well as the growing importance of world economies, world geography, communications networks, migration, cultural values and traditions, and religious diversity.

The effects of 9/11 remain with us. Workplace complaints filed by Muslims have increased significantly since the 2001 attacks. According to a recent survey by the Pew Research Center, more than one-third of respondents report having an unfavorable view of Islam. At the same time, a majority of respondents report knowing "not very much" or "nothing at all" about the Muslim religion. This same survey shows that as people become more knowledgeable about Islam and develop relationships with individuals who happen to be Muslim, the more positive their views of Muslims in general.[21] Since 9/11, in an effort to promote awareness of their cultural practices and religion, Muslim groups

> I am a citizen, not of Athens or Greece, but of the world.
> —Socrates

have become much more active in presenting educational programs to police, hospital workers, teachers and students, therapists, corporations, and community groups.

As the world continues to shrink, global competition and cooperation are pushing diversity issues into the forefront of the workplace. As Friedman acknowledges in *The World Is Flat*, economic change and culture are interdependent. Economic performance hinges to a great degree on *glocalization*, a culture's openness to diverse influences and ability to blend foreign ideas and best practices with one's own traditions. Although Friedman discusses **glocalization** as a cultural trait, this type of openness can be developed by individuals as well. In a flatter world, cultural isolation, intolerance, and an inability to communicate with others and value their contributions will put us at an economic disadvantage. From Friedman's perspective, a constantly changing global environment will be hardest on those who are not prepared, both culturally and technologically. Similarly, a heightened awareness of diversity coupled with a new skill set will empower us to take advantage of the staggering opportunities afforded by this new landscape.

Scholarship on the subject of diversity has mushroomed in recent years. Diversity itself has become a thriving industry. Books, Web sites, diversity consultants, courses, workshops, and conferences have proliferated as more and more money is spent in this area. Pride in our cultural roots is championed by popular music, movies, ethnic festivals, and cultural exhibits. As diversity has become more visible in everyday life, it is more apt to become an issue that we address, discuss, and debate publicly and privately. For instance, the election of President Obama in 2008, and his re-election in 2012, generated considerable discussions on many issues, such as race, ethnicity, religion, sexual orientation, and the ability of candidates to reach out to diverse constituencies.

Continued Cultural Separation in the Midst of Diversity

Although some parts of our cultural landscape are becoming more diverse, other parts show little of this change. Sociologists refer to this as **cultural lag**, a condition in which one part of a culture is not keeping pace with another part. This lag or gap becomes increasingly evident when we look at where we live, worship, go to school, and work. Consider the following examples.

1. While residential segregation has declined in many areas, U.S. residents continue to live in neighborhoods that are divided along racial, ethnic, and economic lines. Rich and poor are increasingly unlikely to live in the same neighborhoods and attend the same schools. Neighborhood diversity is uneven. In some neighborhoods, white flight continues. But in other areas, there has been a significant upturn in *global neighborhoods*, communities where large varieties of people from diverse cultures and ethnicities live together.

2. To a large degree, gender segregation exists in the job market. In some cases, jobs are overwhelmingly held by either men or women, such as the male-dominated fields of engineering and coal mining and the preponderance of women found in nursing and textile manufacturing. Within occupations in general, gender segregation can also be found at different levels of the organizational hierarchy. For example, the U.S. Labor Department's Federal Glass Ceiling Commission reported that the upper levels of big business remain mostly White and mostly male.[22]

   According to the Commission, the **glass ceiling**—attitudes and actions that block the promotion of women and minorities into top management positions—was firmly in place. More recent studies show some incremental progress, although barriers remain.[23]

 Thinking Through Diversity

Have you or any member of your family ever encountered a glass ceiling? Explain.

These barriers include informal networks that exclude women, pervasive stereotypes of women as weak and soft, and a lack of women role models in leadership positions. Fortunately, the track record of Fortune 500 companies shows that improving opportunities for women in top executive positions is not only a moral issue but a market-based issue.

3. Martin Luther King once referred to the weekly worship service as the most segregated hour of the week. Despite a trend toward more integrated neighborhoods, especially in some suburbs, racial segregation remains firmly in place at many religious services, as evidenced by recent data from a nationwide poll by the *New York Times*. Ninety percent of Whites who attend religious services at least once a month said that none or only a few of their fellow congregants were Black. Similarly, 73 percent of Blacks said that almost all of their fellow congregants were Black.[24]

4. Although the percentage of students of color in U.S. public schools is increasing significantly, racial diversification among teachers has not kept pace. Data show a widening demographic mismatch between students and their teachers (see Fig. 1.6). Furthermore, future U.S. census projections leave little doubt that this gap will continue for some time.

5. Recently, there has been a resurgence of intergroup hostility and intolerance. This is not simply the work of a select few. When we think of intolerance, how many of us visualize a member of the Ku Klux Klan (KKK) or a skinhead? Unfortunately, intolerance can also come dressed in a three-piece suit, a military uniform, or more casual wear. Schools, places of worship, and job sites have witnessed an upsurge in hate crimes during the past few years. Hate literature, graffiti, symbols of hate such as nooses, threatening e-mail and phone calls, property damage, and physical violence point to a continuing cultural lag between the diversity we encounter and our ability to respect or at least tolerate that diversity.

People react differently to the changes that continue to transform our cultural landscape. Some adapt while others resist or remain oblivious. In a way, it is a lot like the growing importance of computer technology. We may adjust and learn more because we know that if we do not become computer literate, our chances for success will be severely limited. The same holds true for diversity. Whether we realize it or not, diversity touches each of us on a daily basis. If we are not in a position to capitalize on diversity, we will be at a disadvantage socially and economically.

> The real voyage of discovery consists not in seeking new landscapes but in having new eyes.
> —Marcel Proust

Demographic Profiles of U.S. Public Schools: Students and Their Teachers

Key:
- Students
- Teachers

Other — 8% / 4%
Black — 16% / 7%
Hispanic — 24% / 6%
White, Non-Hispanic — 53% / 84%

Figure 1.6 Public School Students and Teachers: A Growing Racial and Ethnic Gap. *Source: National Center for Education Information.*[25]

A RANGE OF REACTIONS

As individuals, how do we react to our changing cultural landscape? Reactions may vary depending on our awareness of others and ourselves, our comfort level with the situation at hand, and our ability to transform understanding into action. Furthermore, our reactions may show a range of competencies, from being unaware of the landscape and fixated on ourselves and our world, to being able to shift gears and easily adjust to a multitude of individual and situational factors.

 Thinking Through Diversity

As you read the following scenarios that represent a range of reactions (Cultural Cruise Control, Beginning Adjustments, and Fine Tuning), with whom do you most identify? Why?

Cultural Cruise Control

When we shift into **cultural cruise control**, we act as though our own values, beliefs, and experiences are universal. When we find ourselves in this mode of thinking and acting, we are oblivious to different cultural cues and individual perspectives. We simply adhere to our own cultural rules. Our self-awareness is minimal or nonexistent. If we acknowledge differences, we tend to view them as important for other people in other settings.

Although cruise control makes interacting with others easier for us, it also leads to misunderstandings, conflict, and lost opportunities. The following real-life scenarios illustrate some of the pitfalls that are inherent in simply using our own culture to guide our actions.

Good Teachers, So Why Change?

A teacher who grew up in a small New Jersey town talks about his students with coworkers. "In my hometown, my neighbors were people with a Polish heritage just like me. My dad was a blue-collar worker. My family didn't have much and what we did have, we worked hard for.

My best friend went to high school and college with me. His family was pretty much the same as mine. We got teaching jobs together in a suburb. When we started out, the students in the school were a lot like we were as kids. We got to be really good teachers.

Then the neighborhood started to change and we were having more and more Black kids in our school—then Hispanics. And a lot of the neighborhood apartments began to fill up with families that were much poorer than the students we were used to. Both of us knew what it was to struggle, and we had a few Black friends in college, so we didn't think this was any big deal. We were really good teachers—so why change? After all, we've both always treated all our students the same.

Now administrators want us to change the way we teach these poor minorities. They say the way we teach doesn't work for these students. We need to go to workshops and learn new methods. We were poor once. Nobody changed the way they taught for us. We just worked hard. And look where we are. I'm not changing anything. These kids can learn from me if they want to bad enough. They've just got to learn how to work."

A Rabbi Shops at Walmart

After making some selections at Walmart, the shopper brings his items to the checkout. When his total was announced, he proceeds to pay for the items by placing money on the counter directly in front of the cashier, who picks up the cash and makes change. She holds the change out for the shopper. Not looking up to see the cashier, the shopper taps on the counter to indicate he is waiting for his change. Once she realizes the shopper is refusing to take money from her hand, the cashier grows angry, utters a profanity, and slams the money on the counter. A friend of the shopper then asks to speak with the cashier. After ten minutes of heated conversation, the cashier replies, "Y'all gotta learn how to act right if y'all gonna say you're God's chosen people, especially them Rabbis."

The friend had explained to the cashier that Talmudic Law forbids most physical contact between a male and females other than direct relatives. The shopper, a Rabbi, follows an ultra-conservative form of Judaism. The passing of items from one sex to another and most eye contact between the sexes is forbidden. Furthermore, exchanging money is done with minimal discourse.

I have a one-track, one-culture mind, and I thought it was normal.

—Another perspective

Beginning Adjustments

As we unlock cruise control, we learn to adjust or shift gears. We move beyond the "I don't see differences" mindset. This can be a slow, arduous, nonlinear process. For example, as we begin to uncover differences and recognize their relevance, we may find ourselves stereotyping people or pushing them all into a box that does not represent who they really are. Depending on the situation, we may revert back to cruise control. And as we explore and become more open to diversity and all of its nuances, we may become more aware of just how superficial our understanding is. But with the necessary motivation, we learn to adjust our thinking and behaviors. Such is the case with the following three scenarios.

"Yes" at the Help Desk

Leonard works at a help desk. He and other coworkers assist staff employed by the U.S. Department of Justice. These staff members, who track time sheets for entire offices, input the time into a system. When they encounter technical problems, they call the help desk.

One woman of Asian descent repeatedly calls and is extremely difficult to understand. Her English is not proficient and her accent is very noticeable. She also has a lot of trouble understanding Leonard, as a recent call reveals. When she tries to explain her question to him, he responds, thinking he understands what she was asking. As Leonard continues to offer his explanation, she seemingly affirms with "uh huhs" and "yes." Leonard then asks her, "Does that make sense?" and there is silence.

By shifting perspectives and actively listening, Leonard realizes that his client's affirmations are not affirmations in the sense that she understands what Leonard is saying. Rather, his client is simply affirming that she hears him. However, these conversations, which happen repeatedly, leave Leonard feeling extremely frustrated, confused, and helpless. Soon thereafter, Leonard asks a coworker for advice and does some research on his own. He becomes more aware of what "yes" might mean in different cultures, and he develops some communication techniques to ensure understanding. For example, Leonard tries to check whether he is making himself clear by asking his client to explain certain things back to him. But Leonard still finds it difficult to talk with this client, especially at the end of a long workday.

An Airport Security Guard's Encounter

At Heathrow Airport in London, a 20-something woman is traveling with a middle-aged woman. They go through the security check process. The younger passenger has a carry-on and a large pocketbook. As they go through security, the guard abruptly tells her she cannot pass through security with two bags because airport regulations stipulate only one carry-on. At this point, the passenger tucks her chin toward her chest and clasps her hands behind her head. She starts to cry out loudly, "No, I can't do this. No, I can't do this. I just want to go home." Soon, she starts to cry.

The security guard's response is immediate. He stares at her disapprovingly, shakes his head, and rebukes her. He says, "You need to get yourself under control. Save your tantrums for somewhere else." Another passenger in line then catches the guard's eye and says, "Sir, that young lady has problems you and I don't have." The guard stops what he is doing, pauses thoughtfully, and responds "I'm sorry." By this time, the distressed young woman has left with her companion. For the guard, this is a learning experience, something to reflect upon throughout the day, and reconsider the next time he is tempted to react without thinking.

The passenger who had spoken sensed the young women was "different" rather than just acting spoiled or trying to bring attention to herself. Why did she feel this way? She attributed her response to years of teaching in a public school setting where mainstreaming is commonplace. As a teacher, she often has classes in which a student with special needs exhibits unusually inappropriate behaviors. When this happens, other students tend to react by being loud and critical. After the student in question is removed from class by a professional, the teacher talks to the students saying, "That student is dealing with problems you and I don't have."

Stereotyping at the Office of Child Support

Tamara, an employee who works at the Office of Child Support Enforcement in a large city on the West Coast, recounts one of her many interactions with people who collect public assistance. Tamara assists customers from different cultural backgrounds and income brackets who need assistance, mostly from fathers who will not willingly subsidize their children's care. Often, when customers inquire about their child support case via phone or in person, employees are prone to stereotype.

For example, if a coworker hears a television show such as *The Price Is Right* in the background during a call, Tamara might hear a comment such as, "The customer needs to get off her bottom and get a job." On the other hand, people who are thought to be working parents receive more respect. If a call comes in from someone who is whispering, this is seen as an indication that the customer is at his or her workplace and wants to be discreet when inquiring about child support.

Although Tamara hears and even jokingly voices these stereotypes at times, she manages to treat her customers as individuals, or at least so she thought. She clearly remembers one woman who arrived at her office desperately seeking assistance. The young woman, who was articulate and well dressed, told Tamara she was a graduate of a nearby university. When Tamara finally accessed her case, she was taken aback by the fact that this woman had five children by three different men and was currently receiving welfare. Tamara began to ponder how she herself would react if she hit "rock bottom."

Tamara knew her job well, but her perceptions were limiting her ability to meet customers' needs. How many other times had she unknowingly made false assumptions? The magnitude of the difference between her initial perception of this customer and reality made Tamara reevaluate her entire way of thinking. Since that day, Tamara is much more mindful of how she views and treats each person she interviews.

Thinking Through Diversity

Describe a life experience in which you were in cultural cruise control. Then describe another experience in which you were engaged in beginning adjustments or fine tuning. Compare these two experiences.

Fine Tuning

As we survey the landscape, shift gears, reevaluate, and then fine-tune our thinking and behaviors, we become more comfortable in the midst of diversity. This happens over time, as the following scenario illustrates.

Improving an Online Tutorial

In a suburban school district in southern Florida, Web developers are in the process of creating an online tutorial for teenagers to help them in math. The team, working with materials given to them by a number of math teachers, is constructing math word problems. Mindful of the diversity of the students who will be using the tutorial, their problems include some racially and ethnically diverse names and pictures. Moreover, the math problems revolve around what the developers consider to be interesting and engaging everyday life experiences for adolescents. These include:

- Renting bicycles on vacation

- Taking a "road trip"

- Getting a summer job at the beach

- Saving to buy computer games

Before making this new resource available to students, one member of the team suggests hiring a diversity consultant to review it. After some debate about whether this is necessary, the team hires a consultant who has an extensive background in both Web design and diversity.

In her report to the team of Web developers, the consultant comments on the (lack of) inclusiveness of the problem sets. She writes, "Minority students, especially those who are economically disadvantaged, often find they have to constantly step outside of their culture or relate to experiences outside their daily lives. For many students, so-called real-life examples such as these are not something they experience. Of course, all of us feel that way on occasion, but for these students it is more likely to be an everyday, ongoing experience that contributes to their feelings of alienation toward school."

According to the consultant, middle- and upper-class students are more likely to identify with the experiences just listed. For many disadvantaged students, these experiences are outside their realm, both economically and socially. For example, taking a "road trip" is a concept that might be completely unrealistic because it requires leisure time and money. The same applies to renting a bike while on vacation. And many of these students have no computer at home, much less their own personal computer.

With the consultant's help, the team begins to shift their thinking. Using multicultural names and images is a good start, but for all students to feel that this resource is designed for them, it needs to be more inclusive in terms of the cultural context of the problems. If the context of life experiences is varied, all students will need to sometimes step out of their cultural environment. Furthermore, all students will know their lives and lifestyles are important enough to be included.

With this awareness and knowledge, the team begins to examine math problems from a wider range of perspectives. Suggestions regarding possible scenarios include:

- Renting carpet cleaning equipment for a relative or neighbor

- Traveling to visit relatives

- Saving money for items that are more affordable, such as a pay-as-you-go cell phone

- Getting a job at the local mall

As the Web developers become more sensitive to diversity and its implications for student success, they gradually become more able to critique their own work. A greater variety of names, such as Carlos, Tran, Kashif, Shakisha, and Jorge, appear in word problems. Instead of a young white boy animation at the end of each and every lesson, the animation figure is now more abstract and inclusive. Although there are still too many math problems that are set in an upper-class White context, the team is aware of this bias and is systematically revising the tutorial with input from teachers and students alike.

Regardless of our competencies in the area of diversity, we will make mistakes, often unknowingly. What we learn from these mistakes allows us to move beyond cruise control and continue making adjustments.

VIEWS OF DIVERSITY: ASSIMILATION AND PLURALISM

Throughout our nation's history, our diversity has been described as a *melting pot*, *tossed salad*, *rainbow*, *quilt*, and *kaleidoscope*. These images illustrate the fact that we are different. Our differences, and the way we view them, change constantly.

In the early twentieth century, a Jewish immigrant named Israel Zangwill offered this description of the United States in his book *The Melting Pot*: "There she lies, the great melting pot—listen! Can't you hear the roaring and the bubbling? There gapes her mouth—the harbour where a thousand mammoth feeders come from the ends of the world to pour in their human freight. Ah, what a stirring and a seething—Celt and Latin, Slav and Teuton, Greek and Syrian, Black and Yellow … Jew and Gentile."[26]

According to Zangwill, European immigrants would gradually lose their traditional ways of life and blend together. A new mixed culture would emerge from this process. This is commonly referred to as **assimilation**, the process in which people lose their cultural differences and blend into the wider society. International students as well as those born and raised in the United States sometimes sense their culture slipping away. They have many ways to deal with the pressure to assimilate. Some see it as inevitable and desirable. Others see it as something to avoid at all costs. Still others find themselves assimilating, but not completely. As one student put it, "I do it up to a point, as long as it does not rob me of my identity."

Assimilation may have negative as well as positive consequences for immigrants or society in general. For instance, it can mean learning good or bad habits or values. Research has shown that sometimes students who work the hardest and show the most respect tend to be the most recent immigrants. To some immigrants, negative

What Is an American?

How would you define the term *American*? For some, the term applies solely to those living in the United States. Others maintain that those who inhabit any of the countries in North, Central, or South America are Americans. Still others feel that the term has a racial connotation. Toni Morrison, in her book *Playing in the Dark*, observes:

"…deep within the word 'American' is its association with race…. American means white."[29]

A student of color sums up her feelings this way: "Being an American is a phrase way down on my list of descriptive words. America has caused me to describe myself in a lot of ways—Black, woman, minority. The word *American* is not part of that list. I wish I could feel a part of this country. But every day I am quickly reminded that I am not an American but a nuisance."

Work is a perfect example of how I assimilate my identity so that I feel comfortable. If changing the way I dress and act makes me feel more accepted on the job, then that's what I want to do.

My personal background provides me with a very strong belief that I am to be who I am. I think my Jewish background as well as my mother's influence help me deal with assimilation. I know who I am, as far as race, culture, and personality. And I know that I'm not changing for anyone. Therefore, when the idea of assimilation is presented in any way to me, I instinctively decline.

In America, everyone at some point and time will be forced to assimilate themselves with another culture or group. Being a young Black male, assimilation is probably the most frequently used pattern of interaction in my life. In my neighborhood, especially with my circle of friends, it is a cardinal sin to assimilate with the White culture. We see ourselves as the shunned group. At every possible opportunity, we thumb our collective noses at White society. By learning the "rules of the game" a long time ago, I know that assimilating with the majority society is a must. When forced to assimilate, I just separate my two worlds. I'm always going to be Black with Black sentiments and I'll never compromise that for anything. However, I will play by the rules dictated, at least to an extent, to further myself and my people.

—Other perspectives

influences are a constant concern. They see their children taking on negative values that create tensions within families. One 32-year-old mother from Mexico worries about her children: "In the Hispanic tradition, the family comes first, not money. It's important for our children not to be influenced too much by the 'gueros,'" a term she uses to refer to "blondies" or Americans.[27]

Other studies have found that some immigrants consciously choose when and where to assimilate. In *Accommodation Without Assimilation*, anthropologist Margaret Gibson shares findings from her study of Asian-Indian students in a city in the Sacramento Valley of California. She discovered that the students did well in school, often outperforming their Euro-American peers, by following the advice of their immigrant parents. The Asian-Indian students were told to follow rules and regulations at school and adopt only "desirable" aspects of Euro-American behavior rather than assimilate completely.[28]

Do you feel that you are an American? What does 'American' mean to you? What does an American look like? In his book *A Different Mirror: A History of Multicultural America*, Ronald Takaki describes a personal experience while riding in a taxi in Norfolk, Virginia. The driver, who looked to be in his 40s, asked Takaki how long he had been in the United States. He replied that he had been born in the United States. He further explained that his family came here from Japan more than 100 years ago. The driver's assumption was that Takaki didn't really "look" American.[30]

Why do people make this kind of assumption? According to Takaki, schools have to accept at least part of the blame. He argues that from kindergarten to college, teachers and textbooks cultivate a narrow view of U.S. history. Typically, the experiences of African-Americans, Hispanics, Native Americans, and Asian-Americans have been ignored. In addition to schools, our upbringing can influence our thinking. A college student elaborates: "The way I was brought up was to think that everybody who was the same as me were 'Americans,' and the other people were of 'such and such descent.'"[31]

Many now question whether the model of the melting pot fits our society. They argue that people want to be accepted for who they are. A growing number of people are

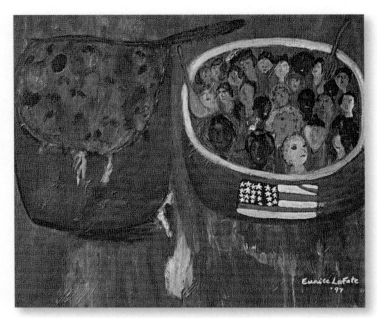

Photo 1.3 The Melting Pot vs. The Salad Bowl.
Source: "The Melting Pot vs. The Salad Bowl" by Eunice LaFate for Everyday Democracy, formerly the Study Circles Resource Center, info@everyday-democracy.org.

unwilling to give up what makes them distinctive, even for only a certain period of time each day. When they go to work or school, they do not want to leave their culture at home. They feel that, like the ingredients in a salad or the colors of a rainbow, differences can coexist and complement each other (see Photo 1.3).

Pluralism is a process through which cultural differences are acknowledged and preserved. By way of illustration, advocates of multicultural education argue that the study of U.S. history should be more pluralistic. History should reflect the distinctive cultural experiences of all people. According to this perspective, courses in history often ignore the experiences, perspectives, and contributions of women or people of color. Those who share this opinion argue that if history courses were truly inclusive, there would be no need for a Black History Month or a Women's History Month.

Whether pluralism is positive is subject to debate. Those who oppose pluralism argue that it promotes tension and conflict at a time when we need to ignore our differences and come together as one, much as we have done in the face of natural disasters, mass killings, and threats to our national security. Proponents of pluralism maintain that cultural diversity is a national resource that we should preserve. Furthermore, they maintain that when people preserve their cultural identity, including language, religion, and customs, it can be a source of pride and motivation.

I think it is important to hold on to one's culture; it is a means of guidance. For instance, my great grand-dad was born in Cameroon in a place called Douala. In Douala, the people were said to be very wise. The story went on to say a bird used to fly around them trying to get their knowledge; and this bird actually was a human being. So they used to hide their knowledge by wearing a hat. I still do this. For me, it's fun, but it reminds me of where I am from. It reminds me I am supposed to be a wise man.

—Another perspective

DIMENSIONS OF DIVERSITY

Dimensions of diversity refer to specific traits viewed as distinguishing one person or group from another. Race, gender, and ethnicity are three examples. **Race** refers to a category of people who are *perceived* as physically distinctive on the basis of certain traits, such as skin color, hair texture, and facial features. Notice that what makes this group distinctive is our perception of differences. The concept of race is discussed later in more detail.

Whereas race relates to physical differences, ethnicity focuses on cultural distinctiveness. **Ethnicity** is defined as the consciousness of a cultural heritage shared with other people. **Gender** has to do with the cultural differences that distinguish males from females. For instance, in any given culture, people raise males and females to act certain ways. Do not confuse the term *gender* with *sex*. Sex refers to biological differences, such as hormones and anatomy.

Social Class Differences in the United States

Social class refers to one's status in society. In the United States, status is usually determined by a variety of social and economic criteria, including wealth, power, and prestige. Even though social class influences where we work, live, and go to school, its importance is addressed infrequently. Perhaps class distinctions are downplayed or ignored because we are uncomfortable, psychologically speaking, acknowledging the tremendous inequality that exists in the larger society. Moreover, the concept of social class is fuzzy and inconsistent. For example, how would we classify other students or employees with whom we interact? *Lower, middle,* and *upper class* mean different things to different people.

A groundbreaking study of social class was undertaken by Barbara Ehrenreich, a well-known author who has written extensively about women and poverty. She decided to assume a secret identity as a waitress to research the ramifications of changing her social class. In *Nickel and Dimed: On (Not) Getting By in America*, Ehrenreich discusses her life as a waitress, working 10-hour shifts for $2.43 an hour plus tips. She worked in Florida, Maine, and Minnesota. With her Rent-A-Wreck car and a laptop, her goal was to earn enough money for basic necessities and to pay rent.

She soon discovered that she needed additional income to keep her afloat, so she took second jobs as a motel housekeeper, professional maid, nursing home dietary aide, and Walmart employee. To Ehrenreich, the experience was mentally as well as physically challenging. She says, "I wasn't prepared for how mentally challenging this was going to be. I mean intellectually challenging. I knew I was going to have to work hard and I was afraid it was physically maybe too much for me. Actually, I did fine physically—though I don't know how fine it would have been after many months. But here I am with a Ph.D. in biology and I was struggling to master all these things that were being thrown at me."[32] Ehrenreich recounts how her coworkers roomed together in hotels, slept in cars, and medicated themselves because they had no money for doctor visits. As a result of her research, she became much more aware of the separate, distinct worlds of the haves and have-nots in U.S. society.

Thinking Through Diversity

If you were to determine people's social class, what criteria would you use and why?

Social class, another dimension of diversity, is a complex subject. However, as Julio Alves points out, even if "the definition of class evades us . . . the consequences certainly don't."[33] Clearly, grasping the significance of social class in all of our lives is fundamental to our awareness and understanding of differences among individuals, groups, and societies.

When we talk about dimensions of diversity, factors such as social class, sexual orientation, religion, personality type, learning style, communication style, and family background are typically overlooked, yet some people may perceive these and other dimensions to be more important than race or gender. When I conduct workshops and ask participants what makes them unique, their answers reflect a very inclusive view of diversity (see Fig. 1.7).

The meaning of the term *diversity* is expanding continually. The late Roosevelt Thomas, a pioneer in the field of corporate diversity, made this point in his book *Beyond Race and Gender*. He defines diversity in a way that includes everyone. According to Thomas, workforce diversity is not something that is simply defined by race or gender. Rather, it encompasses a variety of other dimensions, such as age, personal and corporate background, education, job function and position, geographic origin, lifestyle, and sexual orientation.[34] To this list we can add ancestry, national origin, creed, religion, social class, leadership style, personality type, family background, marital status, military background, and disability status. The list goes on and on. In short, it includes whatever we think distinguishes us.

As you read about diversity and, in particular, various dimensions of diversity, keep these points in mind.

1. *Dimensions of diversity may be hidden or visible.* Diversity is not only skin deep. According to one theory, diversity is like a cultural iceberg. Only about 10 percent of it is

Figure 1.7 Who Am I? Participants in a diversity awareness workshop wrote down four things that describe each of them. Some of their descriptors appear in this figure.

visible. To illustrate, most dimensions mentioned by the workshop participants alluded to earlier (see Figure 1.7: Who Am I?) are not readily apparent. For example, we would not know that someone was a descendant of slaveholders, vegetarian, or born-again Christian unless the person chose to share this with us.

2. *Dimensions of diversity are found within groups as well as within individuals.* Certain dimensions, such as abilities, talents, and interests, vary from person to person. Likewise, everyone seen as belonging to a group may not identify with the group, or they may identify with different group characteristics. Differences within a group are often ignored when we distinguish between groups. Diversity within groups is addressed later in this chapter.

3. *Dimensions of diversity are in a constant state of flux.* In different situations, we see ourselves and are seen by others differently. In some situations, a student might want to be seen as a Muslim female. In another situation, she might simply want to be viewed as a student.

4. *Dimensions of diversity are not always clear cut or easily defined.* Diversity means different things to different people. A good example is the term *race*. Even though we talk about race as if it can be biologically defined, there is no scientific way to distinguish people based solely on their skin color, hair texture, shape or color

Master Status

People are often identified and distinguished by their **master statuses**, positions that stand out in the eyes of society and hide one's individuality. Ask yourself, what is the first thing that people see when they look at you? Is it your race, gender, age, disability, or some other master status? Perhaps, acquaintances notice, first and foremost, our religion, our failing health due to a serious illness, or our lack of a job. When we view people in terms of their master status, we assume one label or one aspect of their identity is much more important than any other. In *The Nature of Prejudice*, Gordon Allport describes a master status as the "label of primary potency."

How we may view transgender persons illustrates the problematic nature of master statuses. **Transgender** does not imply sexual orientation; rather, it refers to a category of people who identify with a gender that is different than the sex they were assigned at birth. When transgender takes the form of a master status, it can lead to false and potentially harmful assumptions. For instance, we might assume that the

life experiences of transgender persons necessarily relates to their gender. If a transgender teenager lives a very isolated life, our thinking might erroneously establish gender identity as the reason why. Perhaps an older, Native American transgender person encounters discrimination when he applies for a position at a clothing store. Our immediate reaction might be that gender identity is behind this unequal treatment, when in reality, discrimination of this nature might be due to this individual's age, ethnicity, and/or some other factor.

All of us identify with numerous statuses, groups, roles, and labels. How we see ourselves may not align with how others see us. Moreover, the salience of different identities may vary from situation to situation, or society to society. Knowing one or two things about someone, whether it is their status as a transgender person, their socioeconomic status, or some other aspect of who they are, provides us with an incomplete picture. Consequently, it is important to look beyond master statuses in order to better appreciate and value what is really important to individuals.

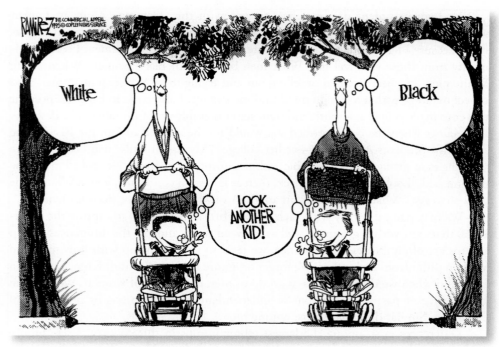

Figure 1.8 Race is Socially Defined.
Source: By permission of Michael Ramirez and Creators Syndicate, Inc.

of their eyes, or any other physical trait. Racial mixing has blurred the boundaries among races. Skin color, for example, is a common but unreliable indicator
of race. There are Whites who are more dark skinned than some Blacks. Many
Hispanics have dark skin but do not consider themselves Black. Anthropologist
Ashley Montagu addressed this issue in his book *Man's Most Dangerous Myth: The
Fallacy of Race.* According to Montagu, the term *race* has no scientific basis and
cannot be applied to real life.[35] There is almost total agreement among scientists
today that race is arbitrarily and socially defined. Yet it is important because we
make it important, and we model its importance for children (see Fig. 1.8).

5. *Dimensions of diversity interrelate.* For example, a recent Pew Research Center
   survey shows the interrelationship of race and social class. Many African-American respondents in this survey see a widening gap between the values of middle
   class and poor Blacks. Specifically, less than a quarter (23 percent) say that middle
   class and poor Blacks share "a lot" of values in common. In this survey, **values**
   refer to things that people view as important or their general way of thinking.[36]

In summary, diversity is multidimensional. Various dimensions may be hidden or
visible. Moreover, they may or may not have anything to do with race or gender.

DIVERSITY BETWEEN AND WITHIN GROUPS

The United States is home to one of the most culturally diverse populations in the
world. Nevertheless, we often ignore or gloss over these differences. When we focus
our attention on race, we may think in terms of Blacks and Whites or sometimes
Asians and Whites. Our societies, and even our communities, are described as biracial
rather than multiracial. This can be particularly uncomfortable and offensive to those
who are constantly stereotyped or left out of the picture.

An Iranian student describes her struggle with this dilemma: "I am an Iranian woman, one who can't pass as White because I'm too dark, but certainly can't pass as Black because I have Middle-Eastern features…. When I date Black men, I receive animosity from those who feel that Black men belong with Black women. When I date White men, I've been accused of selling out and trying to be White. Iranian men who expect me to fit within a certain mold find me strange. I also seem to have this peculiar power to make people at airports and train stations visibly uncomfortable." She describes her feelings when she was informed she would not be allowed to join the BLSA—the Black Law Students Association—at her college. "My first impulse had been to argue with the man sitting behind the table with the introductory flyers. He looked me in the eye and said, 'Look, if you're not Black, then as far as I'm concerned, you're White.'" She goes on to say, "What was I to do, start an 'ILSA' of which I would be the sole member?"[37]

We may paint diversity with such a broad brush that we fail to capture the differences that exist within groups as well as between them. Indeed, the differences within groups are often greater. For instance, we tend to get caught up with how men and women differ from each other. We forget or ignore the significant differences that can be found when we simply look at a group of men or a group of women. Women can be assertive or passive, dependent or independent, and supporters or opponents of feminism. Similar differences exist among men.

Differences exist among the largest ethnic groups in this country. These groups include African-Americans, Latinos, Asian-Americans, and Native Americans. For this reason, we cannot talk about the Latino family any more than we can talk about the White family. Discussing *the* Asian-American or *the* Latino experience in this country ignores the diversity that exists within groups and individuals from these populations. Asian-Americans and Pacific Islanders include Chinese, Japanese, Filipinos, Vietnamese, Laotians, Cambodians, Hmong, Koreans, Samoans, and many others. Latinos are also distinguished by a wide range of skin colors, socioeconomic backgrounds, ethnic or cultural lifestyles, religions, and languages. Many object to the term *Latino* or *Hispanic* because it masks the uniqueness of the particular culture. *Mexican, Puerto Rican, Cuban,* or some other term identifying one's nationality may be preferred.

Sociologist Douglas Massey reminds us of the vastly different histories shared by Latinos and the salience of their social class backgrounds. "They may be fifth-generation Americans or new immigrants just stepping off the jetway. Depending on when and how they got to the United States, they may also know a long history of discrimination and repression or they may see the United States as a land of opportunity where origins do not matter. They may be affluent and well educated or poor and unschooled; they may have no personal experience of prejudice or discrimination, or they may harbor stinging resentment at being called a 'spic' or being passed over for promotion because of their accent."[38]

DIVERSITY MYTHS

Diversity is a concept that means many things to many people. It can trigger a wide range of positive and negative feelings. Unfortunately, what we learn about this subject is often incomplete and inaccurate. Some of the more common misconceptions that surround diversity follow.

Myth 1: Diversity = Women + Minorities

Diversity includes everyone. All of us, for example, bring different talents and perspectives to school and work. This includes White males.

Myth 2: Diversity Is a New Phenomenon

There has always been diversity, but now it is receiving more attention. Some changes are not as new as we might believe. As an example, statistics indicate that more women are entering the job market than ever before. This masks the fact that a large percentage of women of color have always worked.

Myth 3: Diversity = Deficiency

This myth is based on the premise that diversity results in standards being lowered. Today, professionals increasingly view diversity as a resource rather than a deficit. Big businesses such as IBM, Marriott, American Express, and PepsiCo approach diversity as good business for a number of reasons. It makes companies more attuned to markets at home and abroad, it expands their talent pool, and it contributes to the creativity that fosters the development of new, innovative products.

Myth 4: Diversity = Divisiveness

Many assume that our society is divided because of our differences. Does the problem lie with our differences or our inability to respect and learn from these differences? Being exposed to diversity can bring people together. As an example, service learning, study abroad, and diversifying our social network can expand our appreciation of diverse people and cultures and promote understanding as well as tolerance.

Myth 5: Diversity Is to Be Feared

By focusing exclusively on our differences and ignoring our similarities, we create fear. Fear is cultivated by our ignorance of differences and similarities. Fear is compounded by our inability to communicate effectively with people who disagree with us about difficult issues. People often shy away from talking about diversity because it is so emotionally charged. As one student put it, "All it takes is one slip of the tongue." How we approach diversity can make all the difference. If we approach it with a sense of humility and a sincere desire to learn more about others and ourselves, it need not be something to fear or avoid.

In a film entitled *The Color of Fear*, a group of men of varying racial and ethnic backgrounds attend a retreat and open up to each other about the issue of race. After a few days, it appears the racial divisions among the men are insurmountable. Their fear and mistrust almost make it impossible for them to communicate effectively. Toward the end of the retreat, they begin to connect with each other by confronting their fears, sharing intimate feelings, and really listening. They become more aware of some of the feelings they have in common.

The kind of dialogue that unfolds in this film is rare because it is genuinely open and honest. Consequently, it can be very painful at times. Toward the end of the film, one of the participants comments on the anger and hurt that surfaced during the group's discussions. "Sometimes," he says, "the cure for the pain is in the pain."[39]

Differences aren't necessarily a burden but a blessing.

—Another perspective

WHAT IS DIVERSITY CONSCIOUSNESS?

The definition of *consciousness* in the dictionary is being fully aware or sensitive to something. Another way of defining it is the full activity of the mind or senses. This state of mind is necessary to develop **diversity consciousness**: understanding, awareness, and skills in the area of diversity.

 Thinking Through Diversity

Should we always treat everybody the same and ignore differences? Are there any situations in which we should treat people differently?

Diversity consciousness is not simple and straightforward. It cannot be manufactured during a one-hour TV talk show or a day-long training session. Try to keep the following points in mind as you read about diversity consciousness.

Diversity Consciousness Is NOT . . .

- *Simply common sense*—Common sense is not sufficient; rather, we need to educate ourselves and each other. For example, common sense might tell us that individuals share our **ethics**, those standards that guide behaviors and help us determine what is right or wrong. Yet others, raised with different teachings and cultural values, may abide by a different set of standards. Consider the issue of plagiarism. A professor may assume that *all* of her students understand that plagiarism is unethical, and why. But is this assumption accurate? If she were to reexamine the context of her values, it might become evident that some of her students may come from different cultural backgrounds where they have been taught that knowledge belongs to society, not to the individual. Therefore, these students do not necessarily recognize that information borrowed from others requires appropriate citation. Since common sense can prove unreliable, especially in a global environment, it becomes clear why recognizing, understanding, and evaluating ethical dilemmas can seem like a daunting task. For this reason, many organizations offer workshops and training to help professionals develop their diversity consciousness in order to understand better how to manage workplaces where professionals from all over the world have different ideas regarding proper conduct.

- *The result of good intentions*—You may have heard people say, "If my heart is in the right place, that is enough." Trying extra hard to be fair and respectful of others or having the best of intentions is a good start, but only a start. It is possible to show insensitivity and ignorance even though you mean well. People who talk to adults with disabilities in a childlike manner may think that they are being kind. People who tell you to forget our differences and just "be human" may think they are offering helpful advice. Leonard Pitts, a columnist for the *Miami Herald*, writes, "I've lost count of the times well-meaning white people have advised me to quit being black and 'just be a person.'"[40]

- *The result of some simple formula or strategy*—This is a reflection of what George Ritzer terms the "McDonaldization" of our society.[41] Sociologists use this phrase to describe our preoccupation with doing things quickly and efficiently, much like McDonald's restaurants. However, diversity consciousness requires lifelong soul searching, self-reflection, and active learning.

- *Important for just some of us*—Are events held during African-American History Month more apt to attract African-Americans? How many men are in attendance at

Women's History Month events? To survive and succeed in the twenty-first century, all of us need to be culturally literate and responsive. According to Dr. Benjamin Carson, one of the world's most renowned surgeons, it is a mistake to think that someone else's problems or struggles do not affect us. "All of our ancestors came to this country in different boats. But we're all in the same boat now. And if part of the boat sinks, eventually the rest of it goes down too."[42]

- *Simply ignoring differences and treating everybody the same*—It is necessary to distinguish between sameness and equal opportunity. Should an instructor, for example, always treat everybody the same? On one hand, she should have high expectations for all of her students regardless of who they are. That same instructor, however, will have to distinguish among students in determining how she can teach the material most effectively and how she can help individual students succeed.

- *Some "feel-good" activity*—Diversity consciousness is not a matter of merely feeling good about ourselves and others. It goes deeper. Superficial acceptance is replaced by a deeper and more critical understanding.

- *A passing fad*—Diversity has always been with us, and responding to it with ease and competence will become more and more important. A good example is our increasing life span. Hallmark Company reports selling thousands of centenarian birthday cards each year, and recently introduced their first 75th wedding anniversary card. Census predictions point to a much "grayer" population by the year 2050 because we are living longer. America's earliest "Baby Boomers" have already begun to reach age 65. By 2020, nearly a fifth of the U.S. population will be 65 years of age or older.[43] People are not only living longer, but they are also healthier and retiring at a later age. Therefore, the older population will be a growing part of the diversity that surrounds us daily.

DIVERSITY EDUCATION

Diversity education refers to all the strategies that enable us to develop diversity consciousness. Through diversity education, we develop awareness, understanding, and a variety of skills in the area of diversity. Throughout this book, these skills are referred to as **diversity skills**. Among these are flexible thinking, communication, teamwork, leadership, and social networking, as well as the ability to overcome personal and social barriers.

Diversity education takes many forms. It is something we can initiate and control, such as reading a book, volunteering to help others in need, attending a workshop, and exchanging ideas about diversity issues with thousands of people over the Internet. One form of diversity education, which has proliferated throughout the country in recent years, is study circles. Anyone can form a study circle.

Although much of the literature uses the terms *diversity education* and *diversity training* interchangeably, there are important differences. Unlike training, diversity education is a lifelong process. The term *education* refers to a complex and unpredictable process that is both cognitive and affective. Training, however, tends to be more straightforward, standardized, and descriptive. Education, as opposed to training, is more apt to entail questioning, disagreement, and reflection. In essence, diversity training may constitute one component of diversity education.

Much of the dialogue in recent years regarding diversity equates diversity with diversity education. They are not the same. Diversity simply refers to our individual and collective differences. Without formal and informal education, diversity is simply untapped potential.

The Circle of Learning

The idea behind study circles is to involve communities in ongoing dialogues on diversity. Anyone or any group can initiate a study circle. In many communities, organizations such as churches and temples, businesses, schools, and clubs sponsor study circles. Everyday Democracy (formerly the Study Circles Resource Center) provides free discussion materials and assistance.[44]

People who join study circles agree to meet regularly over an extended period of time. This long-term proactive approach to dialogue allows study circle participants to get to know one another and begin to share their innermost feelings. Everyone is given a "home" in the conversation. By participating in study circles, everyday people gain ownership of issues that relate to diversity. Typically, the discussion focuses initially on personal experiences and perspectives. Participants then examine how personal and community issues interrelate and what action needs to be taken. Unlike many other forms of diversity education, which do not go beyond dialogue, study circles combine talk with action.

The experiences of study circles throughout the country and the world show promise. Study circles in Australia and Sweden have been used extensively to engage citizens in various political and social issues. In the United States, hundreds and even thousands of people participate in community-wide dialogues. For example, a statewide program in Oklahoma helped initiate sweeping changes in the corrections system. In Montgomery County, Maryland, more than 1,700 parents, staff, and students representing 57 countries participated in study circles to address racial and ethnic barriers to student achievement.

One parent reflects on what she learned as a participant, "I don't think this group will heal the world...[nor] completely understand the complexities of being in the other person's shoes. I do, however, believe that it is important to know that we are all human and everyone has a story.... We're not obligated to agree with one another, skip off and sing 'Happy Together.' I think varying people having an open space to respectfully share and listen to the viewpoints of others is something I can really get down with."[45]

> Typically, long-term relationships form out of circles. I have a best friend that I met in a study circle. Often, there is a need for a second level of the same circle that further narrows the focus. If the first circle was good, the participants are reluctant to leave. There is a bonding that takes place that transcends culture and race. This makes us simply human beings who have gained a wiser understanding of one another and the need to know more.
>
> —Another perspective

Unlike many other forms of learning, true diversity consciousness requires continual, fundamental change. Change of this nature, what best-selling author Stephen Covey termed *real change*, takes place "from the inside out." In *The Seven Habits of Highly Successful People*, Covey elaborates. Real change "doesn't come from hacking at the leaves of attitude and behavior with quick fix personality ethic techniques. It comes from striking at the root—the fabric of our thought, the fundamental essential paradigms which give definition to our character and create the lens through which we see the world."[46] In other words, fundamental changes involve growing as a person, both intellectually and emotionally. Although change of this nature is not easy, the rewards are worth it.

In summary, the cultural landscape in the United States is changing due to the influence of demographic, technological, and social changes. The term *diversity* has gained new meaning; it is not limited to racial, ethnic, and gender differences. Despite the attention diversity receives, our views and understanding of diversity are often influenced by myths about diversity and the role it plays in our lives. Diversity education enables us to move beyond these myths and develop our diversity consciousness.

 Case Studies

The following three case studies introduce three individuals (Ligua, Mary, and Michael) who you will follow through subsequent chapters. Even though the stories are rooted in real-life experiences, the characters are fictitious. You will learn about each of the three— their backgrounds, day-to-day challenges that revolve around diversity, and how they attempt to resolve certain complex issues addressed in each chapter. After reading each case study, you will be asked a series of questions about Ligua, Mary, and Michael that will challenge your diversity consciousness. The final chapter brings each case study to a close.

Case Study One

Name: Ligua Querling
Education: High school diploma
Marital Status: Married
Children: Kenneth, 3 years; Lisa, 6 years; Michael, 8 years
Hometown: San Miguel, El Salvador
Current Residence: Northern California

Ligua, an immigrant from El Salvador, aspires to be a high school math teacher. Like many of her friends, she somehow manages to find the time to be a mother, an employee, and a part-time student. She is taking courses at a predominantly White, suburban community college that is a short commute from her two-bedroom apartment. Ligua works a full 40-hour workweek as a salesperson at a nearby car dealership.

As a working mom, Ligua feels her biggest challenges are giving 100 percent at her job, 100 percent at school, and most importantly, 100 percent to her family. Given all there is to do in the course of a day, she tries to make every minute count. Often, Ligua's own needs are an afterthought. **Role conflict** (interference among the duties associated with the multiple positions held by an individual), stemming from her multiple statuses as a mother, wife, student, and employee, consume her at times. For financial reasons, she needs her job. But she wants her job too. Her husband, a building contractor who works long hours, helps out when he can. Ligua feels there's nothing balanced about her life at home and at work. Sometimes, she feels like she neglects her family because she is playing "catch-up" at work and school. At other times, the scale shifts much more toward her family, with family illnesses, running errands, and just "being there" when her children and husband need her.

Case Study Two

Name: Mary Stuart
Education: College senior
Marital Status: Single
Children: None
Hometown: Rushville, Illinois
Current Residence: Chicago, Illinois

Mary is a 21-year-old White woman attending an undergraduate university in a large city. Mary's family, which she describes as upper middle class, lives in a rural area of the state where she attends college. Going to school in a large city enables Mary to experience new ideas and cultures. Mary is currently in her fourth year of the university's social work program. She is completing two practicums, one at a children's mental hospital and one at a private, nonprofit agency that provides both outpatient services and in-home family preservation counseling services. After graduating with her bachelor's degree in social work, Mary wants to pursue a master's degree in social work and become a licensed clinical social worker. The majority of Mary's friends are White women with similar backgrounds.

Mary is a descendant of highlander Scots (whose ancestors, in turn, originated in four different regions of Europe). During the last few years, Mary has taken a much greater interest in her cultural heritage. She enjoys taking part in Scottish games and Celtic festivals. The atmosphere is very sociable, especially with the "clan" gatherings. Clans are groups of families or households, the heads of which claim descent from a common ancestor. Music is a big part of the festivals. Also, clan gatherings provide a time to reflect on more traditional times when community values seemed to hold more importance. Modern community life seems more impersonal to her.

Case Study Three

Name: Michael Butler

Education: College degree in computer engineering

Marital Status: Divorced; custody of only child

Children: Aaron, 11 years

Hometown: Greensboro, North Carolina

Current Residence: Atlanta, Georgia

Michael is multiracial but identifies himself as African American. His mother identifies herself as part Cherokee Indian, part African-American. His father refers to himself as Black, although his ancestry is mixed (African-American, Caucasian, Asian). With so many different racial groups running through his bloodline, Michael rejects any attempt to categorize himself into one race. If he did, he says that he would be depriving himself of much of his heritage.

Michael works as a senior manager for a small consulting firm. The job requires quite a bit of travel and a great deal of networking. Michael's performance evaluations have been excellent. He enjoys the long hours his job requires.

Over the years, the firm's workforce has become more diverse, especially in terms of race, ethnicity, and age. With regard to gender, however, few women can be found at the management and decision-making levels.

When life gets difficult, Michael takes comfort in his strong spiritual background. He was brought up as a Baptist and is an active member of his church. According to Michael, his religious and ethnic background gives him peace and helps him get through the day. Michael is intent on passing on his strong religious beliefs to his son.

 ## Key Terms

Diversity	Cultural lag	Social class
Diversity consciousness	Glass ceiling	Master statuses
Culture	Cultural cruise control	Transgender
Cultural landscape	Assimilation	Values
Millennials	Pluralism	Ethics
Minorities	Dimensions of diversity	Diversity education
Globalization	Race	Diversity skills
Global perspective	Ethnicity	Role conflict
Glocalization	Gender	

 ## Exercises

Exercise 1: **What Is Diversity?**

1. Ask ten students who are *not* in this class to complete the sentence:
Diversity is: _____.
Record their responses.

2. Write a paragraph describing the similarities and differences in the responses of the ten students. Do any of their responses reflect diversity myths? Explain.

Exercise 2: **What's in a Name?**

1. What is your full name? How do you feel about your name? Why?

2. Find out as much as you can about your name. For example, what is the history and significance of your name? What is the meaning of your name?

 ## Notes

[1] Michel de Montaigne, "Of the Resemblance of Children to Fathers," *The Essays* (Simon Millanges, Bordeaux, 1580), Ch. 37.

[2] Geert Hofstede, *Culture's Consequences: Comparing Values, Behaviors, Institutions, and Organizations Across Nations* (Thousand Oaks, CA: Sage, 2001).

[3] Katti Gray, "Linguists and Tribe Members Work to Restore Native Languages." Online, November 29, 2012. Available: http://diverseeducation.com/article/49809/.

[4] Sam Roberts, "In Name Count, Garcias Are Catching Up to Joneses," nytimes.com. Online, November 17, 2007. Available: http://www.nytimes.com/2007/11/17/us/17surnames.html?ci-5088&cn-9449f09cf7ac21c.

[5] "Why No One Under 30 Answers Your Voicemail," *DiversityInc.*, September/October 2010, 47.

[6] Vincent N. Parillo, *Diversity in America* (Thousand Oaks, CA: Pine Forge Press, 1996), 65.

[7] U.S. Bureau of the Census, *Historical Statistics of the United States, Part II*, Series Z, 20 –132 (Washington, DC: U.S. Government Printing Office, 1976).

[8] CIA, *The World Factbook*, Available: https://www.cia.gov/library/publications/the-world-factbook/fields/2212.html, accessed November 9, 2012.

[9] Carol Morello and Dan Keating, "Census Confirms Skyrocketing Hispanic, Asian Growth in U.S.," *The Washington Post*, March 25, 2011, A17.

[10] Richard Rodriguez, "Se Habla Espanol." Online, May 9, 2000. Available: http://www.pbs.org/newshour/essays/may00/rodriguez_5-9.htmlrl.

[11] Kip Fulbeck, *part asian—100% hapa* (San Francisco, CA: Chronicle Books, 2006), 12.

[12] Sharon Jayson, "U.S. Rate of Interracial Marriages Hits Record High" *USA Today*. Online, February 16, 2012. Available: http://usatoday30.usatoday.com/news/health/wellness/marriage/story/2012-02-16/US-rate-of-interracial-marriage-hits-record-high/53109980/1.

[13] Clara Rodríguez, "Latina America," *Latina*, July 2001, 87.

[14] Migration Policy Institute, "ELL Information Center Fact Sheet Series," No. 1, 2010.

[15] "The Nation: Students," *The Chronicle of Higher Education Almanac*, September 1, 2000, 24+.

[16] "More International Students Enroll at U.S. Campuses," *Huff Post College*. Online, November 8, 2012. Available: http://www.huffingtonpost.com/2011/11/14/more-international-studen_0_n_1092602.html.

[17] Marshall McLuhan, *The Mechanical Bride: Folklore of Industrial Man* (Boston: Beacon Press, 1967).

[18] Reuters, "Victims by Country." Online, September 20, 2001. Available: http://www.cnn.com/SPECIALS/2001/rade.center/interactive/victims.map/mpa.exclude.htmlrlUntitled.

[19] E. T. Hall and M. R. Hall, *Hidden Differences: Doing Business with the Japanese* (Garden City, NY: Anchor Press/Doubleday, 1987).

[20] Jane Pinchin, "Let Them Go—Because 60 Seconds of World News Is Not Enough," *The Colgate Scene*, March 2002.

[21] Pew Forum on Religion and Public Life, "Public Remains Conflicted Over Islam." Online, August 24, 2010. Available: http://www.pewforum.org/Muslim/Public-Remains-Conflicted-Over-Islam.aspx.

[22] Federal Glass Ceiling Commission, *A Solid Investment: Making Full Use of the Nation's Human Capital* (Washington, DC: U.S. Department of Labor, 1995), 6.

[23] Michelle Ryan, Michael Schmitt, and Manuela Barreto (eds.), *The Glass Ceiling in the 21st Century: Understand Barriers to Gender Equality* (Washington, DC: American Psychological Association, 2009), 1.

[24] Kevin Sack with Janet Elder, "Poll Finds Optimistic Outlook But Enduring Racial Division." Online, July 14, 2000. Available: http://www.nytimes.com/library/national/race/071100sack-poll.html.

[25] C. Emily Feistritzer, "Profile of Teachers in the U.S. 2011," National Center for Education Information, July, 2011; and Pew Research Center, "Hispanic Student Enrollments Reach New Highs in 2011." Online, August 20, 2012. Available: http://www.bing.com/search?q=Pew%2C+Hispanic+Student+ Enrollments+Reach+New%22&form=DLCDF8&pc=MDDC&src=IE-SearchBox.

[26] Israel Zangwill, *The Melting Pot* (New York: The Jewish Publication Society of America, 1909), 198–199.

[27] William Branigin, "Immigrants Question Idea of Assimilation," *The Washington Post*, May 25, 1998, A1.

[28] Timothy Fong and Larry Shinagawa, *Asian Americans: Experiences and Perspectives* (Upper Saddle River, NJ: Prentice Hall, 2000).

[29] Toni Morrison, *Playing in the Dark* (Cambridge, MA: Harvard University Press, 1992), 47.

[30] Ronald Takaki, *A Different Mirror. A History of Multicultural America* (Boston: Little, Brown, 1993).

[31] Ruth Frankenberg, *White Women, Race Matters: The Social Construction of Whiteness* (Minneapolis: University of Minnesota Press, 1993), 198.

[32] Athima Chansanchai, "She Walks the Line of Poverty, Incognito," *The Baltimore Sun*, September 16, 2001, 1N+.

[33] Julio Alves, "Class Struggles," *Chronicle of Higher Education*, 53 (8), 2006, Available: chronicle.com/weekly/v53/i08/08b00501.htm.

[34] Roosevelt Thomas, *Beyond Race and Gender: Unleashing the Power of Your Total Work Force by Managing Diversity* (New York: American Management Association, 1991).

[35] Ashley Montagu, *Man's Most Dangerous Myth: The Fallacy of Race* (Cleveland, OH: World Publishing, 1964).

[36] Pew Research Center, *Optimism About Black Progress Declines: A Social and Demographic Trends Report*, 2007.

[37] Amanda Enayati, "Not Black, Not White," *The Washington Post*, July 13, 1997, C1.

[38] Douglas Massey, "Latino Poverty Research: An Agenda for the 1990s," *Social Science Research Council Newsletter*, 47, March 1993, 7–8.

[39] *The Color of Fear* (video) (Oakland, CA: Stir Fry Productions, 1994).

[40] Leonard Pitts, Jr., "Watching Whites Struggle to Understand Their Whiteness," *The Baltimore Sun*, April 21, 1997, 9A.

[41] George Ritzer, *The McDonaldization of Society* (Thousand Oaks, CA: Pine Forge Press, 2000).

[42] Benjamin Carson, "Carson Philosophy Is 'Think Big,'" *The Baltimore Sun*, August 24, 1997, 6H.

[43] Richard W. Judy and Carol D'Amico, *Workforce 2020: Executive Summary* (Indianapolis, IN: Hudson Institute, 1997), 3.

[44] For more information, contact Everyday Democracy, 111 Founders Plaza, Suite 1403, East Hartford, CT 06108; tel: 860-928-3713; fax: 860-928-3713.

[45] "A First-hand Account of the Dialogue Experience." Online, January 14, 2011. Available: http://thebeautyjackson.com/2011/01/14/im-black-and-therefore-i-am-diverse/.

[46] Stephen Covey, *The Seven Habits of Highly Effective People* (New York: Simon & Schuster, 1989).

2

Diversity Consciousness and Success

Learning Outcomes

Upon completion of this chapter, you will be able to:

- Analyze diverse definitions of success.
- Explain the connections between sociocultural theory and success.
- Create a list of diversity skills.
- Compare and contrast individual and organizational benefits of diversity consciousness.
- Discuss the benefits of exemplary diversity training programs for the workplace.
- Enumerate the costs of inadequate diversity consciousness.

We define **success** in a variety of ways. One meaning, according to the dictionary, is the attainment of wealth, honors, and position. Another is simply to achieve what you want to achieve. In this book, success is the process of achieving our goals, whatever they might be. Continual growth and learning are an integral part of this process—whether the goal is getting a good job, earning a degree, developing a talent, or simply doing one's best.

DEFINITIONS OF SUCCESS

Definitions of success vary from culture to culture. Depending on our background, we might focus more on materialism, power, and status, or we may view one's success in life as determined by forces beyond our control. When asked to think about our success, perhaps we immediately think of ourselves and what we as individuals have achieved. Or, maybe we have been raised to view success in terms of our social, economic, and emotional ties with families, communities, and others. For some of us, success is more about living our life in accordance with certain principles. Clearly, cultural values and beliefs shape how we define success and whether we consider ourselves successful.

My uncle, who owns a trucking company, visited a new car lot to look at trucks for his highly successful business. He arrived at the lot dressed in the clothes he wears when he is working on the trucks. Inside the showroom, he spent a long, long time walking and looking around. Rather than offer help, all of the salespersons looked conveniently busy and totally ignored him.

Finally, he went outside in the car lot and found a young man who was washing the trucks. My uncle asked him about the different trucks and what he thought of these vehicles. The young man's face lit up when asked, and he enthusiastically shared everything he knew.

My uncle then went back inside the showroom and found the manager. He said, "I want to buy ten new trucks with cash, but only under one condition." The manager asked, "What's the condition?" My uncle replied, "That boy over there gets the commission." At that point, the manager balked and fussed, but my uncle made it clear this was the only way he would buy the trucks. The deal was made.

—Another perspective

 ### Thinking Through Diversity

How do you define success?

How do students define success? Often, the emphasis is on achieving a personal goal: getting through another day or earning a certain grade. Other definitions tend to focus more on helping others: being a good role model or learning to work with others. Sometimes, students equate success with certain personal qualities such as character, self-awareness, or peace of mind. The following definitions reflect some of the markedly different ways in which students view success.

Success means establishing goals for yourself, and then not allowing anything to stand in your way.

Success is having the bills paid, food in the fridge, a place to live, a car to drive, and the opportunity to live just one more day.

Success is not only materialistic. It is having a spiritual belief that values every person as your brother.

Success is striving to be a better person by learning all that I can from numerous sources. Success for me is being able to learn something from a 2-year-old to the drug addict on the corner. It is being grounded enough to be able to communicate to people on their level and accept them for who they are.

Success is being aware of oneself. It is learning and growing from new experiences, being able to examine your strengths and weaknesses honestly, and having the courage to change if needed.

—Other perspectives

When I ask my students whom they consider to be highly successful, many list big-name entertainers, sports stars, and well-known political and business leaders. Interestingly, many more students include the names of people they know on a personal basis, including parents, friends, teachers, and others. Once in a while they mention themselves. Often, success is not seen as the result of a single accomplishment. It is a work in progress, the culmination of numerous events: some positive, some negative.

Too often, we sell ourselves short. We fail to appreciate just how much we have to offer and all that we have accomplished. One of the things I do at the end of each semester is ask students to bring something to class that makes them feel special and successful. I tell them it should be something they feel comfortable sharing with their classmates. It is one of my favorite class sessions because it brings out a wonderful mix of success stories.

It is impossible to predict what students will choose to "show and tell." For instance, in one class, a student brought a picture of her family. Her pain was etched in her face as she recounted how she was abused as a child and how she has coped. One older student showed the high school diploma he earned in 1993. He explained that he was supposed to graduate in 1961 but dropped out of school during his senior year. "I was never satisfied until I got it," he said. A middle-aged man passed around a 50-cent coin that he had found as a little boy. As he described it, the coin had a picture of Booker T. Washington's face on one side and a slave cabin on the other. "My father," he explained, "preached to me that the only thing out there for black men is to be laborers. As long as I held on to that coin, I felt I could do more." With each student, a success is revealed and acknowledged. Even though their successes are markedly different, they unite through feelings of accomplishment and pride in themselves and each other.

When I listen to society's definition of success, I have to keep reminding myself that even though I am a part of society, I don't have to fit their mold. Success is contentment and it is something that is learned. It does not matter whether I have a lot or very little because it will not change who I am. My success is achieved through a peaceful heart, a calm spirit, and a content state of being.

—Another perspective

Success stories are all around us and within us. They come in a wonderfully diverse assortment of shapes, sizes, and colors. Some are more obvious than others. As one of my students suggests, they can be found by looking for beauty in the ugliest of circumstances. At times, only we can appreciate the grandiose nature of what we accomplish.

What constitutes success and the paths to success vary from person to person. Consequently, there are an infinite variety of success stories. Too often, we hear only the success stories that make the news and involve the "rich and famous." It is of utmost importance to remember that success is relative. It depends on where we start, how far we come, and the obstacles we encounter along the way.

> I have learned that success is to be measured not so much by the position that one has reached in life as by the obstacles which he has overcome while trying to succeed.
> —Booker T. Washington

SOCIOCULTURAL THEORY AND SUCCESS

Although any attempt to make sense of your success must focus on you, you are only part of the picture. The bigger picture includes your social environment, both past and present. This explanation of success is closely tied to **sociocultural theory,** a perspective that focuses on the social and cultural context of one's thoughts and actions.

According to sociocultural theory, we do not live in a vacuum. Interaction with **social forces,** or those omnipresent social influences that surround us, goes a long way toward explaining our attitudes, character, knowledge, feelings, and other individual attributes. Social forces even shape the way we view success and the explanations we offer for success. Olson's study found that women and men explained their successes and failures differently during a mock interview. In comparison to men, women were more likely to see their successes resulting from luck. Olson concludes that this viewpoint may stem from social relationships that teach women to appear modest and avoid self-serving explanations.[1]

Each of us has a choice in how we react to situations, people, and events. *Every* response to *every* situation is something we can choose and ultimately control. Although our life experiences may *influence* who we are, they do not *determine* who we are. In *Sermons from the Black Pulpit,* Samuel Proctor says: "It does not matter where we were born, what kind of rearing we had, who our friends were, what kind of trouble we got into, how low we sank, or how far behind we fell. When we add it all up, we still have some options left, we still have some choices we can make."[2]

> I'm 27. I live in a homeless shelter with other women. Living in that homeless shelter and coming to college is hard. When I'm at the shelter, I don't really get into what I'm doing that much because there is the envy and the jealousy among the other women and the counselors. I do a lot of downplaying. I keep it real low key. It can be very stressful. It's not that I feel I'm trying to be better than them. I feel there is enough for everybody. I always stress that you can do what I am doing if you really want it. I have to build my self-esteem. That's a daily thing. I think what helps me is my will, my determination. I am strong willed. I've been down. I want to be a power of example to the best of my ability. I want to be able to say "Look at me. I did it. You can."
>
> —Another perspective

Too often, we arrive at simplistic explanations of success by failing to look at an array of individual and external influences and the interrelationships among them. The idea that "no one is going to hire me because of the way I look" ignores the importance of motivation and hard work. These and other individual traits can help us overcome such barriers if indeed they exist. Equally naive is the thinking that "I don't need anyone" and "I can make it on my own."

Maureen, a college student, offers a more inclusive and empowering perspective. She acknowledges the origin of her values: "My mother instilled good values in me just like her mother did for her. She always told me I could get anything I want out of life if I work hard enough." Furthermore, Maureen is aware that her ethnic background shapes her goals and influences the way some people view her. In Maureen's case, this awareness becomes a motivator. "I feel as though some people view Latinos as lazy people who don't want to better themselves. They think all Latinos want a free ride, or welfare, which is not true because I go to college and I also work at night. It is this perception of Latinos that motivates me to work hard at making life better for my daughter."

Thinking Through Diversity

One way of relating sociocultural theory to your life is to think of the bridges you have crossed to get where you are. People, both past and present, can be bridges in that their efforts make it possible for you to do the things you do. Oprah Winfrey talks about the bridges in her life: Sojourner Truth, Harriet Tubman, Fannie Lou Hamer, and others. Which people have been bridges for you? Why?

By relating sociocultural theory to our own lives, we will be better able to understand the importance of diversity skills. For example, my son Jimmy has autism. Autism is a severely incapacitating, lifelong disability. People with autism have a difficult time relating to others and dealing with change. They frequently act in a way people find strange and unacceptable. These autistic behaviors, which may be continual and almost impossible to control, seriously limit the person's ability to be independent.

As Jimmy's father, I become more empowered in many different realms as I realize I need the help of my wife and family, friends, social agencies, support groups, teachers, and therapists. For a long time, I was tempted to isolate myself from the rest of society. However, to get through each day and find the support and services Jimmy and I need, I have to develop my teamwork and interpersonal skills. I am more sensitive to others who may encounter the looks, ignorance, and insensitive comments that continue to be part of my daily life. Because I chose not to remain isolated, I developed diversity skills I would not have otherwise. Being aware of sociocultural influences helps us make the connection between our own lives and the resources that surround us.

WHY DIVERSITY SKILLS ARE IMPORTANT

An integral part of developing diversity consciousness is developing **diversity skills,** those competencies that allow people to interact with others in a way that respects and values differences. Diversity skills such as communication, teamwork, leadership, and social networking are key components of diversity consciousness. Diversity consciousness is more than just being knowledgeable about or aware of differences. It is the awareness, understanding, and skills that allow us to think through and value human differences. As our awareness and understanding expand, so do our diversity skills. Similarly, developing and refining our diversity skills increases our awareness and understanding (see Fig. 2.1).

We often ignore or trivialize the relationship between diversity consciousness and success. This is due, in part, to our limited perception of diversity. Traditionally, the idea of diversity has revolved around some of the more obvious differences among people, such as race, ethnicity, and gender. In this book we adopt the more current, inclusive view of diversity. Dimensions of diversity also include learning styles, multiple intelligences, personalities, personal expectations, and a wide variety of other differences that often remain hidden. By broadening our conceptualization of diversity, we are better able to develop an array of skills that can motivate and empower us. These skills are referred to as diversity skills.

Success at School

If we develop our diversity consciousness, we can be more successful academically. Research, case studies, and student experiences underscore the importance of diversity skills. As you read about five of these skills, examine yourself. Which are strengths of yours? Which need a little or a lot more work? What might you do to improve certain skills?

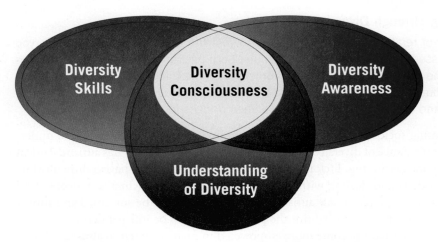

Figure 2.1 Diversity consciousness consists of three interrelated components: diversity awareness, understanding of diversity, and diversity skills.

1. *Ability to expand one's repertoire of learning styles.* **Learning styles** refer to the way we learn. A good deal of research has identified numerous learning styles. For instance, some people find they learn best when they interact with others in small groups. Others prefer a highly structured lecture format. Students may find they are visual or auditory learners. There are those of us who can learn from anybody, and those individuals who find learning nearly impossible if they cannot relate to the instructor. Research has shown that we can change and expand our learning styles.

   We can be more successful by taking control of our own education. Being aware of our learning styles as well as becoming more flexible learners can help us identify our strengths and shortcomings, minimize problematic situations, and develop coping strategies. Begin by asking "How do I learn best?"

   Numerous testing instruments have been developed to assess learning style preferences and strengths.[3] However, it is important to remember that no one assessment can definitively tell us what we can and cannot do when it comes to learning. It can, however, indicate possible tendencies and habits.

Thinking Through Diversity

What is the best way for you to learn? What do you do when you find yourself in a learning environment that does not match your learning style?

   The concept of cultural learning styles suggests that cultural upbringing plays a critical role in determining someone's learning style. Cultural values may influence child-rearing practices and, in turn, the learning styles children develop. Numerous studies have attempted to identify learning style preferences among students from diverse cultural backgrounds. For example, in their review of research, Irvine and York found that Native American students tend to be **field dependent.** Field-dependent students like to work with others to achieve a common goal and are more sensitive to the needs of others than **field independent** students, who prefer to work independently and compete for individual recognition. Their study also revealed that Native American students tend to prefer learning in private rather than public. Moreover, they prefer learning by watching and doing.[4]

   In spite of research findings that point to cultural learning styles, there remains significant intracultural variability. For example, within any cultural group, ways of thinking and speaking vary with age, income, education, and class status. Hence, broad depictions of African-Americans, Native Americans, or Latinos as having different learning styles are likely to be stereotypical and resented by members of these groups who are not accurately represented by these generalizations.

Once you have a better idea of how you learn, you are better able to monitor, adapt, and ultimately improve your learning. In a given class, you may determine that your learning style conflicts with your instructor's teaching style. Perhaps you learn best when *you* talk about something but your instructor is a straight lecturer. Knowing this, you might compensate by forming a study group and talking about the lecture after each class.

> I have a physics instructor who speaks and pronounces words a lot differently than I do. These differences between her language and mine created a conflict at first because I kept telling myself I can't learn from this woman. But I began to pay closer attention and improve my listening skills. She also helped me learn I cannot depend on my instructors to teach me everything. I also have to use my textbooks and talk to others to get a full understanding of the subject at hand.
>
> —Another perspective

Researchers have also examined different intellectual strengths or intelligences. These strengths may come into play during the learning process (see Diversity Box: Multiple Intelligences). A greater awareness of the variety of *multiple intelligences* as well as learning styles can empower us and maximize our chances for success. Also, it can help us acknowledge and value the large variety of individual capabilities we will encounter. Consequently, we are better able to appreciate that an individual's lesser abilities in one intellectual area do not imply lesser abilities in all intellectual areas. Some of us may be artistic, whereas others may show more promise in science or music. It is important, however, not to use our own differences in multiple intelligences as an excuse.

Multiple Intelligences

Some years ago, Harvard University professor Howard Gardner identified a number of different intelligences.[5] Gardner theorizes that although each of us possesses at least eight intelligences, some are more fully developed than others. This theory may help explain why we can pick up some things very easily and other tasks come much harder. It also sheds light on why a particular subject might be difficult for you but not for some other individuals.

Gardner identifies the following eight intelligences: verbal-linguistic, logical-mathematical, spatial, bodily-kinesthetic, interpersonal, intrapersonal, musical, and environmental. Each of us has at least some ability with regard to each intelligence, and our intelligences can diminish or expand over time. Throughout our school years, most of us are taught by teachers who use verbal-linguistic and logical-mathematical strategies. Our ability to understand these teachers depends on our capacity to use language and understand logical reasoning and problem solving. Those of us with underdeveloped skills in one or more of these areas may be at a disadvantage. In some other classes, however, we may encounter teachers who use alternative teaching methods that tap other types of intelligence.

(continued)

(continued)

Picture yourself in Professor B's math class. You are someone who has a long history of problems in math. However, your grades in this class are good for a change. You think it might have something to do with the way Professor B teaches: She seems to connect very well with students and employs a variety of teaching styles. One technique in particular seems almost funny at first, but you find it helps. She creates raps out of different formulas and mathematical definitions. The class then does the rap together and some of the students really "get into it." The following is one example: it is a rap that helps you remember the steps to follow when graphing a line.

The Slope-Intercept Form Rap

$y = mx + b$

b's the y-intercept, so plot it first, ya' see?

m is the slope—rise over run.

So go up or down and to the right and then you're done.

According to Professor B, raps such as this make learning easier because they draw on a number of different intelligences, including musical, interpersonal, and bodily-kinesthetic. The rhythmic nature of rap, for example, appeals to those students who have a well-developed capacity to hear and remember musical patterns. Bodily-kinesthetic intelligence, the capacity to use hands, arms, and other body parts to take in knowledge, feeds into the rhythmic feel of rap. Furthermore, the fact that it is an interpersonal activity utilizes still another type of intelligence.

What can we learn from this experience? It is not enough to view this one class as a positive unique experience and leave it at that. It might be helpful to seek out other teachers who teach this way. But realistically speaking, how many Professor B types are there? Maybe a better strategy is to realize how much this way of remembering helps you and use this technique in another class. In your next math class, you might try putting some of the new formulas to a rhythm. Another idea is to get together with a group of other students from Professor B's class and try to create similar ways of remembering math or maybe another subject.

To learn more about Howard Gardner's life and work, google "Gardner Multiple Intelligences." As you become more familiar with his research and theory, consider how you might nurture and expand your own intelligences.

2. *Ability to appreciate and maintain pride in one's background and culture.* In her book *Affirming Diversity*, Sonja Nieto describes her research on a diverse group of "successful students." In this study, success means that the students are still in school and planning to complete high school or have recently graduated. They also have good grades, generally enjoy school, have plans for their future, and describe themselves as successful. Nieto concludes, "One of the most consistent, and least expected, outcomes to emerge from these case studies has been the resoluteness with which young people maintain pride and satisfaction in their culture and the strength they derive from it."[6] Furthermore, Nieto states that learning about one's culture, and how it informs and enriches us, is not easy.

I am an Orthodox Jew and it is very important for me to practice my religion. I cannot go out and act any old way. Two nights a week I go to Talmud classes and I am not allowed to go to school or study on the Sabbath or Jewish holidays. When I am at school, I say a blessing before and after I eat lunch. I also pray three times a day. When I am studying with someone during the time I observe afternoon prayer, I simply tell that person I have to stop and pray for a few minutes. I understand that the world does not revolve around the Jewish calendar. Therefore, I have learned to focus on my religion no matter who is around or what the situation is. This has made me a stronger Jew and a stronger student.

My grandparents were both from France. My grandfather served in the French cavalry and lost his leg in World War I. Henriette, my grandmother, came to this country alone. Even though she only knew a few words in English, she somehow managed to find a job and save enough money to buy a house. Her husband and children then joined her. Henriette and I were very close. She made me proud of my French and American heritage. When things get stressful, especially at school, thinking of Henriette puts things in perspective, and gives me strength.

My relatives raised me to have self-esteem, to know of my history. We were taught that from the time we could read, when there weren't any black coloring books. My mother used to color the kids in the coloring books black. Jack and Jill were Black. They might have been coal Black but we understood where they were coming from. Later on, I went to a racially mixed high school and I never felt inferior to anybody. And it got me into trouble because I do not allow that kind of stuff to filter into my mindset. I was always arguing with the teachers because I refused to answer questions a certain way. I would say, "Look at Ethiopia, look at the pyramids, look at this, look at that."

—Other perspectives

3. *Ability to network and learn from everyone and anyone.* Experiences that expose us to diversity are a critical component of a quality education. For example, medical schools have transformed their curriculum with an eye toward improving health outcomes by bringing society and diversity into their students' education. Depending on the school, medical students may be required to tutor neighborhood children or interact with senior citizens on an art project. To promote teamwork and break down hierarchal structures, students studying to be physicians may be expected to interact on "an equal basis" with nurses and other health professionals as part of their training. Yet another medical school requires their students to learn Spanish.

   We increase our chances for success by expanding and diversifying our learning experiences and social networks. In so doing, we learn more about who we are and our ability to relate to others. This, in turn, helps us develop our diversity consciousness.

4. *Ability to deal effectively with barriers.* Much research examines the relationship between expectations and success. In many cases, our own expectations or the expectations of others act as barriers. According to the concept of the self-fulfilling prophecy, students may conform to the expectations of teachers. However, students' expectations of themselves are equally, if not more important. For example, there are teachers who begin by saying their course is hard and half of the class will drop by mid-semester. Some students respond by mentally preparing themselves to drop the course, but others react differently. They view expectations of this nature as a challenge and do everything in their power to complete this course "successfully."

My cultural background has been an important factor in my success at school. Because of my major, I had to take biochemistry at the beginning of my sophomore year. The class I attended had only three African-American students. About three weeks into the course, we had our first test. All three of us failed. I remember feeling embarrassed and very intimidated. I felt like quitting, but I didn't want my classmates to think that all African-Americans are dumb plus quitters. I vowed that I would be in the top percent of my class. When the next test was announced, my instructor publicly informed the other two students and myself that we needed to study because there was an academic standard that must be upheld at this school. I felt she had purposely singled us out because other students had failed and yet they didn't get the same kind of warning. At this point, it became a matter of principle to do well on the test. Initially I was going to do well just for my own pride. But after the teacher's remark it became something more. It seemed to me that if I didn't do well on this test, she would forever think that I and all other African-Americans were not capable of meeting

(continued)

(*continued*)

the academic standards of the school. On that test, I made a 97, which was the second-highest grade in the class. I continued to study hard and made very good grades until I received my diploma.

—Another perspective

Punjabi Student Expectations

The Punjabi families who reside in the California community of "Valleyside" are immigrants from India. They offer valuable insight into the relationship between expectations and success. Punjabi students are highly successful. Their families teach them that they are responsible for their own success. These students have high expectations of themselves. They know they must study hard and succeed in school for the honor of themselves, their families, and their community. If not, they put themselves at risk for being withdrawn from school and sent back to work in the fields.[7]

Thinking Through Diversity

If someone were to write your life history, what would we learn about the relationship between expectations and academic success?

5. *Ability to balance "fitting in" and "being yourself."* When students attend college, they may encounter a cultural setting that is unfamiliar and uncomfortable. As one example, due to their social class background, students might encounter an environment that makes it difficult to learn and succeed. Some students may feel they have to deny or cover up their social class to fit in with students from higher or lower socioeconomic backgrounds. Making this cultural adjustment on a daily basis can have profound implications. Like other diversity skills, the ability to fit in and be yourself is connected with your diversity consciousness. More specifically, each of us can develop this skill as we learn to understand and value ourselves, individually and culturally.

Sometimes, certain ways of accommodating or fitting in are necessary. For example, certain rules and expectations must be followed. Mastery of English or the language of instruction is critical. Some students resist talking standard English or even getting good grades because they equate it with "selling out." Willie Jolley, a motivational speaker who grew up in one of the poorer neighborhoods of Washington, D.C., recounts how one of his friends took his books to and from school in a plastic bag because he did not want to appear too studious. Stacie, one of my students, describes how her own family criticizes the way she speaks. "A lot of times at home they would say, 'Why are you talking like you're White?'" Her response was, "I'm not talking like I'm White. I'm just trying to speak correct English."

Findings from research[8] point to the potential benefits of transculturation. **Transculturation** is the process by which a person adjusts to another cultural environment without sacrificing his or her own cultural identity. In analyzing the factors that affect the academic achievement of Native American and White students attending college in South Dakota, Huffman discovered fundamental differences. High school grade-point average and parental encouragement to attend college relate significantly to the academic success of Whites. Among Native Americans, the retention of traditional cultural heritage is the most important predictor of success.

My culture is in my soul all the time.

I had a professor tell me that she hated my tattoo and it wasn't a good way to represent my grandmother. I was widely offended on many levels and also really hurt by it. I felt like she was telling me I should be something I am not, or not participate in a certain aspect of my culture.

—Other perspectives

A middle-aged woman talks about making the necessary adjustments at college without assimilating or losing her cultural distinctiveness. "When we go to school we live a non-Indian way but we still keep our values.... I could put my values aside just long enough to learn what it is I want to learn but that doesn't mean I'm going to forget them. I think that is how strong they are with me."[9] Although this study focuses on Native Americans, transculturation can benefit all of us. We empower ourselves when we learn we can adjust to any situation without sacrificing or compromising our beliefs.

Thinking Through Diversity

When you find yourself in a cultural environment outside of your own, how do you know when to adjust and when to resist?

Success at Work

There is a mismatch today between the skills that college graduates bring to the workplace and what employers need. More and more employers need workers who can cooperate, collaborate, build trust and contribute to teams, negotiate disagreements, and constantly learn and adapt in any situation. Unfortunately, many employers complain about new hires as well as more experienced workers lacking these skills. Consequently, key interview questions often target how well one relates to and works with others (see Fig. 2.2). Some common examples follow:

- With what type of people do you have the most difficulty working? Why?

- Which of your skills would you rate higher—your "technical" or interpersonal skills? Why?

- What do you do when someone is critical of you and seems not to like you?

- If you sensed that your work group was not accepting you, what might you do?

According to research by Hart Research Associates, higher education institutions need to place more emphasis on a number of learning outcomes that enhance diversity consciousness (see Fig. 2.3). In order for employees to excel in today's global economy, both employers and recent college graduates identify certain areas as being most in need of greater emphasis. These include teamwork skills in diverse groups, oral and written communication, critical thinking, proficiency in a foreign language, and awareness and knowledge of global issues. According to this study, the vast majority of employers and college graduates emphasized the importance of moving beyond book knowledge and connecting education to "real-world settings and situations."[10]

Clearly, diversity conscious individuals are very much in demand. Employers value them. Thus, developing this consciousness enhances your chances of landing a job and becoming a highly valued, successful employee. With this in mind, ask

I would rate my interpersonal skills as excellent.
But why would you ask such a stupid question?

Figure 2.2 Do your skills match what employers need?

yourself the following question: Given your background, knowledge, and experience, how well can you meet employers' needs in the following areas?

1. *Interpersonal skills.* In subjects ranging from business management to healthcare to teacher education, it is not uncommon to see entire chapters in textbooks devoted to the subject of interpersonal skills. Increasingly, educators and employers are realizing that strong people skills are just as important as technical expertise. In a study of financial professionals, chief financial officers (CFOs) were asked, "Would you be willing to hire someone with fewer technical skills

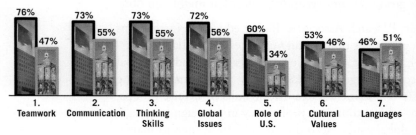

Colleges Should Place More Emphasis Than They Do Today on Selected Learning Outcomes: Employers vs. Recent College Graduates

Key:
■ Employers   Recent Grads

Figure 2.3 Views on College Learning.
Source: Hart Research Associates, Raising the Bar, 2010.

Learning Outcomes

1. Teamwork skills and the ability to collaborate with others in diverse group settings.
2. The ability to effectively communicate orally and in writing.
3. Critical-thinking and analytical-reasoning skills.
4. Global issues and developments and their implications for the future.
5. The role of the United States in the world.
6. Cultural values and traditions in America and other countries.
7. Proficiency in a foreign language.

Diversity Consciousness and Success

Emotional Intelligence

In his best-selling book *Working with Emotional Intelligence,* Daniel Goleman analyzes those skills that distinguish average performers from superstars.[13] On the basis of data collected from more than 150 business firms, he concludes that emotional intelligence skills are the key.

Emotional intelligence is the ability to acknowledge, value, and manage feelings so that they are expressed appropriately and effectively, laying the groundwork for meaningful relationships and true teamwork. Goleman goes on to say that it is not enough to be technically proficient and possess a high IQ. Although school smarts might get you into the office, your ability to handle emotions and relate to people effectively allows you to excel on the job.

As an example, Goleman points to a study cited in the *Journal of the American Medical Association.* This study reveals that physicians who lack empathy get sued more often. However, physicians who never had a malpractice suit possess better interpersonal skills. They are empathetic and take time to communicate at length with their patients. These physicians tell their patients what to expect from treatment, check their understanding, and ask their opinion. They encourage questions and even laughing and joking.[14]

if the candidate had stronger soft skills, such as communication and interpersonal abilities?" More than half (53%) of the national sample of 1,400 CFOs responded yes.[11] In another study, 73 percent of human resources managers said they would not hire someone whose interpersonal skills were lacking, even if they had solid technical skills.[12]

Employees need to relate effectively to the customer at the point of encounter. This requires interpersonal skills that some businesspeople refer to as *emotional intelligence* (see Diversity Box: Emotional Intelligence). Profits in any service-oriented industry depend to a large degree on employees who greet and service the public. A well-trained receptionist with excellent interpersonal skills can make a customer feel valued. Conversely, a salesperson or security guard who lacks these skills and is insensitive to diversity can hurt business.

2. *Flexible thinking skills and adaptability.* Perhaps you are a single parent who has struggled through difficult times. Maybe you have a military background that has given you the opportunity to live in other countries throughout the world. These kinds of experiences help you think creatively and flexibly. To well-known author and management expert Peter Drucker, living in more than one world provides us with new insight and leadership experiences.

Flexible thinkers do not lock themselves into one mode of thought. Rather, they can adjust mentally to different situations. More and more employers need and want workers who are problem solvers, who can do more with less by examining both the familiar and unfamiliar from a variety of perspectives. This kind of thinking requires practice and a will to learn.

Thinking Outside the Box

In the business world, flexible thinking is sometimes described as thinking outside the box. This kind of thinking is necessary to solve the following problem.

```
•   •   •
•   •   •
•   •   •
```

Directions: Draw four straight lines, without lifting your pencil, that touch all the dots. (Note: See the answer at the end of the chapter.)

In his book *A Kick in the Seat of the Pants,* Roger von Oech describes the flexibility of thought that characterizes creative thinkers. "Like race-car drivers who shift in and out of different gears depending on where they are on the course, creative people are able to shift in and out of different types of thinking depending on the needs of the situation at hand. Sometimes they're open and probing, at others they're playful and off-the-wall. At still other times, they're critical and fault-finding. And finally, they're doggedly persistent in striving to reach their goals."[15]

Consider the reaction of IBM managers to security concerns in the aftermath of the 9/11 terrorist attacks. They had to balance safety considerations with respect for cultural differences. In one instance, a Muslim IBM employee who wore her veil to work was issued two identification cards. One ID, with a photograph of herself wearing the veil, was shown to male security personnel. Cultural norms dictate that observant Muslim women do not show their face to males who are not family members. When necessary, another ID, with her picture without the veil, was shown only to female security.

3. *Teamwork skills.*   More and more organizations are turning to teams to solve problems and create better products and services. Consequently, people need to prepare themselves to join and contribute to teams. Leveraging diversity and meshing dissimilar personalities and backgrounds into a highly cohesive, effective unit can be extremely challenging and rewarding. Andrew Sobel, an author and leading authority on developing business relationships, looks at the Beatles for insight into diversity and teamwork. Besides their obvious talent, the Fab Four "was greater than the sum of the parts." Through their teamwork skills, the four of them were able to create and produce far superior music than any of them could have on their own. They not only recognized their diversity, they embraced it, and used it to establish an emotional connection with their audience, generate new sounds and beautiful harmony, and sell over 1 billion records, tapes, and CDs.[16]

The seemingly effortless chemistry of the Beatles was the product of hard work, unmistakable talent, and diversity consciousness. But like any other collaboration, their ability to respect and value each other took time. When teaming, it is important to remember "you're working with people from a variety of age groups and with different events in their lives—people with elder care issues or children, for example. Have respect for the differences among people in your workplace."[17]

4. *Cultural awareness and understanding.*   Awareness and understanding make it possible for you not only to recognize cultural differences and similarities, but also to grasp their meaning and significance. This learned skill is absolutely essential, at home or abroad, given a customer base that is becoming increasingly multinational and multicultural. As the buying power of minorities in the United States increases, businesses are directing more of their attention to minority marketing. According to the Selig Center for Economic Growth, the combined buying power or disposable personal income of African-Americans, Asian-Americans, and Native Americans is in excess of $12.2 trillion. This figure represents an increase of 188 percent from 1990 to 2012.[18] Numerous advertising agencies now specialize in Asian-, African-, and Hispanic-American marketing. As the marketplace expands, a lack of cultural awareness and understanding is even more of a liability. It is clearly difficult to design and develop merchandise for markets you do not understand. Kentucky Fried Chicken found this out the hard way. Their advertising slogan "finger-lickin good" became "Eat your fingers off" when translated into Chinese.

5. *Self-evaluation skills.* According to the late Stephen Covey, best-selling author and business consultant, business leaders frequently cannot find workers who will take on the responsibility for making good things happen.[19] To do this requires continuous self-evaluation. This skill is particularly critical for managers. According to Daniel Goleman, research reveals that exceptional managers have faults like anyone else; however, "they are *aware* of their limits—and so they know where they need to improve, or they know to work with someone else who has a strength they lack."[20] By being open to feedback from others and monitoring yourself, you are more apt to realize why diversity consciousness is so important and what skills you may need to develop. Rather than simply relying on someone else to make this happen, you take the initiative. Self-evaluation is a key area in the development of diversity consciousness.

Employers are in need of workers with an array of well-developed diversity skills. The benefits of these skills are numerous. We grow more aware of the value of human differences and the limitations imposed by close-mindedness. At the same time, we do not preoccupy ourselves with differences. This means that we can acknowledge, respect, and see beyond differences. In so doing, we relate to others more effectively and capitalize on human potential—our own as well as that of others.

INDIVIDUAL/ORGANIZATIONAL BENEFITS

Thinking Through Diversity

Select one organization of which you are a member. If you were to grade this organization on its ability to capitalize on diversity, what grade would you give, and why?

The Individual

Increasingly, "qualified" is synonymous with college educated *and* diversity conscious. As organizations compete for the best talent available, both in the United States and abroad, it is prospective employees' diversity consciousness that gives them a competitive edge (see Photo 2.1). Take a look in the employment section of any major newspaper in the United States. What follows are some actual typical ads for a variety of positions.

- "One of the most important contributions you can make to meeting our mission is enabling others to understand world cultures. Your native-level fluency and expert knowledge of a foreign region's history, customs, politics, and economy will strengthen your students' ability to communicate with others and work in locations around the world." (foreign language instructor for a governmental agency)

- "We require excellent communication and customer service skills. Fluency in French or Spanish strongly desired." (sales and service representative)

- "Excellent interpersonal and communication skills. Communication experience on a global level a plus." (marketing/promotional writer)

- "The position requires an individual who is a quick learner of new technologies with proven qualities of leadership, effective teamwork, and communication.... Our people are diverse, and we capitalize on that diversity as we help each other grow and develop our talents in our areas of expertise." (Web application development and support)

- "Outstanding client relationship skills. Outstanding communication (written and verbal) skills. Strong self-starter, self-motivated, and willing to take on responsibility as an absolute team player." (computer assurance services)

Photo 2.1 The ability to recognize the power and possibilities of diversity has increasingly become a requirement for success in today's competitive, global business environment.

- "We develop innovative programs and treatment modalities to meet the complex needs of an increasingly diverse population . . . need someone to help foster effective interaction with facility staff, patients, consumers, their families, and locally based providers to deliver a progressive continuum of mental health services." (mental health facility director)

- "Candidates must have strong computer and analytical skills, leadership potential, and the interpersonal skills needed to work effectively in a demanding team environment." (technical associate—information)

- "We are looking for a team-oriented professional to provide leadership, direction, and technical expertise to support the current reporting infrastructure across our global enterprise-wide organization." (program analyst)

One indication of the importance of diversity consciousness is the emergence of diversity training into a highly competitive and profitable industry. Schools, government agencies, and major companies such as Levi-Strauss, IBM, Dow, Marriott, and Avon spend millions each year on training of this nature. In some cases, the evaluation of an employee's contributions in the area of workforce diversity is one of the performance criteria that determines his or her salary and bonuses. A more detailed discussion of diversity training and its role in diversity education appears later in this chapter.

The Organization

Why is it important for you to understand why organizations attach so much importance to diversity consciousness? In the course of your lifetime, you will deal with many **organizations,** groupings of people structured to achieve one or a number of goals. Many organizations are employers, including businesses, government agencies, educational institutions, and charitable agencies. Examining how and why organizations operate the way they do will allow you to assess what skills are in demand. Also, you will be better able to understand how diversity consciousness affects the organization and its members. Why, for example, do people at all levels and in all positions need diversity skills? How do these skills affect productivity? Why do surveys consistently show that CEOs of large and growing companies believe diversity is essential to their ongoing success? Whatever your position and function, you need to develop a perspective that is organizational as well as individual.

At the organizational level, the advantages afforded by a diversity conscious workforce are numerous.

1. *More innovation and adaptability.* Diversity consciousness generates a variety of innovative responses to challenges. In dealing with technological advances, international developments, and other social and economic changes, there is less reliance on tradition and more of a focus on creative problem solving. In the business world, the result is typically better products and better services, new customer/client populations, and the expansion of existing markets. For example, U.S. companies alter their marketing strategies as they grow more aware of the buying power of all types of minorities. American Telephone and Telegraph (AT&T) mailed brochures depicting three couples in affectionate poses: two women, two men, and a man and a woman. The slogan reads "Let Your True Voice Be Heard." Other companies, such as Saab, are now running their usual ads in gay publications.

2. *Better communication.* It is not enough to have employees with diverse talents and backgrounds. In sports, this is why the team with superior talent may not always win. Teams with less talent, but better communication skills and a stronger commitment to the group, are able to maximize their collective talent. They put the team first and reach a consensus on their goals and roles.

   The same thing holds true in the workplace. Without effective communication, teamwork suffers and talent is wasted. An example of this is **groupthink,** going along uncritically with the expectations of a group, which in turn limits understanding of an issue. Groupthink, a dynamic identified by Irving Janis, is one of the great challenges of homogeneous groups. When group members share similar backgrounds and beliefs, cohesion and conformity can become an end in itself. People fail to think independently as they quickly agree with what appears to be the consensus of the group.[21] For example, an employee might think of a radically different approach to a group problem. Reluctantly, she keeps it to herself because of the vibes she has gotten from other group members in the past. Her ideas are often dismissed as far-fetched and idealistic. Rather than take a chance, she ends up going along with the group because she doesn't want to "rock the boat." This scenario, which is very common in work teams, produces mediocre solutions to difficult problems.

3. *Recruitment and retention of the best employees.* Those organizations with the best reputation for attracting and maintaining an inclusive and highly competent workforce will be at an advantage in terms of recruiting and keeping the best talent. The consequences of limiting the talent pool are obvious when we examine the history of intercollegiate athletics. Formerly all-White southern colleges and universities did not recruit Blacks and other students of color. Consequently, they denied themselves some of the best athletic talent available at that time.

4. *Less likelihood of incurring the costs of workplace biases.* Bias is very expensive. It creates conflict, siphons off people's talents and energies, and leads to the

underutilization of human potential. Consider the findings from a new study by the Center for Work-Life Policy, *Asians in America: Unleashing the Potential of the "Model Minority."* The study found that Asians in U.S. corporations struggle with a "bamboo ceiling" that prevents them from moving into upper-management. Because of subtle biases, Asian men and women report struggling with "fitting in," finding mentors, and developing the requisite connections and networks necessary to advance.[22]

5. *Greater productivity.* If you feel valued, you are going to be more productive. This is the rationale behind "managing diversity." **Managing diversity** does *not* imply control or manipulation; rather, it means creating an environment that enables everyone to contribute their full potential.

People who develop their diversity consciousness are more valued employees. They can help members of any organization work together to improve the quality of their product or service. This, in turn, will increase profits. Therefore, the importance of diversity consciousness is not some "feel good" issue. It relates directly to the "bottom line"—productivity and profit.

DIVERSITY TRAINING IN THE WORKPLACE

Diversity training, or any activity which promotes awareness and knowledge and builds the skills necessary for operating in a multicultural, global environment, is a form of diversity education. The nature and content of these activities often depend on the organization's definition of diversity and its commitment to effective training. Activities might include teaching managers how to construct and conduct performance appraisals of employees from different cultures, or offering CD-based and Web-based cross-cultural programs to assist employees who are relocating to another country.

Given the challenges of creating a diversity-conscious workforce, many employers in business, government, healthcare, education, and numerous other fields have begun to offer and even require diversity training. Spurred on by demographic data that point to a continually shrinking percentage of white men in the workforce, many human resource departments now send workers to lectures and workshops to help them work with colleagues and relate to customers in a multicultural, multiracial environment. Recently, there has been a proliferation of instructional materials, seminars, books, and journals on managing and valuing diversity. "Diversity managers" are now commonplace in Fortune 500 companies.

In recent years, diversity training programs have been criticized for being ineffective, inflammatory, and even counterproductive. Although this is certainly true of some programs, others have much more positive effects. The efficacy of the program depends on a number of factors, including the motivation for training, support from leadership, the duration and focus of training, and follow-up (see Fig. 2.4).

Ideally, diversity training is a multifaceted, comprehensive program that is linked to organizational priorities such as attracting and retaining talent, building managerial competency, opening up new markets, and improving customer service. Furthermore, it should incorporate a variety of well-integrated initiatives and resources that reflect an ongoing, organization-wide commitment to continuous learning. Among these initiatives are network groups and mentoring; blogs, social networking, webinars and other online learning activities, community outreach, social and educational

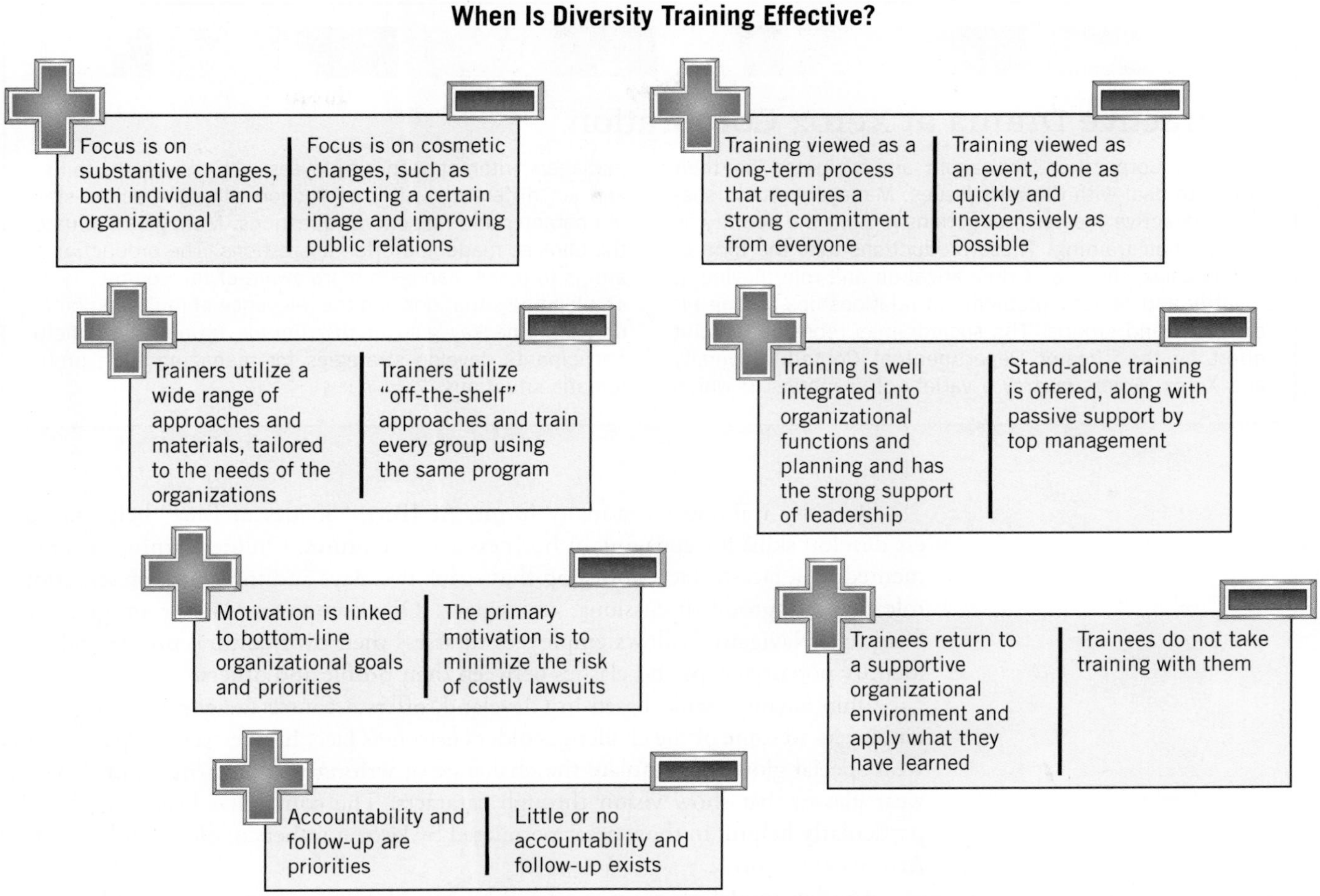

When Is Diversity Training Effective?

Focus is on substantive changes, both individual and organizational	Focus is on cosmetic changes, such as projecting a certain image and improving public relations

Training viewed as a long-term process that requires a strong commitment from everyone	Training viewed as an event, done as quickly and inexpensively as possible

Trainers utilize a wide range of approaches and materials, tailored to the needs of the organizations	Trainers utilize "off-the-shelf" approaches and train every group using the same program

Training is well integrated into organizational functions and planning and has the strong support of leadership	Stand-alone training is offered, along with passive support by top management

Motivation is linked to bottom-line organizational goals and priorities	The primary motivation is to minimize the risk of costly lawsuits

Trainees return to a supportive organizational environment and apply what they have learned	Trainees do not take training with them

Accountability and follow-up are priorities	Little or no accountability and follow-up exists

Figure 2.4 When Is Diversity Training Effective?

events; learning centers with books, videos, and a variety of other learning materials and resources; and workshops on subjects such as leadership, team-building, and customer service. Today, companies are increasingly combining pedagogical approaches in the form of **blended learning,** the integration of online and traditional face-to-face approaches to learning.

Organizations need to insure the effectiveness of diversity training. This might mean varying the delivery of diversity training. According to a recent poll by Workplace Options, younger workers (ages 18 to 29) are much more likely than older workers to prefer training that is shorter and available remotely through mobile devices. Dean Debnam, CEO of Workplace Options, observes that younger professionals "are more inclined to communicate and interact effectively through technology, so the standard model of one person lecturing to a room full of people may not be the most productive approach to reach this age group."[23]

Specific goals of diversity training might include understanding the challenges and benefits of diversity, relating diversity to organizational values and initiatives, identifying assumptions that interfere with teamwork, and developing specific diversity skills. Programs may target change in an individual's awareness, attitudes, and behaviors, or change in the *culture of an organization,* meaning its programs and policies, chain of command, and generally the way it conducts business.

Interactive Drama at Xerox Corporation

At Xerox Corporation, managers are evaluated on their ability to deal with diversity issues. Managers attend special interactive theater productions around the country as part of their training. These productions take the form of **sociodramas,** the use of dramatization and role playing to identify and remedy problems in relationships among individuals and groups. The sociodramas represent a joint effort by the Theater Department at Cornell University and Xerox. Actors portray a variety of scenarios in which managers interact with employees who may look, think, and act differently. After each short play, the actors stay in character and respond to questions. Managers evaluate the choices made and offer suggestions. The productions' aim is to make managers more aware of the complexity of challenging situations and the relevance of multiple points of view. One key goal of this unique training is to help participants develop strategies for managing such problematic situations.

Diversity training takes many forms. At IBM, "Shades of Blue" helps managers develop skills for engaging in business across cultures. Online learning is supplemented by a face-to-face workshop that spans two days and integrates presentations, role playing, group discussions, and videos. One component of the program, the "Cultural Navigator," allows employees to assess their own cultural profile and then identify potential gaps and clashes between their profile and others.

Ohio Savings Bank, based in Cleveland, offers a course designed to sensitize its employees to some of the challenges older customers face. In one exercise, participants wear special gloves to simulate the challenge of writing with arthritis, and they also wear glasses that show vision through cataracts. The course has been found to be particularly helpful in those areas populated by large numbers of older adults, such as Arizona and Florida.

Another model program is offered by MGM Mirage, one of the world's leading hotel and gaming industries. Before beginning work each day, employees gather to discuss daily happenings, service standards, and any diversity issues that need to be addressed. Guest service training emphasizes the importance of creating a welcoming environment for *all* guests and treating everyone with the same care and quality of service. A critical mass of employees, who receive extensive training in diversity, is certified as "diversity champions." Through education, they build high performance teams, foster better employee communications, and generally champion the value of diversity across the entire organization.

An increasingly important focus of diversity training is ethical conflict. Most people associate ethics with standards or moral principles that help us determine the rightness and wrongness of human conduct. In a diverse, unpredictable marketplace and workplace, deciding what is right is increasingly difficult. Because of cultural differences there is often a difference of opinion; therefore ethical conflicts can arise. For instance, until recently it was generally believed that physicians knew what was in their patients' best interests. Therefore, they took it upon themselves to make medical decisions regarding treatment, diet, disclosure, and truth telling in cases involving the terminally ill and end-of-life decision making. Now, many patients and their families want to be involved, and their values and priorities may generate ethical dilemmas. Constantly changing ethical issues in the field of healthcare influence a variety of professionals, including physicians, nurses and other healthcare providers, social workers, lawyers, and chaplains.

The success of diversity training has been mixed. One of the biggest challenges for trainers is the mindset of the audience. Typically it ranges from reverence and approval to indifference to disapproval, confusion, and possibly outright hostility. This is especially true if upper management has not identified diversity as a priority. Moreover, expectations are often unrealistic. Exploring diversity issues and developing diversity consciousness take a lifetime, yet the goals of many programs do not reflect this.

For example, participants in a daylong workshop may at best be taught to recognize certain biases they possess and, with additional work and commitment, suppress those biases, and even begin to unlearn them. Nevertheless, it is not uncommon to see unrealistic goals that target massive individual and organizational changes in a short span of time. Attitudes and behaviors evolve over years and are reinforced repeatedly. Rather than changing those attitudes in the span of a few hours, it is more fruitful to think in terms of identifying and recognizing the need for personal growth and development in this area. With a strong sense of commitment and clear, achievable goals, each training session becomes one more opportunity to do just that.

Examples of ill-conceived training abound. For example, teachers in one school system decided to create a poster for each classroom. The poster, which read "In this classroom, all people are treated with respect," was distributed to all teachers. Unfortunately, there was no systematic effort to ensure that people knew what concerns gave rise to this initiative and how students and teachers from various social backgrounds might define respect differently. And there was no follow-up to make sure that teachers were taking this statement seriously. What began as a promising idea became, in the eyes of some, a shallow and meaningless publicity effort.

Certain training programs are held up for criticism because they are combative and guilt-driven, and therefore end up alienating and offending employees. Others exacerbate stereotyping. In an effort to highlight group differences, some trainers inadvertently promote rather than ameliorate stereotypes. Sometimes, participants are left wondering how diversity training relates to an organization's mission and core values.

Diversity training produces better results when it has the support of top leaders, and is proactive, non-confrontational, relevant, and ongoing. Assessment is also a key component of any successful diversity training. In many cases, a positive or negative evaluation hinges on whether employees view the training as enjoyable, and whether they feel they learned something valuable given their job and function. For example, did the training increase some skill, improve their knowledge, or change an attitude? However, the relevance and value of training can and needs to be assessed in other ways. Specifically, do participants apply and continue to use what they learn, and does the training impact organizational productivity, perhaps by reducing turnover and absenteeism or improving communication. Much of the carry-over effect of training depends on the culture of an organization and management. Culture of this nature is instrumental in designing, "selling," and reinforcing the training. By the same token, if employees have doubts about the commitment of management, diversity training, however good, will have limited value.

A sizable number of research studies in recent years have provided medical schools with the impetus to focus more of their coursework on helping healthcare providers become culturally competent.[24] **Cultural competence** refers to a set of attitudes and skills that make it possible for organizations and staff not only to acknowledge cultural differences but also incorporate these differences in working with people from various cultures. The term *cultural competence* is similar to *diversity consciousness*; however, the latter term emphasizes competencies of this nature need to be more holistic and transformational. In the process of learning to be diversity conscious, healthcare providers undergo profound personal change.

A diversity-conscious healthcare provider must be sensitive to patients' language preferences and religious beliefs, in addition to expectations regarding diet, modesty,

Profile in Diversity Consciousness

As an educator in the 1970s, Marylen Mann became increasingly aware of the lack of meaningful and stimulating opportunities afforded mature adults in her hometown of St. Louis and throughout the country. She recounts spending a day touring senior centers in St. Louis, Missouri, with the city's commissioner of aging. The senior centers offered activities, but they were typically childish activities meant to keep people busy. Mann spent many more days in senior centers, talking with older adults as well as staff.

With adults living longer, healthier, and more independent lives, Mann saw that the needs of a growing segment of the population were not being met. With the help of a friend, she created an organization called OASIS in 1982. In creating OASIS, she defied the commonly held notion that older adults had already made their contribution to society and were readying themselves for increasing dependence on others.

OASIS is an organization designed to engage people over 50 in challenging and productive roles in the community. Mann felt it was critical for OASIS to take a holistic approach to the individual—physical, social, and psychological. Consequently, OASIS created a wide range of programs that utilized the expertise of mature adults.

When OASIS was created, people questioned whether adults would want to tutor children, serve as peer counselors, and teach classes. There was skepticism about whether people over 50 would sign up for eight-week classes in subjects as diverse as creative writing or biblical archaeology. The response was phenomenal; so much so that now more than 59,000 adults in 43 U.S. cities are involved in OASIS-sponsored programs. Recently, AT&T has partnered with OASIS to offer computer training to the increasing number of baby boomers who plan to continue working and need technology skills to compete.

sickness, death, and bereavement, and norms governing the role of the family in healthcare. One program, piloted at the University of Michigan, seeks to provide first-year medical students with a variety of integrated learning experiences. These include discussions that require students to examine their own value systems, their perspectives on caring for patients from different cultures, and specific methods of care that involve the patients' families, members of the healthcare team, and the wider community. The students listen to fourth-year medical students' personal stories about treating diverse patients and working with diverse colleagues. Another component of the program asks students to critique a videotape in which patients recount their experiences with cultural insensitivity in the healthcare system.[25]

THE COSTS OF INADEQUATE DIVERSITY CONSCIOUSNESS

Imagine that you are a doctor. You have been asked, along with a large number of other doctors, to participate in an experiment designed by a team headed up by Dr. Schulman of the Georgetown University Medical Center in Washington, D.C. You agree, and make the necessary arrangements. Once you arrive at the site of the experiment, you are taken to a private room where you are shown a video. You observe a patient describing heart pain, and recommend what you consider to be appropriate treatment. You are told the results will be published, but that your individual response will be kept confidential.

Later that same year, the results of this study are made public in *The New England Journal of Medicine*. Evidently, you were one of 720 doctors who watched videos with actors as patients. Actors wearing plain white hospital gowns read identical scripts describing heart pain. The actors included Blacks and Whites, men and women. Findings revealed that the doctors who participated in the study were generally much less likely to recommend appropriate treatment for the Black and female patients. After subjecting data to statistical tests to ensure reliability and validity, the study's authors conclude that the disparity in what are potentially life-and-death decisions with regard to medical care is most likely due to the doctors' unconscious gender and racial biases.

As a professional, you find this very hard to believe. As far as you are concerned, you do not have a prejudiced "bone in your body." Not only do you see yourself as highly educated and open-minded, but you also think you relate extremely well to a very diverse group of professionals at the hospital where you work. After thinking back to the study, you begin to wonder if the patient's race or gender did make a difference. This may be the first time that you have ever even entertained this notion. It is something you begin to struggle with, at least momentarily.

The aforementioned study by Dr. Schulman[26] is part of a growing body of research that has brought to light significant gaps in the quality of healthcare due to race, gender, ethnicity, and social class. The consequences of inadequate healthcare affect one's quality of life and, in some cases, mean the difference between life and death. Upon reviewing more than 100 studies, a 15-member committee of the Institute of Medicine concluded that racial minorities in the United States receive worse healthcare than Whites, even when the minorities had the same income and health insurance as Whites. The biggest discrepancies in the quality of healthcare were found in the areas of cardiovascular disease, HIV/AIDS, cancer, and diabetes. Researchers identified a number of reasons for inferior treatment. Among these are language barriers, patients' mistrust of healthcare providers, bias among doctors and nurses, and a lack of awareness among doctors and nurses regarding cultural beliefs that can affect health.[27]

Regardless of your education or career plans, your failure to develop diversity consciousness will, in all likelihood, have far-reaching and serious consequences. As a student, you may find it difficult to learn from instructors and other students who do not share your background, personality, values, or learning style. Lacking the skills to be a "team player" may make it difficult for you to work with others in study and work groups. Poor communication skills can make it difficult for you to find the help you need in and out of class. At work, you may not know how to interpret and respond to both verbal and nonverbal cues. When you interact with someone who does not share your point of view, you may find it difficult to listen actively and think flexibly. As a result, you may unconsciously alienate others and sabotage future opportunities in the process.

Organizationally speaking, people who lack diversity consciousness will strain interpersonal relationships, threaten team spirit, and waste time. Costly lawsuits are more likely. Ultimately, the reputation of an individual or organization may be undermined.

Thinking Through Diversity

In today's workforce, many individuals do not use all of their potential, and particularly their insight, resourcefulness, and talent. Does a lack of diversity consciousness shown by employees or their managers contribute to this situation? Explain.

With each of the following real-life examples, the costs are significant.

1. In 2003, the California state pension fund agreed to pay $250 million to more than 1,700 retired public safety officers. The age-discrimination lawsuit, filed by injured police officers, firefighters, and other safety officers, was based on a bill enacted in 1979. The bill stipulated that disability retirement benefits for officers were to be based on their age at the time they were hired, rather than the severity of their injuries. Injured workers hired at a younger age received a significantly higher percentage of their salary than workers hired at an older age. The rationale for this differential treatment, according to the officers' lawyers, was lawmakers' concern that older officers might not work as hard or they might feign injury in order to avoid work.

2. In 2004, Wall Street brokerage Morgan Stanley paid $54 million to hundreds of female employees who claimed widespread sex discrimination. The lawsuit contained allegations that women were groped and subjected to other demeaning behavior such as breast-shaped birthday cakes and strip-club outings with clients.

3. Lockheed Martin, the giant military contractor, agreed to pay $2.5 million to a former employee. The settlement, announced in 2008, is the largest payment ever obtained by the Equal Employment Opportunity Commission on behalf of an individual in a race discrimination suit. The employee, Charles Daniels, claims he was threatened and subjected to racial epithets by coworkers and a supervisor. When he complained to the Human Relations Department at Lockheed, Daniels said he was told, "Boys will be boys." Also, he was warned not to prosecute the company.

4. In 2008, Golf Channel anchor Kelly Tilghman was chatting on air with another analyst, Nick Faldo. When the subject turned to golfers who might challenge superstar Tiger Woods, Faldo said, "To take Tiger on, maybe they should gang up for a while." Tilghman laughingly retorted, "Lynch him in a back alley." Given that Tiger is the son of an African-American father and an Asian mother, and considering the role lynching has played in our nation's history, it is not surprising that her reference to lynching stirred considerable controversy nationwide. The Jena 6 incident and the increasing appearance of nooses in workplaces, schools, and communities have made the public even more aware of this racially charged symbol. Responses to Tilghman's comments ranged from demands that she be fired to acknowledgments that it was a poor choice of words and nothing more. Tilghman apologized to Woods, a friend of hers. He accepted her apology and stated he was not upset.

   Days later, the cover of *Golfweek* showed a swinging noose along with the words, "Caught in a Noose: Tilghman slips up, and Golf Channel can't wriggle free." Many commentators were even more disturbed by the cover image, arguing it was deliberate and unnecessary. Whereas Tilghman was suspended for two weeks, the editor of *Golfweek* was fired.

5. In 2010, the federal government agreed to compensate thousands of African-American farmers, who claimed that because of racism, the U.S. Department of Agriculture (USDA) denied them loans and other assistance for a period of ten years, starting in 1987. In commenting on the historic $1.25 billion settlement, President Obama commented on the importance of bringing these "long-ignored claims" to a just conclusion.

6. A few years ago, more than 200,000 African-American and Hispanic borrowers filed a lawsuit against Bank of America, alleging that they were charged higher rates because of their race or national origin. The settlement in the amount of $335 million is the largest in the history of residential fair lending practices.

Many times, monetary amounts do not begin to capture the full cost of inadequate diversity consciousness. Tony Hayward, CEO of British Petroleum (BP) during the time of the BP drilling rig explosion in the Gulf of Mexico, failed miserably when he tried to reach out to those affected by the biggest oil spill in U.S. history. Two of his comments illustrate his inability to shift perspectives and connect with his audience affectively as well as intellectually. Hayward said, "The Gulf of Mexico is a very big ocean. The amount of volume of oil and dispersant we are putting into it is tiny in relation to the total water volume." Later, he commented, "There's no one who wants this over more than I do. I would like my life back."[28]

According to one highly respected economist, "the labor force of the early twenty-first century is a potential powder keg for discrimination suits."[29] The reasons are numerous. In addition to becoming a larger part of the U.S. workforce, minorities continue to encounter discrimination in terms of hiring and promotion. Overall, many workers question whether merit is the determining factor in job advancement. Some analysts argue that upper-level management at many companies has been reactive rather than proactive. They have been slow to acknowledge the existence of discrimination. Others say that when companies have programs to guard against bias, it can be difficult for executives to ensure that managers and workers fully commit to them.

The relationship between diversity consciousness and success has been examined throughout this chapter. Numerous research findings, personal anecdotes, and workplace data attest to the critical importance of specific diversity skills. Through education, and constant practice of these skills, you have the power to improve your diversity consciousness. This will enhance your chances for success. By developing these skills, you will become a better student and a more valued employee. Conversely, ignoring these skills will be very costly.

Case Studies

Case Study One

Ligua, who identifies herself as a Salvadorean-American, is a car salesperson (plus part-time student, wife, and mother) who works on a commission basis. On Ligua's job, everybody seems to be "out for themselves." With the emphasis on individual accomplishments and evaluations, competition is the norm. Ligua is much more comfortable helping others. But if she tries to be nurturing, coworkers think she is weird or they see it as a weakness. They don't see that she's doing this on purpose so that the entire staff can do the job more efficiently.

A few months ago, she discussed this situation with a friend. Her friend, Katina, could readily identify with her situation. Katina, who was raised to help people in need, said, "If I see you struggling, I will stop and offer help." But where Katina works, it's not that way either. When she reaches out to a coworker, her supervisors want to know, "Why are you concerning yourself with someone else's problems?" Trying to fit in has been a constant source of stress for Katina as well as Ligua.

Questions:

1. If Ligua wants to be successful, does she have to buy into a work culture that values independence and individual accomplishments? Explain.

2. How could the work setting be changed to accommodate individuals who may feel more comfortable in a group-oriented atmosphere?

3. What diversity skills might Ligua work on developing to help her with these conflicts? Explain.

Case Study Two

Mary is a White social work student who plans to go on for a MS degree and work in a clinical setting. She attends an urban university and enjoys the diversity and energy of city life, but in her free time is actively involved in social activities centered around her Scottish background. She is taking a class from a professor who is of a different nationality than she. Although the professor has lived in the United States for several years, he has a very pronounced accent and she finds his English difficult to understand. Mary feels that this particular professor is very knowledgeable and has a lot of relevant personal experiences to share with the class. The class is a lecture class, with the professor talking for the majority of the time. Because the material is new and somewhat difficult to understand, the language barrier can make it more difficult at times.

Mary actively listens and follows along in the book. She raises her hand when she does not understand what the professor is saying. He is always more than happy to explain further. Also, he is aware that at times students may find it difficult to understand him, and he is not embarrassed to ask for help from the class. Mary has discovered that she is actually learning more from the class because she is following in the book and attending more closely to the professor's words than she would otherwise.

During class, it is easy to hear mumbling about the professor from some of her classmates. After class, these same students openly share their feelings within earshot of the professor, saying he is not a good teacher and does not know his subject matter. Mary is upset by the students' comments, which she attributes to their unwillingness to work at understanding what he is saying.

Questions:

1. If you were in Mary's situation, how would you view the class and the professor?

2. If you were in Mary's situation, what would you say to your classmates who you feel are being unfair to the professor?

3. Which diversity skills do Mary's classmates need to develop in order to be more successful in this class? Explain.

Case Study Three

Michael identifies himself as African American. He is a college graduate and the divorced father of a teenage son, Aaron, who attends a private school in the well-to-do suburb where they live. Dennis, a new employee who reports to Michael at work, is a native of Brazil. Dennis asked Michael to approve his request for personal leave. Dennis wants to take paid leave to attend the funeral of his "compadre"—a close personal friend.

Company policy grants five days of paid, excused absence from work for "Death in the Family." Because his friend's funeral is in Brazil, he needs to take a full week off. Nothing in the company's leave policy covers this situation. Dennis feels a deep commitment to the family of his compadre. According to Dennis, a compadre is far more than a friend; a compadre is like family. In his request, he points out that there is no direct English translation for the word *compadre*. Michael is not sure how he feels about this. Although he sympathizes with his friend, he thinks that agreeing to Dennis's request establishes a bad precedent.

Questions:

1. Do you think Michael should approve Dennis's request? Can this request be justified given company policy?

2. If Dennis is allowed to do this, should the company treat all other employees who have a very close friend the same?

3. Dealing with Dennis's request will require Michael to use a number of diversity skills. In this situation, which of Michael's diversity skills do you think will be the most critical? Why?

 Key Terms

Success	Field independent	Diversity training
Sociocultural theory	Transculturation	Blended learning
Social forces	Emotional intelligence	Sociodramas
Diversity skills	Organizations	Cultural competence
Learning styles	Groupthink	
Field dependent	Managing diversity	

 Exercises

Exercise 1: Social Relationships, Diversity, and Your Success

1. Think of the people, both past and present, who have been bridges in your life. Which of these people have played a major role in shaping your thinking about success? Explain.

2. Which of your diversity skills have been instrumental in your success at work and at school? Explain.

Exercise 2: Your Learning Style Preferences

Go to Google.com and type "learning styles inventory" in the search box (be sure to include the quotation marks). You will see many options listed where you can take a test and determine your learning style preferences. Choose two of these inventories and complete them. For each test, follow the directions to determine your preferences.

1. Compare and contrast the results for the two tests.

2. Do you agree with the results? Explain.

3. How can knowing your learning style preferences help you become more successful?

ANSWER to Diversity Box: "Thinking Outside the Box" (see page 45)

Directions: Draw four straight lines, without lifting your pencil, that touch all the dots.

This problem illustrates the idea that sometimes the only way you can solve a problem is to go beyond your usual way of thinking. Most people when trying to solve this problem will not extend their lines past the dots—staying "in the box." The only way to solve the problem is to "think outside the box."

 Notes

[1] C. B. Olson, "The Influence of Context on Gender Differences in Performance Attributions: Further Evidence of a 'Feminine Modesty' Effect," paper presented at the annual meeting of the Western Psychological Association, San Francisco, CA, 1988.

[2] Samuel D. Proctor and William D. Watley, *Sermons from the Black Pulpit* (Valley Forge, PA: Judson Press, 1984), 38.

[3] Al Heredia, "Cultural Learning Styles," *Eric Clearinghouse on Teaching and Teacher Education*, December 1999.

[4] Jacqueline Irvine and Darlene York, "Learning Styles and Culturally Diverse Students: A Literature Review," in James Banks (ed.), *Handbook of Research on Multicultural Education* (New York: Simon & Schuster, 1995), 484–497.

[5] Howard Gardner, *Frames of Mind: The Theory of Multiple Intelligences* (New York: Basic Books, 1983).

[6] Sonia Nieto, *Affirming Diversity: The Sociopolitical Context of Multicultural Education* (White Plains, NY: Longman, 1996), 283.

[7] M. A. Gibson, "Parental Support for Schooling," paper presented at the annual meeting of the American Anthropological Association, December 1986.

[8] Terry Huffman, "The Transculturation of Native American College Students," in Young I. Song and Eugene C. Kim (eds.), *American Mosaic: Selected Readings on America's Multicultural Heritage* (Englewood Cliffs, NJ: Prentice Hall, 1993), 211–219; Sonia Nieto, *Affirming Diversity: The Sociopolitical Context of Multicultural Education* (White Plains, NY: Longman, 1996).

[9] Terry Huffman, "The Transculturation of Native American College Students," in Young I. Song and Eugene C. Kim (eds.), *American Mosaic: Selected Readings on America's Multicultural Heritage* (Englewood Cliffs, NJ: Prentice Hall, 1993), 211–219.

[10] Hart Research Associates, *Raising The Bar*, Washington, DC, 2010.

[11] Robert Half Management Resources, "CFOs Seek Soft Skills," *SmartPros*. Online, December 19, 2007. Available: http://accounting.smartpros.com/x60128.xml.

[12] Office Team, "Fitting In, Standing Out, and Building Remarkable Work Teams," 2007. Available: http://officeteam.rhi.mediaroom.com/index.php?s=260&item=199 (accessed October 4, 2013).

[13] Daniel Goleman, *Working with Emotional Intelligence* (New York: Bantam Books, 1998).

[14] Wendy Levinson, Debra Roter, John Mullooly, Valerie Dull, and Richard Frankel, "Physician–Patient Communication: The Relationship with Malpractice Claims Among Primary Care Physicians and Surgeons," *Journal of the American Medical Association* (February 19, 1997), 553.

[15] Roger von Oech, *A Kick in the Seat of the Pants* (New York: Harper & Row, 1986), 5–21.

[16] Andrew Sobel, "The Beatles Principles," *Strategy and Business*. Online, February 28, 2006. Available: http://www.strategy-business.com/article/06104?gko=8e481.

[17] Sheryl Silver, "New Grads: Make the Most of Your First Job," *The Washington Post High Tech Horizons*, August 3, 1997, M19.

[18] The University of Georgia Terry College of Business, "News Release: Hispanic Consumer Market in the U.S. is Larger than the Entire Economies of All but 13 Countries in the World." Online, May 1, 2012. Available: http://www.strategy-business.com/article/06104?gko=8e481.

[19] Stephen Covey, "How to Succeed in Today's Workplace," *USA Weekend*, August 29–31, 1997, 4–5.

[20] Daniel Goleman, *Working with Emotional Intelligence* (New York: Bantam Books, 1998), 64.

[21] Irving L. Janis, *Victims of Groupthink* (Boston: Houghton Mifflin, 1972).

[22] Center for Work-Life Policy, "Asian Americans Still Feel Like Outsiders in Corporate America." Online, July 20, 2011. Available: www.worklifepolicy.org.

[23] "Poll Reveals Generational Gap in Workplace Training Programs," *Workplace Options News*. Online, July 11, 2011. Available: http://www.workplaceoptions.com/news/press-releases/press-release.asp?id=AC3DEC48BC3 9412B93CF&title=%20Poll%20Reveals%20Generational%20Gap%20in%20Workplace%20Training%20 Programs.

[24] Brian Smedley, Adrienne Stith, and Alan Nelson (eds.), *Unequal Treatment: Confronting Racial and Ethnic Disparities in Health Care* (Washington, DC: National Academies Press, 2002).

[25] Lynne Robins, Joseph Fantone, Julica Hermann, Gwen Alexander, and Andrew Zweifler, "Improving Cultural Awareness and Sensitivity Training in Medical School," *Academic Medicine*, 73(10), October Supplement, 1998.

[26] George Strait, "Health Care's Racial Divide." Online, March 7, 1999. Available: http://more.abcnews. go.com/sections/living/DailyNews/racial_healthcare990224.html.

[27] Ceci Connolly, "Report Says Minorities Get Lower-Quality Health Care," *The Washington Post*, March 21, 2002, A2.

[28] Richard Wray, "Deepwater Horizon Oil Spill: BP Gaffes in Full," *The Guardian*. Online, July 27, 2010. Available: http://www.guardian.co.uk/business/2010/jul/27/deepwater-horizon-oil-spill-bp-gaffes.

[29] Ian Simpson, "U.S. Race Bias Suits on the Rise, Putting Companies on the Defensive." Online, July 14, 2000. Available: http://news.excite.com/news/r/000714/13/economy-race-suits2.

3

Personal and Social Barriers to Success

Learning Outcomes

Upon completion of this chapter, you will be able to:

- Differentiate between personal and social barriers.
- Explain how limited perceptions can be a barrier to success.
- Explain how ethnocentrism can be a barrier to success.
- Analyze the impact of stereotypes on success.
- Compare prejudice to prejudice plus power as barriers to success.
- Discuss each of the four combinations of prejudice and discrimination.
- Summarize how discrimination can be a barrier to success.
- Assess various strategies for overcoming diversity barriers.

I think my personal barriers can be attributed to my social barriers. I think they go hand in hand. I face a lot of social barriers because of my skin tone (dark), my sex (female), and my sexual orientation (lesbian). I often feel like I wasn't put on this earth to make anyone comfortable. I think we all have a purpose and when you find your purpose, align them with your principles, and match that with your intentions; that will display what type of person you are. Having all these social barriers and experiencing the type of discrimination I have has helped me to develop a sense of self that would not have been achieved without going through these experiences. I went through a period of intense agitation, I was constantly told what to do, who to be, who to love, how to dress, and I emerged with a sense of self that can't be diminished. I can't do anything but accept who I am and battle those who can't.

—Another perspective

MyStudentSuccessLab

MyStudentSuccessLab (www.mystudentsuccesslab.com) is an online solution designed to help you 'Start Strong, Finish Stronger' by building skills for ongoing personal and professional development.

SIX BARRIERS TO SUCCESS

How do we explain why some people are more successful than others? Is it simply a matter of individual talent and motivation? Cornel West, a prolific writer and widely cited scholar, is highly critical of conventional explanations of success. In his writings, West zeros in on the issue of race and its implications for climbing up the social ladder. However, his analysis could apply to gender, class, and any number of other dimensions of diversity.

At first, West takes issue with the idea that people can solve problems such as poverty and inequality simply by changing individual values and behaviors. He rightly points out that many poor African-Americans remain poor despite their strong work ethic. Second, he criticizes the notion that more government and economic programs can eliminate racial inequality. West argues that the problem is not strictly a matter of economics. In short, he views approaches to racial inequality that focus entirely on the individual or the larger society as simplistic and incomplete. West maintains that we will be successful only if we stop pointing our fingers at a single source of the problem.[1]

We can take West's analysis and apply it to our discussion of diversity, success, and the barriers to success. Barriers to success may stem from the individual or may be found in the larger society. **Personal barriers** refer to those individual factors that get in the way of our success. Our focus is on factors that relate to diversity. These barriers include one's lack of self-awareness, lack of self-discipline, cultural ignorance, and underdeveloped diversity consciousness. Personal barriers also include a person's biases and discriminatory behaviors. **Social barriers** focus more on society. They refer to those factors that are external to the person and impede her or his success. Among these barriers are the perceptions, thoughts, and actions of others. Ethnocentrism, stereotypes, prejudice, and discrimination are barriers that can be personal and/or social, depending on the situation. Also, it is important to remember, as West mentions earlier, that interrelationships exist between personal and social barriers. For example, encountering prejudice and discrimination in the larger society may reinforce our personal biases. Similarly, our bias can trigger bias from others.

 Thinking Through Diversity

If someone were to write your life history, what would we learn about personal and social barriers?

> I am from a small island in the West Indies. I have an accent where I do not speak clearly. People do not understand me, or laugh. As for my instructors, they look at me as spaced out. They think I do not know what is going on because I do not talk a lot in class. Sometimes if I think I have a good answer, I will second-guess myself. When the instructor asks me something, the first thing I'll do is get hot and sweaty and scared. I'll feel like my answers are not as good as anybody else's.
>
> —Another perspective

In this chapter we examine personal and social barriers that impede our success (see Fig. 3.1). We focus on those barriers that are obvious as well as those that are not easily recognizable. Additionally, we examine a number of strategies for overcoming such barriers.

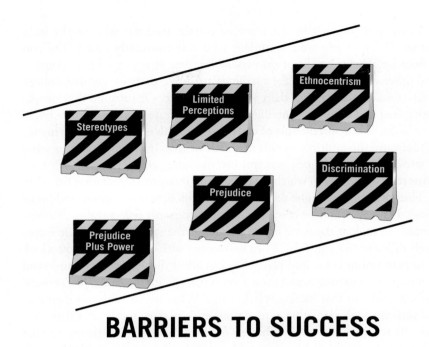

BARRIERS TO SUCCESS

Figure 3.1 Six Barriers to Success

Barrier 1: Limited Perceptions

The scene: You just returned to campus after the spring break. As you approach the library, you see a number of statues. Upon closer examination, you notice that each of these statues represents a student. Two appear to be African-American students. One of the African-American students is twirling a basketball and the other is balancing a book on her head. The single Asian-American student is carrying a violin. Each of the White students is shown holding a number of books. What are you feeling as you study each of the statues? Individually and collectively, what do these statues say to you? Are you offended? Do you plan on sharing your thoughts and feelings with anyone else? Why? Will you be able to put your feelings aside and concentrate on your studies for the rest of the day?

This scene took place at the University of North Carolina (UNC). Each year the graduating class gives the university a gift. Not long ago, one class hired a well-known sculptor to create a number of statues depicting the diversity of UNC's student population. The artist sculpted the figures described earlier. Once they were placed in a prominent place on campus, they immediately caused an uproar among students. Many complained that the statues reinforced stereotypical images. The African-Americans, they argued, were portrayed as being less studious and less intelligent than the Whites and Asian-Americans, reinforcing the stereotype that African-Americans are athletes first and students second. Other students felt that people were making a big fuss over nothing. In response to the growing tension among students, the statues were relocated to another spot on campus that was much less visible. Later on, two of the statues somehow disappeared.

The scenario just described provides insight into the potential barriers that limited perceptions of diversity can create. Did the sculptor consider the different messages these statues might convey? Did the sculptor have any understanding of the backgrounds and perspectives of the students, faculty, and staff at UNC? What about the people who hired this sculptor and oversaw the project? Most important, what did the students learn from this?

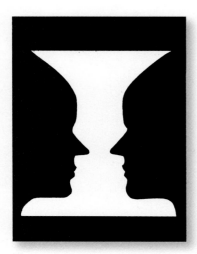

Figure 3.2 What do you see? Two faces looking at each other? A vase? Because of the shapes and coloring in the picture, you might see either. This image, which appears in the book *Can You Believe Your Eyes?* by J. Richard Block and Harold Yuker (New York: Brunner/Mazel, 1992), was first published around 1915.
Source: Used with permission from Archives of the History of American Psychology–The University of Akron.

"The stranger sees only what he knows."
—African proverb

For a moment, put yourself in the place of certain students who might walk past these statues. What if you were a student who was constantly asked "Do you play sports?" because of your height or skin color? Suppose that you often encounter instructors and other students who make a habit of assuming that you got into college because of your athletic talent rather than your intelligence. Or imagine that people assume you are gifted and extremely intelligent simply because of your cultural background or your looks. Taking on the role of each of these students, or at least trying to, can help us understand the multiple worlds in which we live. It can also make us more aware of the barriers we create by our perceptions, thoughts, and actions.

Perceptions refer to the way in which we receive and interpret information from any of our senses. Thus perceptions can be understood as a link between a person and his or her surroundings. However, what we perceive does not necessarily reflect reality. Furthermore, two people can look at the same image or witness the same event and see something completely different (see Fig. 3.2). When we interact with others or even take a look at ourselves, our perceptions come into play. They can affect the way we feel, think, and act. Hence, it is important to understand those factors that can influence our perceptions.

Common sense tells us that "seeing is believing." What we see with our own eyes or what we absorb through our other senses must be true. Yet social scientists have discovered that the reverse is also true. What we *believe* may very well determine what we see. In other words, we do not interact with others with an entirely blank mind. Rather, our perceptions are rooted in past experiences. Throughout our lives, we are exposed to a variety of human images via our interaction with the media, school, peers, friends, family, community members, and others. The images we experience and how we interpret these images color our perceptions.

A well-known psychological experiment illustrates how our beliefs may distort our perceptions. In this experiment, a person is shown a picture of a White man standing next to a Black man. The White man is holding a knife. The person is asked to describe the picture to another person, who then relays what he or she was told to the next person. This process continues until everybody in the group has a turn. When asked to describe what the first person saw, the last person explains that there are two men standing next to each other, one Black and one White, and the Black man is holding a knife. The experiment shows how our racial biases can radically alter what we perceive.

Psychologists conduct extensive research on perceptions. Research indicates that we can only experience and digest a certain portion of our vast social world. Because

A Beginner's Mind

Steve Jobs, co-founder of Apple, was a serious student of Buddhism. A large part of what made Steve Jobs such a successful leader and innovator was his ability to live and promote a principle in Buddhism known as a "beginner's mind." A beginner's or a child-like mind is not encumbered with traditions, routines, or expectations that smother curiosity. When leaders act with a beginner's mind, they are more apt to be creative and focused. Jobs' diverse life experiences shaped his thinking and philosophy. He dropped out of college, traveled to India, was fired from the company he created (Apple), and fought multiple bouts of cancer. He learned from his successes as well as his failures, keeping in mind that every day could be his last. As he said, "I am the only person I know that's lost a quarter of a billion dollars in one year. . . It's very character-building." To Jobs, intellectual diversity is thwarted by limited perceptions and preconceived notions. Hence, Jobs promoted a workplace where workers were encouraged to be genuine, and follow their heart as well as their minds, just like children. In a speech from Apple's "Think Different" ad campaign, Jobs promoted the virtues of intellectual diversity; namely the "crazy ones, the misfits, the rebels, the troublemakers, the round pegs in the square holes."[2] Lastly, he offered this valuable advice to a group of college graduates at Stanford University, "Stay young and stay foolish."

of this, we have a tendency to take shortcuts to understanding others. Dan Keplinger (see Photo 3.1) is well aware of the shortcuts people take to understand him. He says, "If I could change one thing about my disability, it would be the way I speak. When the world cannot understand my words, I'm assumed to be deaf or retarded…I hear people talking about me in front of me, sure that I cannot make decisions for myself, that I can't think for myself."[3]

We often perceive what we want to perceive. This is called **selective perception**. In other words, we focus on those things that support our thinking and ignore information that refutes it. In this way we can store and process information in neat, simple categories.

Our perceptions of poverty reveal the potential dangers of selective perception. Football coach Barry Switzer once said, "Some people are born on third base and go through life thinking they hit a triple."[4] A recent nationwide poll reveals that a significant percentage of people place the blame for poverty on the individual. More than one in four respondents agreed with the statements, "People are poor because they are lazy," and "Poor people usually have lower moral values."[5] Being born into wealth and privilege or even growing up in an environment where one's basic needs have always been met may make it difficult to grasp the many, complex reasons for poverty. For example, we may assume that one's standing in society is simply a result of a strong work ethic and a positive attitude, since we selectively perceive those traits in ourselves. Consequently, we may view the poor as deserving of their status since we define their values as deficient and deviant. However, this view largely ignores the fact that many of the poor in the United States are people with disabilities, children, and women, particularly women who head households and often work multiple jobs.

Limited perceptions work against us for a number of reasons:

Photo 3.1 Dan Keplinger, featured in this award-winning ad by Cingular Wireless, is an accomplished artist who has cerebral palsy. He is a graduate of Towson University, with a Bachelor of Science in Art. This ad, and Dan's work as an artist, is about much more than his disability. Art provides Dan with the tools to express himself, counter limited perceptions, and remind us of our ability to persevere in the face of barriers that all of us encounter at some point in our lives.
Source: Courtesy of Cingular Wireless.

- We tend to be unaware of the blinders or obstructions that distort our perceptions in some way. This makes it difficult to acknowledge, much less remove, these obstructions. Consequently, our senses do not operate at peak efficiency, and our personal and professional relationships suffer.

- We absorb only a small fraction of the world around us. In other words, we experience only a slice or, in some cases, a sliver of life. More often than not, we experience things from one perspective rather than from a variety of perspectives.

- We tend to tune into those things with which we agree. Although this might make it easier to make sense of the world around us, the end result is that we miss out on a lot. In an increasingly diverse world, we fail to experience and appreciate much that the world has to offer. Moreover, there is a tendency to view more and more people as homogeneous masses with whom we have little in common.

- Our perception of others reflects on ourselves. According to an African proverb, "when you judge others, you do not define them … you define yourself."

If I am to have a successful medical career, I can't afford to walk around with blinders on or refuse to treat someone because that person is "different" from me.

—Another perspective

Barrier 2: Ethnocentrism

Culture envelopes us so completely that sometimes it is difficult to realize that our perspective is one of many. **Ethnocentrism** refers to the assumption that our way of thinking and acting is naturally superior to any other. As a result, we use ourselves or our culture as the yardstick by which we measure what is right or desirable or normal. It follows that if we display ethnocentrism, we naturally assume that behaviors and customs that appear different to us are necessarily abnormal and inferior. This kind of thinking produces "tunnel vision." Rudyard Kipling, in his poem "We and They," describes how ethnocentrism locks us into an "us and them" mindset. "Father, Mother and Me, Sister and Auntie say All the people like Us are We, And everyone else is They."[6]

Ethnocentrism is widespread. A survey, administered as part of the Pew Global Attitudes Project, asked more than 45,000 people in 47 countries if they agree or disagree with the statement, "Our people are not perfect, but our culture is superior to others." In 20 countries, more than 70 percent agreed with this statement. In only four countries—Germany, France, Britain, and Sweden—did more than half the respondents disagree with this notion of cultural superiority (see Fig. 3.3).

Selected Countries and Percent of Respondents
"Our people are not perfect, but our culture is superior to others"

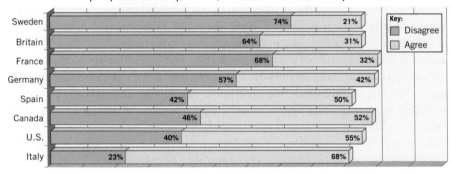

Figure 3.3 Cultural Superiority?
Source: The Pew Global Attitudes Project (2007). "No opinion" and "Don't know" not shown.

Taking a Critical Look at Maps

Since maps shape our thinking about our surroundings and our place in the world, it is important to consider the way we look at maps. We are taught to read maps, not question them. After all, the world can only be drawn one correct way, right? Imagine a sphere like a hollowed-out pumpkin or an orange peel. What happens if we try to make it flat? It would not be possible without damaging or wrinkling it in some way. Now think of what happens when we take the Earth's curved surface and try to make it lie down on a map. There has to be some distortion. This is why mapmakers utilize projection. Over 200 techniques have been used to project the Earth onto a flat map. All are distorted to some degree.

Many schools in the United States still use the Mercator Projection Map. This map was created by Gerardus Mercator in 1569 in Germany. At this time, European colonial powers dominated much of the world. Although the Mercator Projection has navigational benefits, it also reflects the Europeans' sense of importance and power at that time. It makes European countries look bigger than the rest of the world. Other areas, such as China, Mexico, and Africa, appear much smaller than they really are.

During the past few decades, Arthur Robinson is one of a number of cartographers who has created a projection that corrects this bias. Cartographers consider his map, the Robinson Projection Map, to be a major improvement. It displays the relative sizes of continents and countries much more accurately. For example, the true relative size of Africa is shown on the Robinson Projection Map. Unlike the traditional Mercator Projection, the Robinson Projection shows that Africa is actually much larger than Greenland (see Fig. 3.4 on the next page).

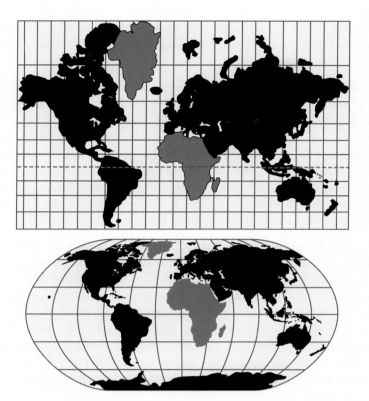

Figure 3.4 Mercator (top) and Robinson (bottom) Projection maps of the world. Compare the size of the continents, particularly Europe and Africa, on the traditional Mercator Projection and the Robinson Projection. Similarly, compare the size of Greenland and Africa. The Mercator map is also often shown without Antarctica, making Europe and North America appear in the center of the world.

It is important to realize that no one person, group, or society has a monopoly on ethnocentrism. We are all ethnocentric to some degree. To illustrate, we might view our customs as the right way and, in some instances, the only way. When we encounter someone from another culture, we might think to ourselves: Why can't she think the way I think? Talk the way I talk? Act the way I act? Wear her hair the way I do? This kind of thinking can build group solidarity and pride. It becomes a liability when we get so caught up in our own thinking that we cannot see the value of other ways of life.

Ethnocentrism can be very subtle and difficult to recognize. In the examples that follow, ask yourself, What assumptions are being made? What are the implications for success?

1. Gloria is a manager of a large department store. She feels very proud of her success on the job and takes pride in being the only employee with a college degree. Gloria attaches considerable importance to academic degrees and credentials. When she meets with store employees, she tends to be close-minded even though she pretends to listen. She finds it particularly difficult to give much credence to the views of lower-salaried employees who only possess a high school diploma. Many of these employees sense this and keep their ideas to themselves.

2. Karlton is completing a lengthy research study in which he examines the short- and long-term effects of daily doses of aspirin. In compiling his data, he relies exclusively on research that studies only men. He operates under the

assumption that what he finds true of men also applies to women. Now, a prominent fellow researcher is criticizing this assumption and questioning the validity of his research.

3. Bob is a 54-year-old single White male. As a veteran lawyer, he is proud of his accomplishments working for a large law firm in Chicago. He attributes his success to the tremendous amount of time and energy he invests in his job. Recently, he attended a diversity training workshop. Along with other participants, he was asked to make a list of the firm's unwritten rules. The lists were then shared. One rule mentioned by a number of minority lawyers was "If you're not a White male, you won't succeed." Although Bob did not say anything at the time, he thinks any mention of race or gender is a "cop-out." According to Bob, "These people have to be willing to sacrifice like I did."

4. Freida, a 35-year-old African-American female, is a human relations manager at a large firm that manufactures hard drives for personal computers. While planning a diversity workshop, she hears of a "diversity trainer," someone who is described as an outstanding presenter with impeccable credentials. He comes highly recommended for his strong academic background and his exceptional ability to relate to diverse audiences. She is ready to ask him to facilitate the workshop until she discovers that he is White. Freida questions whether he can really understand some of the diversity issues that may be addressed in the workshop. Being relatively new on the job, she feels that choosing a person of color is a "safer" choice.

Ethnocentrism is universal. It affects us all. The challenge of ethnocentrism is realizing not *if* but *when* it influences our thinking and judgment. Similarly, it is necessary to recognize the *costs* of putting ourselves and our culture at the center of everything. We become narrow-minded and lose sight of opportunities in realms outside our own. We impair our ability to relate to others. Most important, we fail to learn and benefit from the collective wisdom and experiences of all people.

Barrier 3: Stereotypes

As you were growing up, what stories or comments did you hear about people who were viewed as different for one reason or another? They might have been members of another race, social class, or religion. From whom did you hear these things? Did you believe them at the time? What about now? Often, what we hear and accept as true takes the form of a **stereotype**, an unverified and oversimplified generalization about an entire group of people. Our social environment provides us with a set of images. Many of these images reflect stereotypes. When we stereotype, we lump people in a category and assume they are all alike.

Each of us is exposed to stereotypes starting at an early age. Wilma Mankiller, former chief of the Cherokee Nation, recalls her first encounter with stereotypes. Her schoolmates would sing a song, "Mankiller, Mankiller, how many men did you kill today?" or they would make war-whoop noises. We learn stereotypical images of Native Americans or any other group through our interaction with family, peers, school, religion, the media, and other social influences. Over the course of many years, these stereotypes are reinforced and internalized. As a result, stereotypical thinking tends to be very rigid and difficult to change.

Gary Foster, a sociologist, has studied the persistence of "hillbilly" stereotypes in the media and in popular culture. What is interesting, he says, is that images of

I was raised in a single-parent household headed up by my mother, as were most of my friends. As a result, I grew up believing that African-American men were irresponsible, selfish, and afraid of commitment. They cared nothing about their children or the women who bore these children. As I've grown older and explored other communities and cultures, I've learned to question what I see around me. I've learned that the absentee African-American father is not the norm.

Being a Black man in this society, I am viewed as someone to fear and avoid. Stereotypes typically portray me as someone who shuns responsibility, is not to be trusted, is prone to violence, and is unwilling to commit to any long-term relationship related to marriage and family.

—Other perspectives

hillbilly men and women endure despite the trend toward repudiation of racial and ethnic stereotyping. Foster supports his argument by pointing to television caricatures found in *The Simpsons* and reruns of *The Beverly Hillbillies* or *Green Acres*. Hillbilly men tend to be lazy and unkempt, and have a taste for moonshine. Hillbilly women come in two types: They are either oversexed and underdressed, or gaunt with unkempt hair, tattered clothes, and high-topped work boots or no shoes at all. Foster suspects that we tolerate these stereotypes, sometimes accompanied by labels such as "rednecks" or "White trash," for two reasons: First, those most offended by the stereotype, such as poor, rural Whites, lack the political or economic power to protest effectively. Second, because hillbilly stereotypes are associated with Whites, we may not give these characterizations the same degree of attention and scrutiny.[7]

There is no shortage of stereotypes in today's world. Stereotypes revolve around every dimension of diversity, such as job position and function, race, ethnicity, religion, social class, language, learning style, and sexual orientation. In many instances, stereotypes relate to physical appearance, such as skin color, age, or gender. Another dimension, one that is more subtle and rarely mentioned, is physical attractiveness. Psychological research shows that many people in our society equate character with looks. According to the *attractiveness stereotype*, we view people who are attractive as "more sensitive, kind, interesting, strong, poised, modest, sociable, outgoing, and exciting, sexually warm, and responsive." Furthermore, we tend to assume that they will be more successful, more powerful, and more competent.

Like other stereotypes, the attractiveness stereotype can affect the way we think and act. This was borne out in research by Wesley Kayson and Andrea DeSantis of Iona College. These researchers recruited 160 college students, faculty, and office workers. Each participant was asked to serve as a juror in an imaginary burglary case. After reviewing a fact sheet describing the crime, the participants studied the photographs of men and women described as defendants. The attractiveness of each defendant had already been rated by ten psychology students on a scale of 1 to 7. The participants were then asked to recommend a jail sentence. On average, good-looking defendants received much shorter sentences than those rated as less attractive.[8]

Before we can change our thinking, we need to acknowledge our stereotypical assumptions. However, this is not easy. Coming to grips with a stereotype we have held for a long time can make us feel uncomfortable and vulnerable. Additionally, we tend to be more aware of other people's stereotypes than our own. As one of my students said, some stereotypes are "difficult to see because they are buried deep within our souls."

If students feel a certain level of trust and comfort, the classroom can be a place where students take a more critical and rational look at their thinking about diversity. In my classroom, I use an activity that brings certain stereotypes to the surface. Students and I sit in a tight circle. I ask them to recount a story or comment they have heard about members of another racial or ethnic group. One by one, each student gets a chance to share his or her story. What they share is typically negative and stereotypical.

Once every student has had a chance to participate, I ask questions to help them examine critically what was shared. Are any of these stories based on fact? Why? How do we share and perpetuate these stories? What assumptions are found in each story? Can we make these assumptions about all members of a racial or

---

In elementary school, I was taught that Africans lived in huts, in villages. They were starving and poor. Even though my mother is from Zambia, I still had trouble picturing Africans having the same things Americans have, such as homes, communities, and streets.

I grew up thinking that Asians, Vietnamese, Chinese, and Japanese were all the same. For a long time, I believed that all Asians were smart.

Growing up, I viewed the English as very uptight, unathletic human beings. I pictured them as always wearing suits and trench coats. I pictured the women always dressed as if they were going to a ball. I figured all of the English drank tea and ate only freshly cooked, expensive dinners.

When I was growing up, I heard that you can't trust White people. They'll act like they're your friends and they'll laugh and joke with you. But when it comes down to a confrontation, they'll turn on you.

As a child, I heard that people from Haiti and the Islands in general always lived with like 30 people to a bedroom. So many lived in an apartment they had to sleep in shifts.

—Other perspectives

---

ethnic group? Inevitably, the students teach each other. For example, the comment, "All Whites can't be trusted" is picked apart. What does this mean? How do we know for sure? Does this apply to all Whites or just some? Can people of the *same* race necessarily trust each other? For some students, it is the first time they openly discuss issues such as this in a racially and ethnically diverse group. The value of critical thinking becomes more apparent as students weigh whether the evidence supports certain assumptions. They also begin to share how their thinking is changing as a result of personal experiences.

Interestingly, many of the stereotypes students mention revolve around two sensitive subjects we rarely discuss in public: sex and hygiene. For example, many students have been "taught" that certain other races are unclean and sexually deviant. Cornel West, in his best-selling book *Race Matters*, addresses the interrelationship of race and sexuality. He argues that a candid dialogue is virtually impossible because both are taboo subjects. When we cannot bring ourselves to address a subject openly and honestly, we rely on secondhand information that is full of inaccuracies, ignores diversity within diversity, and becomes highly impervious to change over time.

It is not enough to recognize and critically evaluate stereotypical thinking. We also need to understand that this kind of thinking can limit our opportunities. When we stereotype, we see people as labels rather than individuals. We base our actions on images that are distorted, incomplete, and usually negative. Even so-called positive stereotypes, such as all women are nurturing or all Asians excel in math and science, are damaging because they imply that everyone within a group manifests that trait. Furthermore, the group's potential is limited to that trait.

When others stereotype us, we may feel vulnerable and our self-esteem may suffer. Claude Steele refers to this as **stereotype vulnerability**; the danger of not performing up to our ability because of our anxieties and fears about perpetuating a stereotype.[9] For instance, Paul is an older employee who hesitates to ask for help when he has computer questions at work. He has to deal with a supervisor and others who assume that he cannot keep up with younger coworkers when it comes to computer technology. Because of this stereotypical assumption, he keeps to himself and does not ask questions because he does not want to appear computer illiterate. Consequently, his skills rarely improve.

Steele, a social psychologist at Stanford University, has conducted experimental studies revealing that vulnerability to stereotypes is a significant factor in academic achievement. According to Steele, certain groups of students find themselves constantly wrestling with stereotypes. As an example, women deal with the image of being weak in math and African-Americans contend with assumptions about their lack of academic ability. Steele maintains that fear of conforming to stereotypical expectations creates a pressure-packed situation for these students. As a result, students who are otherwise competent often do not perform up to their ability.

"They Think I'm Dumb"

Carol, a visually impaired African-American student, is a friend of mine. Recently she confided in me that she was having problems in school. When I asked if she had met with her teachers to discuss her poor grades and some of the difficulties she is having, she said no. Surprised by her response, I asked why. After a moment of hesitation, Carol said, "I didn't want them to think I was dumb." Still I did not understand. Carol is intelligent, outgoing, and a hard worker. She then elaborated. "My teachers think I'm dumb because I'm blind. They think I'm dumb because I'm Black. And they think I'm dumb because I'm a female. I just don't want to give them another reason to think I can't do the work."

Steele's research focuses attention on cultural expectations that undermine achievement, but it is equally important to examine the reactions of many different students. For some, stereotypes can motivate them to work that much harder. Some students manage to turn the negatives they encounter at school into a positive.

I believe my cultural background has definitely affected my success in school. My parents, who are not very familiar with this country and did not feel very safe, push me in the only way they know to secure a decent future for me, and that is through studying and working hard. My gender and skin color also make a difference. In some instances, I feel that being a female makes it more of a challenge for me, and that I have to prove myself. In other instances, the color of my skin makes me instantly

(continued)

(continued)

stupid. In still other instances, I am expected to be a genius. These dramatically contrasting experiences teach me more than anything to do the best I can. In instances when less is expected of me, I actually work harder to prove the teacher wrong. It is almost a personal challenge that I am determined to win.

I sat down in my statistics class, looked around, and saw that the students appeared to be about 10 percent African-American, and 90 percent Asian and European mixed. As the African-American students entered, they would look around to see who was in the class. This did not appear to be unusual to me. Once the instructor entered the class, the majority of African-American students grabbed their books and exited the room. I found it hard to believe that they were all in the wrong class. Later on that day, I ran into one of the African-American students and asked him why he left. He informed me that he noticed that the majority of the class was Asian and the probability of him getting a good grade was slim because Asians "mess up a curve." As one of the few remaining African-American students, this made me even more determined to stay in the class and be successful.

—Other perspectives

Stereotyping is a way of putting people in our own mental boxes. The problem with these boxes is we do not individualize them; rather, we use a one-size-fits-all mentality. Therefore, something important gets left out. When we put others into a "box," we lose or distort potentially valuable information and diminish our ability to relate effectively to others. Plus, in those cases in which we are targets of stereotyping, we may feel vulnerable and less confident in our abilities.

Barrier 4: Prejudice

Prejudice is an irrational and inflexible opinion formed on the basis of limited and insufficient knowledge. The derivation of the term *prejudice* can be traced to two Latin words: *prae*, "before," and *judicum*, "a judgment." Hence, prejudice represents a judgment before all the facts are known. In his landmark study, *The Nature of Prejudice*, Gordon Allport points out that prejudice is based on inaccurate information and/or illogical arguments. Therefore, it is not only a *pre*judgment; it is also a *mis*judgment.[10]

I think my instructors feel that because I am older, I should perform at a higher level. Some don't seem to understand that some of the material is just as new to me as to my younger classmates. I notice irritation and disappointment from some of my instructors when I do not perform up to their expectations.

There are people who assume certain things about me because I am White. Even though they don't know me, they act like they're angry at me. They assume that I think I'm superior. They assume my parents do not have to struggle to make ends meet. They assume that being White is a ticket to success.

—Other perspectives

Stereotypes, discussed earlier, often give rise to prejudice. Exposure to exaggerated and rigid images of a particular group can lead us to prejudge anyone we identify with that group. A good example is what followed the attacks on September 11, 2001. Innocent Muslims or people who appeared to be Muslim were indiscriminately blamed for terrorism. Not only was their safety threatened, but also many Muslims found their patriotism questioned. It is worth remembering that people did not make similar prejudgments about all fair-skinned, Christian army veterans when it was discovered that Timothy McVeigh was responsible for the Oklahoma City bombing.

Sikhs, who practice a religion that is distinct from Islam, felt particularly threatened because their faith requires them to wear turbans and grow beards. Mistaken for followers of Osama bin Laden, Sikhs endured harassment, beatings, and vandalism, and one Sikh gas station owner was murdered in Arizona a few days following the attacks. Although some Sikhs tried to blend in and hide their identity, others sought to educate the public about Sikhism, a religion founded in India in the fifteenth century.

Following the 2007 Virginia Tech massacre, there was apprehension that a backlash would take place, similar to what occurred against Muslims in the aftermath of the 9/11 attacks. When word got out that the Virginia Tech shooter, Cho Seung-Hui, was South Korean, Facebook groups, such as "Cho Seung-Hui does NOT represent Asians," sprung up, amassing new members. However, the media generally focused on Cho's mental state rather than his ethnic background. Experts continued this line of discussion, choosing to focus on Cho as an individual and comparing his profile with that of the Columbine shooters.

More often than not, talk about prejudice focuses on "them" rather than "us." Many of us can readily sense prejudice in others, but seeing it in ourselves is a challenge. When someone mentions the word *prejudice*, what comes to mind? Is prejudice something ordinary or extraordinary? Do prejudiced people look and act like you?

It is important to understand that we learn prejudice just like anything else. Research indicates that children as young as 4 or 5 years of age begin to show signs of racial prejudice. At a young age, we are more apt to simply believe what we hear. By the time we are adults, prejudging people for whatever reason can become almost an unconscious habit. Additionally, prejudice affords us a quick and easy way of categorizing all the new and different people we meet each day. It takes much more time and effort to withhold judgment until we really know someone.

> "It is never too late to give up your prejudices."
> —Henry David Thoreau

If we view prejudice as something that each of us learns, it is easier to examine ourselves. We begin to realize that uncovering prejudice in ourselves does not make us bad people. Rather, it simply shows us that we have some work to do. Ask yourself the following questions:

- Do you feel uncomfortable around certain people? Does your body language provide you with any cues? For example, are you comfortable talking to someone whose sexual orientation is different than yours? Are you comfortable sitting next to this person?

As a gay man, I don't live my life looking for sex. My relationships are based on friendship, not sex. As a student, I remember being confronted by a student who lived in the same living unit as I did. He said, "I don't care if you live here as long as you don't come on to me." His assumption was that if you were gay, you wanted to have sex with any man. Who that man was did not matter.

—Another perspective

- Do you have a tendency to judge other people because of the way they look, dress, and speak? Even the cars we drive can give rise to certain assumptions. Lorenzo, a young man who describes himself as White, Black, and American Indian, drives a nice car to work. He constantly runs into people who assume that he stole the car or bought it with drug money. Getting stopped by police is a common occurrence. "It messes my whole day up," says Lorenzo. He now carries his pay stub beneath his license to prove he can afford the car.

- Are there times when you form an opinion about a person because he or she belongs to a particular group? Rafael Olmeda, past president of the National Association of Hispanic Journalists, resents it when people assume they know something important about him because of his name. He remembers being a senior at the Bronx High School of Science. One day, Olmeda received a packet of unsolicited Harvard admission materials. Included was a Minority Student Information Request Card and information about the experiences of Hispanic students at Harvard. Even though he is proud of his Puerto Rican heritage, he resents being categorized this way. What did the people at Harvard really know about him?[11]

Thinking Through Diversity

Frequently, we can see prejudices all around us but not in us. Why? When you recognize prejudice in yourself, how do you respond?

If we are honest with ourselves, we can begin to be more critical of our mental pictures of others. Only then can we begin to acknowledge that prejudice does exist. If somebody does complain about prejudice, it is important not to discount it. As one of my students says, sometimes the greatest gift you can give to other people is just to listen to them.

Some people minimize the importance of prejudice in the workplace. Because an employer cannot know what you are thinking, they argue prejudice becomes an issue only when we act on it. Consequently, you can be held accountable only for your actions, not for your thoughts. The problem with this argument is that we cannot analyze behavior and perceptions as distinct entities.

Picture yourself driving to work. Your commute takes you by two men who appear to be Latino standing on a street corner. You pull up next to them as you stop at a red light. You wonder why they are not working. Trying to be as inconspicuous as possible, you check to make sure that your door is locked and continue on to work. At the office, you ready yourself for a series of job interviews you will be conducting throughout the day. When the last interviewee walks into your office, you notice that he is one of the two men you passed on the way to work. What are the chances that you will be able to judge this person fairly?

We cannot neatly compartmentalize prejudicial thinking. It is messy and can influence our behavior at the most inopportune times. Just ask people who are fired from their jobs because an ethnic slur they use at home finds its way into their conversation at work. We cannot turn prejudice on and off like light from a lamp. Whether or not we are conscious of it, our thinking can and does affect how we behave.

Prejudices, no matter how much we think we can cover them up, work against us. This is true of prejudices that we hold or those we encounter. Consider the implications when prejudice:

- *Leads to inaccurate judgments about people.* According to various studies and court rulings, sometimes police stop a disproportionate share of minority drivers simply because of their racial or ethnic background. Many are searched as well. This practice is called *racial profiling*. More than half of all African-American men report they have been victims of racial profiling by police at some point in their lives. One in five Latino and Asian men report they have been victims of racially motivated police stops.[12] Police, as well as the public, have recently focused more attention on the role of racial bias in police–citizen interaction and possible safeguards to ensure the equal treatment of all motorists.

- *Becomes a source of distraction.* *Race*, a book by Studs Terkel, captures the feelings of ordinary Americans about the sensitive subject of race. One person interviewed by Terkel shares what it is like to deal with racial prejudice in the United States. He compares it to wearing a shoe that does not quite fit. "It squeezes, it pinches, it cuts off circulation and sometimes it drives people to varying forms of distraction."[13] He goes on to say that it is not your race that has this effect. Rather, it is the assumptions that people make about you because of your race.

- *Results in resentment and fear.* Consider **xenophobia**, people's unreasonable fear of foreigners. Throughout the history of immigration in the United States, write Portés and Rumbaut, "a consistent thread has been the fear that the 'alien element' would somehow undermine the institutions of the country and would lead it down the path of disintegration and decay."[14] People who are xenophobic often resent the academic and economic success of certain groups of immigrants. Furthermore, they devalue cultural differences, and no one benefits. A series of *Doonesbury* cartoons makes this same point. In the cartoon, neighbors complain to the parents of an Asian-American student. The parents are told that teaching their daughter to value discipline and hard work gives her an unfair advantage.

> "Immigrants negatively influence America by infusing it with their spirit, warping its directions, turning it into a heterogeneous, incoherent distracted mass."
> —Thomas Jefferson

- *Impacts one's health.* A study from Yale University suggests that prejudices can impair a person's mental and physical health. Ninety men and women between the ages of 60 and 90 were divided into two groups. Using a technique known as subliminal priming, researchers flashed words on a computer screen. One group saw entirely negative messages, including words such as *decrepit, senile, decline,* and *confused.* With the other group, all the messages were positive, including *alert, astute, enlightened,* and *creative.* Participants who got negative messages were more likely to show a greater response to stress and a significant increase in blood pressure. Conversely, those exposed to positive messages tended to improve

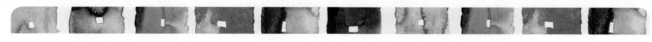

Religious Profiling

Recently, concerns about terrorism and security have made religious profiling more common and visible. Passengers who appear Muslim have complained that airport security authorities single them out for scrutiny and possible abuse. An American-Islamic civil rights organization has received complaints from a number of Muslim women who have been forced to remove their head scarves, or hijab, in front of others at airports. Because removing head scarves in public violates Muslim teachings about modesty, the organization says it should be done in a private area and in front of a female security screener.

memory performance and views of aging. Becca Levy, an assistant professor of epidemiology and public health at Yale University, suggests that these results show the potential consequences when older people in our society internalize chronic negative messages.[15]

- *Results in "coping fatigue."* Through interviews with successful Black professionals, Ellis Cose discovered that many of them suffered from psychological wear and tear that he terms "coping fatigue."[16] Howard Ehrlich, research director at the Prejudice Institute, reviewed research on the effects of prejudice on students at a number of college campuses. Based on his research, Ehrlich estimates that one in four minority students is "victimized for reasons of prejudice."[17] Many of these students report that prejudice interferes with their ability to study. For them, stress and discomfort may be an everyday occurrence.

 Thinking Through Diversity

Some government officials have argued that profiling is needed to track potential terrorists. They argue that it is negligent not to look at everything, including racial and religious factors. Others say that the United States should not use any kind of profiling in the war on terror. They argue that it is reckless and there is no proof it works. What is your opinion? Is profiling justified in order to combat terror, and if so, under what circumstances?

Your prejudices, or the prejudices you encounter, can make it that much more difficult for you to achieve your goals. Prejudice can undermine relationships, reduce productivity, and be a source of distraction and stress. It can lead to mistrust, misunderstanding, resentment, and fear. Your job performance may suffer when prejudice comes between you and a manager, coworker, or client. Ultimately, no one wins in a situation such as this.

Blue Eyes and Brown Eyes

In 1968, Jane Elliott was a third-grade teacher in a small, rural town in Iowa. She conducted an experiment in her classroom so that her students could learn a valuable lesson about the workings and effects of prejudice. She divided them into two groups based on the color of their eyes. For Elliott, it was essential for her students to experience just how easy it is to prejudge people, explain behavior in terms of that prejudgment, and build a reward system around virtually any characteristic that distinguishes one person or group from another. Even though everyone does not neatly fit into distinct categories of eye color, the same is true for other socially constructed categories on which prejudice is based, such as race and social class.

Over the period of a week, Elliott treated the children differently based on the color of their eyes. Elliott and the blue-eyed students initially treated the brown-eyed students as if they were inferior. The "brown eyes" were told to wear collars around their necks so they could be identified easily. It was not long before their schoolwork suffered

and they felt angry and frustrated. Furthermore, blue-eyed students who had always been their friends turned on them.

Midway through the experiment, Elliott convinced her students that she had made a terrible mistake—in fact, the brown eyes were superior. Each brown-eyed student was instructed to take off his or her collar and put it on a classmate with blue eyes. Almost immediately the brown-eyed children started feeling better about themselves and the quality of their schoolwork improved dramatically. A group lesson that had given them trouble when they were assumed to be inferior was now completed with ease. Now that they were viewed as superior, they refused to associate with the inferior "blue eyes." At the end of the experiment, even Elliott was amazed by the students' transformation. When asked what they learned from the experiment, one student mentioned how the collar made it difficult for her to think and pay attention. Another student said the collar made him feel like "a dog on a leash."[18] (To learn more about Elliott's experiment, google "Jane Elliott blue eyes brown eyes.")

Barrier 5: Prejudice Plus Power

When people in power show prejudice, the consequences can be that much more severe. **Power** refers to the ability to influence others and bring about change. Therefore, people with power are in a position to affect many more people by virtue of their prejudices. Imagine that you are looking for a highly competitive job and no one in upper-level management considers you a serious candidate because of your gender or class or ethnic background. Prejudice of this nature is more potent because it is backed up by economic power. This is particularly true if you encounter this kind of thinking everywhere you go.

The various "isms" are at work when we talk about prejudice plus power. **Isms** refer to the thinking by those in power that certain types of people are inherently inferior; therefore, unequal treatment is justifiable. A variety of isms exist, each focusing on a different dimension of diversity (ageism, sexism, classism . . .). One of the most volatile and difficult to understand is racism.

Definitions of **racism** vary. In some instances, it refers to discrimination based on the belief that one race is superior to another. According to this definition, anyone can be a racist. From another point of view, racism requires more than just acting out racial prejudice. It requires power. This means that those in power are the only ones who can be racist. The question then becomes who has the power. For some, only Whites can be racist because they have the economic, political, and social power in the wider society. Still there are those who maintain that power shifts from place to place. For instance, in a specific locale, Latinos or African-Americans may be in a dominant position in terms of their economic or political status.

No matter how we define racism, we need to understand the importance of power and its implications. David Shipler examines the effects of racism in his book *A Country of Strangers*.[19] A former reporter for the *New York Times*, Shipler describes a workshop in which White participants are paired up with minorities. The facilitator asks participants to stand if they have to leave their culture at the door when they go to work. He then asks participants if they believe they have been stopped by police because of their color. Finally, did any of the participants consider not having children because of racism? After each of these questions, a number of minority participants stand up—but none of the Whites.

When I ask these same questions in a number of my racially mixed college classes, the pattern of responses is the same. It is important to note that *acknowledging* racism is not the same as *using* racism as an excuse for not getting ahead. When we discuss social inequality, minority students in my classes are generally highly critical of those who blame their lack of success on White racism or "the system." The views of some of my White students, especially those who are poor, are noteworthy as well. They repeatedly cite instances when being White and poor works against them or someone they know, in part because people assume they do not need help because they are White. They feel denied rather than privileged. Clearly, it is difficult to talk about racism without addressing isms that connect with class, gender, and other dimensions of diversity.

In the larger society, we rarely talk about the issue of racism in public or in racially mixed company because it can be such an inflammatory and divisive issue. However, there have been times when discussions of racism tend to be more open and inclusive. One recent example is the debate about the role of race and class in our response to Hurricane Katrina (see Diversity Box: The Response to Hurricane Katrina).

The Response to Hurricane Katrina

How do we perceive the response to Hurricane Katrina? Was racism a factor in the speed and nature of the response? Did people with more wealth and connections receive preferential treatment? There are those of us who see the response as having nothing to do with race and class. Nature does not discriminate, nor did the recovery effort. And any attempt to inject racism into this discussion is seen as political and biased. Others argue that what took place in the aftermath of Katrina is just one more example of who wields the power in the United States, and who has access to resources in times of crisis. According to research, race figures prominently into our perceptions. Polls show that African-Americans (60%) were much more likely than European-Americans (20%) to feel that the government's response to Katrina would have been faster had most of the victims been White.[20] The tendency to see racism may reflect one's definition of racism. Whereas White Americans are more apt to see racism as a localized or as the exception rather than the rule, African-Americans are more apt to see racism in broader, more systemic terms. For instance, White Americans might argue that someone's skin color was irrelevant to individual rescuers or government officials who doled out aid. On the other hand, African-Americans tend to see how the media was more inclined to stigmatize African-American victims, portraying them as outsiders and even criminals. With greater access to resources in the form of transportation, social networks, credit cards and cash, well-to-do citizens, many of them White, generally had more options in terms of fleeing New Orleans ahead of the hurricane and dealing with its aftereffects. Findings from a study of students who attended Tulane University shed further light on this matter. Students who were more apt to define racism in systemic terms were more apt to perceive racism in Katrina-related events than those who saw racism as an individual, more isolated occurrence.[21]

What might account for this perceptual gap? Some maintain that African-Americans see the significance of race and racism as endemic rather than sporadic. Legal scholar Patricia Williams asks, "How can it be that so many well-meaning white people have never thought about race when so few blacks pass a single day without being reminded of it?"[22] Whites may deny or underestimate the role played by racism since it raises questions about justice and equality in the United States, as well as their role in perpetuating racial discrimination. Moreover, Whites may downplay the existence of racism because it is not part of their reality. They may be unaware of historical events that show a pattern of racism. For example, in the face of flooding from the Mississippi River in the early 1900s, wealthy residents of New Orleans sought to protect their residences by dynamiting the levees and flooding other areas inhabited largely by poor Blacks. Many of these displaced residents were denied aid, ignored by rescuers, and forced to live in temporary shelters without basic necessities.

Sociological and psychological research points to different forms of racism. When people hear the term racism, they typically think of an individuals' overt, racial bigotry. *Individual racism* refers to people's beliefs that support the idea of racial superiority and, therefore, the unequal treatment of different races. Increasingly, definitions of racism focus on **institutional racism**, racism that is built into the customs, norms, and practices of social institutions. Among these institutions are religion, education, government, health care, and the economy. For example, it is one thing to talk about an individual's belief in racial superiority. It is quite another when that belief or doctrine becomes embedded in the way a company does business, a school system distributes resources, or a police department targets criminals and enforces the law. Individual racism cannot be examined apart from institutional racism. They are interconnected and reinforce each other.

One recent example provides insight into the lens through which we view individual and institutional racism. In 2012, Trayvon Martin, an unarmed African-American teenager, was shot and killed in Florida by George Zimmerman, a neighborhood watch volunteer. The case, like many in recent history, raises questions about the racial bias of people who enforce the law and the fairness of the criminal justice system. Reactions to the shooting and the criminal trial of Zimmerman reveal a continuing, deep divide between Blacks and Whites. Was

Martin shot because he was Black and wearing a hoodie or because he attacked Zimmerman? Given the evidence, should Zimmerman have been found not guilty? Other questions examine broader, institutional issues such as how this case would have played out if Martin had been White, and the impact of the "Stand Your Ground Law" in this part of Florida, which gives authorities more leeway if they feel threatened (see Fig. 3.5).

> "Trayvon Martin could've been me 35 years ago."
>
> —President Barack Obama

Our views of racism illustrate that even though we inhabit the same society, we see the world in distinctly different ways. In her book *Why Are All the Black Kids Sitting Together in the Cafeteria?*, Beverly Tatum compares the images and messages that convey racial superiority to the smog that each of us breathes in each day because it surrounds us. In other words, sometimes racism is thick and visible and sometimes it is less apparent and harder to see, but it is still there.[23]

No one is immune from the effects of racism. In his book *No Future Without Forgiveness*, Nobel Peace Prize recipient Desmond Tutu examines the long history of racism in South Africa and its insidious impact. On his first visit to Nigeria, he recounts traveling in a plane piloted by Nigerians. After taking off smoothly, the plane hit turbulence, shuddered, and dropped suddenly. He remembers with shock his immediate reaction. "I found I was saying to myself, 'I really am bothered that there's no white man in the cockpit. Can these blacks manage to navigate us out of this horrible experience?'" He continues, "It was all involuntary and spontaneous. I would never have believed that I had in fact been so radically brainwashed. I would have denied it vigorously because I prided myself on being an exponent of black consciousness, but in a crisis something deeper had emerged. I had accepted a white definition of existence, that whites were somehow superior to and more competent than blacks. Of course those black pilots were able to land the plane

Racial Divides Over Trayvon Martin Case

Do you think Blacks and other minorities receive equal treatment as Whites in the criminal justice system?

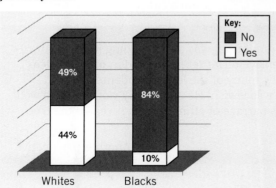

How much of a factor was racial bias in the events that led up to the shooting of Trayvon and the shooting itself?

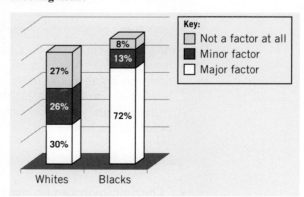

Figure 3.5 Racial Divides in Our Perception of Justice.
Sources: Washington Post ABC News Poll, 2012; USA Today/Gallup Poll, 2012.

quite competently."[24] From this experience, Tutu learned to be a little more forgiving of others when they succumb to racism.

Have instances of sexism, racism, heterosexism, and other isms decreased? According to Derald Wing Sue, a multicultural scholar, the answer is no. Rather, modern-day isms are more ambiguous and therefore difficult to discern. Sue encourages us to shift our attention from Skinheads, White Supremacists, and other conscious perpetrators of hate to people who often have the best of intentions and espouse the value of fair play and equal rights. Sue's extensive research underscores the importance of microaggressions, "brief everyday exchanges that send denigrating messages to certain individuals because of their group membership, such as people of color, women, and LGBTs."[25] In his book, *Microaggressions in Everyday Life*, Sue describes how you and I may unknowingly and repeatedly degrade others by engaging in microaggressions.

When prejudice is coupled with power, diversity becomes a negative rather than a positive for everyone. Mistrust and divisiveness interfere with communication. Teamwork suffers. It becomes a matter of my group versus your group. People may start doubting themselves and assuming the worst about others. What is certain is that human potential will be wasted.

Barrier 6: Discrimination

Unlike prejudice, discrimination refers to behavior. More specifically, **discrimination** is defined as the denial of equal rights and opportunities to individuals and groups. Unequal treatment of this nature varies because of race, age, gender, social class, religion, or any number of other dimensions of diversity. As an example, consider weight discrimination. Research findings show that weight discrimination is all too common nowadays, especially among people who are obese. A scarcity of laws against weight discrimination and attitudes toward obesity contribute to this social problem. One study, coming out of Yale University's Rudd Center for Food Policy and Obesity, examines weight discrimination in various interactions and situations including education, employment, and medical care. Interestingly, researchers found that women are significantly more likely than men to experience discrimination because of their weight. And for women, it starts at a much lower bodyweight. Rebecca Puhl, one of the study's authors, adds, "I think women in our culture face very strict ideals of physical attractiveness that are often very unrealistic." Furthermore, Puhl thinks weight discrimination reflects society's belief that controlling our weight is simply a matter of willpower and choice. But, she cautions, scientific evidence does not support this belief.[26]

> As long as I can remember, my grandfather was always telling jokes about Jews, though he used a more offensive term. Yet he worked in public education, was highly respected, even by many of the Jewish students that had been in his care. In fact, his boss was Jewish! He apparently worked quite well with the man, yet the continuous barrage of ethnic slights revealed the true nature of his heart.
>
> —Another perspective

Discrimination assumes many forms. There are times when it is obvious and clear-cut. At other times, we are not so sure that behavior is in fact discriminatory. According to a study by Pew Research Center, our racial and ethnic background may exert a strong

Combinations of Prejudice and Discrimination

Whereas some people seem to see prejudice and discrimination everywhere, others are certain that prejudice and discrimination no longer exist. As difficult as it is, try to evaluate each situation with an open mind. Although prejudice and discrimination often go hand in hand, they do not have to. Four combinations may occur in a variety of situations (see Table 3.1).

1. *The prejudiced discriminator.* This is someone who holds personal prejudices and discriminates. Example: A manager's age-related prejudices influence her decisions in a variety of personnel actions. The manager evaluates a younger worker more favorably than she does an older person who performs just as well.

2. *The prejudiced nondiscriminator.* In this case, a person's prejudicial attitudes do not lead to discriminatory behavior. Example: A male employee feels prejudice toward his female supervisor because of her gender but does not show it for fear of the consequences.

3. *The unprejudiced discriminator.* Someone who is not prejudiced discriminates nonetheless. There are times when a person may discriminate unknowingly by following certain commonly accepted policies or practices. In addition, someone may belong to a group and discriminate to conform to group expectations. Example: Even though a person is open-minded about the subject of homosexuality, he caves in to group pressure at school and discriminates against certain people who "act gay."

4. *The unprejudiced nondiscriminator.* This person is not prejudiced and does not discriminate. Example: An employer conducting a job interview notices that an interviewee with a noticeable accent shies away from direct eye contact. As in every other interview, the employer puts the candidate at ease and focuses solely on the person's ability to do the job.

It is important to remember that each of these combinations applies to the thinking and behaviors of people in situations, not to the individuals themselves.

influence on whether we perceive discrimination to be a rare or common occurrence, at least in the day-to-day life experiences of Blacks (see Fig. 3.6). Although an individual might discriminate openly against members of another group, there are other instances involving more subtle, institutional, and intragroup behaviors. What follows are some major forms of discrimination:

1. *Blatant versus subtle discrimination.* Discriminatory acts, some more obvious than others, are an everyday occurrence in public places. In towns and cities throughout the United States, certain people are stopped on a regular basis and required to prove their citizenship for no other reason than because of their skin color, accent, or surname.

   The prevalent practice of harassment or name-calling constitutes another example of blatant discrimination. Deliberate insults and derogatory remarks toward women

Combinations of Prejudice and Discrimination	Is the Person Prejudiced? (Attitude)	Is the Person Discriminating? (Behavior)
Prejudiced discriminator	✓	✓
Prejudiced nondiscriminator	✓	✗
Unprejudiced discriminator	✗	✓
Unprejudiced nondiscriminator	✗	✗

Table 3.1 Prejudice and Discrimination.
Source: Adapted from Robert Merton, "Discrimination and the American Creed."[27]

Who agrees with this statement:
Blacks face discrimination almost always/frequently when they...

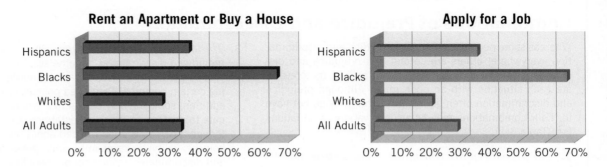

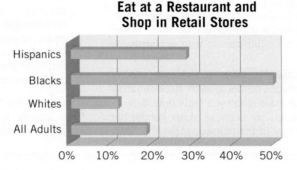

Figure 3.6 How often do Blacks encounter discrimination?
Source: Pew Research Center.[28]

and minorities or anyone labeled as different are standard practice in some work-place settings. What's more, managers and employees often close their eyes to such mistreatment.

Instances of more subtle discrimination are also commonplace, such as certain looks or what one Hispanic woman terms that "spoken or unspoken word." "Because I'm dark and have dark eyes and hair. …. If I entered a department store, one of two things was likely to happen. Either I was ignored, or I was followed closely by the salesperson. The garments I took into the changing room were carefully counted. My check at the grocery store took more scrutiny than an Anglo's. My children were complimented on how 'clean' they were instead of how cute."[29]

Because subtle discrimination, such as exclusion from informal social networks, is so indirect and inconspicuous, it is unlikely to lead to a formal grievance or lawsuit. Knowing how to respond effectively to subtle discrimination can be a challenge.

2. *Individual versus institutional discrimination.* Individuals are not the only ones who discriminate. Sometimes, institutional policies and procedures put certain people at a disadvantage. For example, an employee who is also a cancer patient might have to deal with a supervisor who decides on his own that he wants to limit her workload, even though she is capable of working full-time just as she did before the diagnosis. While this is an example of individual discrimination, this same company might also habitually fire or lay off employees with serious illnesses like cancer or AIDS, regardless of whether they continue to perform at 100 percent. Since this type of unequal treatment is built into the way this *company* operates, it constitutes institutional discrimination.

Thinking Through Diversity

What subtle forms of discrimination have you encountered? How have you dealt with them?

Another form of institutional discrimination concerns the practices of the U.S. Treasury Department. Recently, a ruling by a U.S. District Judge found making U.S. paper currency the same size, shape, and feel puts the blind at a disadvantage. For example, someone with a visual impairment may find it difficult to distinguish a one dollar bill from a twenty dollar bill. In addition to changing the size, the American Council of the Blind suggests other options, such as raised letters or numerals, Braille dots, and rounded edges or punched holes.

3. *Intragroup versus intergroup discrimination.* *Intragroup discrimination* occurs *within* groups, whereas *intergroup discrimination* takes place *between* groups. We often assume that discrimination occurs only between groups such as Latinos and Whites. However, intragroup discrimination is common and may be just as painful. One African-American student recounts how she got teased because of her skin complexion. In her case, most of the people who treated her differently were not Whites; they were people of her own race and even members of her family. "I was seen as a white girl and an albino. People gave me names like 'goldie-locks' and 'light bright.' They called me 'light bright' because they said I was 'light, bright, and damned near White.' It was very humiliating as a kid because I got teased constantly about my complexion. My sister was the worst of them all because when she got mad with me she would tell me that I was the mailman's baby."

Discrimination is a losing proposition for everyone. When discrimination occurs, factors other than merit become important. The financial and human costs are undeniable. Beside costly lawsuits, valuable human resources are lost. Discrimination feeds anger, tension, and fear. When this happens, we sabotage teamwork and close lines of communication. Consider the amount of time and energy that is spent discriminating or coping with discrimination and its aftereffects. What would happen if we could somehow refocus this time and energy in a more positive direction?

OVERCOMING DIVERSITY BARRIERS

Take a Mexican-American man in his early 20s and put him in a situation where he forces himself to go out into an all-White or predominantly White community. He's going to get some negative feedback, whether it's just looks or whispering. It can be anything. . . . there's all types of negative feedback. It doesn't have to be verbal or physical. When things like that happen, that in turn makes that person not even want to try to interact or push himself into that kind of situation. It's like a foreseeable risk.

—Another perspective

Effectively dealing with barriers is a challenge. Although particular barriers by themselves may seem insignificant, the cumulative effect of all types of barriers can be overwhelming. Joe Feagin calls this a **pyramiding effect**, meaning the cumulative impact of encounters with barriers is much more than the sum of individual instances. In his research, Feagin discusses how one respondent compares the pyramiding effect to ergs of energy. To paraphrase, the mind only has so many ergs of energy. If we use up 50 percent of those ergs doing the creative things that we want to do each day, 50 percent remains. But if we need to use a good portion of those precious, remaining ergs to deal with innumerable, everyday barriers, we don't have as much energy left. Because our mind is not free, we cannot do what we are capable of doing.[30]

Thinking Through Diversity

Given the magnitude of this challenge, how do you summon the energy that is necessary to deal effectively with prejudicial beliefs, discriminatory behaviors, and other social barriers that you may encounter? To flourish in the face of adversity, what can you do?

How do you overcome barriers that you encounter in your environment? It is important to realize no single strategy is right for everyone or appropriate for all situations. What may work for you may be ineffectual for someone else. One CEO says that he counters prejudice by doing his job beyond expectations. His habit of doing more than he is asked to do wins people over. A student of mine resorts to writing whenever she feels the sting of prejudice. For her, writing provides an emotional release. "Writing down what happens and how it feels puts some distance between me and the incident. I can look at it later with less emotion." Still another effective strategy was employed by author Zora Neale Hurston. When people discriminated against her, Hurston did not get angry. Instead, she saw discrimination as a way in which others lost out. In effect, they denied themselves the pleasure of her company.[31]

Regardless of what strategy or strategies work for you, keep mindful of the following:

1. *Recognize that barriers sometimes exist.* Before we overcome barriers, we have to acknowledge them—in ourselves, others, and in our communities. That does not mean that you have to let them get in your way. In Ellis Cose's book *The Rage of a Privileged Class*, he discussed the anger of highly successful African-Americans. Repeatedly, he heard variations of the same complaint; that is, "regardless of what I do, and how hard I work, I can never make it to the top." Even as opportunities continue to expand in the twenty-first century, barriers remain for men and women from all walks of life. As Cose says, we need to acknowledge that reality and deal with it in a way that is "inclusive rather than polarizing."[32]

> Prejudice . . . I can get over it, around it, above it. Sometimes I'm just too busy to even deal with it.
>
> When you feel comfortable in your own skin, you simply find a way to get around the obstacles that roll down the road.
>
> —Other perspectives

2. *Develop and maintain pride in yourself.* Eleanor Roosevelt once said: "No one can make you feel inferior without your consent." Stephanie, a former student of mine, has had to deal with what she describes as "life's little cruelties and

discomforts" because of her obesity. She recalls standing in a college biology class for two hours at a time, week after week, because she could not find suitable seating. No one, including the instructor, seemed concerned. Additionally, she remembers the instructor maintaining almost constant eye contact with her one day as he lectured about the dangers of being overweight. As she left the campus that day, she had no plans to return and continue her college education. But she drew strength from her obese mother, who taught her that she is unique and deserves to be heard. Stephanie gradually changed her thinking. "I learned that I have a place in this world that is beyond the shadows. I learned I don't have to accept whatever is given to me. I have a right to be out there and make a living for my children."

3. *Develop and maintain pride in your culture.* When combating intolerance, cultural pride can be a source of strength. Jorge, a student from Mexico who attends a small rural college in Maryland, emphasizes how important it is for him to be grounded in his culture. People who lack this grounding, according to Jorge, tend to be more confused and vulnerable. In Photo 3.2, he is shown with folk art he brought with him from Mexico.

4. *If you encounter diversity barriers directed at you or others, speak out if at all possible.* What you say does matter, according to research. In one study, individual students were interviewed after hearing people express their views about racism. Those students who heard someone else condemn racism were more likely to express antiracist sentiments than those students who heard someone express equivocal views or condone racism.[33] Using the *I feel formula* to convey how you feel about an incident can be particularly effective. Explain to others how *you* feel and why *you* consider it inappropriate. If you or others are personally offended by something that takes place in a group setting, consider the pros and cons of dealing with it immediately. If it involves only one or two members of a larger group, you might be better off waiting

Putting a Price Tag on Discrimination

Andrew Hacker's widely acclaimed book *Two Nations* analyzes inequality between Black and White Americans.[34] Hacker, a college professor, discusses an experiment he conducted with his White students to illustrate the costs of being treated unequally. He creates a scenario in which an official visits the students to tell them a mistake has been made. Newfound evidence shows that their race was identified incorrectly. They should have been identified as Black at birth. The official emphasizes that the mistake must be corrected immediately. From now on, the students will live their lives as Blacks. The official's organization is willing to pay them for the inconvenience of changing their race. When Hacker asked his White students how much money they would request, most of them asked for approximately $1 million a year for the rest of their lives. Hacker analyzed this amount as the price these students attach to prejudice and discrimination.

For a moment, consider what Hacker might discover if he varied this experiment. In my classes, I modify Hacker's experiment to take into account that race, however important, is only one dimension of diversity and one possible reason for inequality. Moreover, I give students a choice. I simply ask students how much money they would want to change any of the following: race, sex, sexual orientation, or age (add ten years to your age). Interestingly, the vast majority of them would not change any of their statuses for any amount of money. They express satisfaction with their current status, even if it makes them the object of discrimination. Of those who do elect to change their status, most choose to add ten years to their age. The price tag for doing this is typically in the millions. Interestingly, one category that is rarely changed is sexual orientation.

and talking to these people in private. However, speaking right away may result in a valuable learning experience for the entire group.

In determining how to respond to discrimination and other barriers, consider whether your safety is an issue. If it is, use your common sense and do what is in your best interest. You may elect to ignore it, at least for a period of time, or deal with it indirectly and remain anonymous. If you think that a law has been broken, report the incident to someone in authority—preferably a person or group you know and trust. It may be necessary to consult a lawyer or the local human rights commission. If you record what happens, this can be useful if you pursue the matter further at a later date.

5. *When people judge you immediately because of your distinctive looks or behavior, try to be as patient and understanding as possible.* In interviews with minority men and women who have thrived as community leaders and advisers, researcher John Moritsugu found that showing compassion was one of their most important coping responses. Even though the respondents were enraged by racism and other acts of intolerance, they were not angry at the perpetrators. Instead, they considered them to "be victims of miseducation or a lack of experience." Furthermore, the respondents addressed the importance of acting rationally and weighing the alternatives. Rather than acting on emotion alone, they considered what they hoped to accomplish by responding a certain way.[35] Did they want to change behavior, raise awareness, or simply "blow off steam"?

It helps to remember that others' perceptions may have nothing to do with you as a person. More likely, they result from ignorance, mistrust, and even fear. Viewing other people's stereotypes and prejudices in this manner helps us deal with the walls of misunderstanding and mistrust that we encounter. Keep in mind those times when *you* jump to conclusions about others.

Because of numerous past encounters with prejudice, sometimes you may sense prejudice where none exists. To illustrate, parents of a child with severe facial anomalies were attending a high school musical. The child remained at home with a relative. Throughout the entire performance, the parents could not help but notice two young people seated in front of them who continually turned around to look at something. On the way home that night, the parents tried to make sense of the strange looks from the couple. Only then did they realize that if their son had been with them, they would have been overcome with emotion. Moreover, they would have been *positive* that the looks were directed at him.

As a graduate student, I attended a small, rural, private college. I had just moved from a large city. I was very open about being gay. I felt like "I'm gay and damn you're going to like it." One night, I remember visiting one of my friends in his dormitory. On the way up to his room, I saw the quarterback of the football team. We knew each other and had talked before. Up to that point, I had always looked at him as a "dumb jock" and he saw me as a "stupid faggot." This time it was different. We related as humans, not as categories. I came to realize that if I tried to push my "category" on someone else, we would end up relating as categories.

—Another perspective

Photo 3.2 Jorge, a student, shares his Mexican heritage with his college community by assembling an altar in memory of a Mexican hero, Emiliano Zapata.

6. *Fine-tune your anger.* Many people who constantly face petty and not so petty slights find it necessary to pick their battles. Some pick their responses: shouting, whispering, or conversing. It may depend on the situation or how one feels that day. Karen Bates and Karen Hudson coauthored an etiquette book for African-Americans entitled *Basic Black: Home Training for Modern Times.*[36] Part of the book offers advice to those who suspect they are being treated a certain way because of how they look. Bates and Hudson give the example of poor service at a restaurant. Perhaps the server is rude to you and polite to others. What if the host or hostess ignores you and your guests or your request for seating in a certain area of the restaurant? The authors suggest asking the person in charge if the server is having a bad day. If you suspect that your race is the reason for your treatment, ask the manager: "Can I assume that your restaurant does not want customers who look like me?" Low-key responses to subtle but hurtful slights can get results.

7. *Resist the urge to scapegoat.* When we **scapegoat**, we unfairly blame others for our own problems. In essence, scapegoating allows us to look outward, not inward. For example, some majority group members blame affirmative action for the ills of society. They argue that affirmative action has given minorities an unfair advantage and puts Whites at a disadvantage. When a close relative or friend is not promoted or hired, an underqualified minority is assumed to be the reason. In reality, maybe this relative or friend was simply not the strongest candidate for the job. Similarly, some minority-group members see the White man as the root of all evil. One student of color comments: "A lot of the blame is toward the White man. When do we stop blaming and just accept that it happened and go on? They say the White man has oppressed us and is still oppressing us. I think in the long run we're oppressing ourselves because of our attitude. We have a lot of opportunities we are not taking advantage of."

8. *Try to keep the focus on the behavior in question rather than the person.* This can be done by maintaining one's composure, using the "I feel" formula, or possibly turning a question around. Instead of trying to answer an insensitive question by justifying or defending your behavior, turn the question around. By doing

this, you keep the focus on what is said. For instance, a student who is gay might respond to the following questions this way:

Question: When did you know you were gay?

Answer: Well, when did you know you were straight?

Question: When did you come out of the closet?

Answer: Good question. When did you come out of the closet?

Question: Why do you like someone of the same sex?

Answer: Why do you like someone of the opposite sex?

9. *Seek out others for support.* Harvard psychiatrist Alvin Poussaint emphasizes the importance of sharing one's experiences and emotions with others.[37] Mentors, or people who serve as guides, role models, and teachers, can provide much needed support, counsel, and friendship. Mentors can offer a different perspective, help you understand the issues that you and others like you may be facing, and reinforce your confidence. Chris Gardner, whose autobiography, *The Pursuit of Happyness*, documents his "rags to riches" story, explains the importance of mentors. "I had so many mentors. Sometimes you meet somebody and it just clicks. Other times you have to look hard to develop them. I had to pursue one of mine for years…Those people (mentors) can make all the difference in the world in what you do."[38]

   Often, people assume that what they are going through is unique to them and may be their fault. By building relationships with others who have had similar experiences, you can release emotional pressure, realize you are not alone, raise your consciousness, and work for change. Support groups take many forms. You can join or create one at school, work, or in any social setting. Another option is networking, online and face to face, with individuals and community groups that foster public dialogue and distribute accurate information (see Diversity Box: Combating Genetic Discrimination).

10. *Work with others to find new and effective ways to combat barriers and promote the value of diversity.* Consider joining a community-, work-, or school-based organization. For example, at one college, a conflict resolution team offers assistance to students who request it. Team members include racial and ethnic minorities who speak a variety of languages, students with physical and learning disabilities, as well as students who are gay, lesbian, and bisexual. After a period of intense training, they work in small diverse groups to help disputants settle their differences.

11. *Combat your own ignorance and intolerance.* When we look for barriers to diversity and ultimately our success, all too often we look outward rather than inward.

Combating Genetic Discrimination

Community groups, such as the Council for Responsible Genetics (CRG), play a crucial role in educating and mobilizing the public. This nonprofit, nongovernmental group of scientists, public health advocates, physicians, lawyers, and concerned citizens disseminates information and promotes dialogue regarding the social and ethical implications of biotechnology. According to CRG, there have been a number of cases of genetic discrimination across the United States. In such cases, employers have used genetic information to dismiss or not hire workers who they found had a predisposition to a serious disease. Their underlying motive was to minimize potential healthcare costs. CRG's efforts include providing public education in areas such as cloning and genetic privacy, creating model legislation, and writing position papers.

Profile in Diversity Consciousness

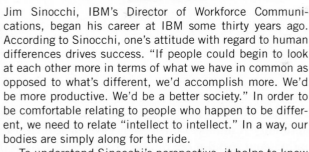

Jim Sinocchi, IBM's Director of Workforce Communications, began his career at IBM some thirty years ago. According to Sinocchi, one's attitude with regard to human differences drives success. "If people could begin to look at each other more in terms of what we have in common as opposed to what's different, we'd accomplish more. We'd be more productive. We'd be a better society." In order to be comfortable relating to people who happen to be different, we need to relate "intellect to intellect." In a way, our bodies are simply along for the ride.

To understand Sinocchi's perspective, it helps to know something of his background. At age 25, after working at IBM for five years, he broke his neck while surfing in Puerto Rico. That accident left him paralyzed from the neck down. Following the accident, he was flown home by IBM. He underwent intensive rehabilitation for months, learning to adjust both mentally and physically to paralysis.

After being out of work for two years, IBM asked Sinocchi where in the company he would like to work, and for how many hours each day. IBM agreed to make the necessary accommodations for his wheelchair and work station. Sinocchi, who was shocked by the company's offer, resumed work soon thereafter.

As he became more comfortable working, he saw a need to make people who came into his office more comfortable. He started telling them about the accident, and how they "couldn't catch it." Making others more comfortable allows him to do his job. Sinocchi adds, "When you show understanding, compassion, and leadership, most people will respond in kind. When it works, people will go out of their way to collaborate with you."

Yet, attitudinal barriers remain part of his life. People still sometimes stare, especially in public. When he frequents restaurants, some waiters still ask his companions for his order.

Sinocchi has become a strong advocate for employees with disabilities at IBM and elsewhere. Although he sees technology as a great equalizer, it is not sufficient. From his perspective, business and government must do more to change perceptions and employ people with disabilities, particularly in leadership positions. He sees education as a shared responsibility borne by all of us. "As a society," says Jim, "if we could get to a point where we realize that we have more in common than not, that would be a great beginning."[40]

Irving Horowitz describes our way of life as becoming a "culture of victimization," in which "everyone is a victim" and "no one accepts responsibility for anything."[39] A culture of victimization encourages us to look for simple answers to complex problems, to distrust entire categories of people who we identify as "the oppressor." One of my students describes victimization as "the barracuda syndrome," the feeling that you are constantly under attack and cannot trust anyone. When we look for barriers to diversity, we need to start with ourselves. Only then can we develop a perspective that allows us to recognize and combat both personal and social barriers.

Each of us has the power to choose our reactions and overcome barriers that get in our way. One of the things I admire most about my students is their resiliency. When we talked about this in class one day, one student recalled how she has spent most of her life crying because of something somebody said. "There comes a time," she said, "when you simply have to stop crying and move on." In the course of the discussion, someone else talked about her "survival kit." When I asked her to describe its contents, she said, "a large sketching pad, colored pencils, free year-round movie passes, a full-sized notebook to write down my thoughts each day, uplifting self-help and spiritual books, and a cell phone I can use to call or text supportive people."

Thinking Through Diversity
If we open up your survival kit, what will we find?

At the outset of this chapter, we distinguished between personal and social barriers. Then, we examined a number of personal and social barriers that may interfere with our ability to be successful. These include limited perceptions, ethnocentrism, stereotypes, prejudice, prejudice plus power, and discrimination. Finally, we explored a variety of strategies that can help us acknowledge, find support, and overcome those barriers that can be found within ourselves and society.

 Case Studies

Case Study One

Ligua is a part-time college student who was born in El Salvador. She is also a full-time employee, wife, and mother. Her desire to continue her education makes her feel like an outsider in her community. A number of neighbors have made it clear that she should reevaluate her priorities and spend more time at home. Ligua feels as though she is a dutiful wife who puts the needs of her family ahead of her own. She works because she has to work. Although her family takes priority, Ligua knows that her husband will help too if there is a crisis at home. Nevertheless, she feels guilty because she can't "have it all," that is, be a supermom, a superworker, and a superstudent.

At school, Ligua constantly feels like she is under a spotlight, especially when people want the "minority" point of view, or expect her to be knowledgeable about certain subjects because of her looks and name. When she interacts with certain professors and staff members, she encounters subtle stereotypes. Some people expect her to be inarticulate, submissive, and unexceptional. For example, although she is an active participant in her English literature class, her professor never seems to call on her or look her way when he asks a truly challenging question. In her history class, she feels it's subtler than that. If Ligua answers a difficult question well, she is apt to detect an element of surprise in her teacher's face like wow, did that come from her?

Questions:

1. Role conflict is a constant struggle for Ligua. This conflict is exacerbated by traditional cultural expectations in her community that view motherhood as a full time responsibility. Are Ligua's expectations unrealistic? What can she do to alleviate her sense of guilt?

2. As a student, Ligua feels like some professors do not expect her to excel. Additionally, she feels as if she is being asked to speak for all Latinos any time one of her professors discusses topics such as affirmative action, immigration restrictions, or profiling. Even though she doesn't want to alienate these professors, she feels that she needs to say or do something. What might Ligua do and why?

3. Which of Ligua's dilemmas do you see as personal barriers? Which are social barriers? Explain your reasoning.

Case Study Two

Society can be very judgmental. Mary is a White social work student who plans to go on for a MS degree and work in a clinical setting. She attends an urban university and enjoys the diversity and energy of city life, but in her free time is actively involved in social activities centered around her Scottish background. She has noticed a lot of negative responses from all sorts of different people regarding her personal expression with body modifications (tattoos and piercing). Mary says, "What people don't realize is how much they mean to me, how much beauty I see in them. It's a chapter in my life that I have opened to the outside world. Each one represents a certain moment in my life or defines a part of who I am, little pieces of me stained on my skin in beautiful contrast." Unfortunately, Mary says she encounters people time and time again who prejudge her because they don't understand.

Suspicious looks and comments, or negative "vibes," are more common in the summertime, according to Mary. "There's a seasonal discriminatory policy in effect," she says jokingly. Sometimes she gets bombarded with rude questions or smirks. Occasionally, she does get a compliment because her artwork is done professionally and she puts a lot of time and money into it.

What really worries her is the impending fear instilled in her by her parents and some friends. They have told her that she will never find a decent job or gain recognition or respect with "all those tattoos." Her mother has even gone so far as to beg her to consider tattoo removal. Despite what they say, Mary believes there is a high-paying and respectable job opportunity in her future in the field of social work. She argues that her skills and her credentials are what matter, not how many different colors are on her skin.

Questions:

1. Do you agree with Mary's insistence that her skills, not her extensive body modification, will determine her opportunities in the field of social work? Explain why.

2. If you were one of Mary's friends, what advice would you give her?

3. Do you think Mary's problems are due more to personal or social barriers? Explain.

Case Study Three

Michael is an African American college graduate. Also, he is the divorced father of a teenage son, Aaron, who attends a private school in the well-to-do suburb where they live. Everyday encounters with racial profiling make Michael distrustful of people. When he goes out at night, he cannot walk close to a woman without thinking what she is going to think of him. Usually, he assumes they're negative thoughts.

Michael finds that if he dresses in business attire early in the morning or late in the day, he has virtually no trouble getting a cab. However, if after work he has on jeans and tennis shoes, that same cab driver who picked him up in the morning will leave him standing on the corner.

When Michael shares these stories with his White coworkers, they say he is making way too much out of it. To prove their point, they describe similar situations in which people ignore or avoid them for no apparent reason. For Michael, experiences like these make him extremely reluctant to share anything of a personal nature with his White coworkers, especially if it deals with race.

Questions:

1. What do you think is the cumulative psychological impact of Michael's daily encounters with profiling?

2. What accounts for Michael's response to his coworkers and his reluctance to discuss race-related issues at work?

3. If you were one of Michael's coworkers and he shared these stories with you, how would you react? Be specific.

Key Terms

Personal barriers	Stereotype vulnerability	Institutional racism
Social barriers	Prejudice	Discrimination
Perceptions	Xenophobia	Pyramiding effect
Selective perception	Power	Scapegoat
Ethnocentrism	Isms	
Stereotype	Racism	

 Exercises

Exercise 1: Memory Maps

1. Draw a map of the world from memory alone.

2. Compare your map to a map of the world found in an atlas or other reputable source. What are the major differences? For instance, which hand-drawn continents are closest to their actual size and shape? Which are the least accurately drawn or missing?

3. What does your map reveal about you and the way you view the world? What biases or gaps in knowledge does it show? Which areas of the world are the easiest and most difficult for you to visualize? Why?

Exercise 2: Hate Incidents

On college campuses, an increasing number of students are victims of hate incidents. These incidents affect students directly and indirectly. Indeed, the entire college community can feel the repercussions of a single act of intolerance. Pick one of the following real-life examples. Describe how you could respond effectively as a student. What would you do? Why? At whom would your response be directed? Why?

- In the entranceway to a dormitory, a student writes on the dry erase board a message that describes local immigrants as welfare recipients and STD spreaders.

- A columnist for a student newspaper refers to Whites as "irredeemable racists" and calls for Blacks to "execute" Whites who pose a threat.

- A college fraternity holds a "Mexican Border Party." To gain entrance, students have to crawl under a barbed wire barrier.

- Leaflets depicting the Holocaust as a hoax are handed out in front of a building housing a Jewish student organization.

- A group of students take it upon themselves to sell T-shirts with anti-homosexual slogans. One of the T-shirts advocates violence against gays and lesbians. Another has the words "Homophobic and Proud of It" printed on the front.

 Notes

[1] Cornel West, *Race Matters* (New York: Random House, 1993).

[2] CBS News, "Steve Jobs Thought Different," October 5, 2011, Available at http://www.cbsnews.com/2100-205_162-20116354.html.

[3] "Artists/Daniel Keplinger," Phyllis Kind Gallery. Available: http://www.phylliskindgallery.com/artists/dk/bio.html (accessed June 15, 2013).

[4] Tom Shatel, "The Unknown Barry Switzer," *Chicago Tribune Sports*. Online, December 14, 1986. Available: http://articles.chicagotribune.com/1986-12-14/sports/8604030680_1_big-eight-coach-arent-many-coaches-oklahoma.

[5] "Perceptions of Poverty: A New Report." Online, May 16, 2012. Available: http://blog.salvationarmyusa.org/2012/05/16/perceptions-of-poverty/.

[6] Angus Wilson, *The Strange Ride of Rudyard Kipling: His Life and Works* (New York: Viking Press, 1978), 290.

[7] Richard Morin, "Needed: A Hillbilly Anti-Defamation League," *The Washington Post*, May 4, 1997, C5.

[8] Andrea DeSantis and Wesley Kayson, "Defendants' Characteristics of Attractiveness, Race, and Sex and Sentencing Decisions," *Psychological Reports*, 81, 1997, 679–683.

[9] Claude Steele, "Twenty-First Century Program and Stereotype Vulnerability," unpublished study and program, Stanford University, Stanford, CA, 1995.

[10] Gordon Allport, *The Nature of Prejudice* (Reading, MA: Addison Wesley, 1954).

[11] Jim Slepper, "Liberal Racism," *The New Democrat*, July/August 1997, 8.

[12] Richard Morin and Michael Cottman, "Most Black Men Profiled by Police, Poll Says," washingtonpost.com. Online, June 21, 2001. Available: http://www.washingtonpost.com/ac2/wp-dyn?pagename=article&node=&contentId=A30338-2001Jun21&notFound=true.

[13] Studs Terkel, *Race: How Blacks and Whites Feel About the American Obsession* (New York: New Press, 1992), 124.

[14] Alejandro Portés and Ruben Rumbaut, *Immigrant America* (Berkeley: University of California Press, 1990).

[15] Becca Levy, "Improving Memory in Old Age Through Implicit Self-Stereotyping," *Journal of Personality and Social Psychology*, 71(6), 1996, 1092–1107.

[16] Ellis Cose, *The Rage of a Privileged Class* (New York: HarperCollins, 1993), 63.

[17] Howard J. Ehrlich, *Campus Ethnoviolence: A Research Review*, Institute Report 5 (Baltimore: National Institute Against Prejudice and Violence, 1992), 8.

[18] ABC News, *The Eye of the Storm* (video) (Mount Kisco, NY: Guidance Associates, 1981).

[19] David Shipler, *A Country of Strangers* (New York: Alfred A. Knopf, 1997).

[20] Susan Page and Maria Puente, "Poll Shows Racial Divide on Storm Response," *USA Today*. Online, September 8, 2005. Available: http://www.usatoday.com/news/nation/2005-09-12-katrina-poll_x.htm.

[21] Laurie T. O'Brien, Glenn Adams, and Jessica C. Nelson. "Perceptions of Racism in the Aftermath of Hurricane Katrina: A Survey of Students Living in New Orleans," Unpublished manuscript, 2006.

[22] "Race—The Power of an Illusion," California Newsreel, 2003. Available: http://www.pbs.org/race/000_About/002_05-godeeper.htm.

[23] Beverly Tatum, *Why Are All the Black Kids Sitting Together in the Cafeteria?* (New York: HarperCollins, 1997).

[24] Desmond Mpilo Tutu, *No Future Without Forgiveness* (New York: Doubleday, 1999), 252.

[25] Derald Wing Sue, *Microaggressions in Everyday Life* (Hoboken, New Jersey: John Wiley and Sons, 2010).

[26] Svetlana Shkolnikova, "Weight Discrimination Could be as Common as Racial Bias," *USA Today*. Online, May 21, 2008. Available: http://usatoday30.usatoday.com/news/health/weightloss/2008-05-20-overweight-bias_N.htm.

[27] Robert Merton, "Discrimination and the American Creed" in *Sociological Ambivalence and Other Essays* (Free Press, New York, 1976).

[28] "Do Blacks and Hispanics Get Along?" Pew Research Center. Online, January 31, 2008. Available: http://www.pewsocialtrends.org/2008/01/31/do-blacks-and-hispanics-get-along/, accessed June 18, 2013.

[29] Gabriela Kuntz, "My Spanish Standoff," *Newsweek*, May 4, 1998, 22.

[30] Joe Feagin, "The Continuing Significance of Race: Anti-Black Discrimination in Public Places," *American Sociological Review*, 56, 1991, 101–116.

[31] Zora Neale Hurston, as quoted in Dorothy W. Riley, ed., *My Soul Looks Back, 'Less I Forget: A Collection of Quotations by People of Color* (New York: HarperCollins, 1995), 318.

[32] Ellis Cose, "Revisiting 'The Rage of a Privileged Class,'" *Newsweek*. Online, February 2, 2009. Available: http://www.thedailybeast.com/newsweek/2009/01/24/revisiting-the-rage-of-a-privileged-class.html.

[33] Fletcher Blanchard et al., "Reducing the Expression of Racial Prejudice," *Psychological Science*, 2, 1991, 101–105.

[34] Andrew Hacker, *Two Nations* (New York: Ballantine Books, 1995).

[35] Bill Shapiro, "Speakers Call for Greater Effort in Combating Racism," *American Psychological Association Monitor*, 28 (10), October 1997, 39.

[36] Karen G. Bates and Karen E. Hudson, *Basic Black: Home Training for Modern Times* (New York: Doubleday, 1996).

[37] Ellis Cose, *The Rage of a Privileged Class* (New York: HarperCollins, 1993), 169.

[38] Rebecca Kahlenberg, "The Pursuit of a New Career Takes Persistence," *The Washington Post*, February 25, 2007, K1.

[39] Irving Louis Horowitz, *The Decomposition of Sociology* (New York: Oxford University Press, 1993).

[40] IBM, "Jim Sinocchi: Finding Common Ground," Human Ability and Accessibility Center. Available: http://www-03.ibm.com/able/news/sinocchi.html (accessed January 14, 2008).

4

Developing Diversity Consciousness

Learning Outcomes

Upon completion of this chapter, you will be able to:

- Explain the importance of diversity consciousness.
- Analyze the impact of cultural encapsulation on developing diversity consciousness.
- Discuss the value in examining ourselves and our worlds.
- Analyze the importance of expanding our knowledge of others and their worlds.
- Explain how stepping outside of ourselves enhances our diversity consciousness.
- Justify the importance of gauging the level of the playing field.
- Examine the meaningfulness of checking up on ourselves.
- Describe the need for following through.
- Specify strategies for developing diversity consciousness.
- Elaborate on the significance of developing diversity consciousness as a lifelong, continuing process.

> Not to know is bad.
> Not to want to know is worse.
> Not to hope unthinkable.
> Not to care unforgivable.
>
> —Nigerian proverb

MyStudentSuccessLab

MyStudentSuccessLab (www.mystudentsuccesslab.com) is an online solution designed to help you 'Start Strong, Finish Stronger' by building skills for ongoing personal and professional development.

Participating in the Occupy Movement really helped me to understand the different attitudes as they relate to diversity. One particular incident stands out. During the first week, we had an American flag placed upside down on display for passersby to see when they walked through the Occupy Baltimore campsite. We argued about this amongst ourselves because of the perception it would leave on people unfamiliar with Occupy. We were not trying to take an un-American stance and hanging that flag might give that impression; however, others thought differently. This particular day I was working the outreach table and fielding some pretty tough questions and this Marine stops me and begins asking me questions about the ideologies we express, our world views. He then says he wanted to know because of how the flag was hung. It made him feel uncomfortable. He was not uncomfortable with the Occupy movement but the flag was off-putting to him for obvious reasons and he felt that it was disrespectful. This was one of my first lessons on inclusion and diversity as it relates to soldiers. He fought in two wars and because of his service and the service of his fellow soldiers; he couldn't not say something about the flag. This happened routinely after that but I learned that you can't discuss social liberalism and wholeness when actively and deliberately making a visual statement that could offend others. It's insensitive and does not promote inclusion; it does the complete opposite. I also learned that even though I didn't hang the flag I was also responsible because I'm still affiliated with the group. It was one of many lessons I learned but I'm grateful for all.

—Another perspective

THE IMPORTANCE OF DIVERSITY CONSCIOUSNESS

In this chapter we look at how each of us can develop our diversity consciousness. We examine the roots and impact of our cultural isolation, as well as how we can become more aware of ourselves and others. This ongoing process is not sequential; it does not occur in steps that follow one another neatly. Rather, many things feed into this nonlinear process as we continually open ourselves up to other perspectives.

Regardless of your educational or career goals, diversity consciousness is important for a number of reasons:

1. *It enhances your diversity skills.* These skills include:

   - Teamwork

   - Ability to balance "fitting in" and "being yourself"

   - Flexible thinking and adaptability

   - Ability to recognize and respect diverse intellectual strengths and learning styles

   - Ability to appreciate and maintain pride in your background and culture

   - Ability to deal effectively with barriers to success

   - Interpersonal relations and communication

- Self-evaluation

- Leadership

- Conflict management

- Social Networking

- Critical thinking

These skills will open up your mind to opportunities in all realms of life.

2. *It expands your horizons and empowers you.* Knowledge is power. Knowledge can give you confidence and instill pride in yourself and your culture. Unlike material possessions, it cannot be taken away from you. Vu Duc Vuong, a Vietnamese immigrant, makes this point when he talks about the economic hardships endured by refugees. They "often lose everything they have; everything can be taken away from a refugee: money, house, car, gold, souvenirs, job, status, friends, relatives, spouses, and even their own lives. You have heard these stories, and some of you may have even witnessed them firsthand. But among all the losses, there is one thing that will always be yours, that is your learning. No person, no circumstance, no law, and no catastrophe can take away what is inside your head. So, you owe it to yourself to learn as much as you can the rest of your life. That is one possession that is completely within your control, which is completely yours."[1]

3. *It promotes personal growth and strengthens your social networks.* By making contacts and developing relationships with people from a wide variety of backgrounds, you expand your social networks. Social networking is not only a matter of who or how many people you know. In the course of cultivating relationships, people come to know you. The nature of the relationship and your skills in nourishing and strengthening that relationship are critical. Carol Gallagher, author of *Going to the Top*, conducted in-depth interviews with 200 top executive women at Fortune 1000 companies. She found that the term *networking* did not resonate with certain women because they thought it implied developing relatively superficial relationships. Instead they talked about the importance of developing close relationships that helped them learn and grow and provided them with the connections they needed to get ahead.[2] Being able to draw on a variety of diversity skills will help you expand your circle of friends and develop substantive relationships with new and different kinds of people.

> Knowledge is better than riches.
> —Cameroonian proverb

At school, diversity consciousness allows you to relate more effectively to a wide variety of instructors with diverse teaching styles. It enables you to learn more from other students. Additionally, the skills you develop as you become more conscious of diversity increase your value at work. Your assets will include your flexibility, creativity, and ability to communicate and collaborate with all kinds of people. These same qualities will make you a more effective leader or manager.

> Opportunity isn't necessarily going to come along looking, talking, dressing, and acting like you. The more different kinds of people you can get along with, the more opportunities you will have.
> —Another perspective

CULTURAL ENCAPSULATION

Cultural encapsulation, meaning a lack of contact with cultures outside of our own, promotes insensitivity to cultural differences. Being encapsulated is akin to living in a cultural bubble. This bubble alters our view, making it difficult to transcend our cultural assumptions or even realize how culture shapes those assumptions. Therefore, we are more prone to define reality in terms of our set of experiences and assumptions, making it possible to sort and evaluate people and their cultures all too quickly and easily.

Thinking Through Diversity
Take a look at your close circle of friends. How diverse is this group?

According to an old Asian proverb, there was a little frog that spent his entire life at the bottom of a deep, dark well. When the frog looked around, all he could see was a small circle in the sky. If the frog had climbed to the surface, he would have seen a much different world. But life at the bottom of the well made it impossible for the frog to understand the expansiveness and diversity of the universe.

When we think of what is typical or normal, we tend to start with ourselves and our own little worlds: our families, neighborhoods, schools, and communities. This kind of thinking often gives rise to ethnocentrism, or self-centeredness. Ethnocentrism leads us to judge others or the larger world by our own limited experiences.

Sometimes, our narrow perspective expands a bit through exposure to the media. For most people in the United States, various media are their primary source of information about the larger world. However, this can be dangerous because many people do not critically evaluate what they see, read, or hear on television, in newspapers and magazines, on the Internet, or elsewhere. According to research, the media often provide information that is stereotypical, superficial, and incomplete (see Fig. 4.1).

For example, substantive discussions of poverty in the media are rare. Because poverty is systemic, persistent, and complex, it does not grab the public's attention. Other so-called "breaking news" is more apt to get the headlines. For example, google the word "poverty," then click on NEWS on the Google menu bar. Next, do the same with the name of a currently popular celebrity. When you compare the "results" of these two searches, consider the human and global significance of each.

When poverty is covered, stories are typically superficial and sensational. Very little if any attention is paid to how we define poverty, how poverty has changed, how people in different parts of the world view poverty, how poverty differs within and among racial and ethnic populations, and the impact of poverty on children. Whether the subject is poverty or some other diversity issue, we need to be critical thinkers and users when it comes to the media. More specifically, we need to develop **media literacy**, a skill set that allows us to access, evaluate, and create different forms of media.

If we cannot necessarily rely on the media, what about our personal lives? Why can't we simply fall back on what we know as a result of our past and present experiences? At the beginning of the semester, we discuss this very subject in my Introduction to Sociology classes. One of the criticisms of sociology is that it is common sense. After all, why spend a semester studying human behavior when "street knowledge" or personal experiences will suffice? We analyze a number of statements that reveal the pitfalls of relying solely on experiences,

Gee, you sure don't look like a Muslim.

Figure 4.1 Does the media distort our perception of Muslims?

YouTube: Reaching Minorities

YouTube resonates with minorities in a way that mainstream media does not. As people, and minorities in particular, gravitate to their smartphones, iPads, and laptops, big names in the entertainment industry such as Russell Simmons, Jay-Z, and Queen Latifah are unveiling new YouTube channels. In contrast to mainstream television, a sizable and increasing share of YouTube producers, directors, and personalities are minorities. Similarly, the medium provides a way to counter stereotypes through more diverse and inclusive programming. Instead of trying to appeal to everyone, YouTube thrives by targeting niches that are largely ignored by other media outlets. Therefore, it is not surprising that recent data compiled by Pew Internet and American Life Project show African-American, Latino, and Asian audiences are more apt to watch online videos than Whites. Russell Simmons, hip-hop pioneer and recently named by *USA Today* as one of the "Top 25 Most Influential People of the Past 25 Years," provides insight into the growing popularity of YouTube. "It's not like, 'Do more black stuff.' I'm an American. I don't want to be patronized. I want to be included."[3]

such as "Most of the poor in the United States are non-White minority-group members." Many of my students agree with this statement because they have lived most, if not all of their lives in large, impoverished urban areas with large concentrations of people of color. Others disagree, noting their exposure to White poverty, which they argue is pervasive but more hidden. Still others take issue with the ambiguity of the statement, arguing that *most, poor,* and *non-White* need to be clearly defined. For example, what does *most* mean? Does it refer to the percentage or number of poor? Finally, in the course of dissecting this statement, we begin to realize that because of cultural encapsulation, our view of the world is skewed.

Cultural encapsulation starts at a young age. It is apparent throughout **socialization,** the lifelong process of social interaction that enables us to learn about ourselves and others. We are inclined to make friends with other people who are like us, or at least that is our assumption. In many cases, we attend schools and live in neighborhoods that are racially and ethnically segregated. Cultural encapsulation prior to college is one of the major reasons why college life can be such an adjustment. After living in relatively segregated communities, students tend to become much more aware of their cultural identity when they enter college. One student comments: "Like now, I feel White. I feel different. I feel really different compared to other people."[4]

Profile in Diversity Consciousness

Unlike many individuals, Danny Leydorf's choice of a college reflected his desire to counter his cultural encapsulation. Leydorf had attended a private evangelical school since kindergarten. However, given his desire to enter the field of law or politics, he wanted to test his beliefs in a setting where others did not necessarily share his views. Consequently, he chose to attend a large secular college. Prior to the beginning of school, he was matched up with a roommate who shared many of his interests, including politics and *The Simpsons*. Only later did he come across a Facebook.com profile of his roommate that read, "I hate evangelical Christians."

At college, Leydorf often felt like an outsider. He wrestled with when it was appropriate to talk about his faith. While one student in his dorm invited him to a strip club and another made a habit of playing video boxing games, Leydorf expressed his beliefs on an index card taped to his desk. It read, "I am not ashamed of the Gospel, because it is the power of God for the salvation of everyone who believes: first for the Jew, then for the Gentile" (Romans 1:16).

Leydorf took advantage of opportunities to challenge his thinking, such as attending a Muslim discussion group and a dialogue between gays and evangelicals. In a class on civics, he read a book that is highly critical of anti-gay discrimination. Gradually, he became less comfortable with judging whom God sends to hell. As he remains entrenched in his faith, he fights the temptation to think of himself as better than others because of his adherence to his beliefs.[6]

Cultural Immersion Program

Indiana University teacher education majors participate in a cultural immersion program. These programs take place in multicultural urban centers in the United States, on Native American reservations, and in seventeen countries throughout the world. As part of their student teaching requirement, they are required to teach and live in a predominantly bilingual/bicultural setting in the United States or abroad.

The program addresses the growing need for elementary and secondary school teachers with multicultural skills and training.

Through this experience, student teachers learn to quickly adapt to the cultural and cognitive backgrounds of their students. Further, they gain valuable insight into the development of effective curricular and instructional approaches for linguistically diverse students.

Students may find it difficult to adjust to college life when the cultural backgrounds of their fellow students are unlike those of people in their home communities. Similarly, adjusting to a new cultural environment at work may pose an equally formidable challenge. Faced with either of these situations, people typically become more focused on their own culture and how it makes them feel. As one individual remarked, "I'm used to being the minority, but I wasn't used to living it day by day by day, morning, noon, and night."[5]

Keep in mind that exposure to diversity does not always lead to greater acceptance and interaction across group boundaries. For instance, research shows that throwing diverse students together in the same setting is no guarantee that they will interact or get to know each other. Whites, African-Americans, Latinos, and other minority students find it easier to socialize with others who they perceive as being more like them. Also, negative prior experiences or personal biases may make some students hesitant to develop any kind of meaningful relationship with someone who does not share their background or even their physical appearance.

This kind of self-segregation, in which people "keep with their own kind," is relatively common on college campuses. It occurs in residence halls, athletic teams, social clubs, and support groups. Contrary to popular belief, research findings indicate that self-segregation is more common among White students than among students of color. This is one of the major conclusions found in *The Impact of Diversity on Students*, a research report published by the Association of American Colleges and Universities.[7]

 Thinking Through Diversity

Look back on your education. Did readings, lectures, and discussions reflect the contributions of many cultures? Explain.

SIX AREAS OF DEVELOPMENT

> Many people want to change the world; only a few want to change themselves.
> —Leo Tolstoy

Diversity consciousness is not an ideal level of awareness and understanding that we reach, after which we remain static. Rather, it is dynamic. Developing our diversity consciousness means committing ourselves to constant learning and change. In this sense, it is a lot like developing computer skills. There is always something new to learn and practice.

The development of diversity consciousness can be broken down into six areas (see Fig. 4.2): (1) examining ourselves and our worlds, (2) expanding our knowledge of others and their worlds, (3) stepping outside of ourselves, (4) gauging the level of the playing field, (5) checking up on ourselves, and (6) following through. In the following sections we describe each of these areas.

Figure 4.2 Diversity Consciousness: Six Areas of Development.

EXAMINING OURSELVES AND OUR WORLDS

It is a huge mistake to assume that we already have full knowledge of our own history and culture. Zora Neale Hurston, a well-known writer and anthropologist, stated: "I couldn't see it [culture] for wearing it. It was only when I was off in college, away from my native surroundings that I could see myself like somebody else and stand off and look at my garment. I had to have the spyglass of Anthropology to look through, at that."[8] Like many of us, Hurston was unaware of her culture because she was so immersed in it. When she went to college, she found herself in a different cultural and academic setting. By experiencing and learning about cultural diversity in this new environment, she was able to "stand back" and take a more critical look at her culture.

Before we begin to make sense of other cultures and cultural differences, we need to become aware of who we are. We do this by focusing on ourselves and the enormous diversity that exists within each of us. Each person is different and each is unique.

Our uniqueness is a reflection of both nature and nurture, which work together. **Nature** refers to our biological makeup. This includes our inborn or genetic traits. "Who we are," therefore, has something to do with nature. However, we cannot examine nature apart from nurture. **Nurture** refers to those aspects of the environment that mold and shape us, such as schools, families, and peer groups. Each of us is reared in a distinctive environment. Even children from the same family interact differently with other family members, watch different television shows, read different books, and have different friends.

You can begin to reveal your own diversity by asking a number of questions about your background. What makes you unique? Is it your work ethic, talents, personality, sense of humor, or maybe all these things? Your upbringing, schooling, family background, and cultural roots further distinguish you from other people. Your answers to the following questions will provide greater insight into your diversity.

1. What is your name? What is the meaning or significance of your name?

2. Where and when were you born?

3. What is your family background? Who raised you? As you grew up, who did you consider "family"? Where did you live? Who were your closest friends?

4. What schools did you attend? In general, did you feel like you belonged, or did you feel like an outsider at school? Were the values you learned at school similar to the ones you learned at home? Did you feel the need to "leave your culture at home" in order to be accepted at school?

5. How has your identity been influenced by your race, gender, religion, ethnic background, sexual orientation, (dis)abilities, and/or social class?

6. What about your personality makes you unique? How are you different from other members of your family?

7. What motivates you? What are your interests and hobbies? What are your goals in life? How do you want to be remembered?

8. What kinds of learning experiences are meaningful for you? What kinds are not?

Every person has a name, and also his own story about his name. My name is Yuan Cai. I don't know what you think about that, but to me it just feels upside-down because I used to be called "Cai Yuan" or "Yuan Yuan." That's why when I speak English I just tell you my name is "Yuan." "Yuan" is the end character of my name, so I feel I have told you all. You know, giving best names to children is so important in China. They look up in a dictionary and search for the most beautiful sounds, perfect meanings, special and elegantly simple characters, and require the characters to have some relationships between family members. So you can imagine how hard a job it was for my parents to give me my name.

—Another perspective

Examining our own diversity entails learning about our culture. This is a bigger job for some than others. How much do you know about your ancestors? Although most of us in the United States have an immigrant past, relatively few of us know much about it. Whereas some students are very conscious of their cultural backgrounds, others are hardly aware of it. Still others wrestle with the history of their culture and how it reflects on them.

Sometimes, learning about your history can be difficult. In *Tearing the Silence*, Ursula Hegi talks about "what it means to be linked to two cultures."[9] Hegi, a German-American, devotes much of her book to the personal histories of Germans who were born during or after World War II and later migrated to the United States. When they arrived, they expected to find an open and tolerant society. Instead, they encountered many who scorned and mocked them because they were assumed to be Nazis.

Many of the German-Americans interviewed by Hegi wanted to leave their past behind. As one person put it, "I have a very difficult time dealing with the Holocaust. I think there is a collective burden in our generation because it is just so tremendous, so horrible. On the other side, I must say that we have this 'Gnade der spaten

Geburt'—the grace of late birth. It's an easy way out. . . . But it came to my mind that there is a shadow of a collective guilt. At the same time, I feel it is not my personal guilt, and there's nothing I can do."[10]

Your own cultural identity may be more or less visible to you for a number of reasons. For example, some people are more apt to be reminded of their cultural background on a daily basis. Bong Hwan Kim, a Korean-American man, recalls that his first childhood memory about difference revolved around bringing lunch to school on the first day of kindergarten. His mother had made him kimpahp, rice balls rolled up in dried seaweed and wrapped in aluminum foil. All morning he remembers looking forward to having this special treat for lunch at school. As soon as the lunch bell rang, he pulled out the kimpahp from inside his desk. When he unwrapped it, his classmates "pointed and gawked, 'What is that? How could you eat that?' they shrieked." He continues, "I don't remember whether I ate my lunch or not, but I told my mother I would only bring tuna or peanut butter sandwiches for lunch after that."[11]

Language, music, food, holidays, and customs all serve to reinforce our sense of cultural belonging. Being treated as an outsider serves as a reminder as well. When this occurs, we may continually find ourselves in situations in which we must decide whether to try to "fit in." Frequently, we may have to weigh the pros and cons of being "true" to our cultural roots, assimilating, or some combination of the two. However, if our culture is the norm at school, among friends, and at work, we do not have to make these difficult choices.

There are also times when some feel their culture is slipping away. "I was so anxious to assimilate, to blend in, that I started to forget who I was . . . . I just felt it wasn't cool to be a poor Latina girl from Harlem. It was better to mosh than merengue and to be able to go to a country home on the weekends. I almost forgot who I was and where I came from, and it's important not to do that. Remember, you come from beautifully vibrant cultures filled with rich music and traditions. Share that. Enlighten others with your history. . . . . Try new things but don't forget the old. . . . Remember who you are."[12]

In the course of becoming aware of our cultural roots, it is important to remember that our identities are inextricably linked to the surrounding cultural landscape. An African proverb states: "A person is a person through other people." We cannot escape the influence of culture; consequently, we are not the totally independent thinkers and learners we may think we are.

Up to this point we have focused on who we are and how we are interconnected with others. Frequently, it is difficult to make that connection for a number of reasons, including the following:

1. *The emphasis on individualism in U.S. society makes it difficult to see social influences.* In most cases, people in the United States are raised to believe that they think and act on their own. Consider the sayings, "Be all that you can be," "Pull yourself up by your own boot straps," and "You are your own worst enemy." Now contrast those with the African proverb, "It takes an entire village to raise a child." Asian cultures also tend to be more oriented toward "we" than "me." As an example, Japanese have a saying, "The nail that stands up gets pounded down." This notion that personal goals are not as important as the goals of the group is at odds with the saying in the United States that "The squeaky wheel gets the grease."

2. *Our cultural environment is so close to us that sometimes we do not see it.* This can lead to **enculturation,** immersion in a culture to the point where that way of life appears only natural. Often, we do not even think about certain beliefs that are deeply embedded in each of us. Consequently, it is hard to step back and take a

Baseball: A Cross-Cultural Perspective

Think for a moment about how we view baseball in the United States. How might people in other countries, such as Japan, view it differently? In *You Gotta Have Wa*, author Robert Whiting offers a comparative study of this game.[13] "Wa" refers to group harmony, the embodiment of Japanese "besoboru." Whereas U.S. professional ballplayers are encouraged to "do their own thing," *kojinshugi* (the Japanese term for individualism) is frowned upon in Japan. In the United States, it is commonplace for a player to hold out for more money and sell his services to the highest bidder. This is highly unacceptable in Japan because it shows that a player is more concerned about himself than about his team. In the United States, each player gets himself into shape, whereas in Japan, everyone follows the same training regimen, even the superstars.

long hard look at our environment or imagine that anyone could think any other way. In *Patterns of Problem Solving,* Moshe Rubinstein provides us with insight into how people from different cultures might view the following hypothetical situation.[14] Imagine that you are in a boat on a lake, along with your mother, spouse, and child. The boat capsizes. If you could save yourself and only *one* of these three people who would you save and why? Most students in my classes answer child. They argue their children have their whole future ahead of them. Some students mention that their children are "part of them." Very few choose mom or spouse. Rubenstein relates how a man from an Arab culture chose "mother." Given this man's cultural background, he could not imagine choosing anyone else. His reasoning was that you can always have another child or spouse. However, you can only have one mother.

3. *Some people rarely experience social marginality, meaning exclusion that results from being seen as an "outsider."* Because of this, they have a difficult time seeing beyond their own world. However, if you are constantly being judged because of your race, class, disability, or religion, you are apt to be more aware of the significance of social relationships. For example, consider an American history instructor who repeatedly calls on the only Mormon student in class to get "her people's" point of view. This experience may make this student feel like an outsider because she is constantly being singled out. In addition, the student may realize that other students in class are not called upon to represent their religions.

 Thinking Through Diversity

How can learning about others help you learn more about yourself?

EXPANDING OUR KNOWLEDGE OF OTHERS AND THEIR WORLDS

Learning about others is instrumental in laying the foundation for diversity consciousness. Furthermore, it enables us to learn more about ourselves. Anthropologists, for example, do not just study cultures that differ from their own. They also work to understand and interpret their own culture, often using what they learn about other cultures to do so. Likewise, visiting another country can make you more aware of your cultural biases and provide you with a basis for comparison. After your visit, you may have a whole new outlook on aspects of your culture that you take for granted, such as housing, recreation, education, or friendship.

I come from the Democratic Republic of the Congo, and one thing that I miss here most is the friendship of my neighbors and friends. In my country, and in Africa in general, people are hospitable. Friendship is the most important thing in life. In my country, you can't perish from hunger or illness, because members of your family must assist you and help you to improve your life. It's an obligation. Even the neighbors give you their assistance. For instance, when you are sick and you can't go to a hospital because you don't have enough money or you don't have a car, the one in your neighborhood who has a car must transport you to the hospital without hesitation. He has to do it with all his heart. You can even stop a car passing your way to get help.

In America, however, I think this is not the same. People live in mistrust of each other. You can't count on your neighbors because either they don't know you or don't want to be involved. You are condemned to live without any moral support from anyone in the neighborhood. You can be ill and can die alone in your apartment and no one is likely to notice it. Here I think friendship takes place only when there is an interest. Last week I finished my milk and went to ask a neighbor for a half cup of milk. She gave it to me, but a few days later, she asked for some sugar from me and gave it back to me in the evening. I was very surprised because this is not done among neighbors.

Maybe I am wrong in my opinion, but the facts show that friendships in America are very different from friendships in my country.

—Another perspective

Malcolm X, in his autobiography, talks about his visit to Saudi Arabia as well as a number of countries in Africa as being one of the turning points in his life.[15] His experiences in that part of the world gave him an entirely different view of race relations in the United States. Moving to another country can provide students with new insight into their ethnic background. A college student from Colombia talks about her interaction with other Latin Americans in the United States. "I have met a lot of Latin Americans. Although we have the same cultural background, we are different. We have different accents in our language and use different words to mean the same things. I have learned about exotic foods from other Latin American countries that I have never seen before. It's incredible that I have learned about Latin American culture in a non–Latin American country. When you are in a foreign country, you have the opportunity to recognize your own roots because you see things from a different point of view."

Differences

Typically, we learn about cultural differences by sampling and studying a few noteworthy events and people. A good example of this is the "group of the month" approach adopted by many organizations. With this approach, we are exposed to various elements of African-American culture during Black History Month. Similarly, there are months for women, Latinos, Native Americans, people with disabilities, and other groups.

This kind of approach may be attractive because it is simple and easy to implement. Unfortunately, it promotes a superficial and distorted view of differences. The historical experiences of African-Americans or women, for example, cannot be separated and studied in any kind of meaningful way in a single month. At best, this approach gives us a "taste" of various histories and cultures. At worst, it excludes those who wonder why their groups are never a "group of the month." Such an approach can also lead to even more stereotypical assumptions.

Although sampling different ways of life may have some value, it is not without pitfalls. After riding in a wheelchair for 15 minutes or attending a one-hour lecture on disability awareness, some people may begin to feel that they now know what it is like to have a disability. They may generalize what they learn or experience to all people with disabilities. In addition, they may forget the lesson learned shortly thereafter, unless it is reaffirmed time and again.

What then is the best way to learn about differences? A number of specific strategies are discussed later in the chapter. It is impossible to know every aspect of every culture. However, we need to approach cultural differences with a number of things in mind:

1. *Do not simply sample differences from a distance.* This promotes an "us versus them" attitude. Awareness and understanding change as we get closer to people and engage differences. In the mid-1970s, I remember a student in one of my classes correcting me on something I had said about Black Muslims. The student, Lola X, was a Black Muslim. She then invited me and my wife to her local temple. We accepted. When we arrived, we were frisked for our own safety. At that time there were concerns about the threat of violence. We were then taken into the temple. My wife was seated with the women on one side and I took my seat with the men. We discovered that we were the only two Whites in a congregation of more than 300 people of color. The sermon was powerful and positive. Everybody, it seemed, tried to make us feel welcome. After the service, a number of people came up to us, introduced themselves, and invited us back. As I look back at that experience, I realize how being there helped me learn and appreciate Lola and her religion. Based on what I had read and heard, I fully expected to be surrounded by people who were angry and hateful toward Whites. What I saw and felt were strong, loving people who went out of their way to make my wife and me feel at home.

2. *Seek to understand how the histories, perspectives, and contributions of different cultures are interconnected.* In 1927, the American historian Carter Woodson made this point with regard to "Negro history." Woodson argued that the focus should be on the Negro in history rather than on Negro history.[16]

3. *Try to decrease the social distance between you and those about whom you know little if anything.* **Social distance** is a concept that was coined by a scientist named Emory Bogardus.[17] It refers to the degree to which we are willing to interact and develop relationships with certain racial and ethnic groups. Bogardus created a scale to measure whether we would accept certain people as neighbors, classmates, coworkers, or even spouses. He found that we tend to separate ourselves from others who we think are not like us. This is particularly true of our inner social circles. Take a look at your close friends. How closely do they resemble your racial and ethnic identity? Would you be comfortable bringing someone of a different religion, sexual orientation, or social class home for a few days to spend some time with your family? Our tendency to gravitate toward people who are like us promotes cultural encapsulation, a concept discussed earlier.

4. *Focus on ordinary people and occurrences.* Learning about a few remarkable people and events from another culture is not sufficient. Often, stories like these tell

us very little about a culture. You can learn a lot more from people who do not make the headlines or the history books, such as a friend, an acquaintance, or the employee who works in the cafeteria. Think about the "perspectives" that appear throughout this book. What have you learned from them?

Thinking Through Diversity

In your life, what groups or cultures are most socially distant?

Similarities

Arthur Ashe, in his autobiography *Days of Grace*, writes, "I see nothing inconsistent between being proud of oneself and one's ancestors and, at the same time, seeing oneself as first and foremost a member of the commonwealth of humanity, the commonwealth of all races and creeds. My potential is more than can be expressed within the bounds of my race or ethnic identity. . . . If I had one last wish, I would ask that all Americans could see themselves that way, past the barbed-wire fence of race and color. We are the weaker for these divisions and the stronger when we can transcend them."[18]

Thinking Through Diversity

Describe a specific life experience that made it possible for you to see yourself as a member of the "commonwealth of humanity."

Too often, we preoccupy ourselves so much with individual and cultural differences that we ignore our similarities. Some similarities are harder to see because they lie beneath the surface. In a poem entitled "Underneath We're All the Same," a student addresses the fact that we all share certain feelings.

> He prayed—it wasn't my religion.
> He ate—it wasn't what I ate.
> He spoke—it wasn't my language.
> He dressed—it wasn't what I wore.
> He took my hand—it wasn't the color of mine.
> But when he laughed—it was how I laughed,
> and when he cried—it was how I cried.
>
> —Amy Maddox, as quoted in *Teaching Tolerance* magazine[19]

Picture yourself in one of your classes. With whom do you have the most in common? Perhaps it is someone who looks like you or shares your cultural background. It might be the Hispanic student who sits next to you. Even though your cultural background is different, you both grew up in a middle-class, urban neighborhood and are very close to your families. Then again, it might be the White woman who sits in front of you. Unlike you, she is married and has five children. Yet she is the one person in class who shares your passion for information technology. Our differences often hide our similarities. Until we really get to know a person, we often fail to realize just how much we share in common.

As students encountering each other for the first time, we tend to notice differences. During the course of a semester, similarities among races, cultures, and other groups can become more apparent. The following comments were written by students who were part of a semester-long study group on racial and ethnic diversity.

I look at things differently because with me being a single parent, I do struggle and I realize that it's not just a "black thing." Everybody struggles.

I learned that Whites hurt just like I do, they cry just like I do. I never knew that some Whites have the same fears about race that I have.

I remember the day we listed the qualities that make us who we are. I realize most of us are alike in a lot of ways, and different in fewer ways. It was very reassuring to see other students agree with me on the same qualities.

—Other perspectives

STEPPING OUTSIDE OF OURSELVES

We understand others or at least try to understand others by stepping outside of ourselves; that is, we try to put ourselves in their shoes, so to speak. In effect, we "simulate" how we would feel, what we would think, and how we would respond in a given situation. In *Surviving in Two Worlds*, Terry Tafoya describes this ability as being "able to borrow other people's eyes, to see to learn, and learn to see." For many Native American people, Tafoya says, "there's the idea of understanding life as a crystal. A crystal of quartz has different facets. Every time you turn it you discover a new facet."[20]

The ability to "put ourselves in somebody else's moccasins" increases our awareness, understanding, and diversity skills—our diversity consciousness. By stepping outside of ourselves and our culture, we can gain a deeper appreciation of other people's experiences. We begin to realize that our perspective is just one of many. As a result, our ability to think flexibly and to communicate effectively improves.

Stepping outside of ourselves is important for other reasons as well. It increases our awareness of our own frame of reference and how this shapes what we see. By adopting another perspective, we become more aware of our own. After artist Laura Lee Gulledge spent time as a solo volunteer in Ghana teaching art in a number of villages, her ability to shift perspectives made it easier to see the difference between "local perception" versus the perception of her western eyes (see Fig. 4.3). For example, she explains how the people she met were always so nice, especially in situations where she really needed

Figure 4.3 "African Eyes."
Source: Courtesy of Laura Lee Gulledge.

a helping hand. Often, she responded with suspicion, asking herself, "What does this person want from me?" She became more aware of her own cultural lens after a while, when people showed her time and time again that they were just being nice and showing respect. Laura Lee needed to look at people in this part of the world through her "African eyes," as she calls them, so when someone was nice to her, simply be grateful rather than defensive. In the United States, she still looks through her African eyes in certain situations, like her use of water. After experiencing what it was like to have to carry water around and conserve it, she now views water very differently. She realizes what a precious commodity it is, and it unnerves her to see people wasting it.

Thinking Through Diversity

Imagine that you are being forced to change your sex (select male/female) or your race/ethnicity (select a "new" racial/ethnic group) or your sexual orientation (select homosexual/heterosexual). Which would you change, and why?

For some, learning to step outside of your own world can be a matter of survival. W.E.B. Du Bois addresses this issue in his book *The Souls of Black Folk*.[22] According to Du Bois, **double consciousness** refers to a person's awareness of his or her own perspective and the perspective of others. It is like looking at the same thing in different ways. Double consciousness makes it possible to shift your perspective back and forth continuously.

Why is shifting one's perspective so important? Imagine driving through the Deep South years ago. For many, driving through Mississippi or Texas on a long trip was like driving anywhere else. They drove as far as they wanted and then stopped for gas, food, or rest. They stopped when it was convenient. Others may recall their trips through this part of the country differently. They had to be constantly aware of where they were at all times. Some remember filling their car with gas and then driving for miles without stopping for gas, food, or lodging. Given the racial climate in the area, they may have even feared for their lives. They found themselves in two worlds

Only Skin Deep

Joshua Solomon, a White student at the University of Maryland, remembers the day he read the book *Black Like Me* by John Howard Griffin.[21] He spent the entire day reading it and thinking about little else. Back in 1959, Griffin, a journalist, took a drug to change his skin from white to brown. He then traveled throughout the South and recorded his experiences. (A White woman by the name of Grace Halsell did something similar in the 1970s. Over the course of three years, she wrote three books about life as an Hispanic, Native American, and African-American woman.)

Solomon decided that he too would change the color of his skin and venture into the South. He did some research and talked to a physician at Yale University. He found the drug that Griffin had taken. Once he started taking it daily and spending time at a tanning salon, the effects became very noticeable.

Solomon decided to visit Atlanta, Georgia, first. Almost immediately, he found himself trying to be polite when people stared at him or looked away. Even though he had never had any difficulty making friends, this was no longer true. People acted differently toward him. A hostess at a half-filled restaurant made it clear to him that there would be a long wait. A police officer stopped him and gave him a warning even though he had done nothing wrong. And a lady who sat next to him while he was eating warned him not to venture into an all-White area north of Atlanta. She made it clear that "you people" ruin White neighborhoods.

Solomon cut short his experiment after a couple of days because he had grown increasingly angry and depressed. He had always thought that many Black people use racism as a crutch or an excuse. Because of this experience, he developed new insight into how pervasive and debilitating racism can be.

divided by race. As they drove, they had to understand the perspective of people who lived in the surrounding areas. If they did not, their safety might be at risk.

Perspective shifting, when done repeatedly, allows us to develop greater awareness and then retain and refine it over time. In some situations, switching positions and roles with another person may seem virtually impossible, such as when a person's behaviors or belief systems seem repulsive or incomprehensible. If this is the case, we may develop the understanding that we do not understand. In the process of trying to understand, however, we may unknowingly begin to loosen up our mindset and emotions.

GAUGING THE LEVEL OF THE PLAYING FIELD

For some of us, living away from home is the first time we really wrestle with inequality. This is particularly true if we have lived around people of similar means all of our lives. George Pillsbury, heir to the Pillsbury Flour Company family fortune, recalls that he never saw people living in poverty during his youth. He grew up on a private estate, attended an elite boarding school, and spent his leisure time at a country club. When he started attending classes at Yale University in New Haven, Connecticut, he was exposed to a radically different social world. "It was the first time I'd ever lived in the city—a real city with housing projects with poor people. I began to see poverty where I never had before. . . . I saw the inequities and felt them personally for the first time. I felt a lot of guilt at first, but then it became an emotional and intellectual process toward dedicating myself to positive social change."[23]

As Pillsbury discovered, learning about diversity means coming to grips with social inequality.

Thinking Through Diversity

Are you solely responsible for opening and closing the doors of opportunity in your life?

Social inequality refers to the unequal distribution of resources, such as wealth, power, and prestige. In *Where Do We Go From Here,* Martin Luther King addresses the fact that people have different amounts of power.[24] He says, "There is nothing essentially wrong with power. The problem is America's power is unequally distributed."

As a result of social inequality, we belong to different social classes. A **social class** is a category of people who share similar amounts of wealth, power, and prestige. Social class, a dimension of diversity, is not simply a matter of economics. Education, lifestyle, interests, and values relate to one's class position as well.

Many times, human differences and social inequality interrelate. A sense of worth is often attached to certain differences. For example, in the United States we attach a lot of significance to age. We distinguish between old and young people, and unlike many other countries, we value youth. Billions of dollars are spent each year by people trying to avoid being perceived as old.

One example of social inequality is **ageism,** an ideology that asserts one age category is superior to another. In the United States, ageism may be used to rationalize economic, political, and social discrimination against older people. Other examples of social inequality revolve around other dimensions of diversity, including gender, race, ethnicity, class, religion, and sexual orientation. In each case of social inequality, we categorize certain people as different and treat them unequally.

Gauging the level of the playing field is difficult. Living in the United States constantly exposes us to advantages and disadvantages tied to social inequality. However, in our own lives, we somehow fail to see many of our *advantages*. Think back to the example of George Pillsbury. He was surrounded by economic advantages throughout his childhood, yet he was not really aware of them because of his social isolation.

Why do we remain oblivious to many of our advantages or privileges? Why are we more aware of our disadvantages than our privileges? Why do we assume that we deserve these privileges and others do not? **Unearned privileges** are those benefits in life that we have through no effort of our own. Perhaps we were born into a wealthy family or maybe we have certain benefits in the workplace because of our religious background, gender, or race (see Fig. 4.4).

Unlike my wife, I was challenged by my teachers to pursue science or math as a possible career. I did not think twice about this unearned advantage until my wife shared with me that she was always led to believe that math was for males. As a result, she opted not to pursue her interest in math even though she exhibited a tremendous amount of potential in this field. After graduating from college and teaching music for a number of years, she went back to school to pursue her life-long dream of being an educator—teaching math and Web design, and training teachers.

Privileges are invisible for a number of reasons. When we have something, we tend to take it for granted. For example, we might not truly appreciate freedom until we lose it. Those with privileges naturally want to hold on to them as long as possible. One way of preserving privileges is to discount or ignore them. The education

"Actually, Lou, I think it was more than just my being in the right place at the right time. I think it was my being the right race, the right religion, the right sex, the right socioeconomic group, having the right accent, the right clothes, going to the right schools..."

Figure 4.4 Rethinking Unearned Privileges.

we receive in schools typically focuses on how certain groups are disadvantaged, not advantaged. Discussing individual privileges is seen as too personal and threatening. In the United States, we value individual achievement, competition, and equality; therefore, we do not like to acknowledge our privileges, especially those that we do not earn. If we are privileged in some way, we assume that we deserve it. If others are not, we assume that they are not as good or worthy or qualified.

Thinking through privileges and disadvantages requires more than just learning about these things in an abstract way. Rather, we need to recognize them in our own life and in the lives of others. In each of our lives, we have an assortment of privileges as well as disadvantages. Power and consequences of these privileges varies from person to person, and situation to situation. Ask yourself: How and when are you privileged? What privileges do you enjoy? Did you earn them?

In *White Privilege and Male Privilege,* Peggy McIntosh talks about some of the privileges of being White. She examines an "invisible, weightless knapsack of special provisions, assurances, tools, maps, guides . . ." McIntosh cites some of the privileges operating in her own life, such as "I am never asked to speak for all the people of my racial group." Two more of the 47 unearned privileges mentioned by McIntosh are "I can be pretty sure that if I ask to talk to 'the person in charge,' I will be facing a person of my race," and "I can easily buy posters, postcards, picture books, greeting cards, dolls, toys, and children's magazines featuring people of my race."[25]

Perhaps another privilege of being White is thinking of oneself as an individual devoid of race. Ruth Frankenberg, in her book *White Women, Race Matters: The Social Construction of Whiteness,* writes about one of the White women she interviewed. "Beth was much more sharply aware of racial oppression shaping Black experience than of race privilege shaping her own life. Thus, Beth could be alert to the realities of economic discrimination against Black communities while still conceptualizing her own life as racially neutral. . . ."[26]

> I feel some type of resentment towards white privilege, not necessarily white people. I don't dislike white people but I dislike the system in place that makes their culture the standard for other cultures to be judged by. I understand that it is systematic and white people are just as socialized as other cultures but it doesn't eliminate the feelings of resentment that I have towards them. I think that it has made me more inclined to deal with black people and learn about black culture instead of white culture. I do interact with white people at school and when I participate in social activism but when I do, I am reminded of white privilege so it makes it hard for me to look at them as allies, when the differences are apparent in thought and action.
>
> —Another perspective

There is considerable disagreement when we attempt to explain why everybody in the United States does not have an equal "piece of the pie." Recent polls show that the vast majority of White Americans believe racial and ethnic inequality is largely a thing of the past. Indeed, some even argue that the election of Barack Obama as President shows that we have become a post-racial society, meaning that race and racism are inconsequential in the United States today. Survey data, compiled by the Pew Research Center after President Obama's election, show that in spite of an upbeat in positive views toward the future, Blacks are still much more likely than Whites to question racial fairness in the United States and to favor the need for changes to ensure equal rights.[27]

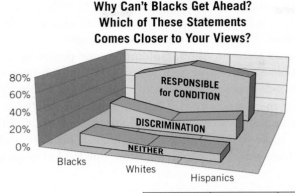

Why Can't Blacks Get Ahead?
Which of These Statements
Comes Closer to Your Views?

	Blacks	Whites	Hispanics
☐ Neither	14%	8%	8%
☐ Racial discrimination is the reason many black people can't get ahead	30%	15%	24%
■ Blacks who can't get ahead are mostly responsible for their own condition	53%	71%	59%

Table 4.1 Perceptions of Inequality.
Source: Pew Research Center.[28]

Ask yourself, "Is racial discrimination the main reason why many Black people can't get ahead?" Answers to this question, from a Pew Research Report (see Table 4.1), point to disparities in the views of Whites, Blacks, and Hispanics. When we examine the answers of *all* respondents, approximately two-thirds agree that Blacks are mostly responsible for their own condition. If we then parcel out responses by Whites, Blacks, and Hispanics, significant intergroup differences emerge. Although majorities of each of these groups place the emphasis on personal factors rather than racial discrimination, Whites (71%) are much more apt to take this position than Hispanics (59%) or Blacks (53%).

In gauging the level of the playing field, it is important to ask yourself the following questions:

1. *Are you blaming the individual or society?* When we blame individuals, we find fault with their characters, work ethic, attitudes, or some other individual difference. We assume that individuals are holding themselves back. Blaming society changes the focus from problem people to people with problems. These problems or barriers, which are found in the larger society, act as obstacles or detours. At times, social barriers take the form of sexism and classism. **Sexism** refers to the thinking that one sex is superior to another and that unequal treatment is therefore justifiable. **Classism** can be defined in the same way, with the focus on social class. Both the individual and societal points of view are shortsighted and incomplete. One assumes total control over one's fate; the other assumes almost a total lack of control. The individual and society are both important and interconnected. Individuals do have the freedom to choose. People are not at the mercy of their environment. However, inequality does exist. We do not live in a **meritocracy**, a system in which people get ahead *solely* on the basis of merit. Factors that have nothing to do with ability can affect your move up the economic ladder, regardless of your motivation. These factors include who you know, your looks, and other people's preconceived notions about you.

2. *Are you assuming that if one person can succeed, anybody can?* How do you feel when people in the public eye are held up as evidence that anyone can make

it to the top? What if your school grades were compared with someone else in your family or with a close friend? We are all different and unique, with our own strengths and limitations. A goal that is realistic or obtainable for one person may be out of someone else's reach or vision. Holding up one person as an example that anything is possible is an example of tunnel vision. People, for example, may point to a female CEO or Supreme Court justice and cite her success as proof of equal opportunity for men and women. We cannot assume that what happens to one person necessarily applies to the entire group. If we focus exclusively on the one or two who "make it big," we may ignore the vast majority who do not. Circumstances vary from person to person and from one field of employment to another.

3. *Do you see power and privilege as an all-or-nothing proposition?* Part of the problem with the terms minority and majority is that they create the impression that we are one or the other. In the literature on diversity, majority does not refer to the size of a group. **Majority** refers to the group with power and privilege. Similarly, a **minority** is not necessarily numerically smaller; rather, it is the group at a disadvantage in terms of power and privilege. In reality, the division between the more and less powerful is not always obvious. As an example, a student's majority statuses might include being White, male, and upper class. This same student's minority statuses might be that he is gay and has a disability. Depending on the situation, people may consider him a majority- or a minority-group member. It is a mistake to ignore our multiple statuses and their impact on us.

4. *Do you immerse yourself in your own victimization to the point that you cannot see or comprehend the victimization of others?* Perceiving ourselves as victims may not only distort our sense of personal responsibility for our actions, but it may also restrict our vision of the role inequality plays in the lives of others. By way of illustration, we may overstate the presence of social barriers for ourselves and underestimate or completely deny their existence for others. We may feel like victims because of our minority and/or majority statuses.

Well-known columnist Leonard Pitts discusses the dangers of blaming one's victimization on the White man. He writes, "Everybody should have a white man. Because when you have a white man, nothing is ever your fault. You're never required to account for your own failings or take the reins of your own destiny. The boss says, 'Why haven't you finished those reports, Bob?' and you say, 'Because of the white man, sir.'" Pitts adds that although it is naive to think that racism no longer exists, we are obligated to "live without excuses" in the face of that reality.[29]

We *can* empower ourselves. Learning from our own experiences and observing how others have resisted victimization can help us think through social inequality. Experiencing what it is like to be a victim may sensitize us to the subtle and not so subtle ways in which our actions victimize others.

> "To be conscious that you are ignorant is a great step to knowledge."
> —Benjamin Disraeli

CHECKING UP ON OURSELVES

Many of us shy away from self-examination. We would rather focus on other people and their shortcomings. In a way, it is much more difficult to confront our own prejudices, stereotypes, and ethnocentrism because it requires us to closely examine our assumptions. These assumptions can be difficult for us to see. They are often so embedded in us that we take them for granted.

A good example is the belief that "women, by nature, make better nurses than men." For some of us, this is an absolute truth. The media, school, and family cultivate and reinforce this assumption. It is difficult to step back and look at this commonplace assumption in an uncommon way. What are the sources of this assumption? Are these sources reliable? Historically, why did the nursing profession become predominantly female? How does this assumption affect our thinking and behavior toward male and female nurses? Wrestling with questions such as these is difficult. It also requires **critical thinking**, the ability to freely question and evaluate ideas and information in a purposeful, goal-directed manner.

Critical thinking is a diversity skill that enables us to recognize our biases and those of others. It can help us understand that our point of view is one of many, and reveal gaps or inconsistencies in our assumptions. Research has shown that one key factor in reducing bias is the ability to think critically. In general, those who question what they hear from others and think things through show less prejudice than those who simply accept things at face value.

Checking up on ourselves requires constant questioning, reevaluation, and self-reflection. Questions, such as those that follow, provide us with valuable insight into our thinking and behavior throughout the day.

1. *Are you more comfortable around certain types of people?* James Box, a paraplegic and founder of a high-tech wheelchair company, implores us to confront our discomfort and wrestle with it. If something "turns us off" or repulses us, we need to examine it for a while and ask questions of others and ourselves until we can figure out why we are uncomfortable.

2. *Do you make snap judgments about people?* When you are walking through a shopping mall, for example, what assumptions do you make based on clothing, hairstyle, and physical features?

3. *Who do you tend to include in your social networks?* Who do you tend to leave out? How might you expand and diversify your social networks?

4. *When you communicate, what messages are you sending?* What about your body language? Do you simply assume that people interpret your communication as you intend? If not, how do you check for possible misunderstandings?

5. *Is your behavior consistent with your thinking?* In *To Be Equal*, Whitney Young addresses the need to do more than use language that is inoffensive. A change of vocabulary, according to Young, is something quite different from changes in behaviors and attitudes.[30]

Self-examination and critical thinking do not occur in isolation. Instead, they go hand in hand with seeking honest feedback from mentors, supervisors, teachers, coworkers, and friends. As our environment changes, our awareness and understanding need to keep pace. We grow and adapt as our world and life experiences continuously expand. Checking up on ourselves gives us direction. Companies, for example, regularly conduct assessments before they draw up a plan of action. Because individual workers need to do the same thing, Northwestern University expects its first-year MBA students to keep a Feeling Journal. The aim of the journal is to help students become more aware of their feelings and the role they play in their work. Before we are able to improve and develop skills such as teamwork, leadership, communication, and social networking, it is necessary to think through where we are and in what direction we are going. This takes time, commitment, patience, and awareness of self.

FOLLOWING THROUGH

Diversity consciousness does not refer simply to our awareness of ourselves and others. It extends to how we behave and interact with others. Think back to those times when your ability to understand something did not translate into doing it. In order to apply our knowledge and awareness to real-life situations, we need to practice, practice, and practice. We learn and "get better" by doing, not by merely listening to a motivational speaker or taking advantage of online or classroom training. For example, taking weekly piano lessons and listening to other pianists will not ensure that you will be able to play this instrument. Rather, you will only learn how to play the piano by constantly practicing and improving your skills.

We can only develop and refine diversity skills through constant application and self-evaluation. For instance, many of us regard listening as passive. However, we can improve our listening skills through **active listening,** taking a more active role in hearing and digesting what is being said as well as encouraging the speaker. By focusing on a specific competency, investing the requisite time and energy, and seeking help if necessary, we can close the gap between "I understood it" and "I actually did it."

Practicing a diversity skill is not necessarily a feel-good activity. There is an element of risk taking. Try not to get too down on yourself or allow others to frustrate you. As time goes by, you will realize that it is worth the struggle.

STRATEGIES FOR DEVELOPING DIVERSITY CONSCIOUSNESS

Developing diversity consciousness is an uneven process, meaning that it is very unpredictable and sporadic. There is no magical moment when you develop diversity consciousness and say to yourself, "Aha, I've got it." You may find the more you learn about diversity, the less knowledgeable you feel. As you grow, you may go from feeling, "I'm not prejudiced" to "maybe I am" to "I am prejudiced."

In the process of developing our diversity consciousness, we change the way we feel, think, and act. Sometimes, changing the way we feel is the most difficult because it is so deep-rooted and holistic. Moving from fixed to flexible thinking requires us to suspend judgment and question received knowledge. Finally, the process is incomplete unless we show the openness, humility, and willingness that is necessary to modify our behavior.

> "Knowing is not enough; we must apply. Willing is not enough; we must do."
> —Johann Wolfgang von Goethe

> The greater our knowledge increases, the greater our ignorance unfolds.
> —John Fitzgerald Kennedy

A Personal Pledge to Listen

Brett Banfe learned to develop his listening skills by making a personal pledge to keep silent for an entire year. During his freshman year at college, he took notes on his digital device and used e-mail to keep in touch with family and friends. Banfe says this year-long experience taught him more about communication and interaction than the first 18 years of his life. Mainly, he grew acutely aware of how little time and effort we invest in listening. "Listening is the most important social interaction we as humans can make to improve human relations, yet we spend the least amount of time on it because it is outward, not inward. We spend our time on appearance, on hairstyle . . . when in my opinion, listening is far more important than all of these, yet it hardly even seems like an interaction."[31]

It is very important for me to maintain control of my wandering mind. I try to avoid all of the listening traps, such as dwelling on one thought while the person continues speaking or thinking about tomorrow's list of errands. Often, everyone is so intent on being able to speak that no one actually listens for content, but for cues that the end of the last sentence is about to arrive. A lot is missed in that kind of environment.

Ultimately, each of us must take responsibility for our development in this area. The following eight strategies, which revolve around education, self-examination, and networking, can help you move toward that goal.

1. *Take an active role in educating yourself.* Developing diverse relationships results in *incidental learning*, meaning that we often unknowingly learn much more about others and ourselves by widening our circle of friends, coworkers, and acquaintances. Reading, especially when we combine it with critical reflection, helps us expand our knowledge too.

   Articles from non-mainstream media, historical novels, and personal narratives can provide us with realistic and dramatic portrayals of diversity. This is especially true of first-person accounts. These accounts or stories tend to be much more real, intimate, and varied. For instance, when we read about American history, different accounts emerge. To illustrate, the westward expansion by early European settlers is a different story when told by Native Americans. For them, the expansion meant encroachment, death, and disease.

2. *Put yourself in a learning mode in any multicultural setting.* Try to suspend judgment and adopt a childlike kind of inquisitiveness when trying to make sense out of a situation. One of my students compared this to starting over or "wiping the slate clean." She went on to say that her English instructor told her on the first day of class to forget everything that she had learned about English. The instructor was pushing her to relearn the subject matter and undo her bad habits. In a similar vein, each of us has to shed what we know in certain situations. Only then can we look at people and lifestyles as if we were encountering them for the first time.

3. *Remember that your own life experiences are one of many important sources of knowledge.* This applies to everyone. In the book *Women's Ways of Knowing*, women who live ordinary lives are interviewed about how they perceive themselves and the world around them.[32] Many of these women had little respect for their own minds, ideas, and experiences. At work, school, and home, they relied on others to feed them information and felt voiceless much of the time. Despite their own feelings of inadequacy, the interviews revealed that these women were extremely knowledgeable as well as talented.

4. *Move beyond your personal comfort zone.* Sometimes, learning can be difficult and uncomfortable. However, this is a necessary part of opening up and growing intellectually and emotionally. For this reason, the company Hoechst Celanese requires its top executives to join two organizations in which they feel like an "outsider." At IBM, a variety of mentoring relationships enable people from dissimilar backgrounds to learn from each other. Cross-cultural training takes place before this process begins. One example of IBM's varied initiatives is **reverse mentoring,** a process in which an older executive pairs up with a younger employee in order to gain a different perspective and learn more about technology and social media. A reverse mentoring relationship is reciprocal; it is not about "us versus them."

5. *Be humble.* A while ago, Bill Cosby told a graduating class at George Washington University: "Don't ever think you know more than the person mopping a floor." Everybody has something of value to share. Be aware that no matter how much you know or have seen, you can still learn from anyone. This perspective will make you more open to differences and more willing to learn from those around you.

6. *Don't be too hard on yourself if misunderstandings arise.* No matter how hard we try, there will be situations in which we show our lack of knowledge of other cultures.

> "If you believe everything you read, better not read."
> —Japanese proverb

We may do this without even knowing it. The important thing is to acknowledge our mistakes and learn from them.

7. *Realize that you are not alone.* There are other people out there who care about you and will support you as you grow, learn, and wrestle with diversity issues. Surround yourself with these kinds of people.

8. *Never stop learning.* Opportunities to learn and grow can arise at any moment. Learning can be triggered by any number of experiences, such as overhearing an insensitive comment, attending a workshop on diversity, or doing something that might seem totally unrelated to diversity. People learn, unlearn, and relearn in a myriad of ways. In the next section we describe a wide range of learning opportunities.

Thinking Through Diversity

Do you think you can honor and respect diversity without working on understanding it?

DIVERSITY EDUCATION—A RANGE OF OPPORTUNITIES

Diversity education is one of the primary ways of increasing diversity consciousness (see Fig. 4.5). We are surrounded by opportunities to learn more about diversity. Whether we avail ourselves of these opportunities to develop our diversity consciousness, and whether we allow ourselves to be transformed, is up to us.

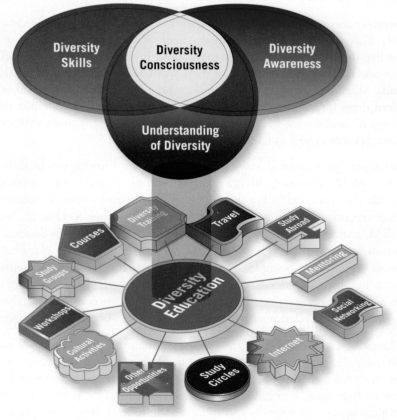

Figure 4.5 Diversity education, in its many forms, is the foundation on which we develop our diversity consciousness.

Vacationers, Prisoners, and Explorers

Lin Dawson, a former professional football player for the New England Patriots, is part of a three-member diversity awareness team that works on behalf of Northeastern University's Center for the Study of Sport. In his work with professional and college sports teams, Dawson knows that members of his audience typically fall into three categories: *vacationers*—those who are apathetic and attend because they have to, *prisoners*—those who are forced to attend and want nothing to do with training, and *explorers*—those who are open-minded and feel there is something to be gained.[33]

Individuals, groups, and entire communities can initiate and participate in diversity education. Five possible activities follow:

1. *Today's technology.* Online social networks, texting, Skyping, online courses, and other cyber-connections make it possible to cross cultural and geographic boundaries very easily and quickly. The Internet provides a window to the world.

2. *Travel and opportunities for study abroad.* Life experiences in other countries, particularly extensive trips abroad which provide opportunities for studying, working, and socializing, enable us to learn the importance of a world view (see Photo 4.1). Moreover, newly published research shows that studying abroad promotes creativity, specifically the "cognitive processes involved in developing innovative solutions.[34]

3. *Racial/cultural awareness training, workshops, programs, and courses.* Schools, workplaces, and community groups frequently offer this type of learning opportunity. Although one two-hour workshop or program is not going to change your thinking and behavior dramatically, it can deepen your understanding of diversity issues and put you in touch with people who may have similar interests and concerns. More and more teachers at all levels of education are integrating diversity into the curriculum. Research suggests that the content of the curriculum as well as the nature of intergroup interaction are both critical.[35] Increasing our knowledge *and* direct engagement with diverse individuals and groups are both essential. To maximize learning we need to work at becoming more comfortable asking tough questions and engaging in courageous conversations.

4. *Cultural activities in the community.* Attending ethnic festivals, museums, and visual and performing arts events provide numerous, diverse opportunities to deepen our diversity consciousness. Sometimes it makes sense to do this with others so that you can share your thoughts and feelings afterward. With a minimal amount of expense or planning, a group can watch classic videos such as *Philadelphia, Talk to Me, Schindler's List, The Joy Luck Club, North Country, Rain Man,* and *Smoke*

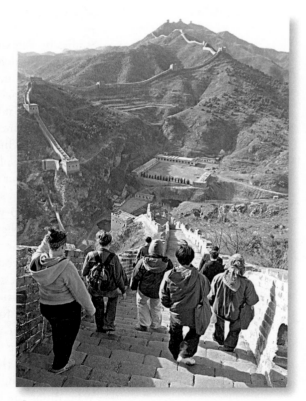

Photo 4.1 Students visit the Great Wall of China. The students, along with faculty, spend a semester on board a cruise ship. Each semester, more than 600 students take classes on board this floating university, and then they bring their studies to life by visiting countries throughout the world.
Source: Courtesy of Semester at Sea and Institute for Shipboard Education.

Signals. This type of experience can "break the ice" and provide insight into history, culture, and different life experiences. It can also make it easier to talk about a variety of issues dealing with diversity.

> Music and art have shown me the common ground between people and what we can do for each other.
>
> —Another perspective

5. *Study circles/groups.* Study circles are small, ongoing group discussions that focus on any number of issues, including diversity. The basic idea is that a group of perhaps 8 to 12 people commit to meeting regularly over a period of time. This type of discussion allows people to get to know each other, discover common ground, and take action. Schools, businesses, and communities throughout the United States and elsewhere have adopted the study circle concept.

> Prejudices, it is well known, are most difficult to eradicate from the heart whose soil has never been loosened or fertilized by education; they grow there, firm as weeds among stones.
>
> —Charlotte Brontë

A LIFELONG, CONTINUING PROCESS

Studies by Pascarella and associates examined what factors had the greatest influence on college students' openness to diversity. What they found should not surprise us. Even though students' academic and social experiences in college made a difference, "precollege variables" had the largest effect.[36] This points to the need to foster openness and combat cultural encapsulation in early childhood.

Children are susceptible to what Carlos Cortés calls the "societal curriculum" very early in life.[37] This curriculum, which includes all those lessons that we learn in school, the family, our places of worship, and throughout society, has a profound and lingering effect on our openness to intolerance in later years.

Imagine observing 3- and 4-year-old children at a pre-school. At nap time, you notice a 3-year-old White girl resting on a cot. She says, "I can't sleep next to a nigger. Niggers are stinky." Later on, during play time, a 4-year-old tells a 3-year-old, "Get off, White girl! Only Black folks on the swing, you see?" These comments, recorded by sociology professors Debra Van Ausdale and Joe R. Feagin, appear in their study entitled *The First R: How Children Learn Race and Racism.*[38] Their examination of the racial attitudes of 58 children at a racially diverse urban school is cause for concern. Notwithstanding the children's progressive teachers who taught from an anti-bias curriculum, many lessons about race and intolerance were learned outside of the classroom. As an example, Whites and people of color often do not occupy the same social space, nor do they share the same social status. What's more, according to the authors, this "lesson" does not go unnoticed by children. Who mops the floors at school, who bags the groceries, and who mows the lawns are important components of a societal curriculum that teaches children what the authors term the "first R"—race.

By doing nothing or very little, we leave our own and our children's diversity consciousness in someone else's hands. By constantly educating and transforming ourselves, we help to restructure the societal curriculum in a way that sheds a more positive light on diversity. To accomplish this, we need to bear in mind that diversity consciousness is not something we can develop, store, and then consult periodically. It is not something that "kicks in" at school or work. Rather, the term *consciousness* implies that these thoughts and feelings become a way of life, second nature, a permanent part of who we are.

As we develop diversity consciousness over the life course, a number of positive changes will gradually occur:

- Our thinking will become less rigid and more flexible.

- Our awareness and appreciation of human differences will heighten our ability to see and value similarities.

- We will move from a perspective that centers on ourselves and our immediate environment to one that is more inclusive and global.

It should be clear from this chapter that it is extremely difficult to develop a high level of diversity consciousness. For many of us, just tolerating certain differences requires radical change. In many cases it means unlearning much that we have been taught. Diversity consciousness moves us well beyond tolerance. Rather than putting up with differences, it makes it possible for us to understand, respect, and value differences. This kind of ongoing, personal transformation requires not only time but also commitment.

 ## Case Studies

Case Study One

Ligua, a part-time college student (plus full-time employee, wife, and mother), is taking a class, "Cultural Diversity," that is required of all education majors. The class examines issues and concepts related to diversity and education, such as cross-cultural communication, teaching tolerance, barriers to achievement, and managing diversity in the classroom. Given her life experiences as a minority and as an immigrant from El Salvador, Ligua feels as if *she* could teach this course. She understands its value, particularly for students who have led very sheltered lives. For such students, according to Ligua, a semester-long course on diversity is not nearly sufficient.

Questions:

1. Do you think a course dealing with cultural diversity should be a requirement for all education majors? Why?

2. What do you think Ligua might learn from a course such as this?

Case Study Two

Mary is a White social work student who plans to go on for a MS degree and work in a clinical setting. She attends an urban university and enjoys the diversity and energy of city life, but in her free time is actively involved in social activities centered around her Scottish background. She is fascinated by different cultures, but because of her upbringing as well as her fear of being put in an awkward situation, Mary has chosen to socialize primarily with people from cultural backgrounds similar to hers. As an aspiring social worker, she realizes she needs to widen her social circle.

Questions:

1. What are three things Mary can do to develop her diversity consciousness?

2. If she chooses to remain culturally encapsulated *outside of work*, do you think this will significantly affect her job performance? Explain.

Case Study Three

Michael is a college graduate who identifies himself as African American. He is divorced and the father of a teenage son, Aaron, who attends a private school in the well-to-do suburb where they live. The students at Aaron's school are predominantly White and most come from wealthy families. Michael struggles with this. On one hand, he wants to prepare Aaron to live in the real world; full of prejudice and poverty, a world in which race is an issue. On the other hand, he wants to protect his son from the racial intolerance that Michael feels is still rampant in our society today.

Ideally, Michael would like his son to attend a quality school in a diverse setting. However, he knows of no such school in his area. Michael worries about the consequences of Aaron's isolated existence. He wonders whether Aaron will develop stereotypical notions regarding inner-city minorities. He is wary of Aaron becoming what he calls an "Oreo cookie," Black on the outside and White on the inside. Because of concerns such as these, Michael does what he can to expand Aaron's world. For example, a segment on the news might turn into a mini-lesson on race relations or Black history. In the aftermath of the death of Trayvon Martin, the issue of profiling becomes a lesson on diversity.

Michael is already starting to weigh the advantages and disadvantages of encouraging Aaron to attend a historically Black college. He thinks that this kind of experience might be good for Aaron, although he is not sure.

Questions:

1. Michael expresses the concern that his son's life is culturally isolated or encapsulated. Do you agree? Why?

2. How might Aaron's education influence his diversity consciousness? Outside of school, what might Michael do to help Aaron develop diversity consciousness?

 ## Key Terms

Cultural encapsulation	Social distance	Classism
Media literacy	Double consciousness	Meritocracy
Socialization	Social inequality	Majority
Nature	Social class	Minority
Nurture	Ageism	Critical thinking
Enculturation	Unearned privileges	Active listening
Social marginality	Sexism	Reverse mentoring

Exercises

Exercise 1: **Shifting Perspectives in the Classroom**

You are sitting in a college classroom. It is the first day of class. Your instructor, whom you have never met, walks in, introduces himself, and hands each student a course syllabus. Prior to going over the syllabus, the instructor reviews his expectations for classroom interaction.

- Students should act as if they understand everything and never ask any questions.

- Students should never raise questions about tests or grades at any time.

- Students should not look directly at the instructor when she or he speaks.

Answer the following questions.

1. In general, how do you feel about these expectations? Why do you feel this way? How does your cultural background relate to your feelings?

2. Talk to other students who have attended schools outside the United States. How do they feel about the expectations just outlined? How do their educational experiences differ from yours?

Exercise 2: **Assessing the Six Areas of Diversity Consciousness**

Imagine that you are in charge of professional development at your place of work. You have been asked by your CEO to create an assessment for the employees. Specifically, you are to measure their competency in each of the six areas of developing diversity consciousness.

For each of the six areas, create four specific questions to measure their awareness, understanding, and/or skills.

 ## Notes

[1] Juan L. Gonzales, Jr., *The Lives of Ethnic Americans*, 2nd ed. (Dubuque, IA: Kendall/Hunt, 1994), 98.

[2] Carol Gallagher, *Going to the Top* (New York: Viking Press, 2000).

[3] Dawn Chmielewski, "YouTube Diversifies with Shaq, Russell Simmons, *Los Angeles Times.* Online, October 8, 2012. Available: http://articles.latimes.com/2012/oct/08/entertainment/la-et-ct-you-tube-diversifies-with-shaq-20121008.

[4] Charles Gallagher, "White Reconstruction in the University," *Socialist Review*, 24, 1994, 165.

[5] Cheryl Tan, "For College Students, Degrees of Ethnicity," *The Washington Post*, September 3, 1996, B1.

[6] Michelle Boorstein, "A Mission of Understanding," *The Washington Post*, January 15, 2007, AO1.

[7] Morgan Appel, David Cartwright, Daryl Smith, and Lisa Wolf, *The Impact of Diversity on Students* (Washington, DC: Association of American Colleges and Universities, 1996), x.

[8] Zora Neale Hurston, as found in Dorothy W. Riley (ed.), *My Soul Looks Back, 'Less I Forget* (New York: Harper Collins, 1993), 81.

[9] Ursula Heigi, *Tearing the Silence* (New York: Simon & Schuster, 1997).

[10] Jonathan Yardley, "Coping with History," *The Washington Post: Book World*, July 6, 1997, 3.

[11] Karen Aguilar-San Juan (ed.), *The State of Asian America* (Cambridge, MA: South End Press,1994), 74.

[12] John Lahr, "Speaking Across the Divide," *The New Yorker*, January 27, 1997, 41–42.

[13] Robert Whiting, *You've Gotta Have Wa* (New York: Vintage, 2009).

[14] Moshe Rubinstein, *Patterns of Problem Solving* (Englewood Cliffs, NJ: Prentice-Hall, 1975).

[15] Malcolm X, *The Autobiography of Malcolm X* (New York: Ballantine Books, 1965).

[16] Carter Woodson, as quoted in Dorothy W. Riley (ed.), *My Soul Looks Back, 'Less I Forget: A Collection of Quotations by People of Color* (New York: Harper Collins, 1995), 189.

[17] Emory Bogardus, "Measuring Social Distance," *Journal of Applied Sociology*, 9, March/April 1925, 299–308.

[18] Arthur Ashe, *Days of Grace* (New York: Ballantine Books, 1993), 186.

[19] Amy Maddox, "Underneath We're All the Same," *Teaching Tolerance*, Spring 1995, 65.

[20] Louis Crozier-Hogle and Darryl Babe Wilson, *Surviving in Two Worlds: Contemporary Native American Voices* (Austin: University of Texas Press, 1997), 139.

[21] John H. Griffin, *Black Like Me* (New York: NAL/Dutton, 1999).

[22] W. E. B. Du Bois, *The Souls of Black Folk* (New York: Fawcett, 1961).

[23] George Pillsbury, as quoted in John Sedgwick, *Rich Kids* (New York: William Morrow, 1985), 120.

[24] Martin Luther King, Jr., *Where Do We Go from Here: Chaos or Community?* (Boston: Beacon Press, 1968).

[25] Peggy McIntosh, *White Privilege and Male Privilege* (Wellesley, MA: Wellesley College Center for Research on Women, 1988), 7.

[26] Ruth Frankenberg, *White Women, Race Matters: The Social Construction of Whiteness* (Minneapolis: University of Minnesota Press, 1993).

[27] Pew Research Center, "Blacks Upbeat About Black Progress, Prospects." Online, January 12, 2010. Available: http://www.people-press.org/2010/01/12/blacks-upbeat-about-black-progress-prospects/.

[28] Jodie Allen, "Obama's Black Audience: What Surveys Show About the Attitudes and Priorities of African Americans," Pew Research Center. Online, July 14, 2008. Available: http://www.pewresearch.org/2008/07/14/obamas-black-audience/.

[29] Leonard Pitts, "It's Time for Men to Act Like Men," *The Baltimore Sun*, July 16, 2001, 7A.

[30] Whitney Young, *To Be Equal* (New York: McGraw-Hill, 1966).

[31] Samantha Critchell, "Silent Since September and Learning a Lot," *The Washington Post*, May 15, 2001, C4.

[32] Mary Belenky, Blythe Clinchy, Nancy Goldberger, and Jill Tarule, *Women's Ways of Knowing* (New York: Basic Books, 1986).

[33] Mark Murphy, "Rocker a 'Prisoner,' At Least When It Comes to Treatment." Online, January 11, 2000, Available: http://cbs.sportsline.com/u/ce/multi/0,1329,1878900_52,00.html.

[34] Tom Jacobs, "To Boost Creativity, Study Abroad." Online, August, 6, 2012. Available: http://www.psmag.com/culture-society/to-boost-creativity-study-abroad-43897/.

[35] Association of American Colleges and Universities, "The Educational Value of Diversity: Research from Louisville High Schools," *Diversity Digest*, Winter 2001, 10, 11.

[36] Ernest Pascarella, Marcia Edison, Amaury Nora, Linda S. Hagedorn, and Patrick Terenzini, "Influences on Students' Openness to Diversity and Challenge in the First Year of College," *The Journal of Higher Education*, Vol. 67, No. 2, Mar. – Apr. 1, 1996; Elizabeth Whitt, Marcia Edison, Ernest Pascarella, and Patrick Terenzini, "Influences on Students' Openness to Diversity and Challenge in the Second and Third Years of College," *The Journal of Higher Education*, Vol. 72, No. 2, Mar. – Apr. 2, 2001.

[37] C. E. Cortés, "The Societal Curriculum: Implications for Multiethnic Education." In J. A. Banks (ed.), *Education in the 80's: Multiethnic Education* (Washington, DC: National Education Association), 1981.

[38] Debra Van Ausdale and Joe R. Feagin, *The First R: How Children Learn Race and Racism* (Lanham, MD: Rowman and Littlefield, 2001), 1.

5

Communicating in a Diverse World

Learning Outcomes

Upon completion of this chapter, you will be able to:

- Discuss how communication and culture interrelate.
- Elaborate on the implications of electronic communication.
- Relate the importance of communication to each of the six areas of development of diversity consciousness.
- Summarize why communication matters.
- Point out the impact of barriers to effective communication.
- Analyze the impact of microaggressions on communication.
- Explain why the ground rules for difficult dialogues are necessary.
- Elaborate on the importance of communicating inclusively.

I think that people within my culture and from other cultures may mistake my lack of eye contact for dishonesty. I feel that staring into someone's eyes lets them see into my soul so instead I focus on something else when speaking.

One day, a man phoned my house taking a survey and he started asking me questions. Before I got a chance to tell him my race, he was already writing down that I was White. I interrupted and told him that I was Black and he apologized and told me that I sound White. I was wondering what Whites sound like.

I have felt like I have represented all Kenyans in all my classes since I'm the only one from that part of the world, standing out sometimes when I dress in African dress or when I speak. There is pin drop silence every time I begin to speak. All eyes are on me when a dub of British is detected in my

(continued)

MyStudentSuccessLab

MyStudentSuccessLab (www.mystudentsuccesslab.com) is an online solution designed to help you 'Start Strong, Finish Stronger' by building skills for ongoing personal and professional development.

(continued)

accent. I wonder what goes through their minds, from my pronunciation to the spelling of certain words. After the first day of class when I introduce myself I face questions about Africa on a daily basis—questions often of places and things I don't even know.

—Other perspectives

Communication takes place whenever meaning is attached to a message. The meaning may be intended or unintended. By developing our diversity consciousness and, in particular, our communication skills, we become more aware of the messages we are sending and receiving. This empowers us and enriches our lives. However, poor communication skills can make it difficult for us to achieve our goals and can alienate, confuse, and hurt others. Communication is clearly one of the most important diversity skills.

COMMUNICATION AND CULTURE

Communication and culture interrelate. Culture is reflected in the way we communicate, and the way we communicate shapes our culture. Because of our upbringing, we attach specific meanings to what people say and do. These meanings may vary within and between cultures. As our work, school, and community environments become more multicultural, it is increasingly important to become more conscious of our cultural differences as well as our similarities. This, in turn, will enable us to become more sensitive to the cultural context of one's words and more proficient in using language precisely and sensitively.

Communication is the process by which people transfer information, ideas, attitudes, and feelings to each other. The word *communicate* comes from the Latin verb *communicare*, which means to share. When people use and share symbols with others who can understand their meanings, they are communicating. A **symbol** is anything that represents something else. Symbols take many forms. Spoken and written words probably come to mind, but we also communicate with nonverbal symbols. Examples of nonverbal communication, or what we refer to as body language, include gestures, facial expressions, body positioning, touching, and eye movements.

I usually fold my arms and I don't walk around smiling. People always comment to me "Is it that bad?" or "Smile; there is nothing to be sad about." I have been told that I look unapproachable because of my stance and facial expressions, but I think I am one of the most approachable people on the streets.

When I smile, there are men who think I'm "coming on to them." All I'm trying to do is be friendly.

—Other perspectives

People throughout the world send messages by a vast array of body language. In *Gestures: The Do's and Taboos of Body Language Around the World*, author Roger Axtell discusses **kinesics**, the study of body movements as a means of communication.

He cites studies by a number of researchers, including Mario Pei and Ray Birdwhistell. Pei estimates that humans can produce approximately 700,000 physical signs. According to Birdwhistell, the face alone is capable of 250,000 expressions.[1] By studying the kinesics of different cultures, anthropologists have determined that people from different cultures may signal each other in very different ways.

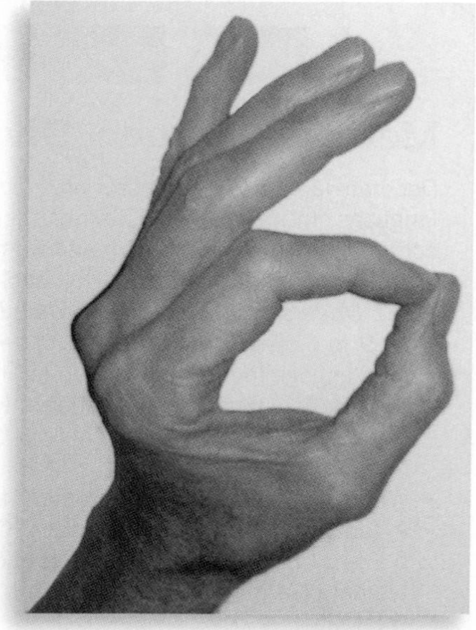

Body language throughout the world is **culturally specific**. If a gesture is culturally specific, it may mean one thing to one culture but something quite different to another (see Photo 5.1). During his presidency, former President George W. Bush, a native of Texas, made a "hook 'em horns" gesture that is well known among University of Texas fans.

Unfortunately, the gesture is culturally specific, and carries different meanings in other regions of the world. Some Norwegians saw this gesture as the president of the United States making the "sign of the devil." Some people in Central and South America were shocked. To them, the president was indicating someone's wife was unfaithful. A Rand Corporation report, commissioned by the U.S. Joint Forces Command, cited this gesture as one example of how misinterpreted symbols have negatively impacted the U.S. government's credibility elsewhere.

Photo 5.1 Is this gesture culturally specific? Google "Okay symbol meaning" to shed some light on the many meanings of this symbol.

Communication allows us to dialogue and feel a sense of togetherness. Also, it can illustrate our differences and drive a wedge between us. This is especially true of intercultural communication. **Intercultural communication** refers to a process in which messages created in one culture must be processed and interpreted in another culture. Misunderstandings can also occur between people who may be different in a variety of ways. Maybe they have different styles of communication. Likewise, differences in gender, age, marital status, or social class may make it difficult to connect with someone.

Miscommunication often results because we attach different meanings to the same symbol. As an example, Nike marketed some of its products by displaying their logo, the word Air, in stylized letters. They soon discovered that the logo resembles the Arabic word for Allah. Under threat of a worldwide boycott of its product by Muslims, Nike agreed to recall and stop selling any shoes with this logo. Muslims found this logo to be offensive, especially when it appeared on shoes. By communicating a totally different message than they intended, Nike learned a costly and important lesson. According to one spokesperson for Nike, "Our company has to be more vigilant and work more with communities on issues of sensitivity."[2]

Most of us think of ourselves as literate. Because of our educational background, we can read and write. But we are literate only in a particular cultural environment. In another setting within our society or abroad, we may have no idea how to communicate ideas and feelings.

There are a lot of beautiful, favorite places in any language in which you feel yourself at home. In English, I don't have such a place yet. All phrases come out from my mouth, rough and heavy . . . the words fall with plops on the floor, like ugly frogs. And I am so waiting for the butterfly.

—Another perspective

Men and Women, Divided by Language

Deborah Tannen is a professor of *linguistics*, the science of language. In her research, Tannen focuses on the different communication styles of men and women.[3] She has written extensively on this subject. Her books, entitled *You Just Don't Understand*, *That's Not What I Meant*, and *Talking from 9 to 5* offer some examples of gender differences.

- Men engage in report talk, women in rapport talk. *Report talk* is a way of showing one's knowledge and skill. *Rapport talk* allows one to share with others and develop relationships.

- When making requests, women tend to be indirect. A female supervisor might ask, "Could you do this by 5 P.M.?" Something more direct and to the point is more typical of a male supervisor: "This needs to be done by 5 P.M."

- Women have a greater *information focus*. They do not hesitate to ask questions in order to understand something. Men have more of an *image focus*. Even though

men may be unclear about an issue, they may forgo asking questions to preserve their image or reputation.

- Women often say "I'm sorry" to express concern about something. Men, however, may interpret this to mean that women are accepting blame or responsibility. This is not at all what women have in mind.

- People tend to judge men for what they say and do, and women by how they look and dress.

Critics argue that Tannen fails to consider the relevance of emotional and psychological issues when evaluating why men and women "don't understand" each other. Tannen admits that these differences do not apply to all men or women in all situations. Furthermore, she states that no one's communication style is absolute. Each person's style may change in response to social context and others' styles. By realizing that differences such as these may exist, we lessen the chances of miscommunication, tension, and conflict.

Imagine sitting in a classroom at Gallaudet University in Washington, D.C., the world's only accredited four-year liberal arts university for deaf and hard-of-hearing people. In *Seeing Voices: A Journey into the World of the Deaf*, Oliver Sacks describes his first visit to Gallaudet. "I had never before seen an entire community of the deaf, nor had I quite realized (even though I knew this theoretically) that Sign might indeed be a complete language—a language equally suitable for making love or speeches, for flirtations or mathematics. I had to see philosophy and chemistry classes in Sign . . . I had to see the wonderful social scene in the student bar, with hands flying in all directions as a hundred separate conversations proceeded."[4] (See Photo 5.2.)

Photo 5.2 Students at Gallaudet University communicate with each other between classes.
Source: Courtesy of the Office of Public Relations, Gallaudet University, Washington, D.C.

Sign language, a visual form of communication using hand shapes and movements to talk or to express an idea, is not uniform or universal. Contrary to popular thought, deaf people all over the world cannot communicate with each other. Sign languages, which have been around since the beginning of recorded history, are as distinct and differentiated as spoken languages. Hundreds of different sign languages exist, including American, British, Mayan, French, and Chinese.

Linguistic diversity refers to the many languages spoken in the United States and throughout the world. Some people speak only one language; others speak more than one. We refer to people who are able to speak two languages fluently as **bilingual,** and those capable of speaking more than two as **multilingual.** Language differences and the way we view these differences affect our achievement. Although proficiency in English is critically important, more and more research shows that fluency in more than one language can enhance one's marketability and job performance.

Perhaps this explains why the CEO of General Motors Corporation asked his Director of Diversity Marketing and Sales to modify the beginning of her presentation to a large gathering of car dealers. The director, who is bilingual, was asked to speak in Spanish for the first five minutes. None of the dealers spoke Spanish fluently. Think of those situations in which coworkers, customers, or acquaintances do not speak "your language." How do you feel, and how do you think they feel? In circumstances such as these, we are apt to feel a range of emotions, including inadequacy, humiliation, and frustration. These are not feelings that make you want to do business with someone. Clearly, the CEO wanted these dealers to experience what it is like when people do not reach out to you and adjust to language differences.

Individuals who speak a language other than English may encounter **linguicism,** a relatively new term that refers to discrimination based on language. How do you feel when you enter a particular class for the first time and you are met by an instructor or teaching assistant who is bilingual and speaks English with an unfamiliar accent? When you are in a group with a number of ELL (English Language Learner) students, do you take the time to listen carefully, and encourage full participation from everyone? Do you accept responsibility for making sure that you understand what is being communicated? When you don't understand, are you comfortable asking people to repeat themselves until you do?

Some of us are apt to view situations such as these as problems rather than challenges. Although communication with the teacher or students just described might be difficult for a period of time, persistence as well as good listening skills can help a great deal. Also, consider what they have to offer. Studies show that people who speak more than one language have higher levels of *cognitive flexibility,* meaning they can adjust more easily to different situations. Someone who is bilingual or multilingual may be better able to share a variety of world perspectives.

Students tell me I have an accent. I usually tell them they have an accent too.

—Another perspective

ELECTRONIC COMMUNICATION

Electronic communication is the imparting or interchange of information through technology, such as cell phones and computers. The capabilities of electronic communication are expanding rapidly. Computer technology is transforming electronic communication. College professors use the Internet to post syllabi, class notes, related links, and other necessary information. As online and hybrid courses proliferate, professors maintain virtual office hours, and many classroom lectures are available online. Increasingly, online universities are creating mobile apps to help students pursue their studies on any Internet-capable device at any time.

Technology is blurring the lines between our working and personal lives. In the workplace, employees telecommute from home or any other location. Unlike the office settings of the past, they communicate by fax, e-mail, cell phones, tablets, and Skyping. And wherever work takes place, advances in technology have improved communication for people with disabilities. For instance, texting has the benefit of being interactive as well as 100 percent visual. Thus, many deaf and hard-of-hearing people prefer texting because it is more practical and faster than a text pager or TTY (Text Telephone), an electronic device providing text communication via a telephone line.

As more and more people throughout the world learn to use new technologies, new communication problems arise. We can easily terminate a conversation, simply because we do not want to entertain other points of view. Because Internet communication relies primarily on text, such as e-mail, blogs, and messaging, people cannot rely on other cues, such as tone of voice or gestures. We do not necessarily know anything about who is sending the message and his or her position, cultural background, or even the person's mood. In fact, an individual is free to create a new identity or a number of different identities.

Electronic messages may result in misunderstandings, name calling, and hard feelings if people are unfamiliar with certain rules of etiquette and cyber shorthand. For example, Internet etiquette defines communicating in all capital letters as YELLING. Some people, who like using "all caps" because they find it easier, do not realize that they may be offending others. Abbreviated messages, such as g2g ("got to go"), lol ("laughing out loud"), and btw ("by the way") as well as *emoticons*, symbols to

E-Mail Privacy?

Many employees converse casually by e-mail each day. In many instances, they mistakenly assume that their messages are private. Consequently they often say things they would not communicate in writing or discuss in public. This includes racist, sexist, and other derogatory messages. Many companies routinely save all e-mail messages. These saved messages are now being used to provide evidence in lawsuits.

Experts say that e-mail is a matter of official record. It is no different than a memo written on company letterhead. A personal password to access one's e-mail account simply provides the illusion of privacy. Former CIA Director David Petraeus discovered this soon after news of his extramarital affair broke. The FBI looked into this affair by examining "private" e-mail he sent to his mistress. The scandal refocused attention on e-mail privacy issues. After all, the argument was made, "If the nation's top spy can't hide his personal communications from law enforcement, who can?"

Jokes, racist and homophobic comments, or other offensive messages circulated through a company's e-mail system may constitute evidence of discrimination. Nowadays, organizations respond to inappropriate e-mail by creating policies regarding e-mail usage and monitoring messages with a variety of software capable of scanning offensive words and phrases. Furthermore, there is growing pressure on lawmakers to revise and update laws governing e-mail privacy.

express the way we feel, fail to capture the range and complexity of our emotions. Also, these quick and easy forms of communication may not be understood by others. Uncertainties also arise because rules governing electronic communication differ depending on the organization or group. As an example, some workplaces permit personal messages while others do not.

Business and educational publications describe the effects of communicating electronically using terms such as *empowerment* and *inclusiveness*. There are a number of reasons for this. When communicating through the Internet, a person with relatively little status can be empowered. This same person's status may be much more of a consideration in a face-to-face meeting. In face-to-face groups, higher-status people tend to talk more, and what they say is assumed to be more important. However, numerous research studies show that the flow of communication online is more evenly distributed and respected, regardless of who occupies what status.

With respect to communication, taking a course online may offer a number of advantages. In general, students of varying ages and backgrounds, who may be unable to attend school physically, can continue their studies. Online courses facilitate lifelong learning regardless of age (see Photo 5.3).

Interaction online affords both students and teachers more time to ask and respond to questions. Discussion boards, where members of a class can communicate freely with each other at their own pace, promote inclusive communication. Learning is *asynchronous*, meaning students can interact in the "classroom" at any time and, therefore, never have to miss a class. Because of the anonymity of electronic communication, people may ask questions online that they would not ask face to face. In effect, race, age, gender, and other dimensions of diversity become less relevant. The message is more important than the messenger.

Photo 5.3 Computer literacy has become a necessity for workers of all ages.

DIVERSITY CONSCIOUSNESS AND COMMUNICATION

Examining the development of our diversity consciousness helps us understand the communication process and specific skills that allow us to communicate effectively as we transition from one situation to another.

Knowledge of languages helps us to extend our circle of friends.

—Another perspective

Areas of Development

Developing our diversity consciousness requires proficiency in the following six areas: (1) examining ourselves and our world, (2) expanding our knowledge of others and their worlds, (3) stepping outside of ourselves, (4) gauging the level of the playing field, (5) checking up on ourselves, and (6) following through. Each of the areas, and its implications for effective communication, follows.

Examining Ourselves and Our World

Before we begin to make sense of communication outside our culture, we need to develop awareness of our own communication style and why we communicate the way we do. Our individual and cultural backgrounds profoundly influence the way we communicate. The most obvious example is the language we learn and use. It is easy to take our own language for granted and assume that everybody interprets words and gestures in the same way. For instance, think about the words you use. If you are majoring in computers, your vocabulary consists of terms such as *gigs* and *terrabytes*, *OS, motherboard,* and *cards*. When you use these terms with people who are not familiar with computers, how do they react?

Even material culture can be interpreted in many ways. **Material culture** is that which we create and can see, touch, or feel. Consider the clothes you wear. What do they communicate to different people in different settings? How do they connect to your culture? For example, what does a pair of $300 jeans symbolize? Does it symbolize the same thing to men and women of varying ages and family backgrounds?

International events can alter the meaning of material culture. The hijab or head scarf, worn by some Muslim women as an expression of female modesty, has taken on added significance in the aftermath of the terrorist attacks on the World Trade Center and the Pentagon. As evidenced by the following comments made by middle school students who attended a Muslim school in the United States, the hijab took on new meaning after September 11, 2001.

> "Before September 11, when we wore scarves, they made us feel special. Now we're just paranoid."
>
> "People, because of our scarves, they think we're something we're not."
>
> "Under our scarves, we're just like other girls. We like to do our hair, and we like to go shopping."[5]

A number of Muslim women's Web sites have blogs to discuss wearing the hijab. For those who feel misunderstood or under attack because of their faith, putting on the hijab may be a way of standing up for their religion and showing pride in being

Muslim. Madeline Zilfi, a professor of Middle Eastern history, says, "It's like when you go to a foreign country as an American and you don't feel patriotic until someone starts attacking your country. Then you find yourself standing up for the good things about it . . . the interesting thing is that the American forum is very open to this kind of expression."[6]

Sometimes, we are ineffective communicators because we fail to realize that everyone does not share our interpretation(s). Furthermore, we may find it difficult to examine our own ways of communicating. In her book *Ways with Words*, Shirley Brice Heath describes a technique that we can use to stand back and look at ourselves. She suggests that we put ourselves "under a microscope" and take the role of an **ethnographer**,[7] a person who spends time living with people in order to research their customs. Using this method, we assume the role of a neutral observer and observe our own communication systematically. We record even the smallest details and try to discover patterns. As an ethnographer, you might focus on how you communicate with others in a variety of settings. What about the tone and volume of your voice? How might your body gestures influence how your message comes across to others? How do you react to people whose accent is markedly different from yours?

Expanding Our Knowledge of Others and Their Worlds

Do we even recognize the presence of others and their capacity or right to communicate? Sometimes, we view women, men, children, lower-class persons, and people with disabilities as unable to speak for themselves in certain situations. Raymond Bingham recounts the assumptions he made one morning while working as a nurse in a newborn intensive care unit. A child with a heart defect needed emergency surgery. The nurse vividly recalls meeting the child's father for the first time. He was "a large Black man, with unkempt clothes, somewhat slurred speech, and at 8 o'clock in the morning a hint of beer on his breath."

The nurse's first impression was not to expect too much from this man. He was soon proven wrong. The father showed a great deal of caring and compassion for his son. When he needed to explain the procedure to the child's mother on the phone, he gave a complete and thorough description of the surgery and why it was necessary. Finally, the nurse remembers the father sitting at the child's bedside and crying. Toward the end of his shift, the nurse reflected back on this experience. "This man, of whom I had thought so little at first glance, who had been so strong, so calm, so resolved throughout a tumultuous day, who had so many things to worry about and take care of . . . had handled them all."[8]

 Thinking Through Diversity

If students sit in the same classroom, read the same assignments, and hear the same lectures, are they all receiving the same education? Might these students interpret the same lesson differently because of the social worlds in which they live?

Frequently, we are unaware of different patterns of cultural differences and the pivotal role they play in communication. Depending on the cultural setting, it may or may not be appropriate to be frank about emotions, to delegate decision making, or to deal directly with conflict in face-to-face meetings. Awareness regarding these differences can help to avoid or resolve misunderstandings or even apologize (see Photo 5.4).

When you encounter cross-cultural communication difficulties, are you mindful of how your cultural background may be influencing your own reactions? Do you listen intently and try extra hard to understand? Are there times when you refuse to

Photo 5.4 A Personal Apology in Tokyo. Citigroup Inc. CEO Charles Prince (right) and Citigroup Japan CEO Douglas Paterson make a deep bow of apology. Under their leadership, the company failed to comply with legal and regulatory requirements in Japan. As a first step toward restoring Citigroup's reputation in Japan, the leaders observed Japanese norms by traveling to Japan to apologize in person. *Source: Courtesy of japantoday.com.*

accommodate or even acknowledge differences? When you go to school or work, are you likely to encounter different communication styles? What do you assume when:

- *People converse with their faces only a few inches apart?* Among some cultures, this is the norm. In others, people like to keep their distance and are uncomfortable if someone stands closer than a couple of feet.

- *A student or a coworker takes a long time to answer a question?* According to researchers who study language, short wait times put some people at a disadvantage. For example, the cultures of many Native Americans emphasize deliberate thought. Before making a decision, they learn to consider all possible implications.

- *People do not look at you when you talk to them?* Among many African, Asian, and Latin American cultures, it is rude to establish direct eye contact with elders or people in authority.

- *People talk informally for a period of time before "getting down to business"?* In many cultures, this is considered good manners. Many Middle Easterners, for example, see this type of "small talk" as a necessary part of business. It is not at all unusual for Asians or Latinos to view the process of getting to know each other as important as the message itself. To many U.S. businessmen and women, it is simply a waste of time.

- *People answer a question with "yes"?* In many East Asian cultures, it is rude to answer a question in the negative. In such situations, people may say "yes" even though they mean "no." It is a way of showing respect or "saving face," saving someone from embarrassment.

- *You see two people verbally challenging each other?* If your cultural background is Greek, Italian, or Israeli, you might view it positively, as a sign of intimacy. If you are from certain Hispanic or Asian cultures, you might consider it more appropriate to repress or temper your feelings and simply smile or change the subject.

When you meet people on the way to class, on the street, in a store, or wherever, they say "Hi" plus they ask "How are you doing?" or "How are you?" even if you are a complete stranger to them. I like when they say "Hi" to me, but what really doesn't make sense is that they add "How are you feeling?" even though they don't care whether I am well or not. I feel like Americans ask this just because they are obliged to do it. In fact, if I answered "I am not OK," nobody would care. In a certain way, this is like a movie where the actors have to say what is written in the script. To the question, you feel obliged to answer you are well no matter whether it is the truth or not. Considering this point, I prefer Italians who just say "Hi" or nothing to the people they have never met before. They don't even think to ask about their health. It could appear colder, but it is certainly less hypocritical.

—Another perspective

Profile in Diversity Consciousness

Curtis Cook was ready to take on a new challenge. After completing some graduate work in linguistic studies in the mid-1960s, he traveled to the Zuni reservation in New Mexico. There, he turned his attention to creating a Zuni version of the Bible. Because the Zuni language is not written, he took it upon himself to talk to the Zuni elders and storytellers, some of whom were 100 years or older. By living with the Zuni Indians, he developed a genuine awareness and understanding of Zuni people and their culture.

Initially, he spent a year learning the Zuni language and developing an alphabet. He approached the Zuni Tribal Council, suggesting that many of the tribe's stories be recorded. The council agreed, and by the time Cook left some 15 years later, 300 reel-to-reel tapes had been produced. Moreover, Cook's work allowed Zunis to teach their written language and pass it on to their children.

Now, Cook makes sure he visits the reservation each year. As he says, "They see me as a novelty, a white man who speaks Zuni."[9] His transcriptions of Zuni stories, biblical translations, photos, and other materials are now part of the Curtis Cook Collection, housed in the Library of Congress's American Folklife Center archives in Washington, D.C.

We cannot be familiar with all variations in communication. Furthermore, we cannot assume that all people from a given culture will communicate in the same way. However, it is important to be open to the possibility that communication differences exist. Keep in mind that despite our differences, we all want people to listen to, acknowledge, and respect us.

Stepping Outside of Ourselves

One of the most important skills needed for effective communication is the ability to process and understand another person's point of view. This skill allows us to step outside of ourselves and become more open and sensitive to others, although it does not necessarily mean that we will fully comprehend or agree with their thoughts and feelings. Certain experiences may teach students the importance of putting themselves in the shoes of friends, family, and others.

Ashley is a high school senior whose best friend is dealing with an unwanted pregnancy. Even though Ashley has never been in this situation, she can "feel her friend's pain" and this helps her know what to say. Judah, a community college student, writes about how he works with a number of people with severe cerebral palsy. Because some cannot communicate verbally, he finds it helps to "put his mind into theirs" and rely on physical cues. Ernestine, an older female student who has a household of daughters, explains how she struggles with their thinking about life. They have watched many of their friends die violently. As a result, her daughters prefer to focus on the present and not think about the future. Says Ernestine, "I try to imagine going to countless funerals of classmates and soulmates and babies, all because somebody dissed them or stepped on their shoes or looked at them the wrong way." These three students—Ashley, Judah, and Ernestine—are more effective communicators because they have the ability to step outside of themselves. They are not locked into their own way of thinking.

When people try to understand a variety of perspectives, it opens up lines of communication. People are more willing to share when they sense that others are really listening and not judging or comparing. Also, stepping outside of yourself can make you more aware of your own thoughts and feelings. In *I Know Why the Caged Bird Sings*, Maya Angelou talks about the development of this kind of self-awareness. "I had gone from being ignorant of being ignorant to being aware of being aware."[10] This revealing, empowering process is not easy. Yari, a college student, describes what it is like to really let herself go into the "inner world of another person." "It is one of the most active, difficult, and demanding things I do. And yet it is worth it because it is one of the most releasing, healing things that I have any occasion to do."

Gauging the Level of the Playing Field

On the surface, this area of development does not appear to relate to communication. What do concepts such as status and inequality have to do with language? Ask yourself whether you address your teacher differently than a fellow student, or your supervisor differently than a coworker. What if you are angry? Would you show that anger differently? The relationship between the speaker and the receiver influences communication. One aspect of this relationship is status and power. **Status** refers to one's position. **Power** is the ability to influence people and bring about change. Our interaction with others takes the form of an equal or unequal status relationship. In the classroom, an unequal status relationship exists between teachers and their students. Simply put, teachers have more authority because of their position. In another setting, this relationship might change and so might the communication between teacher and student.

Differences in power and status can be an obstacle to effective communication. With effective communication, the receiver interprets the message just as the sender intends. Those with less power are often ignored during the communication process. For example, we tend to listen and assign more importance to what an adult says than to what a child says. In the classroom, we want to know what the teacher thinks is important. What students say typically carries less weight. Those who sense they lack power may feel that their input is not as important. However, everybody has something important to offer.

> Every opinion, every voice deserves to be heard. And it is a rare gift indeed to hear voices that are so very different from my own.
>
> —Another perspective

One technique used in diversity training is to instruct people in a group to completely ignore each other's titles and degrees. The idea is to focus on the message rather than the messenger. Although this technique sounds promising, it is extremely difficult to put into practice in everyday life. Actually, young children are more effective communicators in this sense. Unlike adults, they do not get so caught up with the trappings of power.

 Thinking Through Diversity

One of the challenges confronting doctors is to open up lines of communication with their patients. One doctor laments, "People put us on a pedestal. They see us as angels, and this makes communication difficult. They don't ask questions or express their concerns. But we make mistakes like anyone else." In communicating with their patients, what is one specific thing doctors might do to level the playing field and promote more open, honest communication?

Checking Up on Ourselves

Effective communication requires constant practice and self-examination. To improve our communication skills, we need to be open to *feedback*—people's responses to us. Otherwise, we do not know when we are relating well to others.

Despite our knowledge and sensitivity, misunderstandings will occur. Often, we are not even aware of a problem. Therefore, it is important to ask constantly for feedback from others. To illustrate, Michelle, a study group leader, uses several techniques to ensure that she is not simply "talking at" students in her group. As much as possible, she engages each student in a dialogue. She focuses on the students' body language as well as what they say. Furthermore, she is learning to provide more and more wait time. This encourages more thorough and thoughtful questions and answers from a larger number of people.

Thinking Through Diversity

What letter grade would you give yourself for your ability to communicate in a multicultural setting? Why?

In any given situation, ask probing questions of yourself. This enables you to go deeper and examine what messages you send and receive. However, try not to get so caught up with analyzing yourself that it interferes with your ability to listen. Think through the following questions:

1. *Am I considering my entire audience?* This includes people who will hear the message either directly or indirectly. At work, for example, your supervisor may eventually receive your message through someone else. Consider the personal and cultural characteristics of your entire audience, and how much they know and how they may feel about the subject matter.

2. *What is the situation?* What influences outside and within this particular setting might have an impact on communication? What cultural differences may exist? Is the setting formal or informal? Elijah Cummings, a U.S. congressman, describes how he communicates differently depending on the situation. When he is in the halls of Congress, he uses what some might refer to as "paycheck" or "edited" English. But when he is back home, he communicates more informally.

3. *What options are available to me?* In other words, what form or forms of communication might I use? Your message might be written, oral, visual, or a combination of these. A case in point is police work. In response to complaints from the deaf and hard of hearing, police have increasingly reexamined the way they train officers. Some departments have started teaching sign language to selected officers; others have sensitized officers to the importance of using pen and paper to communicate with a deaf person when requested. To deal better with emergencies, departments have begun to recognize the need for having interpreters on call and TTY telephones for the deaf.

4. *What is the specific purpose of the communication?* Perhaps the purpose you have in mind is not shared by others. As an example, Westerners tend to emphasize the end product of communication, the message. In contrast, many Asians place more importance on the people themselves and getting to know each other.

5. *What feedback am I receiving regarding the messages being sent (content) and how they are sent (style)?* Tone of voice, volume, pauses, facial expressions, and gestures can be just as meaningful as words themselves.

6. *What might I do differently to communicate more effectively?* For example, what can I do to listen more actively? How can I make my verbal and nonverbal communication congruent? How can I communicate more inclusively? Toward the end of this chapter, some specific suggestions are offered.

7. *Am I using language that might be viewed as offensive?* Sometimes offensive terms, phrases, or body language known as microaggressions, impair communication. Microaggressions are discussed in more detail later.

> A friend of mine at work told me a story about how she was home alone and two Black guys came to the door selling something. Later I started wondering why she felt she had to describe them as Black.
>
> —Another perspective

Following Through

How did you do that? How did you make it look so easy? People may ask these questions of someone who has refined a skill by practicing it countless number of times—perhaps a great athlete, a computer whiz, or an accomplished musician. What we tend to forget is the same thing applies to communication skills. Constant practice enables us to become excellent listeners as well as competent speakers in a wide variety of settings and circumstances. This is true for all of us.

Developing, expanding, and refining our communication styles and skills is a daily challenge. A teacher who is very task-oriented finds that her relationship with students improves if she makes a habit of engaging in a little chitchat before the start of class. An employee experiments with different ways of listening. He finds that nodding his head, using facial expressions, and making "listening noises" such as "hmmm" and "oh" allow him to show others that he does care. A father discovers that spending time with his teenage daughter and approaching conversations with her a little differently opens up lines of communication on a variety of topics, including dating and other personal issues. Instead of trying to solve all of her problems and telling her what to do, he tries to simply listen much of the time and be more empathetic.

COMMUNICATION MATTERS

In job interviews, employers weed out prospective employees by evaluating their verbal and written communication skills. As the interview unfolds, the employer is getting a live demonstration of how well individuals get their points across to others. In *The Interview Kit*, author Richard Beatty provides numerous examples of questions employers often ask. One series of questions he cites is, "Give me an example of something complex that you needed to effectively communicate to others. What made it complex? Why was it difficult to communicate? What did you do to communicate effectively? What were the results? How might these results have been improved?"[11]

Regardless of the social arena, we can readily observe the value of good communication skills. In school, for instance, why do students like some teachers more than others? Most teachers are well liked because they "know their stuff" and they relate well to students. Relating well has to do with communication skills.

When people talk about the power of communication, what does that mean? Think of the last time you:

- *Heard a dynamic and charismatic speaker.* The message conveyed by that person will probably remain with you for the rest of your life.

- *Had an extremely difficult time communicating with someone who is very close and important to you.* How did that make you feel? How did that affect your relationship?

> Words are powerful and have physical impact on the receiver. They assault
> and abuse if used offensively.
>
> —Another perspective

- *Were part of a team whose members could not communicate very well.* How did this affect your ability to function as a team?

- *Felt hurt by what a teacher, relative, supervisor, or friend said.* This kind of remark can poison your relationship with someone. At the very least, it can be difficult to forget. It can also make you view that person or even yourself in a different light.

To a large degree, your success in all realms of life depends on your ability to communicate effectively. Whenever you encounter someone at school or work, you communicate something even if you say nothing. Each encounter poses a challenge. When communication is ineffective, mutual understanding and joint action are highly unlikely. However, effective communication can promote synergy, creativity, and critical thinking among individuals and teams. Consequently, it should come as no surprise that organizations prioritize communication as well as other requisite diversity skills as part of their annual performance reviews. AMA (American Management Association) and P21, a national organization that addresses the importance of twenty-first century skills for every student, recently surveyed more than 2,000 executives. The results point to the critical importance of effective communication, along with critical thinking and collaboration (see Fig. 5.1).

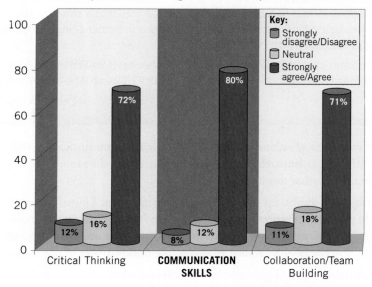

Managers/Other Executives:
"Employees in my organization are measured on these skills and competencies during their annual performance review."

Key:
- Strongly disagree/Disagree
- Neutral
- Strongly agree/Agree

Critical Thinking: 12%, 16%, 72%
COMMUNICATION SKILLS: 8%, 12%, 80%
Collaboration/Team Building: 11%, 18%, 71%

Figure 5.1 Critical Skills in the Twenty-first Century.
Source: AMA and P21 Critical Skills Survey.[12]

BARRIERS TO EFFECTIVE COMMUNICATION

There can be any number of barriers to effective communication, particularly when we communicate across cultures. These barriers include cultural biases, lack of awareness of cultural differences, language differences, ethnocentrism, and inactive listening.

1. *Cultural biases.* In certain situations, we may make unwarranted assumptions about the person or persons with whom we are communicating. A person's dialect, for example, may trigger negative assumptions about a person's education, intelligence, or character. The term **dialect** refers to patterns in the way people use language. These patterns, which reflect people's cultural and regional backgrounds, include pronunciation or "accent" as well as vocabulary and grammar. Children learn dialect prejudice at an early age, as evidenced by comments like "You talk funny" or "Did you hear how she said that?" In the media and in the classroom, accents are described with adjectives such as *foreign*, *hick*, and *weird*. People who are very cautious about saying anything that might have racist or sexist overtones are much more open when it comes to belittling language differences.

   In a film on cross-cultural communication, two people are shown interviewing for a job. Both answer the questions in exactly the same way. However, one of the interviewees talks with a noticeable accent. After hearing both interviews, the narrator of the film poses the question, "Who would you hire?" Too often, a person with an accent is assumed to be less intelligent or less qualified. One study by researchers at the University of North Texas lends credence to the possibility that this kind of discrimination is commonplace. Fifty-six executives listened to a CD of ten men from different regions of the country recite the same 45-second passage. The jobs, and particularly high-prestige jobs, went to speakers with less identifiable regional accents. One of the researchers, Dianne Markley, says her research shows that companies need to monitor their job hirers more closely.[13]

> Personally, when I have had the occasion to speak with students from other cultures I have found myself focusing on how they differed from what I felt normal for me. While focusing on differences, I was really missing the point of what was being said. I found myself making a judgment on the person speaking, based solely on his culture.
>
> Having another language is treated like it's a disease. If you're in America, it is assumed that you ought to automatically speak THE language—that is, English.
>
> —Other perspectives

2. *Lack of awareness of cultural differences.* If you are communicating with someone from a different culture, the two of you may interpret the same symbol differently. As an example, what does:

   • holding your thumb up mean to you? If you are in the United States, most people would probably interpret this gesture to mean "okay." However, in another country, you might interpret this differently. In Ghana and Iran, and parts of South America, it is an obscene gesture, similar to raising the middle finger in the United States.

   • silence mean to you? Generally, in business communications, people in the United States are uncomfortable with a long period of silence. Silence of more than five seconds is something to fill up in order to move the conversation along. This is a reflection of cultural upbringing. Many Native American cultures admire a person who has the ability to remain silent. In many Asian cultures, silence is a sign of respect, in that someone is taking the time to reflect on what was said and not said. Zen Buddhism, which is influential in many parts of Asia, reinforces this lesson. According to a Zen proverb, "He who knows does not speak and he who speaks does not know."

- passing food or gifts with your left hand mean? In many cultures, use of the left hand in any social setting is considered taboo, since this hand is used for personal hygiene, particularly after urinating or defecating.

3. *Language differences.* Communicating in an unfamiliar language can be challenging. For example, some businesses cater to customers who speak a variety of languages. When people try to communicate in a language other than their own, the results can be amusing. The following attempts to communicate in English did not come across as intended:

- "Our wines leave you nothing to hope for." (From a restaurant menu in Switzerland)
- "Ladies are requested not to have children at the bar." (From a bar in Norway)
- "Fur coats made for ladies from their own skins." (From a Swedish furrier)[14]

Even when people speak the same language, such as English speakers in the United States and other parts of the world, they may find it difficult to communicate. To lessen the confusion, the *Encarta World English Dictionary* was recently published. Linked by e-mail, more than 320 lexicographers (dictionary editors), linguists, and other specialists in 20 nations worked for more than two years to define words that can mean different things in different English-speaking countries. In South Africa, for instance, people refer to a stoplight as a "robot." The word *hotel*, in Australia, is an establishment that sells alcoholic beverages. And job seekers in Southeast Asia provide prospective employers with a "biodata" rather than a resume.[15]

4. *Ethnocentrism.* Ethnocentrism shows itself in the language we use. When we talk about the *culturally disadvantaged*, what does this mean? This once commonly used term implies more than just difference. According to this label, anyone who does not share a certain way of life is assumed to be at a disadvantage. Another example of ethnocentric language is the way we fail to differentiate between *arrival* and *discovery*. A number of years ago, many people celebrated the 500th anniversary of Columbus's *discovery* of the "New World." This touched off a heated public debate because Native Americans lived here long before Columbus *arrived* in 1492. Some history books still describe Euro-Americans as defending *their* homes against "Indian" attacks, rather than invading Native American lands. Words such as *primitive* and *backward* have been used to distort history and describe highly defined and complex Native American societies.

5. *Inactive listening.* Poor listening skills can make it much harder to communicate across cultural boundaries. Listening intently and actively helps to overcome misunderstandings and maximize effective communication. Later in this chapter, we examine specific skills to promote active listening.

MICROAGGRESSIONS

I was grocery shopping one day when an elderly woman called me a "nigger." All of the hate and venom was there. I didn't know what to do. I thought of going to the manager and demanding that he do something. But what could he do? I wanted the world to stop and pay attention to me because I had just been

(continued)

(continued)

assaulted! I did my shopping in stunned, confused, and angry silence. Now I am sorry I didn't tell management in the store this happened while I was buying their groceries. I may not have gotten validation, but I would not have kept it quiet.

—Another perspective

Microaggressions, according to Derald Wing Sue, refer to those brief, often subtle and unintentional biases that people communicate by virtue of what they say, what they do, and the environments they create.[16] Microaggressions, whether they relate to race, religion, gender, sexual orientation, social class, or some other difference, do not make us bad people. However, they are a constant reminder that good intentions are not sufficient. Even though microaggressions occur daily, they can be difficult to recognize and address effectively. This is particularly true of microaggressions that are embedded in the environments in which we learn, work, and socialize.

With the best of intentions, someone might say, "I don't see difference; we are all the same" (same species, all members of the human race). Whether the difference being addressed is color, wealth, disability, gender, or culture, the intent may be positive. The individual who makes this statement may be trying to emphasize our similarities and promote equality. While the intent behind this statement may be positive, its impact may be negative. To some, this statement denies who they are, views differences as negative, and posits a world in which we all encounter the same barriers.

For some, the issue of microaggressions is a game of *political correctness*. They feel like they are "walking on eggshells" all the time and cannot be themselves. To others, the issue is simply a matter of being respectful of others. Regardless of where we stand on this issue, it is important to understand just how powerful microaggressions can be. Communicating something offensive, regardless of our intent, can jeopardize communication, create mistrust and hostility, and damage a person's reputation.

Randall Kennedy, a professor of law at Harvard, examines the historical significance and political power of a single word in his book *Nigger: The Strange Career of a Troublesome Word*. "I have invested energy in this endeavor because nigger is a key word in the lexicon of race relations and thus an important term in American politics," Kennedy tells us. "To be ignorant of its meanings and effects is to make oneself vulnerable to all manner of perils, including the loss of a job, a reputation, a friend, even one's life."[17]

Using appropriate language is not something we can easily turn on and off. It always helps to think things through before and after communicating. For instance, change a key word in a phrase and see if it still applies. Suppose that you read an article about "*the* gay lifestyle." Ask yourself, would it make sense to talk about "*the* heterosexual lifestyle?" Someone might consider the phrase "I don't think of you as Latino" a compliment. Change it. Would someone say "I don't think of you as White?"

Another point to consider is the history of a phrase or the context in which it is used. Comparing a hard-driving boss to a slave driver serves to trivialize a period of history that is very painful to some. This same kind of reasoning may apply to fans mimicking "tomahawk chops" and "war chants" at sports events. Whether these actions honor or slight Native Americans is currently the subject of much debate.

Another example of a microaggression is marketing. Sports teams have adopted names and mascots such as Redskins, Redmen, or Red Raiders (see Fig. 5.2). Because of efforts by Native American activists, many of these teams at the high school and college level have changed their names. Professional sports teams, such as the Washington Redskins, Atlanta Braves, and Cleveland Indians, insist on keeping their names. To support their position, they point to research that shows considerable disagreement among fans and Native Americans regarding the use of Indian nicknames, mascots, or symbols.[18]

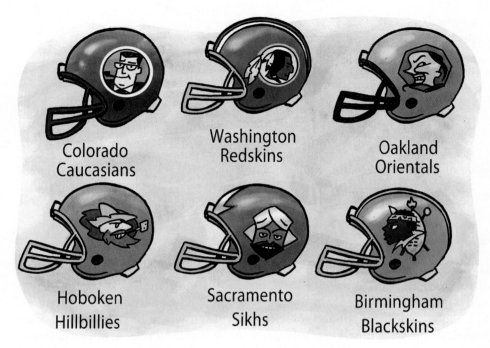

Figure 5.2 Microaggressions?

The controversy over the volatile issue of culturally insensitive marketing is by no means limited to sports teams. A case in point is a company in New York that sells a malt liquor under the name Crazy Horse. The bottle features a Native American in headdress. Although the makers of this product argue they are simply capitalizing on a clientele that identifies with the "Old West," others feel that it is one more example of how Native Americans have been dishonored and dehumanized throughout American history. One state lawmaker, who tried to ban Crazy Horse malt liquor in Minnesota, suggests that this debate illustrates a double standard. "Everybody would understand how insulting it would be to have, say, a Martin Luther King Jr. dark ale or a Golda Meir dark stout. But when it comes to Native Americans, somehow it's a different thing."[19]

Thinking Through Diversity

What microaggressions do you encounter? How do you typically respond? Do your encounters with microaggressions make it difficult for you to communicate effectively?

DIFFICULT DIALOGUES

One day, I called a local radio station. A conservative talk show was on. The only thing I wanted to say was that until Black people and White people, or just people in general, start talking there will always be racism. I was really upset and the talk show host made a fool out of me on the radio. For days after that, he made comments about me . . . like "her name's Utopia (he didn't think that was my real name); she must live in a utopia."

I cried that whole weekend. On Monday I went to school. I attended a predominantly White school. In most of my classes, I was the only Black. I remember walking into class and sharing with them what happened to me. I then said, "I don't know if White people don't understand or they don't want to understand." I was just sitting there crying and that was the first time they all paid attention to me and listened to everything I had to say. That was the

(continued)

(continued)

first day I felt I made a breakthrough with White people. I realized that it's possible that we can communicate, we can talk, and we can listen. Maybe not necessarily always agree but respect what each other has to say. That was the first year I even allowed myself to have White friends.

My sexual orientation is always up for debate, even when I don't want to debate it. I can't walk into any social science course without hearing someone's opinion on why being gay is wrong or why being gay is against religion. Honestly, it's extremely exhausting to have these conversations all the time but if I don't object to intolerance in any form then it is the same as saying it is okay to gay bash. I just can't escape it and I'm not scared of it but it's one of the reasons I'm ready to get out of college.

—Other perspectives

Difficult dialogues are sometimes necessary. If we handle them well, these kinds of discussions can bring diversity issues out into the open and "clear the air." In one study, college students praise professors who know how to create a "comfort zone," and understand the importance of letting discussions continue even if they become heated. At the same time, these professors establish ground rules in advance, emphasize respect, and encourage students not to personalize issues.[20]

Despite the importance of opening up and engaging in difficult dialogues, people rarely do it. This is the case in classrooms, offices, communities, and even on a national level. According to Cornel West, author of *Race Matters*, our society has never had an open and honest discussion about race.[21] The same can be said about many other diversity issues.

Often we reserve difficult dialogues for friends and family. This is because we feel that we know and trust them. In all likelihood, we will not risk opening up elsewhere unless we also feel a certain level of trust or a high degree of anonymity.

In my classes, my students and I work very hard to get to the point where we can talk frankly about race, gender, social class, and other issues related to diversity. This process starts on the first day of class with each of us sharing some aspect of our personal background. Our comfort level with diversity increases as we discuss its relevance throughout the semester. Although students do not always agree, they learn to respect each other's opinions.

Prior to difficult dialogues, it helps to discuss and agree on certain ground rules. Some examples follow.

Eight Ground Rules for Difficult Dialogues

1. Be as open and honest as you feel you can be. Try to move outside your comfort zone.

2. Respect each person's right to be heard.

3. Realize that we are all teachers and learners.

4. Be an active participant, and remember that we participate in different ways.

5. Listen even when you do not want to listen.

6. Do not judge another person's feelings.

7. Focus on the behavior rather than the person.

8. Do not ask people to be spokespersons for their groups.

Negative Messages Surround Adoption

Recently, a teacher e-mailed me regarding a "perspective" that appeared in an earlier edition of *Diversity Consciousness*. A student who is more light-skinned than the rest of her family had shared a perspective that caught the teacher's attention. Because of her skin color, the student explained how people constantly tease her and joke about how she must have been adopted. The teacher, a parent of an adopted child, reacted strongly to this perspective. "As a parent, I feel angry at the implied message—that being adopted is always second class to being 'born into' a family. Being adopted means you don't really belong.

That being 'adopted' was very hurtful to this student is indicative of a prevalent social attitude that those of us who formed our families by adoption frequently encounter. My son has been asked who his 'real' parents are, and I have been asked if I have any kids 'of my own.' Upon finding out how our family was formed, some people express pity that we couldn't have children. Negative language around adoption abounds—we have been asked (within our son's hearing) why his 'real' mother didn't want him, or if we knew his 'father' (with my husband standing there)." By sharing her view of a significant but often disregarded dimension of diversity, the teacher made me more aware of gaps in my thinking.

COMMUNICATING INCLUSIVELY

There is a growing body of literature on multicultural or inclusive communication. As the world grows smaller and our society becomes more diverse, employers are more apt to view people who lack skills in this area as liabilities. Communicating in a way that makes people feel included rather than excluded is not a lesson that can be taught in a matter of minutes, it requires commitment and practice. The following ten strategies provide a good starting point. Rather than focus on all of these at once, it might be helpful to prioritize.

1. *Address people the way they want to be addressed.* Many Native Americans identify with their tribal background. Consequently, they may prefer being called Navaho or Sioux rather than Native American. Do not judge a person's preference. Simply respect it. Also, keep in mind that different people within a group may want to be addressed differently.

2. *Keep an open mind.* People can view the same thing differently. Be open to the "different lens" through which people view the world (see Fig. 5.3). Also, be willing to question your own assumptions and learn from the feedback you receive from others.

3. *Listen actively.* Active listening skills require practice over time (see Diversity Box: Active Listening Skills Checklist). Often, we are so intent on getting our point across that we do not carefully listen to what people are saying and how they are saying it. For instance, we can learn something from inflections in a person's voice, and even from pauses. Remember to focus on what people say, what people do not say, and body language. According to research, most of what we communicate during a conversation is nonverbal.

   In part, effective listening hinges on our ability to attune ourselves to other's feelings. *Mirroring*, commonly used in marital therapy, allows us to build rapport as we listen. When a person says something, we try to repeat or mirror what was said, attempting to capture the person's feelings and thoughts. Without being too obvious, we might start by aligning our body language and noticing the pace and tone of the individual's voice. As we do this, we check to make sure we are on target, and if not, we try again.

Figure 5.3 Different culture, different lens.

4. *Check understanding.* Instead of assuming that someone understands you, assume just the opposite. Ask questions that might pinpoint possible problems. "Is this clear?" "Do I need to explain further?" "What do you think I have been saying up to this point?" Repeat these questions continuously. When you are the receiver of information, ask questions, too. "Is that idea like . . .?" "Are you suggesting that . . .?" "Can you give me an example of . . .?"

5. *Do some research.* Businesspersons who travel abroad or venture into unfamiliar markets at home often ignore this sort of preparation. The Internet can provide a wealth of current information. College libraries or ethnic organizations in your community may be other valuable resources. Perdue Farms is one company that did not do its homework. When its slogan, "It takes a tough man to make a tender chicken" was carelessly translated into Spanish, it read, "It takes a sexually excited

Active Listening Skills Checklist

- Do you listen intently even when you disagree with someone?
- Do you listen intently even when you have a difficult time understanding someone?
- Do you listen intently when someone talks very slowly and deliberately?
- Do you listen carefully, even when you don't want to?
- Are you aware of verbal and nonverbal messages?

- Do you restate, summarize, and question to promote understanding?
- Do you provide positive feedback through body language and "listening noises"?
- Do you give people enough time to respond?
- Do you tune in to people's feelings?
- Do you make sure your biases do not interfere with your ability to listen?

man to make a chick affectionate." Another big company, Adolph Coors, discovered too late that its slogan "Turn It Loose," when translated into Spanish, meant the beer that would make you "Get the Runs."

6. *Think through what you are going to say before you say it.* When you talk about others, do you refer to them by their race, ethnic background, social class, gender, or some other distinguishing characteristic? If so, ask yourself why.

7. *Avoid slang.* Telling someone she has "sick" clothing can lead to misunderstanding. To some Millennials, it can mean awesome or good. To an older colleague at work, it might mean something quite different.

8. *Do not share ethnic jokes.* This is a serious matter, especially in the workplace and at school. To some, ethnic jokes or ethnic humor in general may be acceptable. This is particularly true of self-directed ethnic humor. However, you cannot assume or predict that people will interpret something the same way you do. Jokes are usually made at the expense of others. Think through how you should react if someone decides to tell an ethnic joke in your presence.

Thinking Through Diversity

If a fellow employee tells you a joke about gays during your lunch break, how would you react? Why?

9. *Use as many different styles of communication as possible.* Vary your rate of speech. Use visual aids. You might want to write something down or spell difficult words if simply saying something does not seem to be working. Constantly question your assumptions about the right or preferred way to communicate. Be open to the existence of different cultural norms and their impact on communication styles. At the same time, remember that cultural norms may not apply to the behavior of any particular individual. Numerous factors, such as family background, schooling, and personalities, shape and alter the modes of communication we use and prefer.

10. *Do not assume that you can or should ignore differences.* The problem lies in the value judgments we attach to individual or cultural differences, not in the differences themselves. For example, noticing someone's accent does not make you prejudiced. Having negative thoughts about the accent does.

In this chapter we have addressed the importance of effective communication. Moreover, we have examined the interrelationship of diversity consciousness and communication. Communication is a diversity skill that we learn, develop, and refine throughout the course of our lives. As we become more conscious of diversity, our communication skills will improve. And as our communication skills improve, we become more diversity conscious.

Acknowledge each other's differences and move past them; just don't move too fast.

—Another perspective

 Case Studies

Case Study One

In addition to working full-time, Ligua is a wife and mother as well as a part-time college student. The student population at Ligua's college is predominantly white. In spite of her desire to be as inconspicuous as possible, Ligua often feels the urge to educate other students and even the teachers in her classes. These difficult dialogues often revolve around issues of social inequality. In her history class, for instance, students were talking about the legal, economic, and political changes in the United States that have opened up all kinds of opportunities for minorities. Ligua interjected, "I hope no one here thinks that by earning a degree, and getting an education, that you're going to level the playing field." A heated discussion took place, and the class ended before there was any closure on this subject.

Because of her complexion and Spanish-sounding name, assumptions are made. Even though she was born in El Salvador, Ligua speaks English fluently but finds it difficult to communicate in Spanish. Last semester, in Intermediate Spanish, Ligua's teacher would make references about her knowledge of the language, assuming that the class was easy for her. In reality, Ligua had to work harder just so she wouldn't embarrass herself.

Ligua does not know how to handle these difficult dialogues. She doesn't want to bring attention to herself or alienate the teachers or students, but she feels she must say something.

Questions:

1. What advice might you offer Ligua to help her deal with the difficult dialogues she encounters in her classes?

2. If you were one of Ligua's classmates in Intermediate Spanish, what would you do, if anything? Why?

Case Study Two

Mary, a single, 21-year-old college senior majoring in social work, is currently doing a practicum at a children's mental hospital. In her role as a social worker, Mary often speaks to a family several times over the phone prior to meeting with them. With the background information she receives on each case, Mary is aware of the family's racial background before the family is aware of hers. In one instance, Mary had really connected with the mother of one of her patients. She and the patient's mother, Mrs. K, had talked on the phone several times. Mrs. K made a point of acknowledging Mary's competence and thanked her for how much help she had been.

When Mrs. K and Mary finally met, Mrs. K had a surprised look on her face. From the sound of Mary's voice over the phone and her ability to empathize and understand what the family was going through, Mrs. K had assumed that Mary was African-American. She was shocked to see that Mary was White. The meeting was very uncomfortable. Mary could tell that Mrs. K was hesitant to share information, and the working relationship they had formed seemed to disappear. When Mary came to work the next day, there was a message from Mrs. K stating that she wanted to work with a different social worker, someone who was not White. Mary was taken aback and did not know what she should do. All of the social workers at the hospital were White, and she knew something had to be done so that the patient would continue to receive the best care possible.

Questions:

1. If you were Mary, how would you feel in this situation? Why do you think Mrs.K reacted the way she did to Mary?

2. If you were Mary, what would you do? Specifically, would you call Mrs. K and talk with her, or would you handle it some other way? Explain.

Case Study Three

Michael (African American, divorced father, senior manager at a consulting firm) is constantly reminded that he is exceptional and deserving, unlike so many others. This can be uncomfortable, because the word "others" seems to apply to people who supposedly share his racial or cultural background.

A lot of stress in his life comes from his job as a consultant. For instance, there are people who are comfortable talking to him on the phone but are suddenly uncomfortable when they meet him. They might complain or question his competence by saying, "I don't feel comfortable working with Michael," or "I don't think Michael is the right person for this job." At times like this, he is left wondering and angry.

Questions:

1. Michael is being confronted with a number of barriers to effective communication. Discuss two of these barriers.

2. What microaggressions does Michael encounter? If you were Michael, how would you respond to these microaggressions?

Key Terms

Communication	Linguistic diversity	Ethnographer
Symbol	Bilingual	Status
Kinesics	Multilingual	Power
Culturally specific	Linguicism	Microaggressions
Intercultural communication	Electronic communication	Dialect
Sign language	Material culture	

Exercises

Exercise 1: Ethnic Jokes

Imagine that you and other employees at work correspond by e-mail. You have just received the following message on your computer:

> "Just keeping you informed so that you won't embarrass yourself.
> Due to the climate of political correctness now found throughout
> America, those of us in Tennessee, West Virginia, and Kentucky
> will no longer be 'HILLBILLIES.' Now, you must use the term,
> 'APPALACHIAN-AMERICANS.' Thank you.
> Now, if you don't mind, I've got possums to fry."

After reading this, you decide to respond by sending an e-mail message to the sender of this joke. Type your response.

Exercise 2: Creating an Action Plan

Imagine that you are the director of student affairs at a small liberal arts college in the Midwest. During a staff meeting, the president of the college shares a number of complaints. The complaints allege that many LGBT students encounter prejudice and discrimination both on campus and among townspeople. The students feel that these problems are college-wide and need to be addressed by the president and her staff as well as by community leaders.

The president asks you to create an action plan. She feels that the college needs to open the lines of communication and encourage inclusive, honest dialogue on this issue. Develop a two-page typewritten summary of what you propose. Include the rationale behind your action plan.

 # Notes

[1] Roger E. Axtell, *Gestures: The Do's and Taboos of Body Language Around the World* (New York: Wiley, 1991), 10.

[2] Alice Reid, "Mosque's Children Await Playground," *The Washington Post*, November 22, 1998, B4.

[3] Deborah Tannen, *You Just Don't Understand: Men and Women in Conversation* (New York: William Morrow, 1990); *Talking from 9 to 5: How Women's and Men's Conversational Styles Affect Who Gets Heard, Who Gets Credit, and What Gets Done at Work* (New York: William Morrow, 1994); *That's Not What I Meant* (New York: Ballantine Books, 1992).

[4] Oliver Sacks, *Seeing Voices: A Journey into the World of the Deaf* (Berkeley: University of California Press, 1989), 127.

[5] Jennifer Rudick Zunikoff, conversation with the author, June 4, 2002.

[6] Emily Wax, "The Fabric of Their Faith," *The Washington Post*, May 19, 2002, C1.

[7] Shirley Brice Heath, *Ways with Words* (Cambridge: Cambridge University Press, 1983).

[8] Raymond Bingham, "Leaving Prejudice Behind," *The Washington Post Health Section*, September 6, 1994, 9.

[9] "Preserving a Language and Tribal History," *AARP Bulletin*, November, 2006, 8.

[10] Maya Angelou, *I Know Why the Caged Bird Sings* (New York: Bantam Books, 1993).

[11] Richard Beatty, *The Interview Kit* (New York: John Wiley & Sons, 2000).

[12] American Management Association (AMA), *AMA 2010 Critical Skills Survey*. Online, April 15, 2010. Available: http://www.amanet.org/news/AMA-2010-critcal-skills-survey.aspx.

[13] Nancy Kolsti, "Accents Speak Louder Than Words," *North Texan Online*. Online, Winter, 2000. Available: http://www.unt.edu/northtexan/archives/w00/accents.htmrl.

[14] Charles Goldsmith, "Look See! Anyone Do Read This and It Will Make You Laughable," *The Wall Street Journal*, November 19, 1992, B1.

[15] Anne Soukhanov, *Encarta World English Dictionary* (New York: St. Martin's Press, 1999).

[16] Derald Wing Sue, *Microaggressions in Everyday Life: Race, Gender, and Sexual Orientation* (Hoboken, N.J.: Wiley, 2010).

[17] Randall Kennedy, *Nigger: The Strange Career of a Troublesome Word* (New York: Pantheon, 2002), 4.

[18] S. L. Price, "The Indian Wars," *Sports Illustrated*, March 4, 2002, 67–72.

[19] Michael Fletcher, "Crazy Horse Again Sounds Battle Cry," *The Washington Post*, February 18, 1997, A03.

[20] Barbara Gold, "Diversifying the Curriculum: What Do Students Think?" *Diversity Digest*, Winter 2001, 12–14.

[21] Cornel West, *Race Matters* (New York: Vintage Books, 1993).

6

Social Networking

Learning Outcomes

Upon completion of this chapter, you will be able to:

- Define social networking.
- Compare online and face-to-face networking.
- Explain the significance of the social context of networking.
- Discuss changing dynamics in society that have altered the nature of social networking.
- Elaborate on the role of diversity consciousness (awareness, understanding, skills) in online social networking.
- Give examples of methods for expanding the diversity of online social networks.
- Enumerate key diversity issues in online social networking.
- Define and give examples of the digital divide.
- Discuss various benefits of diverse social networks.

I am proud to be an Orthodox Jewish woman for several reasons. My fellow Jews are always looking out for one another, forming a special bond that I'd like to call a "cultural network." I know that in any time of need, regardless of the problem or barrier, my fellow people will help me out. It is known among Jews that if you have a flat tire on the side of the road, then Jews will stop alongside of you and be of assistance. I'd like to share a story that illustrates this point. A Hispanic man, on his way to New York's Catskill Mountains, got a flat tire. The man was very upset, particularly because no one stopped to assist him. Luckily, he remembered that his grandmother once told him that whenever he needs any kind of help, he should put on a head covering that Orthodox Jewish males wear on their heads. This man always kept this head covering called a "kippa" in his car, but never used it before. He hesitantly placed the kippa on his head and within minutes cars stopped to help him out. They were Orthodox Jews. Without the advice of his grandmother and the kindness of the Jewish people, he might have never made it to the Catskills. I am so lucky to be part of this special network of Jews.

—Another perspective

MyStudentSuccessLab

MyStudentSuccessLab is an online solution designed to help you acquire and develop (or hone) the skills you need to succeed. You will have access to peer-led video presentations and develop core skills through interactive exercises and projects.

During the twenty-first century, our success in many realms hinges on our ability to gain knowledge through a variety of sources, including face-to-face interaction, the written word, the Internet and social media, local and global news, and various societal institutions such as the family, education, religion, and government. In all societies and particularly in a digital society such as the United States, knowledge is power. Therefore, those with limited access to knowledge are at a distinct disadvantage.

Changes in the cultural landscape in the United States and beyond, along with the continuing uncertainty brought about by economic, political, and environmental developments, have made it clear that the ability to connect and form relationships with people from all walks of life is an absolutely essential part of any skillset today. Diversity-conscious social networking makes this possible.

WHAT IS SOCIAL NETWORKING?

A **social network** is a web of connections or ties that link people directly and indirectly to other people. The term *social network* is not new; rather, scientists have been studying social networks for quite some time. Social networks operate at different levels, including ties among individuals, groups and organizations, and societies. **Social networking** refers to the *process* by which we make connections with others. Connections are functional; that is they serve as a conduit for channeling resources such as wealth, power, information, feelings, and awareness. We might use social networking for any number of reasons; to get a job, look for a date, uncover information about our family background or culture, or maybe look into the pros and cons of some medication.

A recent poll of U.S. and Canadian workers reveals that direct, person-to-person networking remains the most effective way to land a new job[1] (see Fig. 6.1). Nevertheless, technology plays a growing role, since we often use the Internet to locate job openings and make the initial contact. Online social networking often works hand in hand with traditional networking; namely direct personal contact.

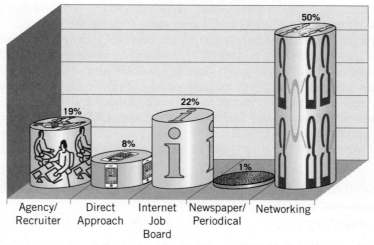

**Networking Is Number One:
How People Find a Job**

Agency/Recruiter	Direct Approach	Internet Job Board	Newspaper/Periodical	Networking
19%	8%	22%	1%	50%

Figure 6.1 Finding a New Job: Networking is Number One.
Source: Right Management

To maximize chances for success, job candidates should generally use as many different approaches as possible.

Social networking is a skill that each of us can develop, improve, and refine. We are all part of social networks. However, all people in our network do not necessarily interact. Our network might consist of people who we know of as well as those who know of us, perhaps through friends, family members, coworkers, or social networking sites such as LinkedIn. On Facebook, our network consists of "friends," and on Twitter and Pinterest we have "followers." The complex web of all of these interlocking connections might look like a large spider web.

It is helpful to map the relationships among individuals, indicating the various ways in which they are connected. Social network theory uses the terms nodes and ties to describe relationships. **Nodes** refer to individuals who share connections in a network, while **ties** refer to the connections themselves. A representation of an individual's network appears in Figure 6.6. In this illustration, the nodes are represented by small circles and the ties are lines.

When we talk about diversity in any type of social network, we are talking about nodes, ties, and the situational context in which these relationships take effect. People in a network may be distinguished by their intellectual, demographic, and cultural differences. A pair of individuals (nodes) may share one relation, such as coworkers in an organization, or they may share a **multiplex tie,** meaning many relations. For instance, two individuals can be coworkers and the best of friends. Or coworkers who are members of the same task force at work as well as travel companions when they attend conferences constitute a multiplex tie as well.

Ties that cut across many different social circles will expose us to more variations in opinions and behaviors than ties that do not connect different circles or clusters of people. Diverse social networks allow us to interact across racial, ethnic, religious, linguistic, and many other boundaries that we may encounter face to face. Moreover, social networks not only connect us to each other; they connect us to bureaucratic organizations and other social units in the larger society.

In this chapter, our primary focus will be on the individual, the ways in which individuals make connections through other individuals online, and the critical importance of diversity consciousness in the process of social networking. As societies have become more modernized and complex, social networks have grown larger and more global. The expansion of these networks has come about in large part due to technological innovations in communications and travel, along with **social media,** or online tools and sites that allow people to network. Diversity-conscious social networking allows us to more effectively navigate and engage these global networks.

Unlike traditional media, social media is interactive, allowing users to generate content and communicate. Examples include online tools such as **blogs,** online personal journals in which authors share their thoughts and feelings to which people can respond, **wikis,** collaboratively built sites of information that allow users to add or change the content, and **discussion boards,** online "bulletin boards" where an ever-growing number of members may comment and discuss issues amongst themselves. Furthermore, sites such as Facebook, Twitter, and LinkedIn may be used to facilitate conversations about personal life experiences, opinions, and perspectives. For example, LinkedIn, a professional networking site, is based on the idea that you are only "x" number of steps or relationships away from the person or persons with whom you want to network. When you share a message with those in your network, these people can then pass it on to their connections, and so forth. Hence, connections such as these can conceivably connect us to other cultures and continents, creating the feeling of a small world. But while the medium and scope of social networking changes constantly, the relevance of diversity consciousness remains the same.

ONLINE AND FACE-TO-FACE NETWORKING

The channel or medium by which we network varies. Communicating online or face to face significantly alters how we connect with each other. And both are intertwined. The Internet makes it possible for people's networks to be much larger and more diverse. Pew reports that Internet users have more diverse networks than non-Internet users.[2] We can interact at any time across economic, political, cultural, and geographic borders. And because online communication is asynchronous, we do not have to adjust to others' schedules.

When we interact face to face, we convey messages in many ways besides words, such as voice intonation, facial expressions, hand gestures and physical contact, and posture. When we communicate online, these forms of communication are not typically available; hence, we may use certain symbols or emoticons to express happiness, sadness, contentment, surprise, or any number of other feelings. Different social norms govern how we communicate, whether we are interacting face to face, over the telephone, using text messaging, or on a social networking site such as Twitter. Another difference relates to the speed and scale of communication. Unlike face-to-face networking, saying something online can spread virally in seconds. Moreover, an online message is permanent and forever available for public consumption.

THE SOCIAL CONTEXT OF NETWORKING

Any and all types of social networking take place in a **social context,** the environment of people, relationships, and cultures that surround us. Social networking involves creating connections with others, including strangers. Sociologists distinguish between social networks and groups. Unlike groups, networks do not necessarily share a common sense of belonging or a common identity; nor do they necessarily interact on a regular basis. If you think of family and friends as groups, think of a social network as extending far beyond these groups. They may know us, but we may not know them. For example, I may get a message from someone who has a son with autism and wants my advice. Perhaps someone who knows of me and my family suggested this person contact me. This person is now a part of my social network.

The number of ties we have is indeed important. More ties can result in more information and, more importantly, diverse sources of information. However, increasing the number of our ties does not necessarily result in stronger or more "quality" contacts. Equally, if not more important, are the people with whom we connect, and how they tie us to other individuals, communities, and cultures. Are members of our social network willing and able to help us? Do they provide emotional support? Do they have knowledge and talents that we value?

As we discuss social networking, it is important to adopt a global perspective and be mindful of worldwide opportunities and disparities among different countries and populations. For example, a study entitled *Women and Mobile: A Global Opportunity* shows the power of mobile phones to promote networks and independence for women. In Senegal and Pakistan, mobiles reinforce women's literacy skills. Women as well as men in Mexico use cell phones to support each

Informal Social Networks and Career Advancement

In their book, *Our Separate Ways: Black and White Women and the Struggle for Professional Identity*, authors Ella Bell and Stella Nkomo share that many women whom they interviewed pointed to the pivotal role informal networks play in career advancement. Excellent job performance is necessary but so too are informal social networks through sponsorships, mentorships, and assistance from colleagues. The authors found that business decisions become more dependent on relationships, especially as those relationships grow and strengthen. Also, Bell and Nkomo point to the continuing influence of informal **old boy networks**, exclusive networks by which men who share a similar socioeconomic background use their power and influence to help others "like them." Women and minorities may advance, but not by breaking down this barrier. They simply find a way to get around it, but the barrier remains intact. It is revealing that in one study of executives, men were significantly more likely to use networking to find new jobs, while women resorted to classified ads.[3]

other as part of an HIV support group. And women farmers in Uganda use mobiles to access information about livestock and find answers to questions about agriculture and business. Unfortunately, even though mobile phone ownership in low- and middle-income countries has increased dramatically in recent years, women in these countries are still much less likely (21%) than men to own a mobile phone. This gap increases to 23 percent in Africa, 24 percent in the Middle East, and 37 percent in South Asia.[4]

In order to understand better the interplay among members of a network, it is helpful to examine how ties vary.

Strong and Weak Ties

Ties vary in terms of strength. **Strong ties** are generally close and frequently maintained; while **weak ties** are more distant and less intimate, infrequently maintained, and extend to more different social circles. According to the Pew Research Center, we increasingly use Facebook to maintain strong, close ties with people whom we have met in person on numerous occasions. Generally, strong ties tend to be more redundant, generating less diverse information. Research shows that weak ties or acquaintances can be a valuable source of new ideas, resources, and information because they typically connect us with people who spend time in social circles that we do not frequent. In his study of professionals and managers looking for jobs in the Boston area, sociologist Mark Granovetter found weak ties to be particularly helpful. Granovetter refers to this as the "strength of weak ties."[5] When we consider that most positions are found on the "hidden" job market since they are not advertised publicly, both strong and weak ties provide crucial resources.

Degree and Degrees of Separation

Degree refers to the number of ties we have with other individuals or a collectivity. *Degrees of separation* is a measure of social distance. We are one degree or tie away from people we know, two degrees away from people they know, and so forth. If people are closely connected, meaning they can be reached in relatively few steps or ties, the implications are significant. For example, consider how having many close ties, within one or two degrees of separation might provide support in the event of a natural disaster or any type of personal emergency.

Trust

The viability and usefulness of a tie may hinge on trust. Members of a social network who trust each other are more apt to be open and honest and listen to each other. We trust people when we assume they have our best interests at heart. This might mean disagreeing with someone even when it is difficult to do, or pushing and challenging certain individuals in our social network to assert themselves in a specific situation or acknowledge their shortcomings. In some instances, a tie based on trust might allow us to be brutally honest even to the point of risking conflict.

Trust can develop through weak as well as strong ties. Bill Gates, former CEO of Microsoft, talks about a concept called the *"trilogy of trust."* By this he means that trust is passed on through networking. For example, Faith, a colleague of yours, asks you if you know anyone who is great at Excel. You indicate that Subash, a person you worked with six months ago, is an Excel expert. The trust that Faith has in you is immediately transferred to Subash, a third party whom she has never met in person. Consequently, Faith is more open to a third party even though she has never met that person. An added benefit is that Subash might speak highly of you because he knows of you. In this way, building connections and trust can multiply with each new contact and conversation.

Building close ties with people who are different from us can promote tolerance and trust over time. Through social networking, initial feelings of discomfort and disengagement with people who seem unlike us can give way to more trust and a greater awareness of our similarities. Individuals whom we feel we can trust may provide us with a good "sounding board," especially with regard to sensitive issues. For example, we might make a comment at work that comes across as offensive, but we are not sure why and we are hesitant to ask just anyone. Asking members of our social network whom we trust might provide us with greater understanding of this comment and its impact.

CHANGING DYNAMICS OF SOCIAL NETWORKING

Sociocultural evolution, the study of changes in societies and cultures over time, provides a more historical, macro-level perspective on social networking. Since earliest societies, people have formed social networks, connecting with individuals, groups and others in and outside their communities. As societies evolved and became more technologically complex, the nature of social networking changed dramatically.

In the past, social networks in rural and even urban areas tended to be smaller and tighter. An individual's support system or safety net might have consisted of family members, close friends, community leaders, churches, and perhaps a few other community groups. When the social networks of individuals began to extend outward, individuals could reach larger numbers of people more easily.

Nowadays, social networking is often more varied and specialized. Utilizing a number of diverse, specialized networks and moving at will among them enables us to gain the psychological, economic, and social support we need. We might look to different people, groups, and organizations for emotional support, professional advice, spiritual comfort, or information on a variety of subjects. The Internet facilitates this process in that it affords more opportunities to interact with more people and more diverse people.

In digital societies, computer technology has dramatically expanded and reshaped people's social networks. Technology changes the way we use social networks to learn, adapt, make choices, and deal with personal and social problems. With the Internet and smartphones, individuals can reach out to more people and more different people in a variety of ways. Because their networks extend outward, some of us can reach large numbers of people very easily. We tell our friends, who in turn inform others, and everyone is "in the know." Other people, however, may have a much more difficult time being heard because the range of their connections is limited. Perhaps these people have quite a few friends, but their networks overlap to a considerable degree.

The Internet also makes it very easy to find and connect with a small number of people who share our exact experience or interest. Imagine you are looking for people with a similar type of medical condition, or perhaps individuals who have lost a young child. Maybe you have a question about your organization's Web site that requires you to communicate with a very targeted group of professionals, such as Java programmers. Prior to the Internet, finding these people was extremely difficult.

Time and space are not the barriers they used to be. We now work with multiple teams in multiple locations. Technology, which allows information to be sent as attachments over the Internet, faxed, or stored in "clouds," permits us to access data, documents, and drawings from anywhere. But social networking, even in a digital society, continues to be a time-consuming endeavor. Whether we are connecting online or face to face, starting and maintaining relationships requires time, effort, and focus, especially with all of our roles and obligations. In a highly mobile, rapidly changing society such as the United States, growth and turnover in many social networks is a constant. People are in a constant state of flux; they travel, change jobs, friends, residences, and develop new personal and professional interests. Moreover, we have gradually become more socially flexible. Traditional social boundaries that revolve around race, ethnicity, gender, religion, and sexual orientation are weakening. While friends, family, and neighbors still represent important socializing agents, much of our networking now extends far beyond these groups.

> I remember the sorrow I felt as I left my native country of Ghana, wondering when I would ever see my parents' and siblings' faces again, knowing how expensive flight tickets were and how difficult the acquisition of a visa was. The only way I communicated with them was by phone and letters until I discovered Facebook and Skype. In fact, the first day we communicated via video call on Skype was the best day of my life. There has not been a day since then that I have not seen their faces. My mother even taught me how to cook, bathe my newborn son, and even coached me through how to swaddle him all through video calls. Although I have not seen any of them in flesh for so many years, I know what they look like, and am now abreast with their day-to-day activities and so are they with mine.
>
> —Another Perspective

Digital Natives

Digital natives, younger people born or raised during the age of digital technologies, are "native speakers" of the language of computers, video games, and the Internet. On the other hand, **digital immigrants** are people who were not born into the digital world but learned the language and the new technology later in life.[6] Consequently, their lives have been transformed by technology. According to a national study by Common Sense Media, a majority of teens report social networking technologies have helped them "keep in touch" with friends or connect with others who have a common interest. Many more teens say social networks help rather than hurt their friendships.

This study's findings are at odds with the idea that technologies such as Facebook isolate teens. Moreover, one in five teens in this survey said using social networking sites makes them feel more confident and sympathetic to others. Interestingly, today's teens still prefer face-to-face communication, and see it as the best way to nourish relationships.[7]

In another interesting global study, nearly 1,000 college students in ten countries were asked to go without all media for a period of 24 hours. These students describe this experience using a language of dependency that brought to mind addictive behavior. One U.S. student from Chile says, "I didn't use my cell phone all night. It was a difficult day . . . a horrible day . . . I need my social webs, my cell phone, my Mac, my mp3 always." Another student alludes to the way social media helps her manage her relations with friends and interact with others. She writes, "There is no doubt that Facebook is really high profile in our daily life. Everybody uses it to contact other persons, also we use it to pay attention to others."[8] Students in this study, who were asked to write about their experiences during this period of abstinence, were most likely to use the words shown in Figure 6.2.

Copyright 2013 tagxedo.com

Figure 6.2 Students Describe Going without Media for a Day.
Source: International Center for Media and the Public Agenda.

The Global Reach of Social Networking

In many ways, our future success depends on our ability to effectively network in a global environment. This significant challenge will test our ability to adapt to individual, organizational, and cultural differences and similarities. While this challenge is no easy task, our diversity consciousness can be a tremendous asset. When we interact, online or offline, diversity consciousness serves to counter *"cultural cruise control,"* the tendency to assume other cultures mirror ours. Cultural cruise control undermines our efforts to network effectively.

The Internet has revolutionized social networking. In the twenty-first century, growth in the number of Internet users throughout the world has been rapid and

Cross-cultural Guidelines for Social Networking

If you find yourself networking in an unfamiliar cultural environment, try to keep an open mind and be observant. Also, keep the following "guidelines" in mind:

1. When introducing yourself to others, be more formal than usual. Use titles and be very respectful. And do not assume that the titles you are accustomed to using necessarily apply in other settings and countries. If in doubt, ask questions.

2. If possible, research ahead of time. Go online and search for information that might be helpful. For instance, what norms govern greetings between men and women, and young and old?

3. Avoid acronyms, idioms, and slang, unless you explain them.

4. Learn "safe" topics of discussion. In many cultures, it is a good idea to avoid initiating discussions about religious and political issues.

5. Be mindful of how you present yourself online. For instance, modesty and colors are associated with different values in different cultures.

6. Be humble. Share your opinion, but listen carefully in order to understand others' opinions as well. For example, we may have been brought up to believe that our work defines us. In other countries, people may very well view their identity and accomplishments outside of work as more important.

7. Respect and engage individuals and their cultures. In so doing, other people are more likely to appreciate your acceptance of them, and value what you bring to the relationship.

8. Manners matter. Being polite and grateful can help set the tone for a meaningful relationship.

9. If communicating with someone who speaks a different language, commit to learning one or two new key words and phrases each day, such as please and thank you, yes and no, hello and good-bye, and I don't understand.

uneven. At the present, one-third of the world's population uses the Internet.[9] As can be seen in Figure 6.3, the **Internet penetration rate,** or the percentage of a region's total population that uses the Internet, varies widely, from roughly 79 percent in North America to 16 percent in Africa.[10]

While English and Chinese are the languages most commonly used on the Internet (see Fig. 6.4), there are apps for mobile devices that instantly translate what we say into more than 30 languages. As translation technology continues to develop in the years

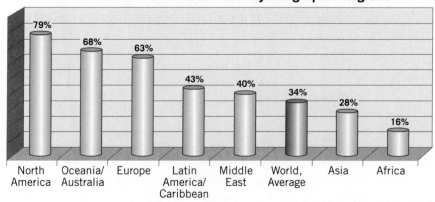

World Internet Penetration Rates by Geographic Regions

- North America 79%
- Oceania/Australia 68%
- Europe 63%
- Latin America/Caribbean 43%
- Middle East 40%
- World, Average 34%
- Asia 28%
- Africa 16%

Figure 6.3 World Internet Penetration Rates.
Source: Internet World Stats.

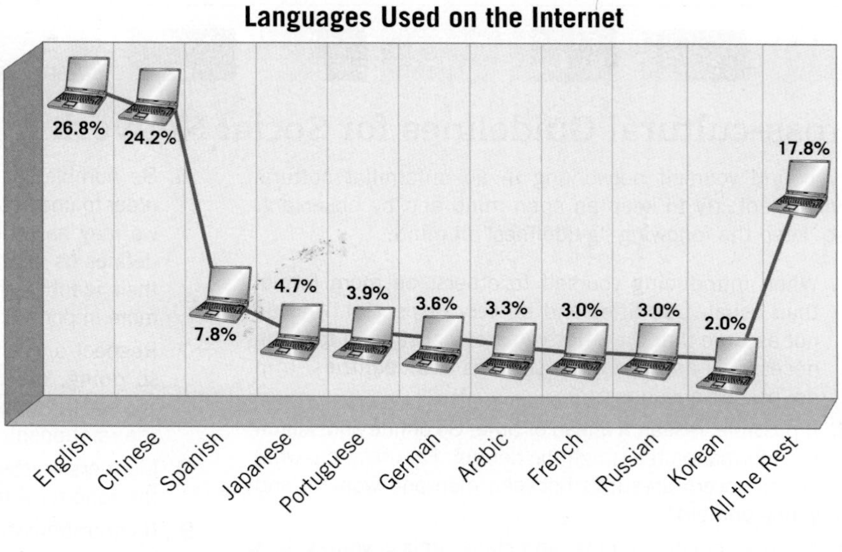

Languages Used on the Internet

Figure 6.4 Internet's Top Ten Languages.
Source: Internet World Stats, "Internet World Users by Language."[11]

ahead, more and more people will be able to use their language of choice to be understood. Direct translations, however, frequently distort meaning.

In spite of its growing influence worldwide, digital communication is not the all-important socializing force it is sometimes made out to be. For the past six years, marketing consultants Keller and Fay have studied all forms of conversations, face to face, online, and over the phone, in countries such as the United States as well as Australia, Mexico, South Korea, and United Kingdom. Data on more than two million conversations indicate that the vast majority (75%) of conversations in the United States are still face to face. In the other countries they studied, the figure is even higher. Less than 10 percent of the conversations in the United States occur through the Internet. Moreover, Keller and Fay found that the increasing popularity of social media, such as Facebook, comes at the expense of e-mail rather than face-to-face conversations. Data from Keller and Fay's study show that face-to-face conversations are generally more positive and perceived to be more credible than online conversations. The subject of the conversations varies as well. When online, what is considered "cool" is more apt to influence conversations. On the other hand, face-to-face conversations are more apt to deal with real life experiences.[12]

DIVERSITY CONSCIOUSNESS AND ONLINE SOCIAL NETWORKING

As mentioned earlier, social networking is not a new phenomenon. However, with the Internet, smartphones, and other new and emerging technologies, we are increasingly able to explore diverse worlds, expand personal networks, and develop our diversity consciousness. At the present, we are only beginning to understand the implications of online social networking for our personal, everyday lives and the interconnected global communities in which we live.

Online social networking, enhanced by diversity consciousness, provides us with indispensable tools to help us crawl out of the cultural silos that isolate us and curtail our opportunities. Research by Robert Putnam, a well-known professor of public policy at Harvard University, shows a trend toward greater diversity *and* cultural encapsulation in the United States. Putnam examined the associations of about 30,000 people across the United States. Putnam's analysis focuses on whether we have become more or less interconnected over time and why. He came to the conclusion that as our communities have grown more diverse, people tend to disconnect and "hunker down." According to Putnam, people are now more inclined to avoid and distrust their neighbors, and even their friends. They volunteer less, show less faith in the leaders of their community, and are less inclined to believe that they can effect change and make a difference in this world.[13]

Putnam's study focuses on face-to-face social networks we develop in our neighborhoods. Perhaps memberships in clubs and organizations have been replaced in part by the social ties we make and develop on sites such as Facebook and Pinterest. In contrast to strong, community-oriented ties, many online ties may be weak and geographically dispersed. The relationship between online networking and neighborhood involvement is certainly a subject that merits further study.

Awareness and Understanding

We can develop a better awareness of ourselves by examining how we present ourselves online. For instance, checking up on ourselves helps us understand why we might "stretch the truth" on Facebook in order to appear wealthier or smarter. Recognizing and understanding which aspects of ourselves we share on different social networking sites, and which aspects we "hide" or do not divulge provide us with insight into ourselves, others, and society.

As we move from one relationship to another, we may engage in **impression management,** tweaking our appearance and changing how we act in order to influence how different people see us. Online, we may consciously or unconsciously project a certain image in order to make a good first impression. This might entail sharing our goals or dislikes, linking ourselves to certain friends who maintain a certain well-to-do lifestyle, or posting pictures that provide insight into our personalities. Also, we may change our image as we engage in impression management with multiple audiences, such as ethnically diverse coworkers, long-time friends, and relatives. Due to the anonymity afforded by online networking, we may have more flexibility to craft and alter impressions of ourselves.

 Thinking Through Diversity

Google yourself. What is written about you? What pictures of you, and messages written by you, appear? What does your online image reveal about you?

It has been said that "googling" one's name is the equivalent of a modern-day resume. Our **online identity management,** meaning how we showcase ourselves to the world online, is an increasingly important component of social networking. With that idea in mind, what do your views on social networking sites, such as blogs, wikis, and Twitter say about you, your character and respect for others, and your expertise? What does your social media presence convey to prospective employers? Findings from a recent survey by CareerBuilder.com speak to the value of online identity management. Of those hiring managers surveyed, one in four makes use of search engines in screening candidates, and one in ten checks the profiles of candidates on various social networking sites.[14]

> The idea of looking for a job now has to come with some type of tweak on my online accounts. I'm not sure if me being Black, woman, or if my general appearance will come into play if someone decides to search online profiles before they call me for an interview. I know that people have prejudices, especially employers. I worked at a small business once and the owner said he would Google and Facebook to search for every applicant who had an interest in the position. It doesn't stop me from applying but it's something I take into account.
>
> —Another perspective

Our awareness of our own diversity and the type of people we choose to include in our networks help explain the self we construct and portray on the Internet and the connections we seek to build. For instance, our Facebook presence may reveal certain aspects of our diversity that we keep hidden in everyday life. Facebook does not classify us by race, but it does ask us to identify our sexual orientation if we so desire. Is this aspect of our hidden diversity something we want to divulge? Clearly, our social networks are an extension of who we are and how we view the world around us. For example, we may assume that our network is diverse because it includes men and women of varying races, religions, and ethnicities. But perhaps it lacks international contacts and resources, or people of diverse socioeconomic backgrounds and political ideologies. Developing a global perspective enhances our self-awareness and opens up opportunities for networking and learning.

Reid Hoffman, the cofounder and chairman of LinkedIn, is the author of *The Start-up of You*. In this book, he talks about being aware of what you already have going for you. This includes your networks. Hoffman states, "If you want to build a strong network that will help you move ahead in your career, it's vital to first take stock of the connections you already have." [15]

> I think that my use of social media has increased my diversity consciousness. I have 287 friends on Facebook, and each of them is unique. Most of my friends are obviously from my country, and still every day I realize that we are diverse.
>
> —Another perspective

In many instances, being aware or taking stock of our connections turns our attention to social networking sites (SNSs). There are hundreds of SNSs, such as Facebook, Twitter, Pinterest, and LinkedIn. With social networking sites, our connections are visible. Therefore, we are better able to understand why and how we develop connections. Some sites may attract people with distinctive cultural identities, such as MyChurch, AsianAvenue, MySpaceLatino, CitySaheli, BlackPlanet, and MilkandMocha. Increasingly, scholars in many different disciplines are looking into the cultures of different sites, and their effect on a number of social issues including privacy, power, philanthropy, generational differences, education, identity, and conflict.

The Diversity of Facebook

In comparison to other social networks, Facebook has by far the largest number of active users throughout the world (see Fig. 6.5). Approximately one in thirteen people worldwide uses Facebook. In some countries, Facebook is blocked (China) or hard to access due to censorship (Iran). In the U.S., research suggests that social relationships and interpersonal feelings distinguish users of Facebook. Specifically, Facebook users:

1. Tend to be more trusting. In comparison to other Internet users and non-Internet users, Facebook users are more likely to feel "that most people can be trusted."

2. Get more social support, including emotional support, companionship, and instrumental aid. Facebook users, who use Facebook multiple times each day, are more apt to receive support of this nature than other Internet users and non-Internet users.

3. Are more politically engaged. Relative to other Internet users and non-users, Facebook users who repeatedly use the site each day are significantly more inclined to say they would vote, try to influence another person to vote for a particular candidate, and attend a political meeting or rally.[16]

The cultures that distinguish SNSs vary considerably and attract different people. As an example, adults who are more educated and have large social networks already in place are more apt to use Twitter and LinkedIn. While many sites support pre-existing connections, others bring strangers together on the basis of their common interests, identities, or activities. SNSs cultivate diverse audiences as well as more homogenous populations such as individuals who share common racial, religious, sexual, or ethnic identities or those who are interested in dating, a hobby, or a particular business. The culture of sites, which is shaped in part by their target demographic, may have broad appeal or seek narrower audiences. Similarly, they may result in more weak ties or strong ties. Communication tools, such as blogging, mobile connectivity, link sharing, and photo/video sharing, serve to distinguish sites as well.

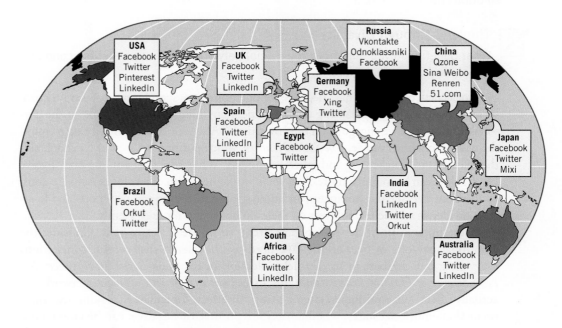

Figure 6.5 Most Popular Social Networks by Country.
Source: themoscownews.com.[17]

Thinking Through Diversity

Google the phrase "unique social networks." Visit at least three online social networking sites geared toward people from cultural backgrounds that are very different from your own. Identify these sites and the audience they target. In general, how do they add to your awareness and understanding of diversity?

Effective social networking is driven by our awareness of commonalities and differences in motivation, communication, and culture. Kim and Choi studied what motivates college students in the United States and Korea to use social networking sites.[18] Students from both countries use social networking sites for the same reasons; namely, to seek friends, and find social support, entertainment, and information. However, Korean students are much more apt to include existing relationships in their online social networks, such as family, friends and others who are socially close. U.S. students are more likely to look for new friends online, while family and friends constitute a much smaller part of their online network.

When we network across cultures, our communication style can be of paramount importance. For example, in the United States, initial contact in multicultural networking is likely to take the form of text messaging, e-mailing, or talking by phone. This mode of communication does not resonate with people from certain cultures who prefer to meet face to face and build a sense of trust before getting down to business. In many cases, for example, Asian and Latino cultures attach more importance to developing relationships at the beginning of a project or collaboration, with task completion coming later, whereas European-Americans are more apt to engage in task completion at the outset or earlier in the process, and let relationships develop as they complete the task.

As we network, it helps to be mindful of different approaches to knowing, or how we gain information and make sense of the world around us. From one cultural perspective, addressing a problem in the community may call for sharing resources and information online. Others might prefer an approach that is more experiential, such as visiting places in the community and elsewhere in order to get a better feel for what solutions might work best.

 Thinking Through Diversity

What benefits do you reap from your social network? Are these benefits economic, social, and/or psychological?

Social networking may have negative connotations. Some employers mistakenly equate social networking with socializing that has little if anything to do with work, or the personal relationships we engage in on our "own time." Also, this concept may bring to mind the widely acclaimed movie, *The Social Network*, which portrays the start of Facebook and the role of Mark Zuckerberg and other cofounders. While social networking may involve Facebook, it can be so much more. And while we connect with others for personal reasons, connections pervade the workplace, and time spent networking can pay short- and long-term dividends and help employees do their job better and more efficiently.

Certain pay-offs of networking are latent, or not readily apparent. Consider the emotional pay-offs of networking. We need to understand that certain connections may bring out the best in us. Daniel Goleman, in his book *Social Intelligence: The New Science of Human Relationships*, discusses how people in our social network can actually affect our emotional state of being. In effect, Goleman is making the argument that emotional states, whether they are positive or negative, can be contagious. Furthermore, social networking can improve our quality of life and our health. For instance, research by the Phoenix Center in Washington, D.C. indicates that senior citizens who network online may be less prone to depression and loneliness.[19]

The personal and professional benefits of diverse networks are noteworthy. However, in order to reap these benefits, we need to recognize, understand, and assess the connections we have and those we seek to develop. Further, we need to understand why "who we know" may be just as important or perhaps more important than "what we know." As an example, numerous studies show a significant relationship between our lifetime income and the nature of our social networks.[20] In essence, social networks play a significant role in hiring, professional success, and job performance. One recent study by Deirdre Royster, for example, examined a group of Black and White men who were all graduates of the same vocational school, and looking for the same kind of jobs in the same areas, and comparable in work ethic and other ways that might impact their employability. She found that the White men did significantly better in finding employment, in large part due to their contacts.[21] While awareness and understanding of our networks does not "level the playing field" by any means, these components of diversity consciousness provide the foundation for creating and strengthening relationships that open doors and allow us to build an impressive resume.

Skills

Anyone can become a more effective social networker by developing their diversity consciousness in addition to their digital skills. *Diversity Consciousness* addresses a wide range of diversity skills. These include communicating, managing conflict, teaming, and leading in such a way that everyone feels valued and respected. All of these skills are invaluable both online and offline. Daily interactions present us with a plethora of opportunities to learn, develop, and refine these competencies. Furthermore, we can expand and leverage the diversity of our online social networks by assuming diversity, seeking diversity, and leveraging diversity.

Assuming Diversity

When we engage in social networking, we should assume our audience is diverse in ways we might not realize. What we share with one member of our social network could at some point be shared with others. Assuming diversity means questioning certain labels and assumptions. For instance, suppose we contact different members of our social network because we think they are experts on certain issues because of their nationality, gender, or religion. We might view women as knowledgeable about issues pertaining to the family and childcare, like balancing family obligations with the demands of work. But is that necessarily true? If we think inclusively, we might realize that some men in our network have more experience and insight on this issue. Men, like women, are multidimensional. Their gender is only one aspect of their diversity.

Traditionally, part of networking requires tailoring one's message to fit a particular situation, being aware that what we say, how we say it, and how we present ourselves may be appropriate for one audience and setting but not necessarily for another. Nowadays, relationships are much more complex. For example, a presentation at work or at a conference may be posted online; making it available to a variety of audiences in a variety of contexts. Consequently, constantly assuming diversity allows us to take this into account ahead of time and tweak our presentation accordingly.

Seeking Diversity

Building the skill set we absolutely need requires a willingness to seek out diversity, and a commitment to follow through when opportunities to learn and grow arise. Indeed, we can be proactive and create those opportunities online. Suppose we wish to learn more about Indonesia, and specifically Indonesians who have moved to the

United States, in addition to U.S. citizens in Indonesia. Also of interest to us are Indonesian expressions, proverbs, and catchphrases, and what topics should not be broached if someone travels to Indonesia. We could reach out to neighbors, coworkers or acquaintances, hoping to connect with someone who is privy to this information. Or we might join an online networking group or create one, inviting people throughout the world to join us, including those born in Indonesia or those with knowledge and ties to Indonesians and their way of life. Another option would be to get virtual pen pals. Using the power of the Internet, we can create a profile, search for pen pal connections using a variety of services, and begin to communicate electronically.

Building diverse professional networks requires us to seek people who broaden and complement our skills and backgrounds. A systems engineer who just began working at a large firm describes her reasons for seeking diversity. Rather than simply network with people with technical backgrounds, she seeks to diversify her skills and network with coworkers in other areas. Specifically, she is looking for "a different perspective of the company and, more importantly, a sounding board and source of feedback that communicated differently than I or most engineers would."[22] She targets people who do *not* engage in "engineer speak," who in effect help her develop the skills she needs to communicate with non-technical people. Lastly, she is thinking of changing careers in the future, and this diverse network allows her to become better acquainted with other job functions and opportunities within the company and elsewhere.

Leveraging Diversity

Besides assuming and seeking diversity, we need to take advantage of it. We might interact with a structurally diverse network. Because of diverse organizational affiliations, job positions and functions, and educational backgrounds, members of this network can expose us to many different sources of knowledge. Hence, diversity of this nature provides us with opportunities to engage and learn from a heterogeneous group of people. However, it does not ensure that meaningful interaction of this nature will necessarily take place. In such an environment, we might stay to ourselves or gravitate to our "own kind." Perhaps we do not process information from certain people because we automatically assume that our way is the right way. Leveraging diversity requires being willing and able to step outside of ourselves. This critical component of diversity consciousness enables us to engage and strive to understand diverse, even seemingly contradictory perspectives, and learn from them.

When networking with community organizers, Barack Obama asked them to shift perspectives and put themselves in somebody else's situation. One day, directing their attention out of the windows of their office, he said, "What do you suppose is going to happen to those boys out there? . . . You say you're tired, the same way most folks out here are tired . . . Who's going to make sure [those boys] get a fair shot?"[23]

 Thinking Through Diversity

According to William Powers, becoming more creative and productive requires us to be disconnected for periods of time. By balancing connectedness with disconnectedness, we can leverage diversity. In an era in which connectivity is the norm, Powers maintains that we need to create time and space for solitude and reflection. Do you agree with Powers? Why or why not?[24]

Expanding and diversifying our connections through networking involves awareness, understanding, and skills. Diversity-conscious social networking is a critical twenty-first century skill. Valuable knowledge, insight, support, and resources of all kinds pass from person to person, both locally and globally. Dr. John Horrigan, head of the

Media and Technology Institute of the Joint Center for Political and Economic Studies, expounds on this idea. "If ideas change the world, then it is increasingly true that networks shape ideas."[25]

EXPANDING THE DIVERSITY OF ONLINE SOCIAL NETWORKS

Throughout our life course, from childhood to retirement, diverse social networks are critically important. They help us find jobs, meet new people, showcase our talents, prepare for different stages in our life, and share valuable resources. For example, a senior citizen may spend time each day online preparing for retirement by looking for new things to do, new people to meet, and new opportunities to consider in retirement.

Expanding and transforming our networks to be more diverse and powerful takes time, effort, and a willingness to venture outside of our comfort zone. Dr. Ivan Misner, who has been called the father of modern networking, explains the rationale behind diversifying one's personal network. Doing so increases the likelihood of connectors in our network or **linchpins,** those individuals who cross over between clusters of individuals or groups. The overlapping interests or connections of linchpins allow them to easily link people with diverse backgrounds, talents, and information. These people might vary in age, profession, education, religion, social class, ethnicity, political ideology, and digital proficiency. Besides sharing our network, they may have very little in common with us.[26]

Researchers at Pew Internet have developed a tool to measure the diversity of our social networks. Rather than focus on race, ethnicity, or gender, this broad measurement of diversity is based on the social locations and resources of the people we know. Specifically, Pew asks people whether they know anyone in 22 different occupations. These occupations, which include CEO of a big company, nurse, teacher, janitor, congressman/woman, police, and professor, vary widely in terms of their **occupational prestige,** meaning the honor or respect society attaches to these positions. Using a scale that ranges from 1 to 100, Pew is able to measure the diversity of our network. In the United States, people's average score on the scale of network diversity is 42. It is interesting to note that LinkedIn users (47) score higher on diversity than users of Twitter (42), Facebook (39), and MySpace (37). Analysis of these differences points to the characteristics of users who gravitate to different sites.[27]

Maximizing Social Capital

Diverse ties allow us to maximize our **social capital,** those actual and potential interpersonal resources embedded in our social networks. Psychological, social, and economic resources flow from social networks and create opportunities for individuals and organizations. As we get to know a larger circle of people different from ourselves, the more likely it is that we will have access to an increasingly wide range of resources. Consider the importance of a social network when we find ourselves immersed in another culture. A social network can help acquaint us with the norms, language, and people we need to know in order to navigate and enjoy the local culture. Or imagine if we were moving off welfare and entering the labor force. A viable network would make it easier to find quality childcare and housing.[28]

According to social capital research, people in our network who feel positively toward us represent an important resource. Furthermore, people who occupy different positions can provide us with different resources. As an example, people in powerful and prestigious positions have resources tied to their authority and their personal and professional networks. People in low status positions have unique talents, insights, and life experiences as well.

Social capital is one of the main drivers behind professional networks throughout the world, as we share with and support one another. Consider the following example. If I ask a favor of a contact, I am spending social capital. Now that person may ask me for a favor at some point in the future, and expect that I will reciprocate. This sounds like "I'll scratch your back if you scratch mine," and there is an element of this. Typically this type of interaction takes place in a socially friendly context. Given this exchange of social capital, we might not want to ask too much of one person if we have not built up that much social capital.

In some cultures, networks are governed by **guanxi,** a mutually beneficial relationship between people in which an individual can be called upon to return a favor of some sort. Like social capital, guanxi involves social relations. Some business professionals mistakenly view guanxi as simply another form of gift-giving and bribery. While this may occur, guanxi is much more. It is rooted in the cultivation of interpersonal relationships over a period time. If gifts come into play, they are symbolic of an attempt to build relationships and strengthen one's ties, resources, and social standing. In China, for example, guanxi is an integral part of everyday life. As such, it is customary to nourish an elaborate set of guanxi, which might involve the exchange of material goods, friendship, or emotional support. The individuals involved need not occupy equal statuses, nor do they have to stay in contact with each other. If guanxi exists, failure to reciprocate at some point in time is considered a serious and even unforgivable offense.

Bridging and Bonding

In research on social capital, a distinction is made between bridging and bonding. **Bridging** is the development of ties with people who are dissimilar to us in important ways. For example, we might develop ties to people of a different generation or a different political ideology. On the other hand, *bonding* refers to the development of ties with people who are similar to us in some important way, be it age, gender, race, religion, or some other dimension of diversity. One does not necessarily develop at the expense of the other; rather, we can have an abundance of ties that take the form of bridging as well as bonding.

> If someone chooses to call him/herself 'catcrazy2215' or 'braniac44,' I can learn a lot about individuals without ever discovering age, race, national origin, religion, or even gender. My only judgment tool is a gut-level, do I like this person?
>
> —Another perspective

Bridging social capital promotes critical thinking. For instance, networking with people who are independent thinkers and who adopt a variety of political ideologies will test and strengthen our critical thinking skills. In addition, we are less likely to experience a phenomenon known as the **echo chamber,** a situation in which like-minded members of online communities echo our opinions and beliefs back to us. The echo chamber serves to reinforce our cultural biases and stifle critical thought in addition to perspective taking.

Bonding has value as well. It allows us to interact with people with whom we can identify and relate. However, when taken to its extreme, bonding can delay our personal growth and intellectual development. The term **homophily,** which literally means "love of the same," is the tendency to limit our networks to people who share similar backgrounds and values, who work in similar types of jobs, who live close by, and have similar contacts. In their review of the literature on this subject, McPherson, Smith-Lovin, and Cook point to more than 100 studies that support the existence of various forms of homophily, such as networking among people who share the same age, class, organizational role, and gender.[29] This study builds upon the work of earlier sociologists, who make the distinction between two types of homophily. In the event of **status homophily,** individuals who possess a similar social status or position are more likely to associate and bond with each other, while **value homophily** explains our tendency to associate with others who think like us and share our values. Moreover, value homophily may occur even when there are differences in status.[30]

> A great many people think they are thinking when they are merely rearranging their prejudices.
> —William James

Education and Diverse Networks

Thinking Through Diversity

Pew Research findings show that education is the best predictor of a diverse social network. How do you think your educational level impacts the diversity of your social network?

According to the Pew Internet and American Life Project, people with more years of education have more diverse networks.[31] Education broadens our perspective. By exposing us to new people, experiences, and knowledge both in and out of the classroom, we grow more aware of the importance and value of diversity. Also, more highly educated people are apt to work and live in a greater variety of social contexts. Because people with more education tend to have more economic and social resources, they can afford to be more mobile and spend more time cultivating and nourishing local and global contacts.

Strategies for maximizing the diversity of our networks

Diversifying our social networks is a process that requires work and commitment on our part. A number of strategies can help us diversify, strengthen, and critique our personal and professional networks.

- Assess the diversity of your social networks, both online and offline. How diverse are your online social networks? For example, ask yourself whether a preponderance of people in your network know each other. By going to LinkedIn Labs, you can produce an image of your LinkedIn contacts. Similarly, Facebook has created an app that enables you to assess the diversity of your "friends."

- Develop ties with people who tend to disagree with you about work-related or contemporary social issues, and coworkers who span different generations and do not share your seniority on the job. For Lee (see Fig. 6.6), this means assessing the diversity of groups that make up her social networks.

- Connect with people who appear to have very little in common with you. These individuals may be connectors or linchpins to perspectives, beliefs, value systems, interests, and lifestyles that you might otherwise never encounter.

- Expose yourself to social networks and other forms of media, particularly those that broaden your global perspective and expose you to cutting-edge, innovative ideas.

- Join groups, associations, and communities that make you feel like an outsider. While you do not have to agree with their point of view or the way they do things, try to engage and understand where they are coming from.

- Avoid the trap of simply believing what people say because of their relation to you, reputation, educational background, title, or position. Question and critically evaluate the thinking and assumptions of all people in your social networks.

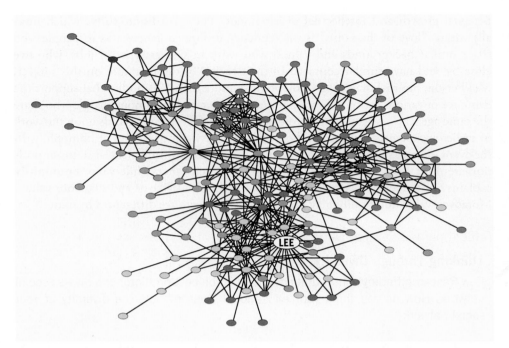

Figure 6.6 Lee's Social Network: The colors represent different groups within Ms. Lee's network, including her place of work (red), family (yellow), religious community (purple), and others (green).

KEY DIVERSITY ISSUES IN ONLINE SOCIAL NETWORKING

In order to understand the dynamics and importance of online social networking, it is helpful to explore diversity issues such as identity tourism, digital divides, and online microaggressions. Each of these issues relate to various dimensions of diversity such as race, gender, social identity, and sexual orientation. Moreover, all of these issues deal with the dynamics of online social networking, the relevance of power and one's status in society, and the role diversity consciousness plays in helping us recognize, understand, and adapt to the wide range of differences we encounter in virtual communities.

Identity Tourism

Unlike face-to-face interaction, cyberspace allows us unprecedented opportunities to represent ourselves any number of ways. Because we "feel" anonymous online, we may be more open and divulge who we really are, or we may fabricate a new online identity. Lisa Nakamura, Professor of Media and Cinema Studies, coined the term **identity tourism,** the process of adopting someone else's identity online, such as taking on a sexual or racial identity other than one's own.[32] Just as people in real life (or "rl" as it is sometimes referred to by participants in virtual environments) engage in different forms of **passing,** pretending to be members of another group, the same phenomenon occurs in cyberspace.

Identity tourism takes place in social gaming networks, virtual worlds, or in other online social networks. For instance, millions of people visit a virtual world known as

Second Life to construct a new persona online. With the help of an orientation session, participants unleash their imagination and create who or what they want to be in their "second life." In customizing their own **avatar,** meaning an online representation of a person, choices are almost limitless, including body type, dress, hairstyle, and skin. Once they leave "Orientation Island," they can further modify their appearance as they interact with other residents in a wide variety of individual and group activities.

On some sites, the profession, race, class, gender, and overall appearance of the avatar we create may be quite different or similar to our actual identity. As players and their avatars interact in a virtual world, they may convey social expectations and promote stereotypes grounded in real-life experiences. By extending our diversity awareness to online interaction, we gain more insight into identity tourism. In one study, participants who were randomly assigned taller avatars acted more confidently when trying to make an offer and negotiate a deal with shorter avatars. In other studies, avatars interacting in a virtual setting were more likely to reach agreement on some issue if their appearances were similar.[33] While studies on avatars provide valuable insight into diversity and its effect on behavior, it should be noted that research of this nature is still in its infancy.

Digital Divides

The **digital divide** refers to the unequal access to information and communication technologies (ICT) among different populations. Unequal access, which is both a local and global phenomenon, impacts who engages in social networking, how they connect, and the social capital they develop through these ties. In essence, the digital divide makes it more difficult for certain people to network, and therefore interact, contribute, and compete on an equal footing.

In making sense of this divide, it is important to examine various ways in which we go online, including using a smartphone as well as a computer. With regard to degrees of access, we get a better picture of the digital divide when we do not simply group people and societies into the "haves" and "have-nots." For example, a gap may exist among people who have Internet access. There are those who have access to high-speed, reliable, and brand new computers and those who only have access to old, unreliable, and slow computers connected by modem. Even the word access can be problematic. Access may range from exclusive to shared to shared public access. And gaps in access can be due to numerous factors, including one's knowledge of computers, one's motivation to make use of opportunities to use ICTs, and the availability of technology itself as well as when, where, and how long it may be used.

The following analysis of some major digital divides focuses on social networking. Furthermore, we will highlight:

- Trends more so than statistical information at any one point in time

- Both local and global social inequalities and divides

- The dynamic, interlocking nature of these divides

Recent data from Pew research show that more than one in five adults in the United States do not use the Internet.[34] A number of factors appear to be at work here, including educational attainment, income, English proficiency, disability status, and rural/urban residence. Of those not using the Internet, some do not have the necessary resources or digital skills. Others see it as irrelevant, a hassle, or not worth the bother. Interestingly, some nonusers have an Internet connection in their home.

Age

Back in 1995, Pew reported that just one in ten adults (ages 18 and older) in the United States were online. At the present, that number has increased dramatically to approximately eight in ten. About four in ten adults do not use high speed connections at home or do not use mobile connections. Variables related to the use of the Internet include socioeconomic factors such as education and household income, English proficiency, and disability.[35]

According to Pew, about 95 percent of U.S. teens go online.[36] In comparison to adults, teens today are much more likely to network via texting. For their entire lives, they have lived in a world where they could converse anywhere with anyone at any time. And like the preceding generation, Millennials (or Generation Y), they have very little tolerance for being digitally disconnected. Texting for these digital natives is part of their daily life and is the preferred application for communicating. The average teen in the United States, according to Pew, sends and receives about sixty texts each day. Not only is texting simple, but it allows teens to converse in private. Interestingly, the vast majority of teens report that they take their phones to bed with them so they can check messages and status updates throughout the night.[37]

When it comes to online social networking, diversity exists within and between generations. For example, young people are not exposed to video games and social networking sites to the same degree. Some youth have virtually no skills or interest in this area, and may have no computers. The stereotypical image of a young, digitally connected generation glosses over the influence of various dimensions of diversity such as wealth, knowledge and skills, education, interests, nationality, and language. Older age cohorts are diverse as well, with online social networking growing dramatically among older generations. As an example, close to one in two individuals 65 years of age and older now use Facebook at least weekly.[38] Data from Pew reveals the average age of SNS users has gradually risen in recent years.[39]

Gender

As with other divides, gender differences are in a state of flux. Whether we conclude that a gender digital divide exists in the United States depends on the data we examine and how we define access. Data from Pew show that the rate of Internet use among adults, both male and female, has increased significantly since 2000.[40] In recent years, more women than men are using social networking sites and are more active in their use of these sites.[41] Use of specific SNSs shows trends that vary by gender as well. For example, women increasingly gravitate to Pinterest, while men trend toward LinkedIn. Data from Nielsen indicates gender differences in online activities. One recent study shows that women are more apt to build or update a personal blog and have a social networking profile.[42]

In spite of the frequent use of the Internet and SNSs by women, researchers and educators point to a different kind of gender divide. Joel Cooper examined numerous studies dealing with whether women are at a disadvantage in terms of learning about computers. His findings suggest that women of all ages continue to deal with gender stereotypes and life experiences that result in computer anxiety. This in turn negatively impacts their computer attitudes and performance. Other trends show that women continue to take fewer technology courses at the high school level and are less apt to graduate from college with a degree in IT fields.[43] These issues may have a profound effect on the nature of women's online activities and their willingness to expand and diversify their social networks.

Race/Ethnicity

Owning a computer and having access to the Internet on a regular basis varies according to race and ethnicity. However, many minorities with unequal access in the past are now going online using smartphones. Significant differences in the Internet access gap continue to exist among non-English speakers in the United States, the White and non-White poor living in rural communities, and those living on Native American reservations.

Historically, Native American communities, and particularly those situated in remote areas of the United States, have encountered a stark digital divide. Their relative lack of information and communication technologies extend to even the most basic of services. To illustrate, 32 percent of this population lack basic telephone service, while 90 percent lack access to high-speed Internet. This gap has put many Native Americans at a disadvantage with regard to employment and educational opportunities, online social networking, language preservation, quality health care, and personal safety.[44]

Another dimension of the digital divide is being seen among Latinos. While lower-income Latinos are less likely to use the Internet, usage by Latinos in families earning $40,000 or more each year is comparable to African-Americans and Whites with similar incomes.[45] Among Latinos, there is also a noticeable divide between native and foreign born. For example, U.S.-born Latinos ages 16 and older are more likely than foreign-born Latinos to go online and use a cell phone. Use of cell phones by Latinos ages 16 and older is also linked to English proficiency; those who are "English dominant" show a greater tendency to use cell phones than those identified as bilingual and those who communicate primarily in Spanish.[46]

As alluded to earlier, Latinos and African-Americans are more likely to access the Internet using smartphones, while Whites are more likely to access the Internet via computers. This has narrowed the racial and ethnic digital divides that have been of concern to educators and policymakers alike. However, more dependency on mobile Internet access may be creating a new divide of sorts. Aaron Smith, a senior research specialist at Pew, says, "There are obvious limitations on what you can do on a mobile device—updating a resume being the classic example."[47]

Social Class

Thinking Through Diversity

In what ways does your social class affect your use of social media?

According to Pew studies, income continues to be a major factor in determining who goes online. A low household income (less than $20,000 per year) and low educational attainment (lacking a high school education) are amongst the strongest predictors for not using the Internet.[48] Because of social class differences, two people may have Internet access but unequal opportunity. As Howard Jenkins states, "What a person can accomplish with an outdated machine in a public library with mandatory filtering software and no opportunity for storage or transmission pales in comparison to what [a] person can accomplish with a home computer with unfettered Internet access, high bandwidth, and continuous connectivity."[49]

Jen Schradie, in her study, *The Digital Production Gap: The Digital Divide and Web 2.0 Collide*, extends the analysis of the digital divide beyond Internet access. She distinguishes between those who produce and consume information. Findings from her analysis of Pew data show that people with lower incomes and less education are less apt to produce online content. Individuals' wealth, educational attainment, time available to work online, and digital literacy, when combined with their access both at work and home, are all factors which may contribute to this divide and in turn, the opportunity to network online.

Disability

Recent statistics from Pew indicate that adults with disabilities continue to be much less likely to go online than adults who do not report having a disability. A number of factors contribute to this vast divide in the United States. As a whole, adults with disabilities tend to have low incomes and high unemployment rates. Their lack of economic resources, coupled with employment discrimination, make it much more difficult for this population to access online content and get Internet access at home. It is worth noting that only a very small percentage of adults with disabilities report that their disability "makes it harder or impossible for them to use the Internet."[50]

People with disabilities, including those with conditions that are physical, mental, and emotional in nature, pay a heavy price for this divide. Someone with a visual impairment or learning disability may find it difficult or impossible to read text online. Similarly, accessibility for individuals with hearing issues may depend on whether closed-captioning or audio content is available. Alexandra Enders, a senior policy analyst, compares lack of accessibility to language barriers. She says, "If you don't read Russian and all the sites are in Russian, you may be able to get to them, but they won't make sense to you."[51] By gaining access, in all its forms, people with disabilities can live fuller lives, expand their social networks, decrease their sense of isolation, and increase their independence. They can shop online, research medical and health issues, take online courses, increase their employability, tele-study and tele-work, and stay connected with family, friends, and acquaintances. As one individual with spinal muscular atrophy says, "My body may be confined mostly to one point in physical space, but my mind looks forward to its weekends in cyberspace."[52]

A Profile in Diversity Consciousness

Shashi Bellamkonda is a humble, tireless, and warm social networker. As the Senior Director of Social Media at Web.com, he helps small businesses reap the benefits of social media. Besides having thousands of followers on Twitter, he is also active on Facebook and LinkedIn. Moreover, he is a consummate face-to-face networker, going out of his way to meet new people and help them in any way he can. As he says, "Be a giver and you will automatically receive."[53] Shashi views networking as a powerful opportunity to help others. But it requires thought, a strategy, and diversity consciousness. Networking takes time. Whether he is walking into a room full of people or doing it virtually by posting and engaging thousands, Shashi believes in establishing clear objectives and understanding the social context of networking. This insight, which enables him to use his time wisely and efficiently, is rooted in his humble beginnings, growing up in India.

Some of the earliest lessons he learned had to do with the power of technology and the importance of giving and sharing. One incident stands out in his mind. When his family got a new television, he heard the news from a neighbor as soon as he returned home after a day at school. Even though his family did not have Internet access at that time, news travelled at the speed of sound. To Shashi, if you have knowledge but you do not share it with people, then "it is gone forever." But if you share it, then it grows as you grow.

Since coming to the United States, Shashi keeps learning new skills. He is multilingual, fluent in five languages. In the midst of juggling multiple platforms, he makes sure to never have lunch alone, meaning he *always* looks for opportunities to converse with people. Why? Because he firmly believes that he is going to learn something from having lunch with another person, who is likely in a different field and brings a different and fresh perspective to the table. Once he leaves lunch, Shashi looks back at that small but significant example of networking and realizes how much he has grown from this experience.[54]

Global Digital Divides

The **global digital divide** refers to the unequal access to information and communication resources among more and less developed regions and nations of the world. As an example, wealthier, more developed nations generally have more resources to develop an infrastructure that results in far-reaching societal changes, such as efficient communications, Internet use and broadband access, extensive and diverse social networks, and online education. Conversely, people in developing countries are apt to find it much more difficult to capitalize on the information age due to a lack of economic, political, social, and educational resources. Also, political, cultural, and geographical barriers compound the problem of disseminating technological tools and information.

A number of variables interrelate to explain the global digital divide. This is the focus of **intersection theory,** the analysis of different dimensions of diversity such as race, gender, age, and social class, which account for multiple, interlocking dimensions of socioeconomic inequality. For instance, in societies throughout the world, women have lagged behind men in terms of access to communications technologies. This gap is tied to women's disadvantaged status, and in turn to **gender stratification,** the unequal distribution of economic, social, and political resources among men and women.

Analysis of data sets from 25 African and Latin American countries shows that women are not at a disadvantage because they are technophobic or refuse to embrace digital tools. Rather, global inequalities in employment, health services, education, and income come between women and their use of information and communication technologies. When researchers control for these variables, women in these countries are actually more inclined than men to make use of digital tools.[55]

Photo 6.1 "Info Ladies."
Source: AP IMAGES, rights as per NAPA.

Bicycling "Info Ladies"

Thanks to the Info Ladies, people in remote areas of Bangladesh now have access to the Internet (see Photo 6.1). Due to this program, tens of thousands of people and particularly women can chat with loved ones far away, discuss issues such as child marriage and the sexual abuse of girls with other members of their network, and qualify for government services. For example, one woman shares how her one hour of Skype time allows her to chat with her spouse who is working in Saudi Arabia. D.Net, a local government group, created this program a few years ago. Once Info Ladies are trained to use computers, the Internet, and cameras, they bike into rural villages where connections are extremely rare. In addition to providing laptops and Internet connections to local citizens, Info Ladies provide a wide range of social services, leading community discussions about social problems and health issues, and assisting students with online college applications. With government support, the program seeks to expand its reach by training as many as 15,000 Info Ladies by 2016.[56]

Online Microaggressions

> Back when I was in high school I was very soft spoken. I didn't speak very much on anything, but on Facebook I could talk up a storm. It was my platform, it was my voice for speaking up to someone that I didn't say anything to in person. But on the other hand, my mouth got really reckless. Facebook gave me the courage to face the ones who constantly bothered me, but it wasn't good courage. With Facebook I was a bully through the computer, but was petrified facing them in real life.
>
> —Another perspective

Microaggressions, daily insults or indignities that demean and stigmatize people who are perceived as different, can migrate from real life to virtual life. And the effect of online microaggressions mirrors what takes place offline. With regard to social networking, microaggressions make it difficult to retain, expand, and nourish valuable ties.

Lisa Nakamura, in her book *Cybertypes*, argues that the Internet is not some raceless utopia. As an example, Nakamura points to pull-down menus with racial classifications. These lists mirror the racial categories that we have socially constructed offline.[57] Those microaggressions that promote anger and alienation in public and private settings also appear online. Examples include offensive displays of nooses and naked pictures, conversations on SNSs that belittle conservative Christians, or teens using language in a text that disparages gays.

Microaggressions that ignore someone's identity can be found on the Internet in various mediums, including text, art, photography, and multimedia. In an online health and fitness class, one student remembers reading about a list of stressors for teens. The list included, "increasing attraction to the opposite sex." As a gay student, this individual felt ignored and invisible. Exclusive language can also be found on online forms and applications. Invariably, the default choice for gender is male.

It is not unusual to find racist microaggressions on YouTube, both in videos and in the comments of the people who respond to them. According to a study by *The Journal of New Media and Culture*, racist messages are commonplace in social media, including Facebook. Facebook photos and pages portray Barack Obama as a monkey, thug, or some other evil or deviant stereotype. His wife, Michelle Obama, has also been the target of microaggressions, including pictures that show her as an angry Black lady with manly features. Comments on Facebook that appear on the "I Hate Obama" page include the N-word, "Frobama," and ". . . he looks like a monkey with large ears." These comments are followed by numerous "likes." Although Facebook prohibits messages of hate, users use their creativity to skirt this policy.[58]

Microinsults, Microassaults, and Microinvalidations

Many individuals use Web forums to comment on diversity issues. Because of their anonymity, these forums allow users to respond openly and honestly. Hence, this type of online forum provides an opportunity to examine types of microaggressions. For these reasons, one recent study examined data from ten blogs. Contributors to these blogs commented on the discontinuation of Chief Illiniwek, the racialized mascot of the University of Illinois. In their analysis of blog data, the study's authors grouped microaggressions into three categories identified in existing literature.[59]

1. **Microinsults,** those subtle, hidden messages that convey stereotypes and demean diversity, were apparent in this study. Some microinsults expressed the viewpoint that Native Americans should blend into White American society. One blogger commented, "It's

high time the Indians assimilate into American life completely."[60] Other microinsults found in the blogs stereotype Native Americans as too emotional and overly sensitive, alleging that their concerns are trivial and they should just "get over it."

2. **Microassaults,** messages that are overt and intentional with the intent to harm the victim, took the form of name-calling and attacks on Native American identities. One contributor, who illustrates this type of microaggression, comments, ". . . Damn the Natives. Don't they just love the fact that white, black, and brown can get a good hoot and holler at the 'injun' everytime Illinois scores [a touchdown]?"[61]

3. Findings from this research also reveal **microinvalidations,** messages that exclude or deny people's feelings, perspectives, or realities. Some posts completely dismissed the idea that Chief Illiniwek was derogatory or racist in any way. Rather, these people saw the mascot as functional and one of the best in the country, fostering campus unity and promoting respect for Native Americans.

Cyberbullying

A relatively new form of microaggression is **cyberbullying,** the use of the Internet, cell phones, or other electronic devices to send messages or post images with the intent to hurt, embarrass, or harass someone. Unlike traditional bullying, cyberbullying is anonymous and can take place anywhere and anytime. Online technologies make it possible for a large number of people to bully an individual via chat rooms, blogs, text messages, and websites. Whereas targets of traditional bullying can retreat to their homes, cyberbullying offers no such refuge. Since cyberbullies can operate anonymously, they are rarely caught or punished. Unfortunately, cyberbullying is growing more common among youth and adults alike. In some cases, it is an outgrowth of traditional bullying. Cyberbullying may have serious psychological, physical, and social consequences for the victim, such as lower self-esteem, emotional trauma, distrust of people, and even suicide.

Cyberbullying garnered considerable public attention following the suicide of Tyler Clementi, an 18-year-old freshman at Rutgers University. Clementi jumped off New York's George Washington Bridge once he discovered that his roommate, Dharun Ravi, had secretly filmed him kissing another man and then posted the video online. The judge who sentenced Ravi to 30 days in jail stated that he did not think Ravi hated Clementi. However, the judge thought Ravi was guilty of what he termed "colossal insensitivity."[62] This tragic example of an online microaggression illustrates the relationship between bullying and an imbalance of power. In this case, power was not a matter of brute strength or physical violence; rather, it had to do with differences in the social identity of young adults. Sexual orientation as well as age, race, gender, disability, and religion are all examples of social identity statuses that confer power on some and enable these individuals to exploit others.

Data from the National Crime Prevention Council (NCPC) indicate that cyberbullying directed at children in the United States is not uncommon. NCPC statistics show that nearly half of teens in the United States report being targets of cyberbullying. A majority of these teens felt that most cyberbullies "probably didn't see the action as a big deal." Moreover, a majority said parents should be less concerned about regulating what their children see on television, and more concerned about what they view online.[63]

Children on the autism spectrum are particularly prone to cyberbullying. There are a number of reasons for this. Many children with autism spend a great deal of time online, often connecting with people like themselves on Facebook, Twitter, and other sites. Given the challenges posed by face-to-face interaction, they may find online relationships to be more satisfying and less stressful. However, children such as these may be vulnerable to cyberbullying because some are not able to discern what is appropriate and who is trustworthy in the course of networking.

Default Whiteness

While the Internet frees us to take on different identities, it does not level the playing field. Differences in power and privilege pervade cyberspace and influence the way we network online. Consider **default whiteness,** the tendency to view White people's behaviors, values, and perspectives as the norm for all people. Consequently, all other racial groups are measured by the degree to which they conform to the White "yardstick." If we live in a society where White standards of beauty, intelligence, and ethics are considered normal, then this type of thinking may very well influence the way we view ourselves and network with others.

Consider how the following scenario could qualify as an online microaggression. When I say the name Heather, what image comes to your mind? A woman named Heather recounts her experiences in a blog, explaining that other members of her online social network assume she is White simply because of her name. Similarly, a Korean-American woman, who communicates with thousands of users in a chat room, shares her frustrations. "I never outright . . . said I was Asian, because I felt that IRL [in real life] people already have stereotypes and felt that it would be at least as bad here . . . But then it bugs me that people just assume you're White if you don't say otherwise."[64]

When people misjudge our identity, racial or otherwise, and make invalid assumptions about us, it is often demeaning and disheartening. In the case of default whiteness, a person's whiteness, goodness, and normalcy may become almost synonymous online. Whiteness can be difficult to see, especially for those of us who, because of our racial identity, do not feel different and excluded. Typically, default whiteness is much more visible to people who are not White.

Impact of Online Microaggressions

Even though social networking brings people of diverse backgrounds together and builds community, it also heightens the potential for cultural misunderstandings, divisiveness, and distrust. As more and more networking takes place online, microaggressions directed at people who seem different have become increasingly problematic. Unfortunately, diversity training and other efforts to combat microaggressions have focused on more blatant, face-to-face acts of bias that are behavioral or verbal.

Online microaggressions tend to be seen as trivial, harmless, and sporadic; but clearly they are not. While the intent behind an online microaggression may be fleeting and difficult to discern, the impact can be widespread and long-lasting. For example, an innocent, ignorant racist or sexist tweet can gain a much wider audience once it circulates around the Internet. Given the nature of the medium, the message is preserved regardless of the circumstances that gave rise to such a message.

> "The axe forgets, but the tree remembers."
> —African proverb

If we are the target, microaggressions can affect us in a number of ways. They can lower our self-esteem, promote anxiety and depression, and make it more difficult for us to focus on a task, be productive, and collaborate with others. If we regularly experience microaggressions where we work or attend school, we may disengage to some degree, wrestle with feelings of insecurity, and even opt to leave an environment that seems hostile and exclusive.[65] On the other hand, if we are seen as perpetrators of microaggressions, it may be very difficult for us to multiply and strengthen our connections, communicate effectively, lead, and earn people's trust when we participate in online social networks.

Coping Strategies

Coping strategies involve acknowledging, recognizing, and interrupting microaggressions, as well as dealing with their impact over time. It is important to keep in mind that each one of us has been both a target and a perpetrator of microaggressions.

Because we tend to see ourselves in a positive light, we may find it difficult to acknowledge our role in demeaning others. Regardless of the situation, our ability to respond effectively will hinge to a great degree on the support and advice we receive from our online social networks, as well as our diversity skills in the areas of self-evaluation, communication, leadership, and conflict management.

> Social networking makes communication intertwined with conflict unpredictable and harder to control. When getting into conflict with friends, you have to wonder if they will slander you online, post pictures of you, or create rumors. Your many roles as a coworker, friend, family member, and so forth converge online, so a rumor or online argument won't just affect how friends view you but generally your whole image.
>
> —Another perspective

Responding effectively requires us to be aware of different forms of microaggressions, and how they can operate both online and offline. This is especially important given the subtlety of many microaggressions. Constantly shifting perspectives helps us to be more mindful of context. People and sites present information from different viewpoints.

Findings from an Associated Press-MTV poll show that more than half of the 14- to 24-year-olds surveyed did not find the word "retard" even moderately bothersome.[66] How many of these young people consider the potential impact of this hurtful word? With regard to online microaggressions, understanding the difference between intent and impact helps us cope. For example, texting, "I don't think of you as Latino" might be intended as a compliment, but it might very well come across as a slight. To some, the hidden message is that one's identity as a Latino is negative and therefore should be hidden or minimized. Or an individual might create an avatar in order to be humorous, but the impact is offensive, at least to certain individuals. Sometimes, online networking makes it extremely difficult to discern context or whether a microaggression has actually taken place. Perhaps this helps explain why one common response to microaggressions is silence.

Online social networking enables us to address microaggressions. Instead of ignoring a microaggression or simply remaining silent, we have the opportunity to interrupt and respond appropriately. Even if we are networking online, finding time to collect our thoughts and gain control of our emotions before we respond is always a good idea. Instead of simply becoming angry or disengaging, we can seek advice and establish a dialogue with other members of our social network.

Findings from a survey of international graduate students reveal a variety of coping strategies in the face of racial microaggressions. Students' responses range from looking for support from an existing network to a strategy the researcher describes as *forbearance*, that is, relying on oneself to overcome the problem. For students in this study, opting to go it alone was more common.[67] As difficult as it is, it is important to seek social and emotional support when we encounter a microaggression online. Engaging others allows us to share, validate, and critique our view of the experience. Another valuable coping strategy is to reflect on what we think took place without trying to fix or blame, and acknowledge what others are sharing with us. All of these coping strategies help us to assess the microaggression from multiple perspectives and respond appropriately.

Thinking Through Diversity

Do your interactions with social networks and social media increase or decrease your diversity consciousness? Explain.

BENEFITS OF DIVERSE SOCIAL NETWORKS

Diverse social networks have numerous, substantive benefits. Among these are cross-cultural collaboration, diversity discussions, the wisdom of crowds, resource sharing, collective action and social change, and personal empowerment.

Cross-cultural Collaboration

Diverse social networks can and do play a critical role in building what Henry Jenkins of the Massachusetts Institute of Technology describes as our **collective intelligence,** "the ability to pool knowledge and compare notes with others toward a common goal."[68] In some cases, our diverse ties can function as **communities of practice,** networks of individuals who commit themselves to interact over time, brainstorming, teaching, and learning from each other in order to improve their ability to understand and deal with a common interest or problem. In *Cultivating Communities of Practice*, authors Wenger, McDermott, and Snyder expand on this concept.

1. Collaboration should be voluntary, ensuring more open and honest dialogue.

2. Multiple means of collaboration might include social media, teleconferences, Web sites and face-to-face interaction.

3. There needs to be a strong commitment by participants to maintain and nourish this collaborative process.[69]

When scientists at a number of biotechnology firms took it upon themselves to share scientific knowledge with scientists at other organizations, including universities, their collective intelligence rose measurably. According to research findings, this type of boundary-spanning networking opens up learning, freeing it from the insular, hierarchal structure of a single organization. Scientists found they became more flexible and knowledgeable in the course of learning and collaborating. Without this social network, their theories might have grown dated and become irrelevant.[70]

Communities of practice hold tremendous potential for communicating and collaborating across cultures. For instance, a community of practice using LinkedIn or any other social networking site can share best practices and develop skills that promote diversity consciousness. This type of ongoing international collaboration allows individuals to learn about each other's cultures and build their competencies as they diversify their networks across cultural, organizational, and societal boundaries.

Diversity Discussions

With diverse social networks, we have the *opportunity* to engage in meaningful discussions about a wide range of diversity issues. Discussions such as these, which require openness and honesty, may lend themselves to an online environment. For example, when the movie *The Hunger Games* came out, a number of fans tweeted their feelings about a Black actress assuming the role of Rue, a supporting actor. Prior to

Twitter: The World's Water Cooler

Twitter lends itself to cross-cultural communication since it is text on a screen. Therefore, body language as well as accents, tone, and other subtle ways of communicating are not as problematic when tweeting across cultures. Apps make it possible to tweet in other languages or translate other tweets. Therefore, we can follow a number of people on Twitter who diversify our network, communicate in a variety of languages, and help us see diversity issues from a more macro perspective. However, Twitter's 140-character limit makes it difficult to discuss and analyze complex cultural issues

Not long ago, Twitter was extensively used as a means to converse cross-culturally about the tragic killing of Trayvon Martin in Florida. Martin, a 17-year-old, unarmed African-American male was shot to death as he walked home after purchasing some candy from a convenience store. George Zimmerman, a neighborhood-watch coordinator, shot the young man even though local police reported Martin was not engaged in criminal activity. In the aftermath of Martin's killing, international discussions focused on profiling, the criminal justice system, and the history of racism in the United States. LeBron James, a superstar on the National Basketball Association's Miami Heat, joined the discussion by tweeting #WeAreTrayvonMartin #Hoodies #Stereotyped #WeWantJustice and a picture of the Miami Heat Players dressed in hoodies.[71] Many other individuals expressed their feelings as well (see Photo 6.2).

seeing the movie, these fans assumed this character was White. Later, they acknowledged caring less about her due to her darker skin tone. One fan commented, "Why does Rue have to be black?" "Not gonna lie, kind of ruined the movie."[72] Shortly after these tweets, a blogger began to assemble and then share them. What followed was an open, honest discussion about racism and default whiteness in Hollywood.

"Y? The National Forum on People's Differences" is one of the more innovative uses of technology to promote diversity discussions. This forum allows people to ask embarrassing, personal questions about our differences in a safe, anonymous setting on the Web. This low-tech site relies on simple text with questions typed in by users worldwide. Interestingly, most of the questions revolve around small everyday issues. Typical inquiries include: "Is there a way to tell the difference in Asian nationalities?", "Is it true that the direction the eyes slant is an indicator?", "Why do Jewish people eat matzos?", "Why is it that Caucasians seem to spend so much time on lawn care?", and "What would take place during a typical weeknight in a Black family?"[73] Questions like these illustrate just how much we don't know about each other and the critical need for honest dialogue.

Photo 6.2 Picture posted on Facebook in support of Trayvon Martin.

The Wisdom of Crowds

In the opening anecdote of his book, *The Wisdom of Crowds*, James Surowiecki describes a county fair he attended, at which fair-goers as well as cattle experts guessed the weight of an ox. The author was surprised to discover that the average of all of the individuals' guesses was closer to the ox's real weight than the estimates made separately by experts and most of the fair-goers. This anecdote points to what Surowiecki describes as the **wisdom of crowds,** the ability of a diverse group of individuals to come up with better choices as well as more innovative solutions than any one person or group of homogenous individuals. This holds true regardless of the latter's IQ or expertise. Surowiecki cites game shows as an example of the wisdom of crowds. When contestants are asked a question and then choose to poll the audience for the correct answer, the audience gets it right more than 90 percent of the time. In most situations, Surowiecki states it is better to have a wide range of views, even if there is disagreement and conflict.[74]

Surowiecke's thesis has implications for diverse social networks. In emphasizing the importance of diversity, he makes it clear that the wisdom of a crowd is due to their diversity and the fact that each person draws on his or her own knowledge and is not influenced by others' opinions. Likewise, when we network, especially online, we often expose ourselves to more diverse sources of information. Online, we may be less conscious of others and less intimidated by somebody's title or ability to communicate. Given our looser ties, we may feel more comfortable sharing our true thoughts and feelings, thereby capitalizing on the diversity of our social network.

Resource Sharing

Resources can take many forms, including invaluable information. In times of war, emergencies, and natural disasters, online networks may be the only or best means available to provide advice, comfort and support, and warnings of impending danger. People with whom we have strong and weak ties are valuable sources of information about medical issues, job prospects, leisurely activities, personal problems, and information we need to know. Rather than wait, answers to parenting questions are available at all hours of the day. For example, a young mother posts on Facebook that her toddler is having constant nightmares. Typically, a number of other parents will respond with suggestions based on what works for them. Several might even include links to relevant articles and websites.

Also, connections can provide access to community resources. As an example, many Sikhs living in the United States have developed a social network with the media, law enforcement, and local education and government agencies. Using these ties, they work to counter stereotypes of Sikhs as terrorists and provide authorities with information about incidents that violate the rights of Sikhs in airports, schools, and businesses. Recently, a Sikh advocacy group launched a free mobile app that makes it possible for travelers at airports to complain if they feel they have been profiled or discriminated against in any way. Complaints are reviewed by the Transportation Security Administration (TSA) and the Department of Homeland Security (DHS). The app, called "FlyRights" is a response to complaints from Sikhs that they are unfairly subjected to more rigorous inspections at airports. More reliable, better data on the frequency of such searches is one of the primary goals.

Creative ideas from a culturally heterogeneous social network constitute another valuable resource. According to Harvard Business School professor Roy Chua, creating a more diverse social network can stimulate new, better, and more novel approaches to decision-making. In his study of executives' professional networks, Chua found that diverse ties can improve performance in the workplace, but only if executives have certain key skills that come from diversity consciousness. These skills included self-awareness, knowledge about other cultures, and the motivation to continue to develop cross-cultural ties in spite of the inevitable challenges and frustrations. It is worth noting that Chua's study emphasizes that these skills help build trust, particularly affect-based trust, which he describes as trust from the heart as opposed to trust from the head. Without affect-based trust, anxiety and feelings of vulnerability make it difficult for executives to disclose new ideas and collaborate effectively.[75]

Collective Action and Social Change

In the past, technologies limited the scope of social networking. For example, individuals communicated by phone or fax. Broadcasting, such as via radio or television, made it possible to reach large numbers of people; however, these technologies facilitated one-way communication. Nowadays, with the Internet, individuals have the power to network and leverage the power of large numbers of people to educate, engage, agitate, and promote social change.

Beginning in 2010, citizens in countries such as Egypt and Syria have used social networks as a tool to organize, gather support, and bring attention to their plight. These uprisings, which spread across the Arab world, galvanized the world's attention and, in a number of cases led to the overthrow of dictators. And because they relied on social networks such as Facebook, Twitter, and LinkedIn, anyone could join these protests and make themselves heard around the world. Unlike traditional media, which is more centralized, these voices were much more difficult to censor or explain away.

The Occupy Movement used social networks to connect individuals and organize protest activities. Its global reach made it possible for the movement to spread beyond New York, through the United States and internationally. For example, police in California pepper-sprayed Occupy Movement protestors. Even though no mainstream media was at the scene, the whole incident was recorded by onlookers, who relied on social networks such as Facebook, Twitter, and YouTube to get their message out to the community, the nation, and the world. Social media protestors could join in and support the Occupy Movement, even if they did not have the time and the resources to join protests in person.

Rather than rely on those in power to provide information and direction, social networking makes it possible to self-organize and access information from any and all sources. However, with so many people participating and communicating in diverse social networks, misinformation can be a problem. Rumors can quickly spread and gain legitimacy, influencing decision-making. Furthermore, digital divides come into play, both locally and globally. Some voices are less likely to be heard; such as those with no Internet access, the homeless, oppressed minorities, and individuals who lack digital skills. And in some countries, censorship of social media, manipulation of Internet content, and repression of Internet users have made it extremely difficult for movement organizers, bloggers, activists, and ordinary citizens to freely share their concerns and push for change.[76]

Personal Empowerment

Each year, *Time* magazine chooses its "Person of the Year." Usually, it is a well-known individual, a mover and shaker who for better or worse, changes the course of history. Not too long ago, *"You"* were chosen for this distinction. Why you? According to *Time* magazine editor, Lev Grossman, "It's about the many wresting power from the few and helping one another for nothing and how that will not only change the world, but also change the way the world changes."[77] As individuals, we control the information age and empower ourselves and others through the content we generate and the connections we make.

Digital citizenship is a vital skill in the twenty-first century. With that said, it is important to remember that we are all works in progress. As we change, grow, and adapt, our ability to network effectively can help us thrive in uncertain and exciting times. Recently, the business world introduced the term **Generation Flux** to refer to those individuals who embrace uncertainty, question conventional assumptions, and understand that their skill set is constantly evolving. Unlike Boomers, Millennials, and Generation X, Generation Flux is not defined by its age; rather, it is defined by a mind-set that capitalizes on constant changes in the larger society. Having diverse networks enables us to grow and thrive in all kinds of situations. Only by constantly recognizing, understanding, and expanding our relationships with diverse individuals and communities can we adapt our thinking and empower ourselves as the world around us changes.

To conclude, social networking is a critical life skill that will only grow more important in the years to come. When we combine this skill with diversity consciousness, it connects us with people of different statuses, cultural backgrounds, perspectives, and life experiences. As this skill set evolves over time, we learn to initiate, diversify, and nourish our connections, and we educate ourselves and grow in the process. By being conscious of diversity, we are able to increase the viability of our network and treat everyone with dignity, empathy, and respect as we negotiate and learn from local and global communities.

 ## Case Studies

Case Study One

Ligua, an immigrant from El Salvador, works as a car salesperson. She is also a part-time student, wife, and mother. In her classes at the local community college, Ligua finds herself in the company of students who seem to be more financially comfortable than her. Many of them have iPhones and 24-hour access to new or relatively new laptop computers at home. Ligua has only a mobile device on which to make calls, and she shares an old desktop computer with her husband and three children. She also does not feel as comfortable with technology as many of her classmates. Her skills are pretty basic—she can surf the Internet, create Microsoft Word documents, and communicate on her mobile.

Ligua feels like she is on the wrong side of the digital divide. She constantly worries about computer viruses and being victimized in other ways. Once, she had to hire a service to fix her computer, and the cost was significant; yet she had no idea if she was being overcharged.

Questions:

1. Ligua's long-term goal is to be a math teacher. As she continues with her education, she feels increasingly confident that she can teach math on the high school level. However, she feels that unless she significantly improves her online networking skills, she will be operating at a disadvantage once she graduates from college and looks for employment. Do you agree? Why?

2. Given her financial situation at the present, what might she do to improve her skills and confidence in online social networking?

Case Study Two

Mary is a White social work student who plans to go on for a MS degree and work in a clinical setting. She attends an urban university and enjoys the diversity and energy of city life, but in her free time is actively involved in social activities centered around her Scottish background. Mary and some of her coworkers have posted pictures online of themselves drinking and partying. In addition, Mary's profile reveals deeply personal information, such as her sexual orientation (bisexual), and where she sometimes goes for drinks after work. Recently, one of Mary's friends, who is also a social worker, commented on Mary's Facebook page, "I work in the most 'ghetto hospital' I know." Her friend has made it clear that these postings are intended for people they know and trust, people to whom they have granted access.

Recently, Mary did a search on Facebook to find a client of hers who had stopped coming to see her for their bi-weekly sessions. When Mary shared that she had done this because she was concerned, the patient was upset. She felt that Mary had crossed the boundary between patient and social worker.

Questions:

1. As Mary has grown older, she has heard "horror stories" about disclosing too much on certain social media sites. Should Mary concern herself with privacy issues and the potential consequences of her social networking?

2. What, if anything, would you recommend to Mary and her coworker?

3. Do you feel that Mary's behavior, in which she searched one of her clients on Facebook, was unethical? Why?

Case Study Three

Michael is a Black college graduate and the divorced father of a teenage son, Aaron. His son attends a private school in the well-to-do suburb where they live. Aaron has become enthralled with his smartphone. In fact, it seems like he never turns it off. As Michael sees it, his son's use of technology has become a problem in that it is interfering with his school work, his chores around the home, and the quality time they used to spend together over dinner and on weekends. Recently, Michael read about a condition the author calls **nomophobia,** the fear of losing contact with one's phone. Michael is not sure that his son is nomophobic, but he is deeply concerned. But he wonders if he is overreacting; perhaps this is simply a "generational thing."

Questions:

1. Are Michael's fears warranted?

2. Is there anything Michael might do to address his son's behavior? Explain.

 # Key Terms

Social networking	Old boy networks	Online identity
Nodes	Strong ties	management
Ties	Weak ties	Linchpins
Multiplex tie	Degree	Occupational prestige
Social media	Sociocultural evolution	Social capital
Blogs	Digital natives	Guanxi
Wikis	Digital immigrants	Bridging
Discussion boards	Internet penetration rate	Bonding
Social context	Impression management	Echo chamber

Homophily	Intersection theory	Default whiteness
Status homophily	Gender stratification	Collective intelligence
Value homophily	Microaggressions	Communities
Identity tourism	Microinsults	of practice
Passing	Microassaults	Wisdom of crowds
Avatar	Microinvalidations	Generation Flux
Digital divide	Cyberbullying	Nomophobia
Global digital divide		

 # Exercises

Exercise 1: **Network Analysis**

Examine one of your social networks (face to face or online).

1. Create a chart that illustrates the diversity of your network. Include at least ten dimensions of diversity, such as social class, race, age, personality type, job function, and so on.

2. In what ways is you network diverse? In what ways does it lack diversity? Explain.

3. Are the ties in this network of yours primarily strong or weak? Explain.

4. What interpersonal resources, or social capital, do you derive from this network?

5. How might you enhance the diversity of your network?

Exercise 2: **Your Use of Social Media**

Over a period of 24 hours, take a critical, in-depth look at your use of social media.

1. Using a log, record your social media interactions. Specifically, notate 1) what you did, such as texting, posting a photo on Facebook, "liking" a comment, tweeting; 2) where you were when you did it, such as home, work, school, the mall; 3) how long this interaction took place; 4) the topic; and 5) your feelings about the interaction.

2. Examine your log during this time. How does your use of social media reflect on you, your priorities, and your diversity consciousness? Explain.

 # Notes

[1] Right Management Manpower Group, "Most Expect to Get New Job by Networking." Online, January 22, 2013. Available: http://www.right.com/news-and-events/press-releases/2013-press-releases/item24727.aspx.

[2] Keith Hampton, Lauren Sessions Goulet, Lee Rainie, and Kristen Purcell, "Social Networking Sites and Our Lives," Pew Internet. Online June 16, 2011. Available: http://pewinternet.org/Reports/2011/Technology-and-social-networks.aspx.

[3] Yvonne Benschop, "The Micro-Politics of Gendering in Networking," *Gender, Work, and Organization,* 16(2): 217–237, 2009.

[4] Anne-Ryan Heatwole and Katrin Verclas, "Women and Mobile: Is It Really a Global Opportunity?" Online, Mar. 8, 2010. Available: http://mobileactive.org/women-and-mobile-it-really-global-opportunity.

[5] Mark Granovetter, "The Strength of Weak Ties: A Network Theory Revisited," *Sociological Theory* 1 (1983): 201–233.

[6] Marc Prensky, "Digital Natives, Digital Immigrants." Online, 2001. Available: http://www.marcprensky.com/writing/Prensky%20-%20Digital%20Natives,%20Digital%20Immigrants%20-%20Part1.pdf.

[7] Common Sense Media, "Social Media, Social Life: How Teens View Their Digital Lives." Online, June 26, 2012. Available: http://www.commonsensemedia.org/research/social-media-social-life/key-finding-2%3A-teens-more-likely-to-report-positive-impact--.

[8] International Center for Media and the Public Agenda (ICMPA) and the Salzburg Academy on Media and Global Change, "Going 24 Hours Without Media." Available: oneworldunplugged.wordpress.com (accessed October 18, 2012).

[9] "Internet World Stats: Usage and Population Statistics." Available: http://www.internetworldstats.com/stats.htm (accessed June 17, 2013).

[10] "Internet World Statistics." Online, June 30, 2012. Available: http://www.internetworldstats.com/stats.htm. For up-to-date information on Internet usage throughout the world, see www.internetworldstats.com.

[11] "Internet World Stats: Usage and Population Statistics." Available: http://www.internetworldstats.com/stats7.htm (accessed June 17, 2013).

[12] Ed Keller and Brad Fay, *The Face-to-Face Book: Why Real Relationships Rule in a Digital Marketplace* (New York: Free Press, 2012).

[13] Robert Putnam, "E Pluribus Unum: Diversity and Community in the Twenty-first Century," *Scandanavian Political Studies*, Vol. 30, No. 2, 2007.

[14] Cristian Lupsa, "Do You Need a Web Publicist?" *The Christian Science Monitor*, November 29, 2006. Available: http://www.washingtonpost.com/wp-dyn/content/article/2007/03/06/AR2007030602705.html (accessed September 11, 2012).

[15] Reid Hoffman, and Ben Casnocha, *The Start-up of You* (New York: Crown Business, 2012).

[16] Pew Research Center's Internet and American Life Project, "Social Networking Sites and Our Lives: Summary of Findings." Available: http://pewinternet.org/Reports/2011/Technology-and-social-networks/Summary.aspx (accessed September 13, 2012).

[17] "World Map of Social Networks." Online January, 16, 2012. Available: themoscownews.com/infographics/20120116/189372325.htm/.

[18] Y. Kim, D. Sohn, and S. Choi, "Cultural Differences in Motivations for Using Social Network Sites: A Comparative Study of American and Korean College Students," *Computers in Human Behavior*, 27(1), 365–372, 2011.

[19] George S. Ford and Sherry Ford, "Internet Use and Depression Among the Elderly," October 15, 2009, Phoenix Center for Advanced Legal and Economic Public Policy Paper No. 38. Available: http://dx.doi.org/10.2139/ssrn.1494430.

[20] Rick Nauert, "Social Networking for Jobs May Add to Income Inequality." Online, July 25, 2012. Available: http://psychcentral.com/news/2012/07/25/social-networking-for-jobs-may-add-to-income-inequality/42207.html.

[21] Deirdre Royster, *Race and the Invisible Hand* (Berkeley, CA: University of California Press, 2003).

[22] DiversityInc., "Mentoring Case Studies – Diversity Best Practices." Available: http://diversityincbestpractices.com/mentoring/mentoring-case-studies/ (accessed September 19, 2012).

[23] Barack Obama, *Dreams from My Father* (New York: Three Rivers Press, 2004), 171–172.

[24] William Powers, *Hamlet's Blackberry* (New York: Harper, 2010).

[25] John Horrigan, "TIG Solutions." Available: tigsolutions.com (accessed September 11, 2012).

[26] N. Lin and B. Erickson, *Social Capital: An International Research Program* (New York: Oxford, 2008).

[27] Keith Hampton, Lauren Goulet, Lee Rainie, and Kristen Purcell, *Social Networking Sites and Our Lives* (Washington, DC: Pew Research Center, 2011).

[28] Yvonne Benschop, "The Micro-Politics of Gendering in Networking," *Gender, Work, and Organization*, 16(2): 217–237, 2009.

[29] M. McPherson, L. Smith-Lovin, and J. M. Cook, "Birds of a Feather: Homophily in Social Networks," *Annual Review of Sociology*, 27, 2001: 415–44. Available: http://arjournals.annualreviews.org/doi/abs/10.1146/annurev.soc.27.1.415.

[30] P. Lazarsfeld and R. K. Merton, "Friendship as a Social Process: A Substantive and Methodological Analysis," in *Freedom and Control in Modern Society*, Morroe Berger, Theodore Abel, and Charles Page, eds. (New York: Van Nostrand, 1954), 18–66.

[31] Keith Hampton, Lauren Sessions Goulet, Lee Rainie, and Kristen Purcell, "Social Networking Sites and Our Lives," Pew Internet. Online, June 16, 2011. Available: http://pewinternet.org/Reports/2011/Technology-and-social-networks.aspx.

[32] Lisa Nakamura, "Race In/For Cyberspace: Identity Tourism and Racial Passing on the Internet." Available: http://www.humanities.uci.edu/mposter/syllabi/readings/nakamura.html (accessed January 1, 2013).

[33] Shyong K. Lam and John Riedl, "Expressing My Inner Gnome: Appearance and Behavior in Virtual Worlds," *IEEE Computer*, July 2011.

[34] Kathryn Zickuhr and Aaron Smith, "Digital Differences," Pew Internet. Online, April 13, 2012. Available: http://pewinternet.org/Reports/2012/Digital-differences/Overview.aspx.

[35] Kathryn Zickuhr and Aaron Smith, "Digital Differences," Pew Internet and American Life Project. Online, April 13, 2012. Available: http://pewinternet.org/Reports/2012/Digital-differences/Main-Report/Internet-adoption-over-time.aspx.

[36] Kathryn Zickuhr and Aaron Smith, "Digital Differences," Pew Internet. Online, April 13, 2012. Available: http://www.pewinternet.org/Reports/2012/Digital-differences.aspx.

[37] Amanda Lenhart, Rich Ling, Scott Campbell, and Kristen Purcell, "Teens and Mobile Phones," Pew Internet and American Life Project. Online, April 20, 2010. Available: http://pewinternet.org/Reports/2010/Teens-and-Mobile-Phones/Chapter-3/Sleeping-with-the-phone-on-or-near-the-bed.aspx.

[38] Merkle Inc., "View from the Digital Inbox 2011. Available: http://www.jonrognerud.com/docs/Merkle_Digital_Inbox_2011.pdf (accessed September 11, 2012).

[39] Pew Research Center's Internet and American Life Project, "Social Networking Sites and Our Lives: Summary of Findings." Available: http://pewinternet.org/Reports/2011/Technology-and-social-networks/Summary.aspx (accessed September 13, 2012).

[40] Kathryn Zickuhr and Aaron Smith, "Digital Differences," Pew Internet and American Life Project. Online, April 13, 2012. Available: http://pewinternet.org/Reports/2012/Digital-differences/Main-Report/Internet-adoption-over-time.aspx.

[41] Joanna Brenner, "Pew Internet: Social Networking." Online, Sept. 17, 2012. Available: http://pewinternet.org/Commentary/2012/March/Pew-Internet-Social-Networking-full-detail.aspx.

[42] Megan Garber, "The Digital (Gender) Divide: Women Are More Likely Than Men to Have a Blog (and a Facebook Profile)." Online, April 27, 2012. Available: http://www.theatlantic.com/technology/archive/2012/04/the-digital-gender-divide-women-are-more-likely-than-men-to-have-a-blog-and-a-facebook-profile/256466/.

[43] Joel Cooper, "The Digital Divide: The Special Case of Gender," *Journal of Computer Assisted Learning*, Vol. 22, No. 5, 320–334, 2006.

[44] United States Department of Commerce, "Closing the Digital Divide for Native Nations and Communities." Online, April 12, 2011. Available: http://www.ntia.doc.gov/blog/2011/closing-digital-divide-focus-native-american-communities.

[45] *Washington Post*-Kaiser Family Foundation-Harvard University Poll, Cecilia Kang and Krissah Thompson, "Hispanics on Web Less Than Others," *The Washington Post*. Online Feb. 22, 2011. Available: http://www.washingtonpost.com/wp-dyn/content/article/2011/02/22/AR2011022207470.html.

[46] Gretchen Livingston, "The Latino Digital Divide: The Native Born versus The Foreign Born," Pew Hispanic Center. Online, July 28, 2010. Available: http://www.pewhispanic.org/2010/07/28/the-latino-digital-divide-the-native-born-versus-the-foreign-born/.

[47] Jesse Washington, "For Minorities, New Digital Divide Seen," *USA Today*. Online, Jan. 10, 2011. Available: www.usatoday.com/tech/news/2011-01-10-minorities-online_N.htm.

[48] Kathryn Zickuhr and Aaron Smith, "Digital Differences," Pew Internet and American Life Project. Online, April 13, 2012. Available: http://pewinternet.org/Reports/2012/Digital-differences/Main-Report/Internet-adoption-over-time.aspx.

[49] Howard Jenkins, with Katie Clinton, Ravi Purushotma, Alice Robison, and Margaret Weigel, "Confronting the Challenges of Participatory Culture: Media Education for the 21st Century," 2005. Available: http://digitallearning.macfound.org/atf/cf/%7B7E45C7E0-A3E0-4B89-AC9C-E807E1B0AE4E%7D/JENKINS_WHITE_PAPER.PDF (accessed September11, 2012).

[50] Pew Internet, "Digital Differences." Available: Pewinternet.org/Reports/2012/Digital-differences/Overview.aspx (accessed September 15, 2012).

[51] Wilson Rothman, "For the Disabled, Just Getting Online Is a Struggle," NBCNews.com TECH. Available: http://www.nbcnews.com/technology/technolog/disabled-just-getting-online-struggle-125501 (accessed September 29, 2012).

[52] Michael Murphy, "Social Networking and Disability," *Quest*. Online, March 31, 2011. Available: http://quest.mda.org/article/social-networking-and-disability.

[53] "You Have To Love People: The Shashi Bellamkonda Interview." Online, December 23, 2011. Available: http://www.firebellymarketing.com/2011/12/love-people-shashi-bellamkonda-interview.html.

[54] Shashi Bellamkonda – YouTube. Online, March 15, 2012. Available: http://www.youtube.com/watch?v=R-tLjMLIF58.

[55] Martin Hilbert, "Digital Gender Divide or Technologically Empowered Women in Developing Countries?" *Women's Studies International Forum*, 34(6), 479–489.

[56] Associated Press, "Bicycling 'Info Ladies' Bring Internet to Remote Bangladesh Villages," FoxNews.com. Online, November 2, 2012. Available: http://www.foxnews.com/world/2012/11/01/bicycling-info-ladies-bring-internet-to-remote-bangladesh-villages-where/.

[57] Lisa Nakamura. *Cybertypes: Race, Ethnicity, and Identity on the Internet* (New York: Routledge, 2002).

[58] Mia Moody, "New Media, Same Stereotypes: An Analysis of Social Media Depictions of President Barack Obama and Michelle Obama," *The Journal of New Media and Culture*, Volume 8, Issue 1, Summer, 2012.

[59] Derald Wing Sue, Christina M. Capodilupo, Gina C. Torino, Jennifer M. Bucceri, Aisha M. B. Holder, Kevin L. Nadal, and Marta Esquilin, "Racial Microaggressions in Everyday Life: Implications for Clinical Practice," *American Psychologist*, Vol. 62 No. 4, p. 271–286, May-Jun 2007.

[60] D. Anthony Clark, Lisa Spanierman, Tamilia Reed, Jason Soble, and Sharon Cabana, "Documenting Weblog Expressions of Racial Microaggressions That Target American Indians," *Journal of Diversity in Higher Education*, Vol. 4 (1), Mar. 2011, 39–50. Available: http://search.ebscohost.com/login.aspx?direct=true&db=pdh&AN=dhe-4-1-39&site=ehost-live, 5 of 13.

[61] *Ibid*.

[62] Associated Press, "Dharun Ravi Sentence in Rutgers Webcam Case Renews Hate Crime Law Debate, *The Washington Post*. Online, May 22, 2012. Available: washingtonpost.com/national/. . ./glQAuiODiU_print.html.

[63] National Crime Prevention Council, "Teens and Cyberbullying." Online, February 28, 2007. Available: http://www.ncpc.org/resources/files/pdf/bullying/Teens%20and%20Cyberbullying%20Research%20Study.pdf.

[64] Matthew Desmond and Mustafa Emirbayer, *Racial Domination, Racial Progress* (New York: McGraw Hill, 2010), 434.

[65] D. Anthony Clark, Lisa Spanierman, Tamilia Reed, Jason Soble, and Sharon Cabana, "Documenting Weblog Expressions of Racial Microaggressions That Target American Indians," *Journal of Diversity in Higher Education*, Vol. 4 (1), Mar. 2011, 39–50; S. A. Fryberg, H. R. Markus, D. Oyserman, and J. M. Stone, "Of Warrior Chiefs and Indian Princesses: The Psychological Consequences of American Indian Mascots," *Basic and Applied Social Psychology*, 30, 208–218, 2008.

[66] Connie Cass and Jennifer Agiesta, "Poll: Young People See Online Slurs as Just Joking." Online, September 20, 2011. Available: http://news.yahoo.com/poll-young-people-see-online-slurs-just-joking-070620137.html.

[67] Enedelia Sauceda, "Ethnic Identity, Perceptions of Racial Microaggressions, and Perceptions of University Environment as Predictors of Coping Among Latino(a) Graduate Students." Ph.D. Dissertation, Oklahoma State University, Stillwater Oklahoma, 2009.

[68] Henry Jenkins, with Katie Clinton, Ravi Purushotma, Alice Robison, and Margaret Weigel, *Confronting the Challenges of Participatory Culture: Media Education of the 21st Century* (Cambridge, MA: The MIT Press, 2009).

[69] E. Wenger, R. McDermott, and W. M. Snyder, *Cultivating Communities of Practice* (Boston: Harvard Business School Press, 2003).

[70] Julia Porter Liebeskind, Amalya Lumerman Oliver, Lynne Zucker, and Marilynn Brewer, "Social Networks, Learning, and Flexibility: Sourcing Scientific Knowledge in New Biotechnology Firms," *Organization Science*, Vol. 7, No. 4 (July-August, 1996), 428–443.

[71] Dan Devine, "LeBron James, Miami Heat Put Their Hoods Up to Show Support in Trayvon Martin Case," sports.yahoo.com. Online, March 23, 2012. Available: http://sports.yahoo.com/blogs/nba-ball-dont-lie/miami-heat-put-hoods-show-support-trayvon-martin-182102000.html.

[72] "*The Hunger Games* 'stomach-turning' racist tweet scandal," *The Week.* Online, March 29, 2012. Available: http://theweek.com/article/index/226225/the-hunger-games-stomach-turning-racist-tweet-scandal.

[73] Philip Milano and Larry Lane, *Why Do White People Smell Like Wet Dogs When They Come Out of the Rain?* (Orlando Park, FL: Y Forum, 1999), 2, 3.

[74] James Surowiecki, *The Wisdom of Crowds* (Harpswell, ME: Anchor Publishers, 2005).

[75] Roy Chua and Michael Morris. "Innovation Communication in Multicultural Networks: Deficits in Intercultural Capability and Affect-based Trust as Barriers to New Idea Sharing in Inter-Cultural Relationships," *Working Paper 09-130*, 2009, 1–20.

[76] Sanja Kelly and Sarah Cook. *Freedom on the Internet 2011* (Washington, DC: Freedom House, 2011).

[77] Reuters, "Time Magazine's 'Person of the Year' Is . . . You," NBCNews.com. Online, Dec. 17, 2006. Available: http://www.nbcnews.com/id/16242528/#.UU8la0xEJcY.

7

Teamwork

Learning Outcomes

Upon completion of this chapter, you will be able to:

- Explain the significance of teams today.
- Describe various methods for developing teamwork skills.
- Discuss the relationship between diversity consciousness and teaming.
- Analyze the proven strategies for building high-performance teams.
- Illustrate obstacles to teamwork.
- Define conflict.
- Elaborate on each of the six approaches to conflict management.

The scene: You are a surgeon in a hospital emergency room in a large city. A patient arrives by ambulance. He is a young child who appears to have a disability. The child's breathing is heavy and he has a fever of 104 degrees. Because he is so anxiety-ridden, he can hardly talk. He seems to be complaining about his stomach.

His parents, who are recent immigrants from Cambodia, are unable to say more than a few words in English. The doctor who is the resident in charge is a Filipino woman born in the United States in 1960. The anesthesiologist is multiracial and hearing impaired. In a few minutes, the radiologist will arrive: a Cuban-American who plans on retiring in a few months. Also present is the registered nurse, a 29-year-old of German and French descent, and a nursing assistant, a young Nigerian man who just completed his education. You and other members of this team must deal with this emergency.

MyStudentSuccessLab

MyStudentSuccessLab is an online solution designed to help you acquire and develop (or hone) the skills you need to succeed. You will have access to peer-led video presentations and develop core skills through interactive exercises and projects.

TEAMS TODAY

The multicultural setting just described requires people from vastly different backgrounds to work as a high-performing team in a pressure-packed situation. If each of these health professionals is not committed to the team and to the task at hand, their effectiveness as a group will be severely undermined. Additionally, each professional needs to be able to relate effectively to people who have different beliefs, communication styles, learning styles, educational levels, and cultural backgrounds. Situations like this, which require working together in the midst of diversity, are commonplace today.

Figure 7.1 illustrates a team with many different components, but one common goal. Each pit crew member has a specific job that requires speed, agility, strength, impeccable timing, and seamless cooperation. Their responsibilities include jacking up the race car, changing front and rear tires, and emptying a 90-pound gas can, all in the span of 12 to 13 seconds. In a close race, the pit crew can mean the difference between winning and losing.

Because diversity can interfere with unity, teams often fall short of their goals. An abundance of research on teamwork, cited throughout this chapter, points to diversity consciousness as a critical variable. Studies show that different perspectives, talents, and experiences make some teams stronger and others weaker. The difference often lies in the ability of team members to appreciate the value of their differences and take advantage of them. In spite of the growing prevalence of diverse teams in diverse settings, this skill is all too rare. Consequently, teamwork is one of the most important diversity skills we must learn, practice, and continue to develop.

Most people think of sports when teams are mentioned. However, athletics is only one of many areas in which you find teams. A **team** is simply a number of people who are involved in a cooperative effort. Each of us belongs to many teams. Sometimes we are put on teams and have no choice in the matter. At other times, we may join voluntarily or even create new teams. Your instructor might put you on a team in class. You may choose to form study groups or join support groups. Additionally, there are numerous teams in the workplace and in the community. These teams might focus on your responsibilities at work, recreational interests, and

Figure 7.1   Formula One racing car at pit stop surrounded by crew.

community activities. The key thing to remember is that you cannot avoid teams—they are part of everyday life.

However, there are instances when teams are not necessary or desirable. Some tasks lend themselves to individuals. It may not make sense to form a team if time is a concern and the task is clear-cut and relatively simple. However, many tasks in the workplace are too complex and too demanding for one person. Moreover, some jobs require more cooperation than others. The same is true of sports and other activities. A long-distance truck driver does not need to possess the same teaming skills as a police officer, an airline pilot, or a member of the pit crew mentioned earlier in the chapter.

When we find ourselves on teams, we tend to want to work with people who are similar to us. However, most teams are made up of individuals who are different in any number of ways. As stated repeatedly, diversity means more than differences in race and gender. When talking about teams in the workplace, the concept of diversity includes many other differences, such as age, personality, leadership style, job function, job position, and tenure. Your success on any job-related team will depend in part on your ability to relate to all kinds of people. As a team player, diversity consciousness will enable you to contribute more. You and your organization will reap the benefits.

Interest in teamwork has grown significantly in recent years. Organizations are becoming more team-oriented, flexible, and collaborative. Businesses are using teams to improve marketing, customer service, and productivity. Employees who formerly worked by themselves are now being organized into teams, and many work in multiple teams. The composition of these teams is also becoming more diverse. As businesses reorganize, restructure, and downsize, people increasingly find themselves on teams with others who differ markedly in terms of their employment and educational backgrounds. Because of demographic changes, cross-cultural work groups are becoming the norm rather than the exception.

Technology, outsourcing, and globalization are also altering the composition of teams. Technological advances are making it possible for teams to overcome geographic barriers in an instant. The ability to communicate clearly and quickly and to work together from anywhere in the world at any time provides teams with a distinct competitive advantage.

> One hand cannot applaud alone.
> —Arabian proverb

LEVERAGING DIVERSITY THROUGH TEAMWORK

Research findings point to the value of diversity and **teamwork**, the coordinated effort by a group of persons working toward a common goal. The benefits of teamwork begin to make sense when we think about the diverse relationships and perspectives we develop and share. Our learning increases when we depend on each other and share new ways of looking at the world. We pay more attention to each person's talents and preoccupy ourselves less with differences that are irrelevant to the purpose of the team. And yet certain differences may play a critical role in the success of a team.

While diversity encompasses racial, gender, and ethnic differences, research shows that other differences may be even more critical to a team's success. For example, consider the relationship among diversity, teamwork, and creativity. Researchers at Northwestern University studied both scholarly and artistic teams. Academic teams' success was measured by their publications in top journals, while artistic teams, made up of choreographers, directors, and librettists, were evaluated on their ability to produce highly successful, long-running Broadway musicals. Their findings point to two

The Jigsaw Method

Elliot Aronson, who is widely recognized as one of the most eminent psychologists of the twentieth century, is best known for developing an educational model of teamwork that cultivates a culture of shared responsibility and support. It addresses academic success by encouraging collaboration, building self-esteem, and reducing intergroup tensions among students. The model, known as the jigsaw method, divides students into small racially and academically mixed teams. As the following real-life example makes clear, the benefits of the jigsaw method extend far beyond academic performance.

Each day, students in each group were assigned one of six subtopics. After learning about that segment of the lesson, each individual taught the other group members. The results showed a decrease in prejudice and an increase in self-esteem among students in the jigsaw groups. The academic test scores of minority diverse students in these groups also improved. Unlike before, these diverse students had to work and fit together like pieces of a jigsaw puzzle. If they were going to do well on the tests, they had to pay attention and support each other. In the process, they learned not only the subject matter but also some valuable lessons about each other.

Carlos, one of the students in Aronson's study, had learned to be quiet in school because he was not very articulate in English. In his jigsaw group of five students, Carlos' experiences were different. "It began to dawn on the students that the only chance they had to learn about Carlos' segment was by paying attention to what he had to say. If they ignored Carlos or continued to ridicule him, his segment would be unavailable to them and the most they could hope for would be an 80 percent score on the exam—an unattractive prospect to most.... And with that realization, the kids began to develop into pretty good interviewers, learning to pay attention to Carlos, to draw him out, and to ask probing questions. Carlos, in turn, began to relax more and found it easier to explain out loud what was in his head. What they (students) came to learn about Carlos is even more important.... They began to like Carlos, and he began to enjoy school more.... After a few weeks, they noticed talents in him they had not seen before."[1]

Schools throughout the United States continue to use the jigsaw method and adapt it to their needs. In the aftermath of the mass shooting that took place at Columbine High School, Aronson has pushed for jigsaw classrooms to help combat the social divisions and conflict that contribute to the increasing incidence of school violence.

> None of us are as smart as all of us.
> —Japanese proverb

defining features of highly successful teams, both of which relate to creativity. First, highly successful teams have a healthy mix of newcomers and individuals with more experience. Another key, at least on these teams, was the inclusion of at least some experienced members who had never worked together. While people tend to want to work with friends and others whom they know, this research indicates that "repeat relationships" work against creativity and success.[2]

Research psychologist John Dovidio argues that getting people to cooperate, to work together as members of the same team, goes a long way toward reducing prejudice. In his experiments, he has put people of different races on the same team in order to examine group dynamics. When competing, the racial makeup of the team is not nearly as salient as the competition against another team. "We" versus "they" supersedes intragroup differences such as Black, White, Asian, and Latino. Furthermore, Dovidio's research reveals that when we categorize someone as belonging to another group, we tend to see that group as more homogenous than our own. These findings show the promise of dealing with prejudice indirectly, that is, getting people who normally would not work or socialize together to collaborate on some project at school or anywhere else for that matter.[3]

At Ford Motor Company, different people with different ideas are included on teams to problem-solve, innovate, and cater to new and emerging markets. A good example is the way Ford ensures that female perspectives are represented in the design of its vehicles. Female engineer and non-engineer workers create and evaluate concepts and features in the design of cars, vans, and trucks. As an example, a team of all female engineers at Ford are working on using green technology, recyclable and renewable materials, to design cars of the future. In their short time together, they have already been awarded ten prize patents.

Teams, particularly those made up of people from diverse backgrounds, are proliferating in the workplace. The accent on teamwork in the workplace is a surprise to many students. In college, the focus is typically on individual success and competition. According to Judy Blair, Vice President of Human Resources for American Management Systems, the teamwork focus "is often an adjustment from school where achievement tends to be individual and aimed at getting the best grade. . . . Although individual contribution matters in the workplace, the teamwork element is also key. Someone may be responsible for a particular aspect of work on a project, but collaboration and cooperation with others on the project is key."[4]

Teamwork is not sold as a technique for promoting human relations. Rather, it is viewed as good business. As more and more companies expand globally, teamwork makes it possible to increase productivity and profits. The idea of bringing the world closer together through teamwork is an effective marketing strategy. For example, Ford's home page for its Web site champions its worldwide connections, and Boeing refers to itself as "people working together as a global enterprise for aerospace leadership."

Research findings point to the benefits of teamwork, especially when it involves people from diverse backgrounds. A number of academic studies show that diverse teams are more creative and innovative. At the University of North Texas, business students were divided into teams for a period of 17 weeks. Teams made up of students who were culturally and racially diverse were pitted without their knowledge against teams who were all White and much less diverse. During the first few weeks, the all-White teams sprinted ahead. But by the end of the competition, the more diverse teams were being more creative and flexible in the way they attacked and solved work-related problems. Larry K. Michaelsen, one of the three professors who conducted the experiment, commented: "Cultural diversity in the U.S. workforce has sometimes been viewed as a dark cloud. Our results suggest that it has a silver lining."[5]

Employees who hoard information or are unwilling or unable to work together waste time and money. However, employees who thrive in a work environment of teamwork and information sharing are highly valued. From top management to workers in offices and factories, people who are adept at working as members of diverse teams can pool their talents and be more productive. This is called **synergy**, the concept that members of a team interacting cooperatively will accomplish much more than if they act alone. Interestingly, this concept has been applied to other areas, including architecture (see Photo 7.1). In his book *The Seven Habits of Highly Effective People*, Stephen Covey used this word to describe a problem-solving approach that is better than compromise. According to Covey, synergy makes it possible for one plus one to equal more than two.[6] Think of a time when you and other people were able to brainstorm about an issue or problem. What you came up with as a group was in all probability more creative and useful than anything originally proposed by a single person.

Photo 7.1 Synergy is a 20-level structure to be built in Business Bay, Dubai. *Synergy* is used here to refer to the integration of more traditional architecture (the skin that envelops the building) with a modern structure that appears as a stack of cuboids. The diverse architectural elements create an enhanced, combined effect. Besides its distinctive aesthetic appeal, Synergy's structure allows it to endure harsh summers by creating cool internal spaces. *Source: Courtesy of Sanjay Puri Architects.*

VIRTUAL TEAMING

 Thinking Through Diversity

How do you effectively team with a group of people you have never met face to face?

Computer technology is revolutionizing the concept of teaming. In today's world, virtual teams are enabling more people to link together at an accelerating rate. Recent survey data from multinational companies in more than 100 countries indicate that the vast majority of their white collar employees work virtually. However, only a small fraction of these employees received training to help them prepare for the challenges they encounter in a global and collaborative environment.[7] In their book *Virtual Teams*, Jessica Lipnack and Jeffrey Stamps contrast conventional and virtual teams. The authors describe a **virtual team** as a group of people that work "across space, time, and organizational boundaries with links strengthened by webs of communication technologies."[8] Virtual teaming allows our individual and group creativity to flourish by enhancing opportunities to express ourselves. It can also significantly increase our ability to draw on the talents of a culturally diverse and geographically dispersed group of people. At the same time, the diversity of the group is often difficult to gauge unless it comes out in the course of communication or face-to-face interaction.

When we communicate on the Internet, individual characteristics such as appearance, religion, and social class may be kept invisible. The physical distance of team members and their use of electronic media can exert a profound influence on relationships. This is particularly true when people communicate anonymously. The message, rather than who is sending it, becomes the focal point. This encourages more input from people with diverse backgrounds and positions. One drawback of virtual teaming is that members tend to ignore each other's individual needs. When communicating from geographically dispersed locations, desensitization to the values, goals, and competencies of individuals can occur easily.

Teamwork on a virtual team poses a number of challenges. Everything that can go wrong in a face-to-face team can also be a problem in a virtual team. A lack of trust, miscommunication, and conflict are even more problematic. Unfortunately, a good deal of training dealing with computer technology ignores the interpersonal dynamics of virtual teaming. This reinforces the idea that computers are tools for individuals, not groups. For members of a virtual team to be successful, they need to learn how to share their beliefs, knowledge, and skills. When communicating across distances, keep in mind the following strategies:

1. Share and clarify your group's mission and goals.

2. Openly discuss the challenges of virtual teaming and communication.

3. Be aware of the value of communication with other locations and invite feedback.

4. Identify and discuss differences. These differences may be cultural, organizational, and geographic.

5. Take advantage of any opportunities to meet face to face. This will personalize and reinforce relationships.

6. Seek and share knowledge. Do not hoard it. Hoarding delays results and works against synergy.

Teaming In a 3-D World

Colleen Monahan, Director of Development at the Center for the Advancement of Distance Education at the University of Chicago, has been working with a large corporation to create a virtual world for employees. This 3-D "virtual company" allows employees to have space somewhere "outside of the corporate firewall" where they can meet, much like a virtual water cooler. Employees use avatars to move around this 3-D world as they interact, converse, and develop a sense of community. Strategizing in a virtual situation room is also an option. Further development is being made to have avatars offering counseling within this virtual world.[9]

DEVELOPING TEAMWORK SKILLS

As part of your education, have you been taught how to work with people who commit themselves to a common purpose? Is your education providing you with opportunities to develop and practice teaming skills? Many employers believe that there is a mismatch between the skills students need when they enter the workforce and those they learn in college. This is particularly true in the area of interpersonal skills. Teaming, teaching others, negotiating, and managing people with diverse backgrounds are essential in today's workplace, although they are not always emphasized in higher education.

Thinking Through Diversity

Given your plans for the future, how will developing teamwork skills benefit you?

Interest in training related to teamwork has grown with the realization that working together does not necessarily mean working together. Good intentions or even a common purpose are not enough. Nor can we assume that people understand teaming is a process that requires education, experience, and trust. A variety of educational and training programs exist to help people learn and develop teamwork skills. Some examples follow:

1. One college program forms teams of engineering and business students to work in the classroom and at job sites on real-life problems. The program is based on the idea that students will be collaborating on teams in the workplace. Many of these teams will be crossfunctional, meaning that people with different areas of expertise, backgrounds, and job functions will be working together.

2. Marines, from raw recruits to senior officers, go through a three-day test. The test emphasizes values, morality, and above all, teamwork. Marines are evaluated on their ability to work continuously as a team for 54 hours; they stand or fall as a group.

3. Organizations are devoting more of their resources to team-building exercises. These exercises range from workshops for coworkers and students (see Photo 7.2) to executive retreats in the wilderness. For instance, a wide variety of programs teach the importance of teamwork, communication, and leadership through physical challenges such as rock climbing and white-water rafting. These experiences, which help us move past our preconceived notions of each other, make it necessary to work as a single unit. Team members who might not completely trust each other have to function as a cohesive unit in order to navigate a rock-climbing

Photo 7.2 A team-building exercise challenges students to work together and trust each other.

exercise or survive in the desert for a number of days. Ideally, this experience will help them adapt, excel, and grow as a team in other challenging situations.

4. Airlines have crew resource management (CRM) training programs. CRM focuses on promoting teamwork among cockpit crew members by improving their communication and decision-making. Crews are put through various flight exercises in aircraft simulators. The trainers videotape and analyze the interaction of crew members and their ability to respond to emergency situations. The possibility that a number of airline crashes have resulted from certain commands being misinterpreted or ignored by the captain or the rest of the crew has provided the impetus for such training.

5. Sports psychology has become a big-time industry in recent years. Sports psychologists are in demand, in large part because of their expertise in the area of team building. Dr. Colleen Hacker, a "mental skills coach" with a degree in sports psychology, works with the U.S. women's national soccer team to improve their team chemistry, focus, and confidence in each other. Hacker challenges people's assumption that "team chemistry" is a noun, a quality that simply exists. She sees it as a verb, as something you do.[10] In one of her team-building drills, the U.S. team drove to the top of a cliff in Portland, Oregon. Hacker blindfolded half of the team, and instructed the remaining teammates to lead them down a steep, narrow ledge. Their biggest weapon, according to the players, is "their uncommon bond as teammates and friends."[11] Like other sports psychologists, Hacker tailors activities of this nature to the age, maturity, and conflict tolerance of the group.

> Teamwork is the ability to work together toward a common vision...It is the fuel that allows common people to attain uncommon results.
> —Andrew Carnegie

DIVERSITY CONSCIOUSNESS AND TEAMING

Diversity consciousness develops over time. As it grows, we become better able to deal with team members, who in all likelihood will have a wide variety of values, personalities, behaviors, and abilities. Thus, we are in a position to contribute more to a team.

Every team is diverse. In any team, group members vary in background, knowledge, and attitudes to some degree. People may even view the concept of team building differently. What is the role of an effective team member? Does it mean being assertive and outspoken or agreeable and a good listener? Is it necessary to build trusting relationships among members before any action can be taken? Is it OK to "rock the boat" or is maintaining harmony of utmost importance? How you answer these questions may depend on your personality or cultural background or even the setting.

Picture yourself in a class of students. You are put in groups at the beginning of the semester. Prior to each test, time is set aside in class so that each group can review the material. Although some students may prefer to defer to other group members, your instructor has made it clear that she wants everybody to be part of the discussion.

Some students may find this experience very traumatic because they are not comfortable in small group settings. A young female, raised to believe that women should be seen but not heard, may struggle with her role in the group. A group member from Japan or Laos might stress the importance of being courteous and cooperative. However, team members who were born and raised in the United States may be more apt to speak their minds, even if it results in conflict and confrontation.

Group differences are only an asset when members develop the competencies needed to utilize the assets and meet the challenges of diversity. By becoming more conscious of diversity, you will improve those skills that are essential for true teamwork; these include communication, conflict management, empathy, self-evaluation, and leadership. In turn, developing these skills will expand your diversity consciousness.

1. *Communication.* Because people process information in different ways, it is important to utilize a variety of communication styles. For example, team members may be more productive and creative if they constantly combine visual, verbal, and experiential modes of communication (see Photo 7.3).

2. *Conflict management.* Dealing effectively with conflict requires fundamental skills in interpersonal relations. These skills, which include showing empathy and listening actively, can help team members work through and benefit from conflict. Conflict in groups is discussed in more detail toward the end of this chapter.

Cooperative Learning Among Hmong Adults

The Hmong are the largest ethnic minority in Laos. Many Hmong refugees resettle in the United States. When Hmong adults participate in American basic education, their cultural background affects their classroom behavior.

Through participant observation, a researcher from the University of Wisconsin was able to study a class for non-literate and low-literate Hmong adults. According to the researcher, these Hmong students view classroom work as a cooperative activity. They are constantly in touch with each other and are hesitant to be singled out as being more able than their peers. The stronger students help the weaker students. Students check each other's books, papers, and worksheets. Interestingly, there is no competition. The researcher observed: "When Mee Hang has difficulty with an alphabetization lesson, Pang Lor explains, in Hmong, how to proceed. Chia Ying listens in to Pang's explanation and nods her head. Pang goes back to work on her own paper, keeping an eye on Mee Hang. When she sees Mee looking confused, Pang leaves her seat and leans over Mee's shoulder. She writes the first letter of each word on the line, indicating to Mee that these letters are in alphabetical order and that Mee should fill in the rest of each word. This gives Mee the help she needs and she is able to finish on her own. Mee, in turn, writes the first letter of each word on the line for Chia Yang, passing on Pang Lor's explanation."[12]

Photo 7.3 For this team at Johns Hopkins Hospital, excellent communication skills are essential. *Source: Courtesy of the Office of Communications, Johns Hopkins Medical Institutions, Baltimore, MD. Photographer Keith Weller.*

3. *Empathy.* To author Stephen Covey, empathy is the most important skill we need for teamwork. Members of a team must really listen and "put themselves in other people's shoes."[13] This skill creates the openness that allows creativity to flourish. It also helps us to realize that there is more than one way to accomplish a task.

4. *Self-evaluation.* As a team member, you need to evaluate your performance continually. This is particularly important in self-managed work teams. To use Langer's terminology, replace mindlessness with mindfulness. *Mindlessness* blots out intuition and much of the world around us. *Mindfulness* raises our consciousness and awareness.[14] Although total self-awareness is virtually impossible, ask yourself questions that focus on how you see yourself and others. Such questions might include:

   • Are there parts of myself that I do not share with others?

   • Am I comfortable with myself and other team members?

   • How well do I listen to all members of my team?

   • What do I know, think, and feel about team members?

   • How do my emotions, values, and experiences affect my ability to work with other team members?

5. *Leadership.* Leaders succeed through the efforts of others. By inspiring a "team culture," leaders help members sacrifice individual goals and agendas for the common good. By moving with ease across personal and cultural boundaries, leaders unify, empower, and, if necessary, heal. When we learn to accept and share leadership, we are able to bring out the best in everyone. For example, you may show leadership when you fill a particular role in a group. Perhaps you take on an assignment that no one wants. Or maybe you help other members work through conflict that threatens your ability to function as a team.

A Profile in Diversity Consciousness

At times, the only way we can survive an unforeseen crisis is through teaming. In situations such as this, one's position, responsibilities, or background may not matter. Rather, the effectiveness of a team may be more a function of how motivated people are to collaborate with each other to achieve a desired result.

Consider the response of employees of the New Orleans *Times-Picayune* during the aftermath of Hurricane Katrina. With flood-waters rising, no working phones, no way to communicate with loved ones, and increased lawlessness, employees of this daily newspaper debated what to do. The company's headquarters in New Orleans was squarely in the path of Katrina.

The staff came together to continue producing a newspaper as they tried to cope with the disruptions in their personal lives. Without any formal plan from senior editors, everybody from newsroom employees to those on the loading docks pitched in to put out a newspaper. Many of these employees were not accustomed to working on the same team. For example, one team kayaking downtown in search of supplies and reporting along the way included the paper's sports editor, an art critic, a religion writer, and an editorial page director.

Staff slept on the floor of the *Times-Picayune* library. A photographer named Brandon swam to the newspaper office. During the crisis, another photographer explained that their motivation went beyond building reputations. "Everyone has something they can give to this effort. We as photographers, that's what we do. We shoot pictures of the tragedy and try to do it in a way that's going to help people, to show the world what's going on here."[15]

 Thinking Through Diversity

Consider the times you have participated on teams. When was diversity within these teams an asset? Why? When was it a liability? Why?

As work teams become more global and heterogeneous, leaders will need to develop their diversity consciousness. Moreover, leadership skills are becoming increasingly important for everyone. Employers typically expect workers with widely different job functions and levels of authority to assume leadership roles. As an example, it is not unusual for management to delegate responsibilities to workers, who then organize teams and get the job done with little if any supervision. These are sometimes referred to as *self-managed work teams*.

HIGH-PERFORMANCE TEAMS

High-performance teams do not just happen. They evolve over time and require people who possess certain talents, a wide range of diversity skills, a common vision, and a strong commitment to the team. They develop something Albert Bandura refers to as **collective efficacy**, people's shared belief that they are capable of effecting change and making a difference.[16] Reflect on the teams to which you belong in school, at work, or in your community. On which teams do people work well together? Which teams do the best job of making people feel included? Which teams accomplish the most? High-performance teams are not necessarily made up of the most talented individuals. In sports, it is not uncommon for a team of superstars to get beaten by a team with much less individual talent. Things such as team togetherness, commitment, and communication can be as, if not more important than raw talent.

 Thinking Through Diversity

More often than not, teams operate at less than peak efficiency. Why?

Research shows that it is not enough simply to include diverse and capable people on a team. High-performance and low-performance teams differ in how they manage

Photo 7.4 A study group can develop into a high-performance team over time.
Source: Courtesy of Colgate University.

diversity. "When well-managed, diversity becomes a productive resource to the team. . . . When ignored, diversity causes process problems that diminish the team's productivity."[17] For a moment, think of the storyline from *The Wizard of Oz*. In a training video, a management expert analyzes the team that Dorothy built. Her team consists of a scarecrow, a lion, and a tin man. Each character has a different talent. Together they delegate tasks, take risks, establish trust among themselves, and pursue a common goal.

In real life, team members need to come together, coalesce, and realize their common purpose in much the same way (see Photo 7.4). According to Tuckman, periods of conflict (called *storming*) will occur. Often, it will take considerable time and effort to develop a sense of trust and cohesiveness, as well as a common understanding regarding the norms or rules of the team and its mission (called *norming*).[18] Although the development of each high-performance team is unique, there are ten proven strategies to keep in mind.

Ten Proven Strategies for Building High-Performance Teams

1. *Get to know each other first.* Before you start focusing on the task at hand, take some time to learn about group members. What are your interests at home and at work? What special talents do each of you have? What is distinctive about your personal and professional backgrounds? Sharing a part of yourself with the group initiates the process of establishing and nourishing a comfort zone in which to operate. It brings out individual differences and similarities and uncovers team members' skills. Although becoming acquainted takes time, it is worth it. If you ignore this step, there is a good chance that you will encounter problems later.

2. *Make sure that you understand your role(s) and the team's goal(s).* High-performance teams unite around a common vision. Team goals, team knowledge, team skills, and even team problems should be your focus. Also, everybody needs to understand what part they play and how every part is vital to their success as a group. If certain people feel that others do not want or value their input, commitment to the group is likely to be weak.

3. *Respect the ideas and feelings of other team members.* This helps to create an open, supportive environment that allows team members to feel comfortable and be authentic. Building your diversity consciousness enhances your ability to value what each member brings to the team.

4. *Manage conflict effectively.* By doing this, different agendas and competitive struggles do not drain the energy of the group or threaten group cohesion and morale. Conflict management strategies are discussed later in this chapter.

5. *Continue to build relations with other team members.* Sometimes, high functioning teams are described as having the right "chemistry." Typically, this is something that evolves over time. To complement others, you need to know something about them. Over time, for example, my wife and I have learned to work as a team. When it comes to computer technology and anything of a mechanical nature, I look to her for help. If we need groceries, she invariably seeks my advice. I cut out the coupons, read the ads, and buy virtually all of the food for our family. With other tasks, our skills are more similar than complementary. It is important to remember that utilizing our respective strengths does not just happen magically. It requires hard work, mutual respect, and continual learning about each other and ourselves.

6. *Think and act like a team.* Put your attitudes and individual egos aside. Bill Russell, one of the greatest basketball players in the history of the sport, explains that he was extremely egotistical. "But my ego always was a team ego," he adds. "My ego was totally linked with the success of my team. It wasn't linked to personal achievement. It was linked to team achievement."[19]

7. *Decenter and recenter.* As discussed earlier, synergy occurs when the sum total of a group is greater than its parts. Decentering and recentering represent two techniques for achieving synergy in a diverse team. When you decenter, you and other team members shift your perspective and adopt multiple points of view. Recentering allows each member to identify and construct a common vision. Both are critically important and interconnected.

8. *Avoid groupthink.* Groupthink is the tendency to go along with a group and discourage differences of opinion. When this happens, every voice is not heard and teamwork suffers. Part of the lure of groupthink is that decisions can be made quickly. This often becomes an overriding concern in a society such as ours which revolves around deadlines and emphasizes immediate results. In a high-performance team, the mindset of the group does not constrain or stifle you. Rather, you are comfortable raising issues, challenging others, and being yourself.

9. *Be flexible.* Exercise "give and take" as needed. For example, be willing to give help and receive help. When necessary, assume the role of a leader in order to mobilize the team for high performance. Similarly, there are situations that require you to be a good follower. This might mean taking directions and accepting criticism from someone who thinks differently than you.

10. *Periodically assess the team's performance.* High-performance teams evaluate their strengths as well as their weaknesses. By making this a group priority, you can examine group processes with more precision and confidence. In turn, the team not only builds on its successes, but also learns from its failures.

Realize the process of building a high-performance team is not linear. It has its ups and downs. Reaching decisions may take longer. You can do your part to construct

> When spider webs unite,
> they can tie up a lion.
> —Ethiopian proverb

a high-performance team by keeping track of where you are and where you are going. Are you helping to create a climate of trust, commitment, cooperation, and flexibility? When you assume leadership, is it empowering or conforming? Finally, do you really believe in the value of diversity and what each member brings to the group?

OBSTACLES TO TEAMWORK

Numerous obstacles can detract from the synergy of a team. Some can be traced to the thinking and behaviors of individual members; others originate outside the team. Obstacles, such as those that follow, compromise a team's potential.

1. *Social values.* Teamwork can be difficult in a society that stresses the importance of individualism and competition. Common sayings in the United States, such as "make your own breaks" and "look out for number one," support values that may undermine teamwork. As an example, U.S. workers are sometimes reluctant to share their ideas because they fear that someone else might get the credit. Contrast this kind of thinking with the African saying: "One finger cannot pick up a grain."

2. *Stereotypes.* One popular exercise used in diversity training illustrates the negative effect of stereotypical images on teamwork. A label is placed on each person in a small group, such as leader, secretary, newcomer, rebel, and idealist. Participants are instructed to treat each other according to his or her label. Then they are assigned a task. What evolves during this role playing is typical of what takes place in teams on a daily basis. If we let stereotypical ideas cloud our thinking, it becomes difficult to see each other as individuals (see Fig. 7.2).

3. *Unequal distribution of power.* In the context of teamwork, power affords you the opportunity to participate in decision-making, access resources, make yourself heard, and make things happen. In some cases, an imbalance of power or

Figure 7.2 Our assumptions about each other can undermine teamwork and productivity.

a disagreement regarding the implications of power can sabotage team goals. As an example, a subordinate may be afraid to talk openly and honestly to his supervisors because of the power they hold. A supervisor may perceive her subordinates as rebellious or militant when they speak out or resist going along with the group.

4. *Disagreement over the roles of team members or the team's mission.* Think of a team as an interlocking set of gears on a machine. Each gear needs to do its part and work together in order for the machine to run smoothly and efficiently. This same set of dynamics governs a team. Team members need to agree and be clear regarding their individual responsibilities and collective goal or goals. If not, roles will overlap and time as well as effort will be wasted.

5. *Unequal treatment or the perception of unequal treatment.* Discrimination is one of the surest, quickest ways to sabotage teamwork. It undermines trust and cohesiveness. It arouses anger and makes it more difficult to focus on the task at hand. Excessive avoidance or acquiescence replaces genuine interaction. Psychologically speaking, the group mentality shifts to "us" versus "them."

6. *Lack of communication or miscommunication.* Communication is the "glue" that holds a team together. It is the vehicle by which people come together, share, and learn from each other. Unfortunately, open, honest, and clear communication is a rarity on many teams. As teams get larger and more heterogeneous, communication styles and skills tend to become more numerous and differentiated. This makes it difficult for a team to develop a common language.

7. *Lack of outside support.* Teams do not operate in a vacuum. They connect to other teams, organizations, and the larger community. External support can take many forms, including funding, volunteer help, and commitments from organizational and community leaders. A team that feels cut off from the outside world will probably find it difficult to sustain any amount of synergy.

8. *Lack of trust.* Through trust, we gain cooperation. Without trust, we do not have complete confidence in the character and competence of team members. In *The Five Dysfunctions of a Team: A Leadership Fable*, Patrick Lencioni defines **trust** as "the confidence among team members that their peers' intentions are good, and there is no reason to be protective or careful around the group; in essence, teammates must get comfortable being vulnerable with one another."[20] When team members show an absence of trust, they are hesitant to ask for help and perhaps even offer help. Additionally, Lencioni states they are apt to hide their weaknesses, hold grudges, jump to conclusions about others' intentions, avoid one another, and overlook each other's talents.

As we develop diversity consciousness, these obstacles to teamwork will become more visible. Furthermore, we will have a vast array of skills at our disposal to possibly prevent, minimize, or overcome such obstacles.

CONFLICT

Conflict is the struggle that results when two or more parties perceive a difference or incompatibility in their interests, values, or goals. It can occur between individuals as well as among and within groups, communities, and societies. Every time we interact with someone, there is the potential for conflict.

A variety of individual, group, and cultural differences may give rise to conflict. More specifically, it may stem from different values and perceptions as well as a lack of agreement regarding needs and priorities. Within a team, potential sources of conflict include cultural misunderstandings, stereotypical assumptions, discriminatory behavior, and disagreements regarding the roles of team members and the team's mission.

What comes to your mind when you hear the word *conflict*? When I pose this question to various audiences, the answers I get typically portray conflict as problematic or negative. Some of the terms people use are *disagreement*, *"attitude,"* *problems*, *trouble*, *fighting*, *frustration*, *anger*, and *tension*.

Traditionally, conflict has been viewed as a negative in the United States. It is seen as something that stands in the way of communication and teamwork. Therefore, some people assume that we should avoid conflict at all costs. Although conflict can have negative consequences, it can have positive outcomes as well. At school, conflict can motivate you to work harder, or deepen your understanding of a problem. Conflict in your personal life can make you stronger and strengthen your relationships with others. In the workplace, conflict can bring certain issues out into the open and in some cases bring people closer together. It can stimulate creativity and signal a need for change.

Richard Tanner Pascale, author of *Managing on the Edge: How the Smartest Companies Use Conflict to Stay Ahead*, examines a number of innovative organizations that actually embrace tension. He cites Honda as an example. With its "contention-management system," Honda seeks to find the proper balance between debate and harmony. Subordinates openly, but politely, challenge their bosses. Takeo Fujisawa, the cofounder of Honda, compared the challenge of fostering openness and questioning to conducting an orchestra. "As president, you must orchestrate the discordant sounds into a kind of harmony. But you never want too much harmony. One must cultivate a taste for finding harmony within discord, or you will drift away from the forces that keep a company alive."[21]

> Without struggle there is no progress.
> —Frederick Douglass

Conflict Management

The effect that conflict has on us depends largely on how well we manage it. **Conflict management**, the process by which conflict is dealt with in an effective and constructive manner, is a key diversity skill. To develop this skill and understand the causes and consequences of conflict, we need some knowledge of subjects such as history, sociology, anthropology, economics, and psychology. Of equal importance are basic interpersonal skills. In some cases the management of conflict results in resolving or eliminating conflict by changing how we relate to an issue and/or each other. There are other circumstances when it makes sense to avoid or smooth over conflict. Although this does not necessarily make the conflict go away, it might very well be the prudent thing to do in a particular situation. A variety of approaches to managing conflict are discussed later.

People who manage conflict well at school, work, and home have an advantage. The issue is not whether people experience conflict but how they experience it. In the workplace, globalization, group decision-making, organizational complexity, and a preponderance of diversity issues result in more time spent on conflict management. Whereas conflict frustrates and stymies some people, others seem to take it in stride and even thrive on it. The difference in how people react has a lot to do with their upbringing, cultural background, and people skills. In his book *Conflict: Resolution and Prevention*, John Burton argues that it is important to take a proactive approach to conflict.[22] Dealing with conflict proactively means that we prepare ourselves for conflict in advance. In other words, it is important to develop and continuously improve our conflict management skills and be ready to use them at a moment's notice.

Learning to deal effectively with conflict is a skill that expands both your diversity consciousness and your chances for success. It builds your self-respect and increases your confidence in yourself. Your interpersonal skills benefit as well. These include your ability to communicate, cooperate, negotiate, manage your emotions, and exercise self-control. In addition, working through conflict in a constructive way helps you to develop your cognitive skills. You will become a better problem solver by developing your understanding of the sources, dynamics, and effects of conflict.

Thinking Through Diversity

Think back to a situation in which there was conflict that you needed to manage. How did you deal with the conflict? What was the outcome? What did this experience teach you about conflict management?

Approaches to Conflict Management

Different situations may require different approaches. Flexibility is key. Sometimes, situations call for strong responses, and sometimes the response needs to be more gentle. The setting, as well as the people and their relationships to each other, need to be taken into consideration. If your boss at work comments "You're so articulate for a foreigner," you might feel rage, hurt, or a mix of positive and negative feelings. Depending on how you feel, you might want to hit her or him over the head, ignore it, or explain why you find this "compliment" offensive. Your ability to control your feelings, consider the consequences of your actions, and act accordingly will be pivotal to your success on the job.

Cultural differences need to be taken into consideration. Although we should not jump to conclusions about people because of their cultural backgrounds, it is important to be sensitive to the impact that culture might have on managing conflict. For example, what do you assume when team members disagree on important issues? When confronted with an argument, do you try to look at all sides or presume automatically that there are only two sides? Do you assume that if people think differently, they must be opposed to each other? People's responses to these questions have a lot to do with their cultural backgrounds. For example, in many Native American and Asian cultures, people view differences or opposites existing in harmony. Humans or things are not either this or that; rather, they overlap and interconnect. The ancient Chinese concepts of yin and yang illustrate this kind of thinking. Differences can be interactive and even complementary. Instead of simply focusing on differences, the concept of yin–yang reminds us to search for common ground.

Yin and Yang ☯

The dark and light halves of the yin–yang symbol represent the two sides of a hill, one shadowy and one sunny. The outer circle of the symbol shows that yin and yang are not two separate things; the small black and white dots in the symbol show that yin and yang contain the seed of its opposite. Like day and night, one cannot exist without the other. Viewing conflict in terms of yin and yang helps us realize that differences do not necessarily have to result in opposition.

According to Deborah Tannen, author of *The Argument Culture*, Americans traditionally assume that opposition is the best way to get things done. As a result, people are inclined to settle their differences by resorting to debate, fighting, and lawsuits. There is an emphasis on finding fault rather than solving a problem, having an argument rather than making an argument, and winning the argument rather than understanding another point of view.[23] We can find evidence of this emphasis in the metaphors we use. Examples include phrases such as the "battle of the sexes" and "war of words." The power of words to shape perceptions has been substantiated by research. Phrasing a conflict as "Black" versus "White," "rich" versus "poor," or "old" versus "young" is counterproductive. It not only forces people into two artificial, opposing camps, but it may also alienate or exclude many people.

 Thinking Through Diversity

What is one issue that elicits considerable disagreement in your community or in the larger society? Can you think of more than two sides to this issue?

Approaches to Conflict Management: The 6 C's

When you encounter conflict, you may choose to communicate, circumvent, confront, conform, compromise, collaborate, or any combination thereof.

Approach 1: Communicate.   With this approach, people who hold conflicting views on divisive and emotional issues come together to talk, listen, and learn. Unlike a debate, the goal is not to score points. As an example, the Public Conversations Project is an initiative that has brought people with strong differences together to converse on such potentially volatile topics as sexual orientation, abortion, and the environment. The project team establishes certain guidelines to ensure that conversations are respectful and constructive. Project leaders encourage participants to avoid name-calling, stay on task, and give everyone "a home in the conversation." Dialogues do not necessarily resolve the conflict or significantly change positions on an issue. However, they can open up lines of communication and help people see each other as people rather than enemies. When this happens, people's views can shift ever so slightly and new options may emerge.

Conflict can make person-to-person communication particularly difficult. Anger and ill feelings can easily get in the way of meaningful dialogue. One way to work through conflict is to view communication as a building process. Breaking the process down into steps can help you take advantage of the opportunities conflict affords.

- Share information. Each person should state the problem clearly; making sure a conflict actually exists. Seek clarification if necessary.

- Try not to blame. Rather, use the "I feel" formula. Focus on how you feel as a result of what happened. For example, I feel ____when you _____ because _____. In stating how you feel, try to avoid words such as angry or mad. Be more specific, such as I feel "left out" or "embarrassed."

- Explore differences and similarities in your assumptions.

- Try to understand the perspectives of others through deliberate, active listening. Chinese distinguish between listening or *ting* (attending to the other person with your ears, eyes, and heart) and simply hearing.

- Brainstorm possible solutions. Determine the advantages and disadvantages of each.

- Try to agree on a solution that is fair to all.

Approach 2: Circumvent.   There are times when it is necessary to avoid or get around conflict in some way. Sometimes, you may feel as though you want to "fight the world." Everything seems to be a source of potential conflict. To keep from being overwhelmed, you may find it necessary to "pick your battles." In other words, you choose what to fight and what to avoid. Sometimes the situation might be too volatile. Maybe the timing is bad and people need to "cool off." After thinking it through for a while, you may even discover that you are at fault or overreacting.

Some of us encounter the possibility of conflict on an everyday basis. A gay woman comments: "Working in a dental hygiene clinic, I have heard negative comments regarding gay people. They come from department coordinators, instructors, and students. The interesting aspect of it is they include me in these discussions, never thinking for a moment that I might be gay. It is funny how people just assume that sometimes. I know in these situations I just have to play the game. There are too many people to deal with, and I know it would not be in my best interest to come out. I have also been warned by other gay women who have graduated from this program to remain discreet. The program is tough enough as it is. I think it is better in this case to avoid unnecessary emotional turmoil."

Approach 3: Confront.   In some instances it is necessary to be assertive and take action immediately. Maybe it is a matter of speaking up for yourself or someone else. A person's safety may be an issue. Certain conflicts may result in people being denied respect or even basic human rights. For example, what if a coworker or your boss tells you the latest "Polish joke"? You might respond by informing the coworker that you find this joke offensive. With your boss, you might simply not laugh and walk away. Remember, confrontation need not be overtly challenging to be effective.

Confrontation may also be necessary when people show a lack of respect for certain cultural traditions. Put yourself in the position of a person who has to take time off from work or school to observe a religious holiday. If you are denied this opportunity or penalized in some way because of your religious beliefs, you have the right to take whatever action is necessary to ensure that your rights are not being violated.

Approach 4: Conform.   There may be times when you feel that you have to smooth over conflict or simply "give in" because you do not want to upset or jeopardize your relationship with others. The people may be more important than the issue. In some instances, conformity is a short-term solution. For example, you may find yourself in a no-win situation with your parents. They make it clear to you that they do not approve of the fact that you are unmarried and living with someone. Consequently, they have asked you to avoid talking about your living arrangement when other people are present. Although you may disagree with your parents and even think of them as old-fashioned, you respect their strong feelings on this issue and conform to their request.

Approach 5: Compromise.   With this approach, all the parties feel they can give a little. A typical example might be balancing responsibilities at work and at home. Take a father who works late on weekdays in order to keep up with the heavy workload at his job. His wife, with three young children, wants to work part-time as a fitness instructor and wants him home for dinner so they can spend more time together as a family. They compromise. He agrees to go into work later so she can teach her early morning fitness classes. And his wife, realizing that dinner on weekdays is out of the question given the demands of his job, settles for dinner as a family on Friday, and weekends in which the family comes first.

A widely used program that teaches students the need for compromise is the "Model United Nations." Using a realistic simulation of the actual United Nations, its purpose is to bring students together to discuss real-world issues. During these discussions, conflicts arise that students need to resolve. A student UN delegate comments: "My experiences as a delegate allow me to see the world through others' eyes. Passing substantive resolutions is extremely difficult. Many end up being watered down to make them agreeable to countries."

Approach 6: Collaborate.   Rather than taking sides or compromising, we may reach agreement by finding some common ground. Collaboration requires creativity and "buy in" from everyone. Maybe you remember a time when you were part of a group that was trying to solve a problem of some sort. No one could agree on a solution. Each person felt strongly that his or her approach was right. Nevertheless, all of you were determined to find a solution that was satisfactory to everyone. After brainstorming for a while, someone came up with a great idea that was surprisingly simple. Everyone immediately felt a collective sense of relief.

There is no one correct approach to conflict management. An approach that works for you in one situation might backfire on someone else. Sometimes, we can use a combination of approaches. As an example, confrontation may lead to communication and even collaboration. The situation as well as your own comfort level with various approaches are factors you need to consider. You may feel more at ease being confrontational at times, whereas someone else may prefer to avoid this approach at all costs. Remember that you will make mistakes. You might not control your anger, or perhaps you will avoid a situation you need to confront. Simply learn from your mistakes. Like diversity consciousness, conflict management is a continual growth process.

Mediation: Empowering Others

Mediation is a give-and-take process in which a neutral third person (the mediator) helps disputing parties reach a mutually fair resolution. Because mediators lack authority or power, their decision is not binding. This distinguishes it from **arbitration**, in that an arbitrator has the power to render a binding decision. Mediation is used in a wide variety of settings, including international conflicts, workplace and public policy disputes, and divorce proceedings. (see Photo 7.5).

Opportunities abound for students and other members of college communities throughout the United States to study and practice mediation. At Virginia Tech University, a core group of staff and faculty are carefully selected and trained to act as mediators. Their success rate is impressive; and even if the conflict is not resolved, disputants typically walk away with a better understanding of the issue and each other. Throughout this confidential process, the mediator aims to empower others to resolve their own disputes and model respect for diversity. In this way, mediation recognizes the positive value of conflict.

Photo 7.5 A mediator facilitates an open dialogue among disputants. Mediation brings to mind a Chinese proverb that says "Observers can see a chess game more clearly than the players."

The Ten Principles of Conflict Management

Regardless of your approach to conflict management, you may not always be able to control your emotions. This makes it more difficult to compromise, collaborate, or even communicate. The following principles of conflict management will help you manage your emotions, relate to others, and maintain your focus.

1. *Manage conflict in the early stages.* Do not wait for it to explode. Conflict that we allow to build up, especially when communicating across a distance, is more difficult to resolve.

2. *Think through conflict.* In other words, what is the conflict about, why does it concern you, and what would be a satisfactory solution for you and the other parties involved? Additionally, what do I need to learn and do to deal more effectively with conflict of this nature?

3. *Take enough time to get your emotions under control and choose your response.* When you are angry, it is difficult to evaluate the situation from different perspectives. Ask yourself "Is this the best time and place to resolve this?" "Are my feelings under control?" "Is there enough privacy?" As you deal with conflict, try to be constantly aware of your own thoughts and feelings. This can help you avoid a destructive power struggle.

As a child, people picked on me because I was the quiet one, the "nerd." I took martial arts. It gave me discipline, self-motivation. It taught me not to resort to violence every time a problem arises. It taught me to tone down my temper, keep it under control.

—Another perspective

---

4. *Listen actively.* Pay careful attention to what you and others are saying and feeling as well as what is not being expressed. Listen to the total message rather than what you want to hear. Try restating what you think the other person is saying before responding. Active listening coupled with good feedback promotes understanding.

5. *Watch your body language.* Most certainly, there are times when you share something very personal and important to you. If the person with whom you are talking appears disinterested, how does that make you feel? How does it affect your communication? As you interact, be aware of your body language. For instance, nodding your head and leaning forward while seated in a chair shows your interest. Leaning back, crossing your arms, pointing your finger, or smiling during a heated discussion might put others on the defensive. Keep your nonverbal language consistent with your verbal message.

6. *Keep an open mind.* Realize that your view is just one way of looking at things. Instead of asking yourself how you can win, ask yourself what you can learn. Also, be alert to the influence of cultural differences. You might discover that because of a person's cultural background, dealing with conflict face to face is not as effective as a written exchange. Or perhaps because of different cultural beliefs, questions that seem only natural to you might be at odds with someone else's attitudes toward disclosure. For example, "What was the conflict about?" "What was your role?" "How do you feel about the conflict?" may come across as intrusive and inappropriate. Therefore, a lack of cross-cultural sensitivity may lead to inaccurate conclusions.

7. *Criticize ideas, not people.* Keep your focus on the issue or issues. Begin by acknowledging and showing your respect for the opinion of others. Then, you can explain why you disagree. Insulting or blaming people blocks communication and results in destructive conflict.

8. *Ask questions rather than assume.* You can only guess what another person is thinking. Keep checking your assumptions with questions such as "Can you help me understand?" and "Why do you feel that way?" Accept and respect corrections from others.

9. *Try to put yourself in the other person's place.* Bernard Guerney states: "Once you have placed yourself 'inside' the other person, 'walk around' in there. Ask yourself: If I were this person, what would I be thinking? . . . How would I be feeling? What would I be wishing for?"[24] This does two things. First, it helps you get a better idea of someone else's perceptions, beliefs, and wishes. Second, it helps you react in a way that is respectful and caring.

10. *Be willing to change.* You are at a severe disadvantage if you are extremely rigid in your thinking and locked into your approaches or solutions to conflict. A willingness to change allows you to turn conflict into opportunity. Consultant Caryn Tilton helps workers manage conflict by assigning communications "homework" as part of their training. For instance, Tilton might instruct employees to walk around at work and change their facial expressions, noting the different responses they get from others. As Tilton points out, even though we may not be able to change the behavior of someone else, we can alter our behavior to elicit a different response.[25]

Like many other diversity skills, the management of conflict is a critical component of teamwork. Although teamwork is not necessarily one long, drawn-out battle, there will be times when conflict occurs. Conflict can tear a team apart and waste human potential. As a team member, you can help make conflict a growth experience. This is clearly not easy. It takes knowledge, skills, and commitment on your part. How well you and your team work together in the face of conflict will have a significant impact on your individual and collective success.

Throughout this chapter we have explored a variety of issues and concepts related to teamwork. We examined how teams are changing and why employers attach so much importance to teamwork. Additionally, we focused on the relationships among diversity, teamwork, and diversity consciousness. Finally, we addressed a variety of obstacles that can make teamwork difficult, if not impossible. Developing and refining diversity skills, such as communication, conflict management, and leadership, make it possible to recognize and overcome these obstacles.

 Case Studies

Case Study One

Ligua is a car salesperson who works on a commission basis, as well as a part-time student, wife, and mother. Usually in meetings on her job, Ligua is very passive. She doesn't speak up. She thinks this might have something to do with her family background. Ligua was raised not to push, not to be aggressive. If she has something to contribute at meetings, she hesitates. If somebody else receives credit for work she does, she finds it difficult to open her mouth and say, "That was my work. I did that."

Ligua has been working at her current job for the past five years. Recently, three individuals with less experience than Ligua were promoted to positions with some managerial responsibilities. She has begun to wonder why she hasn't been offered a similar promotion, especially since her evaluations have been excellent. When she arranged for a meeting to discuss this matter, her supervisor initially was taken aback. He was under the impression that Ligua was content with her position. As they talked, it became apparent that Ligua's supervisor thought she needed to be more outspoken and to assume more of a leadership role. Also, the supervisor made the comment that some of Ligua's coworkers perceive her to be too "soft," someone who needs to be less concerned with people's feelings and more concerned with holding people accountable. However, her supervisor could not be any more specific and refused to mention names.

Questions:

1. When Ligua asks for feedback regarding her prospects for promotion, what might her supervisor do differently?

2. Specifically, what teamwork skills does Ligua need to work on and why?

Case Study Two

Mary is a White social work student who plans to go on for a MS degree and work in a clinical setting. She attends an urban university and enjoys the diversity and energy of city life, but in her free time is actively involved in social activities centered around her Scottish background. At the children's mental hospital where Mary is doing her practicum, a multidisciplinary team is assigned to each child. Mary is part of a team that includes a social worker, psychiatrist, psychologist, psychology intern, psychiatric resident, nurse, and direct service associate. The members of the team are very diverse in terms of ethnicity, race, age, and experience levels. Mary's experience with the team has been great. Although a variety of disciplines are represented, everyone is treated equally and all ideas are heard and critiqued. As a result, the patient receives a high level of care.

Mary has heard from other social workers that at some hospitals not all team members are equally valued. Hospitals that use the medical model may have doctors "running" the teams—doctors who do not place much importance on the opinions of professionals in other disciplines such as social workers. Katie, one of Mary's friends, is also completing a social work practicum at a local medical hospital. She often feels that the doctors do not listen to her ideas because she is "just a social worker." Out of frustration, Katie is debating whether to continue working at this hospital because she does not feel valued. Additionally, she is beginning to have second thoughts about social work as her chosen profession.

Questions:

1. If you were Mary, what advice would you give Katie?

2. If you were Katie, what could you do to try to make the situation better?

3. What are the benefits of the multidisciplinary team approach at the children's mental hospital? What are the implications of this approach for the patients?

Case Study Three

Michael is a Black college graduate and the divorced father of a teenage son, Aaron, who attends a private school in the well-to-do suburb where they live. Michael is a brilliant loner. As a student, he made a habit of avoiding group assignments and group work whenever possible. At work, he prefers to stay to himself. If he has to work with others, he prefers projects in which everyone has individual responsibilities. Teaming with coworkers, he feels, slows him down and lessens the quality of his work. Michael readily points to examples of his work on groups. In some instances, the final product, he thinks, is not nearly as good as what Michael feels he is capable of creating alone. When he is not the group leader, Michael feels as though his talents are underutilized. Invariably, he gets assigned tasks that do not challenge him.

In addition, Michael largely avoids interacting with other employees after work. He does not dislike other employees; rather, he feels somewhat uncomfortable. At company picnics and parties, he has a difficult time finding common ground in his conversations with coworkers. His taste in music, food, and entertainment is clearly not the norm for this group. Because he is often one of only a few African-Americans at these functions, he feels "under the spotlight." Consequently, he relishes his time away from work, where he can be himself, play with his son, and relax.

Questions:

1. Michael's experiences at work illustrate obstacles to teamwork. What are these obstacles, and how do they interfere with teamwork?

2. What might Michael do to become more of a team player? What might his coworkers do to facilitate teamwork and help Michael feel more included?

 Key Terms

Team	Leadership	Conflict management
Teamwork	Collective efficacy	Mediation
Synergy	Trust	Arbitration
Virtual team	Conflict	

 Exercises

Exercise 1: Conflict Management

1. Describe one example of conflict you encounter at work or school.

2. Explain how you manage the conflict.

3. Which of the six C's of conflict management (communicate, circumvent, confront, conform, compromise, collaborate) do you use most often, and why? Do you feel that you manage the conflict effectively? Why?

Exercise 2: **Team Journal**

Select a team to which you currently belong. Keep a journal of this team for a week or more during the semester. Record your thoughts about:

- Conflict and how you as well as other team members manage it
- Team leadership, creativity, and productivity
- Communication among team members
- The team's ability to utilize its diversity

Note: As you and your classmates discuss conflict, communication, diversity consciousness, and other concepts related to teamwork, you may want to share pertinent entries from your team journal.

 # Notes

[1] Elliot Aronson and Neal Osherow, "Cooperation, Prosocial Behavior, and Academic Performance: Experiments in the Desegregated Classroom," *Applied Social Psychology Annual*, 1, 1980, 174–175.

[2] Roger Guimera, Brian Uzzi, Jarrett Spiro, and Luis Nunes Amaral, "Team Assembly Mechanisms Determine Collaboration Network Structure and Team Peformance," *Science*, 308: 697–702.

[3] Ellis Cose, *Color Blind* (New York: HarperPerennial, 1998), 226.

[4] Sherry Silver, "Advice for Adjusting to the World of Work," *Washington Post Advertising Supplement*, Oct. 19, 1997, 60, 65.

[5] Faye Rice, "How to Make Diversity Pay," *Fortune*, Aug. 8, 1994, 79.

[6] Stephen Covey, *The Seven Habits of Highly Effective People* (New York: Simon & Schuster, 1989).

[7] "Survey Reveals Global Employees Not Prepared for Virtual Teamwork." Online, May 4, 2012. Available: http://rw-3.com/2012/05/survey-reveals-global-employees-not-prepared-for-virtual-teamwork/.

[8] Jessica Lipnack and Jeffrey Stamps, *Virtual Teams* (New York: Wiley, 1997).

[9] Robert Mitchell, "The Virtual Office," *Computerworld*, January 8, 2007.

[10] Colleen Hacker, "Team-Building Tips for Coaches." Available: http://www.active.com/mindandbody/articles/Team-Building-Tips-for-Coaches (accessed Jan. 8, 2013).

[11] Amy Shipley, "A Successful Science Project," *The Washington Post*, June 29, 1999, D1+.

[12] Christina Hvitfeldt, "Traditional Culture, Perceptual Style, and Learning: The Classroom Behavior of Hmong Adults," *Adult Education Quarterly*, 36(2), Winter 1986, 70.

[13] Stephen Covey, "How to Succeed in Today's Workplace," *USA Weekend*, Aug. 29–31, 1997, 5.

[14] E. J. Langer, *Mindfulness* (Reading, MA: Addison-Wesley, 1989).

[15] Daryl Lang, "Their City in Ruins, Times-Picayune Photographers Keep Working." Online, September 20, 2005. Available: http://www.pdnonline.com/pdn/newswire/mailto:dlang@pdnonline.com.

[16] Albert Bandura, "Exercise of Human Agency Through Collective Efficacy," *Current Directions in Psychological Science*, 9, 2000, 75–78.

[17] Nancy Adler and Allison Gundersen, *International Dimensions of Organizational Behavior* (Boston: South-Western College Pub., 2007), 140 .

[18] Editor, Management at Work, "Tuckman's Team-building Model." Online, February 12, 2008. Available: http://management.atwork-network.com/2008/02/12/tuckmans-team-building-model-forming-storming-norming-performing/.

[19] Rick Pitino and Bill Reynolds, *Learn to Succeed* (New York: Broadway Books, 2000), 39.

[20] Patrick Lencioni, *The Five Dysfunctions of a Team: A Leadership Fable* (San Francisco: Jossey-Bass, 2002), 195.

[21] R. T. Pascale, *Managing on the Edge: How the Smartest Companies Use Conflict to Stay Ahead* (New York: Simon & Schuster, 1990), 26.

[22] John Burton, *Conflict: Resolution and Provention* (New York: St. Martin's Press, 1990).

[23] Deborah Tannen, *The Argument Culture: Moving from Debate to Dialogue* (New York: Random House, 1998).

[24] Bernard Guerney, *Relationship Enhancement Program*, 2nd ed. (Bethesda, MD: Ideals, 1997), 4.

[25] Margery Weinstein, "Conquering Conflict," *Training*, June 2007, 56–57.

8

Leadership

Learning Outcomes

Upon completion of this chapter, you will be able to:

- Define leadership.
- Give examples of diversity-conscious leadership.
- Discuss myths about diversity-conscious leaders.
- Point out why diversity-conscious leaders need to adapt, communicate inclusively, and assess themselves.
- Summarize questions that assess each building block of diversity-conscious leadership.
- Compare and contrast theories of leadership.
- Differentiate between expressive and instrumental leaders.
- Explain the value of analyzing leadership in a cultural context.
- Discuss Hofstede's six cultural dimensions.
- Distinguish between leadership of the past and leadership in the future.

Like many organizations, orchestras are made up diverse and talented people who gauge their performance through feedback from their colleagues, customers, and management. Orchestra members bring their culture and diverse perspectives to work every day. Moreover, orchestras have a single leader—a conductor, who assumes various roles. Like any leader, the conductor strives to nurture and harness the energy, creativity, and diversity of all the players, training and inspiring them to collaborate and excel in pursuit of an objective (see Photo 8.1). Effective communication and flexibility between the leader and followers is crucial As leaders, conductors may embrace or resist input from the musicians who actually create the music. Finally, the bottom line for an orchestra is delivering a quality product (the music).

MyStudentSuccessLab

MyStudentSuccessLab is an online solution designed to help you acquire and develop (or hone) the skills you need to succeed. You will have access to peer-led video presentations and develop core skills through interactive exercises and projects.

Yet, the analogy between being an orchestra conductor and being a leader in business and other organizations is incomplete. It does not address the different faces and contexts of leadership. In organizations today, the role of leader may be assumed by different individuals and groups depending on the situation. Nor does the analogy consider the influence of other variables, such as the cultural setting in which the organization operates.

Photo 8.1 Leadership takes many forms.
Source: Stockphoto/Thinkstock.

WHAT IS LEADERSHIP?

Despite the voluminous number of books, articles, and studies on the subject of leadership, there is no single agreed-upon definition of leadership. Furthermore, the definitions vary considerably. And as the world grows more complex and individuals and groups of all colors and cultures become more interdependent, definitions of leadership and the characteristics of a good leader continue to change and multiply.

Many definitions include ideas such as exerting influence, motivating, and enabling people to see and realize their potential. In the foreword to the Drucker Foundation's *The Leader of the Future,* a leader is simply defined as "someone who has followers." Increasingly, definitions look beyond leadership as an individual trait and emphasize its relational and collaborative nature.

Leadership, as defined in this chapter, is the process by which people inspire, influence, and empower others to achieve a common goal. Leaders can exert a positive or negative influence. As leaders, we may impact people negatively if we believe we can simply motivate someone because we have more power. Similarly, our behaviors may suggest that what we say and what we do are two different things. In a more positive vein, leaders can help bring out the best in people, both individually and collectively.

Three Key Features of Leadership

Figure 8.1 Features of Leadership.

They may model collaboration, humility, and openness, helping others realize the value of diversity.

Leadership embraces three key features (see Fig. 8.1).

1. Leadership is a *process,* meaning it reflects what someone is doing rather than his or her position. Through influence and inspiration, leaders unite and motivate people in the pursuit of a common goal.

2. Leadership is *interactive,* that is, it focuses on the relationship between the leader and those being influenced. Thus, a leader needs to relate to people's values and cultures.

3. Leadership is *situational,* meaning it cannot be analyzed apart from the context in which it occurs. Time, location, organizational culture, relationships involving individuals and communities, and numerous other individual and cultural variables shape context.

We are all potential leaders, regardless of our background, status, power, or appearance. Therefore, we need to move beyond conventional, monocultural images of leadership. To illustrate, an individual's appearance, including the formality of his attire, may signal a follower or a leader depending on the situation (see Photo 8.2).

Within an organization, leading is no longer the sole responsibility of the CEO, vice presidents, or other people in authority at the top of the organizational hierarchy. Unlike managers or supervisors, who are appointed and have formal authority by virtue of their position, anyone at any level can be a leader. As the hierarchy within U.S. organizations becomes flatter and as **self-managed teams,** relatively small groups of employees who function on their own and are given significant responsibility for planning, organizing, and decision-making, assume more of the workload, there are more opportunities for all employees to lead.

> If you think you are too small to make a difference, try sleeping in a closed room with a mosquito.
> —African proverb

A relatively new concept called "everyday leadership" alludes to the fact that leadership occurs in our daily routines, both in our professional and private lives. Regardless of our title or seniority, we may provide direction, give guidance, or clear up a misunderstanding. And depending on the situation, we may act as a leader or a follower.

Kouzes and Posner argue that leadership is not "the private reserve" of a few extraordinary men and women. Quite the contrary, "it is a process ordinary people use when they are bringing forth the best from themselves and others. What we've discovered is that people make extraordinary things happen by liberating the leader within everyone."[1]

Leadership is a dynamic process. You may or may not assert your leadership depending on the situation. Furthermore, leadership can rotate from person to person, or even group to group. As an example, more than 25 members make up the Orpheus Orchestra, one of the most widely acclaimed musical ensembles in the world. For the last 30 years, the Orpheus Orchestra has rehearsed, performed, and recorded without a conductor. Members select a small group for each piece of music to work out the details and then present their ideas to the entire orchestra. Then, the orchestra refines the final product, rehearsing the piece and checking the sound. At some time, every member is expected to become a leader.

The Orpheus Orchestra has developed training sessions for organizations that are looking to incorporate the **Orpheus Process,** a process in which the sharing of leadership allows everybody to work together and maximize their expertise and creativity. Harvey Seifter, the orchestra's executive director, has collaborated with a business writer to write a book about this fascinating and unusual process, *Leadership Ensemble: Lessons in Collaborative Management from the World's Only Conductorless Orchestra.*

All leaders operate in a multicultural context. Even if leaders and their followers come from the same ethnic group and geographic region, cultural differences exist. As an example, imagine a team of White males who grew up in the same neighborhood. However, their ages differ markedly. This team is made up of Baby Boomers born between 1946 and 1964, GenXers born between 1965 and 1980, and Millennials born after 1980. Because of their age, their views have been shaped by a variety of different life experiences, such as growing up with the Internet and digital media, participating in the civil rights movement, or developing one's cultural identity at a time when international terrorism and security are growing concerns. These and other generational differences may influence team members in numerous ways, including their communication styles, lifestyles, goals, work and family priorities, and cross-racial friendships.

DIVERSITY-CONSCIOUS LEADERSHIP

In order to lead across difference in today's multicultural workplace, what skills are the most important? The Center for Creative Leadership asked this question of a group of small business owners, educators, professional services and public sector leaders, and other people who show leadership in their everyday lives. While their responses point to the importance of technical and organizational skills, even more importance is attached to interpersonal openness and relationship building (see Fig. 8.2).

When leading across differences and working with people made up of diverse cultural or demographic groups, leaders influence others in a variety of ways, including

Photo 8.2 Leadership varies from situation to situation.

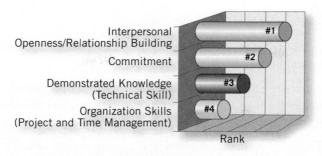

Figure 8.2 What leadership skills are most important today?
Source: Center for Creative Leadership.[2]

problem-solving, team-building, communication, and consensus-building. But how can we empower others if we do not understand them? How do we motivate people whose values are markedly different from our own? And how do we promote teamwork and unity when language differences, biases, and cultural ignorance inhibit communication?

Diversity-conscious leadership refers to the process by which people influence and empower others by recognizing, understanding, and adjusting to diversity in all its forms. Research indicates that diversity consciousness can make the difference between an average, good, or great leader. In part, this is because many leaders, regardless of their job or status, are ill-prepared to relate to others who do not share their personalities, values, and backgrounds. Their insensitivity to individual and cultural differences mitigates their ability to lead others.

For example, diversity-conscious leaders understand that purely research-based decision-making may or may not be appropriate in a particular cultural context. In some cultures or situations, relationships and traditions may take priority over scientific reasoning. On the surface, it might seem counterproductive to consider age, disability, gender, or religious values when making decisions about work schedules or where and when to schedule a meeting or retreat. Yet, such thinking might be prudent.

Diversity-conscious leaders are competent thinkers and actors in a variety of worlds. One of their strengths is their ability to adapt, shift perspectives, and blend leadership styles when the situation calls for it. They stay the course but also shift direction when necessary.

Diversity-conscious leaders do not predict and evaluate the actions of others based on what they would do. **Mirror-imaging**, judging others on the basis of one's own expectations, is something many leaders tend to do because it is easier to question others' assumptions than our own. Likewise, we find it easier to assume others share our backgrounds, motives, emotions, and perspectives than to consider and search for possible differences.

Rather than engage in mirror-imaging, diversity-conscious leaders are aware of the possibilities whenever and wherever interaction takes place. They do not assume similarities any more than they assume differences. For example, even though leaders may view time as a valuable and finite resource, they understand that others may not. Cross-cultural interaction has provided them with insight into societies such as India, Mexico, and countries in South America, where events begin and end by mutual consensus. Punctuality may be a goal, but unless there is an emergency, personal commitments and the event itself are more important.

WHO CAN BE A DIVERSITY-CONSCIOUS LEADER?

Many myths contribute to the idea that only a select few can be diversity-conscious leaders. These are some of the most common:

- *Myth One:* Diversity-conscious leaders are naturally "people persons."
  Reality: There is nothing natural about the ability to relate to others effectively. As with any skill, people develop and improve their competencies in this area.

- *Myth Two:* Diversity-conscious leadership is an extremely rare ability.
  Reality: Everyone has the potential to be a diversity-conscious leader.

- *Myth Three:* Diversity-conscious leaders are intellectually brilliant.
  Reality: Brilliance is not a precondition for diversity consciousness. Any number of brilliant leaders find it difficult to relate effectively to people from diverse backgrounds. Furthermore, people with "average" capabilities can be exceptional leaders.

- *Myth Four:* Diversity-conscious leaders are charismatic extroverts.
  Reality: Some are but many are not. Diversity-conscious leaders do not fit one mold; rather, they display a wide assortment of personalities, behaviors, and communication styles.

- *Myth Five:* A diversity-conscious leader must be able to persuade and control people in spite of their differences.
  Reality: Diversity-conscious leadership is not so much the exercise of power as the empowerment of others.

We cannot narrow any type of leadership down to a specific set of traits. Not only do diversity-conscious leaders possess a wide variety of traits, individuals and cultures perceive leadership traits differently. For instance, one culture may define a leader as a consensus builder; others might see a leader as someone who is more task-oriented and controls others. Moreover, the optimal level of a specific leadership trait varies according to the situation. Consider the trait of flexibility. Leaders who are too flexible may not provide the structure that others need. Similarly, a lack of flexibility may make it difficult to take individual needs and values into account.

 Thinking Through Diversity

Have you ever believed any of these five myths to be true? Explain.

Regardless of age, cultural background, or educational credentials, each of us can be a diversity-conscious leader. There is no magic formula; nor are there any shortcuts. Quite simply, we must be willing to invest the necessary time, energy, and resources and commit ourselves to a lifelong process of learning and personal growth.

Leaders Develop Their Own Potential

John Kotter's *The General Managers* is based on his classic study of the traits of top executives. Although Kotter studied leaders in upper-level management, his findings certainly apply to workers at all organizational levels. The author, a professor at Harvard Business School, found that effective leaders learn to develop their own potential. According to Kotter, their careers are distinguished by almost constant growth in their interpersonal and intellectual skills and in their relationships with "relevant others."[3]

KEY SKILLS OF A DIVERSITY-CONSCIOUS LEADER

Diversity consciousness provides leaders with the skills to promote interpersonal openness and build relationships in a global, multicultural environment. Of these skills, adapting, thinking and communicating inclusively, and assessing as well as monitoring are among the most important.

Adapting

Imagine that you are asked to lead a task force at work. You are given a relatively short period of time to gather information, analyze it, and submit a report to your supervisor. Seven other employees whom you hardly know have also been appointed to work with you. Which type of leader are you going to be in this situation? Are you simply going to adopt whatever leadership style is most comfortable for you? Given the fact that you need to produce a report quickly, you might prefer to focus on making sure that your team completes its job. However, what if the people on the task force find it difficult to get along with each other? Is this something you can afford to ignore?

Diversity-conscious leaders do not necessarily gravitate to what is most comfortable or familiar. Rather, they seek to expand their repertoire of leadership styles and develop their ability to seamlessly shift styles depending on the cultural context. Given the dynamics of a group, they may choose to coach and collaborate with others, or avoid emotional bonds and adopt a more authoritative posture. Reflecting on their knowledge of human behavior and group processes helps them realize that although team members may have the same goals, they may use different means to achieve these goals.

> It's hard for leaders to change without awareness of what they do.
>
> —Another perspective

Actively listening to others can help us adapt and change. Consider Janet, a supervisor for a consulting firm. Her assessments show that her coworkers feel she is impatient and does not care about people. Janet is not happy with this feedback. After all, any advice she offers is aimed at helping people succeed. With a bit of coaching from a close friend, she begins to realize that perception is part of the problem. Although she takes pride in "telling it like it is," people perceive her to be uncaring and unapproachable. As an alternative, she begins to explain that she offers advice to help them succeed, however uncomfortable they might feel. To counter the perception that she is a cold-hearted, career-only woman, she redecorates her office. Realizing that many of her coworkers are having babies and trying to balance work and family responsibilities, she decides to hang pictures of her nieces and nephews on the wall of her office and put some of their artwork on her desk.

The Vietnamese tend to place a high value on adaptability, admiring individuals who do not simply adhere to their position but compromise and adjust to fit the situation. The Vietnamese have a saying, "The supple bending reed survives storms which break the strong but unyielding oak."

Thinking and Communicating Inclusively

In order to think and communicate inclusively, diversity-conscious leaders are students of people and their interrelationships. These leaders are aware of the danger of only internalizing information that reinforces their own beliefs and values while ignoring or rationalizing away information that does not. Furthermore, they appreciate the difficulty of leading in the context of difference and the costs of thinking exclusively.

For example, a U.S. businessman may not think inclusively when he uses sports lingo such as "I'm calling an audible," "Step up to the plate," or "We're under par." Often, people who do not follow sports or do not use sports terminology in a business context have little or no understanding of what these phrases mean. For instance, the Japanese do not customarily use sports analogies in their own language.

Communicating inclusively means developing one's awareness and understanding of different communication styles. As an example, feedback in Asian cultures—whether it be positive or negative—is apt to be directed at a group rather than an individual. The directness of feedback varies as well. U.S. managers are more apt to provide face-to-face feedback, whereas Japanese managers are more likely to convey their thoughts in writing or through someone else.

Another prerequisite for inclusive communication is empathy. Being empathetic moves us out of our paradigms and helps us to recognize others' realities and talents. In *Principle Centered Leadership,* Stephen Covey discussed the value of empathy; that is, how it helps people feel that someone is learning and open to other points of view. According to leadership experts, people can sense whether leaders understand their concerns or if they are just putting on an act. Dotlich, Cairo, and Rhinesmith, authors of *Head, Heart, and Guts,* emphasize that leaders are "thrust into situations where they must work with and lead people who are different from themselves. To handle these situations from a purely cognitive basis (to explain but never be able to connect emotionally) won't work."[4] Empathy allows a diversity-conscious leader to motivate individuals in ways that allow everyone to feel understood and respected.

Assessing and Monitoring

What are the ways in which my cultural background, gender, religion, and race frame my thinking and influence my actions? Do I understand and appreciate the ways my behavior influences others? How do I monitor the degree to which I am responsive to racial, ethnic, linguistic, religious, and gender diversity?

One of the defining traits of diversity-conscious leaders is their quest to continually improve and learn by assessing and monitoring their own competencies. Honest and thorough self-assessment can be a humbling experience in that it helps us realize just how much we do not know. For example, the deeper we dig the more we may become aware of our own cultural illiteracy and bias.

Self-monitoring is the ability to use interpersonal cues to understand better one's own behavior and its effect on others. By self-monitoring, we continually focus on ourselves, others, and the environment. People who self-monitor learn from all kinds of feedback, reevaluate, and then adjust according to the situation.

Continuous self-monitoring and self-assessment enable us to discover our strengths and weaknesses, develop awareness and understanding of interpersonal skills, and expand our knowledge of cultural differences. For example, self-monitors look for cues regarding the appropriateness of behavior. How might verbal and nonverbal reactions point to whether I am seen as listening in an attentive, empathetic, and nonjudgmental way? As a leader, are there any cues to indicate whether my interactions convey respect to both men and women? In an interview, am I acting differently toward certain types of applicants? For example, do I establish more eye contact, ask more follow-up questions, or change my tone of voice with certain individuals? Acquiring a more complex understanding of our actions by asking questions such as these may point to hidden biases.

Monitoring Bias

A recent study by Bertrand and Mullainathan found that a person's name can trigger bias. Resumes of phantom job applicants were randomly assigned White-sounding names, such as Emily Walsh and Brendan Baker, and African-American-sounding names, such as Lakisha Washington and Jamal Jones. All of the applicants' resumes were alike in other important respects, such as education, experience, and skills. The researchers found that White-sounding names generated 50 percent more interviews.[5]

When leading, do we engage in self-monitoring? For instance, are we aware when we tend to be more authoritative or inclusive? Are we more comfortable focusing on the way people interrelate or the task to be accomplished? And if the situation calls for it, are we capable of shifting gears and becoming more supportive, more directing, or more delegating?

FOUR BUILDING BLOCKS OF DIVERSITY-CONSCIOUS LEADERSHIP: AN ASSESSMENT

Self-assessments, such as the one that follows, allow us to recognize and leverage our strengths, and equally important, identify and work on our shortcomings. This assessment focuses on the four building blocks of diversity conscious leadership: awareness, understanding, skills, and commitment (see Fig. 8.3).

Directions: For each statement, write the number corresponding to your answer in the space provided: Almost always (5), Frequently (4), Sometimes (3), Rarely (2), or Never (1).

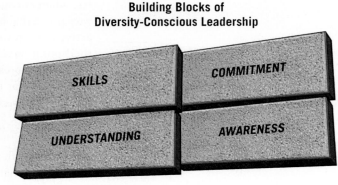

Building Blocks of Diversity-Conscious Leadership

Figure 8.3 The Four Building Blocks of Diversity-Conscious Leadership.

Awareness

When leading across differences, I am aware:

_____ of my strengths.

_____ of my weaknesses.

_____ that diversity is not all about women and minorities.

_____ that people might share the same cultural or racial background but think and act very differently.

_____ of those times when my behavior may or may not bring out the best in people.

_____ of the challenges posed by diversity.

_____ of my own cultural values and beliefs.

_____ of my language, both verbal and nonverbal.

_____ of those times when I assume my cultural values are everybody's cultural values.

_____ of the ways in which my cultural background influences my thinking.

_____ *total out of a possible score of 50*

Understanding

When leading across differences, I understand:
_____ that everyone does not organize and process information the way I do.
_____ the different ways in which people identify themselves.
_____ how culture and communication interrelate.
_____ how my ability to adapt to new cultural contexts impacts my "bottom line."
_____ how cultural differences may influence how and why people disagree with one other.
_____ the cultural complexities of the environments surrounding me.
_____ the importance of inviting honest feedback and open dialogue.
_____ *total out of a possible score of 35*

Skills

When leading across differences, I:
_____ empower others.
_____ am open to change based on input and feedback from others.
_____ check the assumptions I make about others.
_____ use all of my senses to gauge people's expectations.
_____ view situations from a variety of perspectives.
_____ examine the cultural setting in which interpersonal interactions take place.
_____ adapt my leadership style when necessary.
_____ deal effectively with the uncertainty that results from cultural differences.
_____ deal effectively with the "cultural shock" or personal disorientation I may feel when encountering radically different beliefs and values.
_____ vary my verbal and nonverbal communication when a situation requires it.
_____ actively listen to each and every individual, regardless of who they are and their point of view.
_____ am adept at breaking through interpersonal barriers.
_____ reflect on what I might do differently in the future.
_____ *total out of a possible score of 65*

Commitment

When leading across differences, I:
_____ want to do what is necessary to be more aware of diversity.
_____ want to make a difference by modeling respect for diversity.
_____ look for ways to be more inclusive.
_____ am willing to engage in difficult dialogues that deal with diversity issues.
_____ try to assess myself whenever and wherever possible.
_____ am determined to understand the perspectives of people from diverse cultural backgrounds.
_____ push myself to continue despite barriers and setbacks.
_____ am willing to look deep into myself and confront my own prejudices.
_____ am committed to continuous learning and adjustment.
_____ show my commitment to diversity by my actions.
_____ *total out of a possible score of 50*
_____ **cumulative total** *out of a possible score of 200*

By regularly using the preceding self-assessment, you will be able to track your personal growth over time. Personal commitment is key. Without a strong desire to put newfound awareness, understanding, and skills to use, your development as a diversity-conscious leader will be compromised.

Thinking Through Diversity

Reflect on the self-assessment you just completed. In what area (awareness, understanding, skills, commitment) do you need the most improvement? What is one specific thing you can do now to improve?

Understanding *and* Doing

Recently, Goldsmith and Morgan conducted a study of more than 86,000 leaders from major corporations. As part of the study, leaders were given feedback regarding what they could do to increase their effectiveness. Interestingly, results showed *no* correlation between understanding what they needed to do and actually doing it. Leaders who did nothing understood what actions were necessary just as well as those leaders who followed through on their plans for improvement.[6]

LEADERSHIP THEORIES

Traditionally, so-called *trait theories* of leadership were built on the premise that certain people are "born leaders." According to these theories, leaders were distinguished by certain traits. Physiological, psychological, and intellectual traits set leaders apart. However, attempts to identify a cluster of leadership traits proved unsuccessful, in part because these traits are neither universal nor inborn. Any list, no matter how comprehensive, will reflect cultural biases.

 Behavioral theories of leadership shifted attention away from the traits of effective leaders and toward their behaviors. Two major research efforts associated with this school of thought took place during the mid-1900s at The Ohio State University and the University of Michigan. Researchers identified two dimensions of leadership behavior that influenced work performance: leaders who were production- or task-oriented and those who were more people-oriented.

 In contemporary discussions of leadership functions and styles, researchers continue to use these dimensions. Task-oriented or **instrumental leaders** tend to focus more on the task at hand and less on how group members get along. People-oriented or **expressive leaders** take a different approach. Their primary concern is the well-being of group members and their ability to work as a unit. Although each of these behaviors was found to have certain benefits, subsequent research found that effective leaders often combine a concern for people and a concern for performance.

 More recently, researchers have focused on the situations in which these behaviors are found. Situational factors might influence whether a particular behavior is effective. These include the nature of the task, organizational climate, cultural setting, and people's expectations.

Thinking Through Diversity

After a day-long workshop on leadership in the workforce, one of the participants began to rethink his view of an effective leader. "Are effective leaders," he asked, "more like proven gladiators (instrumental) or caring shepherds (expressive)?" Which of these two types of leaders best describes you? Why might you try to develop skills related to both types?

Situational leadership theory posits that different leadership styles are more or less effective in different situations. **Leadership styles**, which refer to the way we influence others, are numerous and varied.

One widely used typology delineates three major leadership styles:

Authoritarian leaders—make all or most of the decisions and keep power to themselves
Democratic leaders—share power and encourage group discussion and decision-making
Laissez-faire leaders—minimally involve themselves in decision-making and encourage group members to make their own decisions

Situational leaders refer to individuals who adapt their leadership style depending on the circumstances. Management guru Ken Blanchard and an internationally known author and consultant on leadership, Paul Hersey, created a theoretical model of situational leadership that involves analyzing the situation and then adopting the most appropriate leadership style.[7]

The Hersey and Blanchard leadership model emphasizes that the effectiveness of different styles depends on the people being led. Followers may differ in terms of their competence and their commitment or motivation to tackle the task at hand. To illustrate, someone with only "low competence" and "high commitment" may lack the necessary skills but be eager to learn and take direction. This type of follower is apt to benefit from an "authoritarian leader" who supervises them closely. On the other hand, a follower with "high competence" and "high commitment" is apt to be more experienced and confident in his or her ability. This situation may call for more of a "laissez-faire leader," in which the follower is given more control and latitude. Another situational variable, hierarchal relations between leaders and followers, may influence whether power is viewed as something to be shared. A "democratic leadership style" might only be appropriate if followers embrace and utilize their decision-making responsibility. In an organizational climate in which top-down decision-making is expected, individuals are apt to prefer a more authoritarian leadership style.

Assumptions underlying leadership theories may reveal a cultural bias. As an example, it is frequently assumed that democratic or participative leadership is preferable and more productive. Although this may be true in some situations, it is not true in all situations. Rather than assume, we need to analyze leadership from a critical, cross-cultural perspective. Indeed, this assumption may reflect U.S. values that support democratic over authoritarian leadership. Such thinking disregards the interrelationship among leadership and customs, traditions, beliefs regarding the nature of power and authority, standards of living, and gender roles.

 Thinking Through Diversity

Do you vary your leadership style depending on the individuals and cultural diversity in a particular setting?

LEADERSHIP IN A CULTURAL CONTEXT

In different cultures, there are different views regarding who should be a leader and what a leader should or should not do. Consequently, cultural context exerts a significant influence on how we influence others and whether one style might be more effective than another.

For instance, people in the United States do not expect leaders to be infallible, but people in many other cultures are much more unforgiving when one of their leaders admits a mistake. Similarly, cultural differences may influence who is seen as "leadership material." For example, a leader who is in his 60s or 70s may command great respect in a culture that equates age with wisdom, but this same leader may be considered past his prime in another culture.

Geert Hofstede, an international management scholar, surveyed more than 116,000 workers in 40 countries, all of whom were employees of International Business Machines (IBM). Not surprisingly, he found that a country's culture had a profound effect on workers' attitudes and values. Leaders, regardless of their position in an organization, need to be constantly aware of this interrelationship. Hofstede's framework for understanding cultural differences helps us understand that principles of sound management, or effective leadership strategies, are not universal.

Data from Hofstede's study show that the countries differ along a number of dimensions.[8] Additionally, findings point to considerable variability within a culture; therefore, each dimension represents an average pattern of beliefs and values found in a particular country. Different countries show greater or lesser amounts of each dimension.

Hofstede's Six Cultural Dimensions

Individualism Versus Collectivism

This dimension refers to the degree to which cultures emphasize the importance of individuals (individualism) as opposed to groups, such as the extended family or an organization (collectivism). **Individualism** reinforces people's reliance on self, and encourages a greater concern with one's own interests. **Collectivism** reinforces a greater reliance on the group, and a greater concern for the welfare of all concerned.

Leadership in collectivist societies is more of a group phenomenon. Workers bring considerable loyalty to their jobs and place their utmost faith in leaders. In return, workers expect leaders to show loyalty as well by looking out for the workers' best interests. Leaders in the United States, found to be highest on the dimension of individualism, tend to prioritize an individual's needs. The self-interests of leaders and followers tend to be more important than the group (see Fig. 8.4).

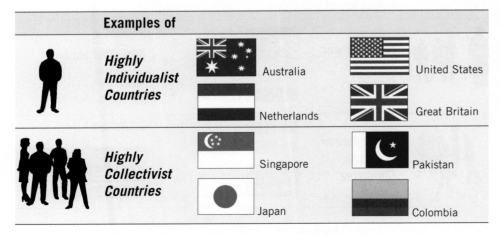

Figure 8.4 Individualism or Collectivism.

Large or Small Power Distance

This dimension refers to the degree to which power is distributed unequally. In **large power distance cultures**, significant inequalities among people are both accepted and expected. On the other hand, **small power distance cultures** play down the importance of inequalities in power and wealth as much as possible.

In a large power distance society, leaders lead autocratically. Employees show a great deal of respect for those in authority. They are hesitant to question their supervisor or even offer up ideas. A person's title and rank is socially significant, and impacts greatly on interpersonal relationships. In schools, for example, students are expected to treat an authority figure such as a teacher with a great deal of respect and deference. Relationships in a small power distance society such as the United States tend to be more egalitarian; however, power still remains with the leader. There is more two-way communication between those in authority and subordinates. For instance, teachers in the United States often seek more input from and delegate more authority to students. Nevertheless, the relationship between students and teachers remains hierarchal (see Fig. 8.5).

Strong or Weak Uncertainty Avoidance

This dimension refers to the degree to which ambiguity and uncertainty are tolerated, and absolute truths are avoided. In societies characterized by **strong uncertainty avoidance**, risk and uncertainty are avoided if at all possible, and absolute truths are embraced. People in **weak uncertainty avoidance** societies tend to avoid absolute truths and do not feel nearly as threatened by behavior and opinions different from their own.

In strong uncertainty avoidance societies, followers create a feeling of security by relying heavily on leaders. Organizational leaders in a strong uncertainty avoidance society are people whose word is accepted as a kind of law. These leaders are apt to have more rules and tolerate less deviance from those rules. In the United States (weak uncertainty avoidance), leaders are more inclined to take risks, tolerate deviance, and encourage employees not to back down but to speak their mind. This type of leadership strategy is seen as a way to promote new ideas (see Fig. 8.6).

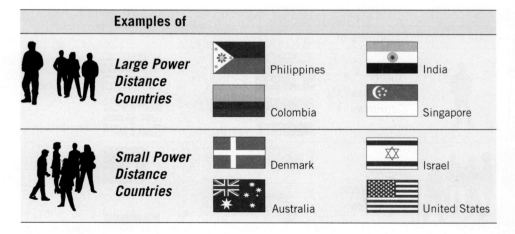

Figure 8.5 Large or Small Power Distance.

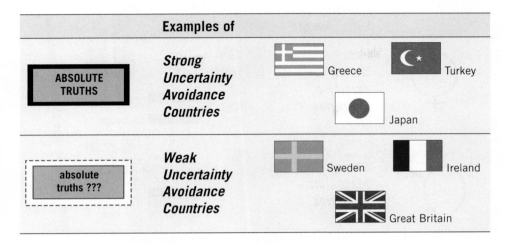

Figure 8.6 Strong or Weak Uncertainty Avoidance.

Thinking Through Diversity

Does your cultural background influence your views about the effectiveness of leaders who show a great deal of interpersonal sensitivity? Explain.

Masculinity Versus Femininity

This dimension refers to the degree to which gender roles are differentiated and valued. Some societies allow males and females to assume many different roles, whereas others make a sharp distinction regarding what males and females should and should not do. Hofstede refers to **"masculine cultures"** as those that sharply delineate gender roles and attach more importance to roles associated with males, such as assertiveness and independence. **"Feminine cultures,"** as defined by Hofstede, are those that distinguish among gender roles to a lesser degree and attach more importance to roles associated with females, such as relationship-oriented activities and interpersonal sensitivity.

Of the countries he surveyed, Hofstede found Japan to be the most masculine country, with very strong sex role differentiation in leadership. More feminine cultures, such as the Netherlands, tend to attach more importance to nurturing and social support (see Fig. 8.7). U.S. culture was found to be somewhat more masculine than feminine. Although leaders in the United States viewed traditional sex role divisions as outdated and stereotypical, expectations based on traditional roles remain.

More recently, Hofstede added two more dimensions: long-term versus short-term orientation and indulgence versus restraint. Societies with a **long-term orientation** place more emphasis on the future and attach importance to values such as persistence and saving. **Short-term orientation** is typical of those societies that direct people's efforts towards the present and past, and value tradition and the achievement of more immediate results. The sixth dimension examines the issue of gratification. **Indulgence** is found in those societies that put less restraint on gratification of basic human drives, while **restraint** typifies societies that rigidly regulate gratification through the imposition of social norms.

Hofstede's model forces us to expand our view of leadership. Traditionally, leadership has been evaluated from a narrow, ethnocentric perspective. Theories on leadership usually reflect a **micro-level orientation**, a viewpoint that focuses on interaction among individuals in specific settings. A **macro-level orientation** focuses on

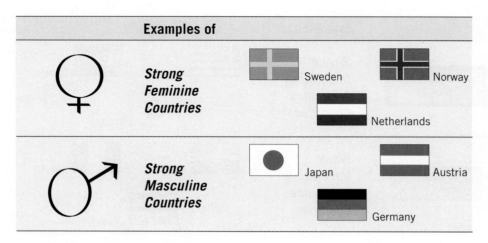

Figure 8.7 Masculinity Versus Femininity.

large-scale patterns of behavior in organizations, societies, and the world as a whole. By viewing leadership from a broader perspective, Hofstede shows the importance of evaluating leadership in a cultural, global context. Given the gap among countries on the cultural dimensions, there is a strong likelihood that the leadership styles among different cultures will be dissimilar and, in some cases, markedly so. As an example, leaders from Australia or the United States (highly individualist, small power distance) will probably have to modify their leadership styles radically if they find themselves in a country such as Colombia or Singapore (highly collectivist, large power distance). If they are not prepared for this degree of adjustment, the result could very well be **culture shock**, feelings of disorientation and stress due to experiencing an unfamiliar cultural environment.

Despite its continued relevance, Hofstede's groundbreaking study is not without its critics. One of the major criticisms is that he tends to portray populations as culturally homogenous and ignores the salience of various communities and subcultures within a nation. Other critics take issue with how Hofstede makes inferences about the cultures of entire countries based on his research of a single company, IBM. Finally, some scholars note that Hofstede's work is incomplete. Further research is necessary in order to examine other cultural dimensions by gathering data using a variety of research methods.

Diversity-conscious leadership is about relationships involving individuals, groups, *and* cultures. Consequently, views regarding what constitutes effective leadership vary. As numerous cross-cultural studies indicate, including Hofstede's research and more recently the GLOBE study,[9] diversity within and across cultures calls for situational leadership, rather than a one-size-fits-all model. Data from the GLOBE Project Team, made up of 170 researchers, point to cultural dimensions in addition to those studied by Hofstede. These dimensions include the degree to which a society encourages people to be caring, generous, and kind (humane orientation) and focus on the job itself (performance orientation). Being aware of these cultural dimensions helps us guard against assuming that a leader should always act a certain way. For instance, performance improvement and excellence may be valued in Hong Kong and the United States. However, in countries such as Russia and Argentina, a greater emphasis may be placed on loyalty and *who* someone is rather than *what* he or she does.

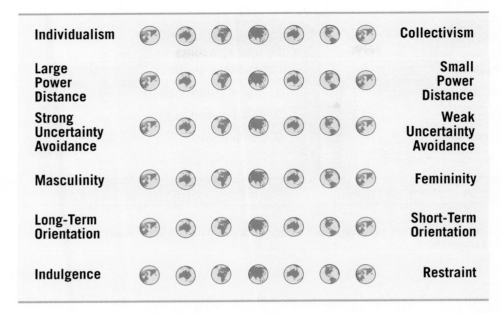

Figure 8.8 Rank Your Cultural Preference.

Thinking Through Diversity

How do you view yourself in terms of Hofstede's six dimensions (See Fig. 8.8)? For each dimension, place an "**X**" on one of the globes to indicate your own cultural preference. Do your preferences show the influence of your cultural background? Explain.

If we are to excel in an increasingly borderless world, we need to look beyond the individual and view leadership in a cultural context. Findings from comprehensive global research show that our views of leadership are shaped by cultural beliefs and values. Hence, the effectiveness of leaders hinges to a large degree on their ability to recognize, understand, and adjust to a wide array of cultural dimensions.

THE DIVERSITY-CONSCIOUS LEADER OF THE FUTURE

As perceptions change regarding key leadership skills, more attention is being focused on the diversity consciousness of leaders. Data from a global survey of organizations by the Center for Creative Leadership illustrate significant changes in our thinking regarding important leadership skills (see Fig. 8.9) As challenges facing both small and large organizations become more complex, leadership will continue to become a more collective, interdependent process that occurs throughout an organization. Interestingly, respondents see leaders of the future being rewarded for the "success of others," rather than for "being a star."

As leaders manage global issues with a global workforce, an emerging skill set will place even more emphasis on cultural issues and collaboration, according to the recently conducted *Developing Successful Global Leaders Study*. Among the most important future competencies of global leaders, participants identified collaborating with peers from multiple cultures, managing innovation in a multicultural setting,

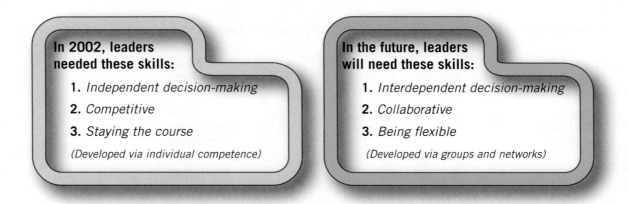

In 2002, leaders needed these skills:

1. *Independent decision-making*
2. *Competitive*
3. *Staying the course*

(Developed via individual competence)

In the future, leaders will need these skills:

1. *Interdependent decision-making*
2. *Collaborative*
3. *Being flexible*

(Developed via groups and networks)

Figure 8.9 Emerging Leadership Skills. Data based on responses from nearly 400 mid- to upper-level managers. *Source: Center for Creative Leadership.*[10]

cross-cultural employee engagement, and managing virtual teams.[11] The diversity consciousness of future global leaders will allow them to:

- *Collaborate across cultures, face to face and remotely, using the latest and most effective virtual technology.* Open to diverse views and new ideas, they will value feedback and not be defensive when their opinions are challenged.

- *Empower and engage employees across cultures.* Working across boundaries will necessitate that future leaders have a flexible coaching style that is encouraging rather than conforming.

- *Apply their broad knowledge and awareness of diversity and cultural issues.* They will educate themselves, drawing on information from a wide variety of international and multicultural sources and life experiences. Their language and communication skills will reflect their understanding of differences in motivation, communication, group processes, and leadership.

In the future, the nature of leadership will continue to change as diversity-conscious leaders find it increasingly necessary to collaborate and communicate across cultures more quickly and efficiently. This will severely test their openness and responsiveness, as well as their knowledge of how subjects such as psychology, sociology, economics, history, and geography all mash together. However, any course of study, no matter how extensive, is only a first step. Because of the subtlety, ambiguity, and complexity of human behavior, no laundry list of facts will cover every conceivable situation.

LEADERSHIP DEVELOPMENT

Thinking Through Diversity

What is one important life experience that helped you improve your leadership abilities?

According to a recent study, companies identified as the "best for leadership" position for the future by developing their leaders at every level. They do this in a variety of ways, including "stretch assignments" and "accelerator experiences" that help leaders grow, engage and enable people, and remove obstacles that hinder followers.[12] Many of these experiences, which require new skills and novel solutions, test their diversity consciousness.

Leadership development often occurs outside of formal training. In a study of leaders, alluded to earlier in this chapter, the Center for Creative Leadership asked respondents to share a significant, leadership-building event in their life. Among the experiences leaders shared were serving in Vietnam, living away from home for the first time, and the birth of a first child. Moreover, it is interesting to note that respondents generally thought of leadership development as a journey rather than an event.

There is no cookie-cutter method of leadership development that applies to everyone. Commitment to developing our awareness, understanding, and skills enables us to learn what is important to people, shift perspectives, and then communicate in a way that illustrates our empathy and grasp of the situation. According to Stephen Covey, leadership "comes from communicating people's worth and potential so clearly they come to see it in themselves."[13]

Each of us has the power to shape and enhance our ability to lead across differences by doing the personal growth work that is necessary. This journey of leadership development might include online learning, formal training, and experiential training. As opposed to a situation that is fabricated, experiential learning allows us to develop skills "on the job." For example, we might learn from our daily experiences with customers and clients. Challenging experiences with culture shock may teach us to observe, reflect, and experiment with new ways of adapting to new situations.

Learning to be a diversity-conscious leader is a cumulative process, making each new challenge a little easier. As we develop, we begin to move beyond superficial understanding and become more open to differences. Over time, we expand the breadth and depth of our diversity consciousness by engaging in continual reflection and self-assessment, learning to assume complexity and deal with ambiguity, and becoming more mindful of context.

A Profile in Diversity Consciousness

Diversity-conscious leaders such as William Pagonis combine expertise and empathy. Pagonis learned to be a leader in places like Vietnam and Saudi Arabia. As head of the U.S. Army's 22nd Support Command fighting in the Persian Gulf War, he came to understand the vital importance of empathy. He says, "We asked ourselves constantly: What do the other people on our team need? Why do they think they need it, and how can we give it to them?"[14] Empathy, according to Pagonis, helped him learn when and when not to adapt.

In one instance, for example, troops were unloading supplies into a building that was situated next to a particularly devout Muslim community. The sight of female soldiers with uncovered hair and rolled-up sleeves offended these Muslims. Before the situation developed into a crisis, it was decided that U.S. military personnel would wear long-sleeved shirts and female soldiers would wear hats. Another point of contention had to do with female soldiers driving vehicles and carrying weapons, activities that were prohibited for Saudi women. This time Pagonis stood firm—making it clear that all soldiers, including females, need to be able to use the tools of their trade.

To summarize, diversity consciousness has become a prerequisite for effective leadership. Diversity-conscious skills, developed through constant practice, assessment, and monitoring, enhance our ability to inspire, influence, and empower all kinds of people in all kinds of situations. By increasing our awareness and understanding of the multiple ways in which people and cultures define and demonstrate leadership, we are better able to know when and how to adjust. In turn, this allows us to cultivate trust, build cohesive relationships, look to others to challenge and complement our thinking, and mobilize people in order to get things done.

 Case Studies

Case Study One

Ligua, a native of El Salvador, is a part-time student, wife, and mother. In addition to her school and family responsibilities, Ligua works as a car salesperson. Her close friend, Rosa works at a retail store. Rosa, who has a noticeable accent, has seen how her accent can work against her in terms of her ability to sell merchandise. Some customers seem to judge Rosa by the way she sounds, rather than what she knows. Her store manager has suggested she enroll in speech training. Specifically, he hinted that if Rosa wants to move into a managerial position, she needs help in reducing her accent. A course entitled, "Your Job, Your Voice," is offered nearby. According to literature describing the course, it enables participants to move toward the standard American nonregional speech, the kind of speech television news anchors use. Her employer is willing to pay for this training.

Rosa is planning on a career in sales, and looking foward to moving into the ranks of management. While she understands the importance of effective communication, how she speaks is part of who she is. Even though some view her speech as a problem, she is reluctant to give up an important part of her identity. Rosa is not sure what she should do and has asked Ligua for advice.

Questions:

1. If you were Ligua, what advice would you give Rosa and why?

2. What are the pros and cons of Rosa's enrollment in such a class?

3. Will changing her accent help make Rosa a more effective manager? Explain.

Case Study Two

Mary is a White social work student who plans to go on for an MS degree and work in a clinical setting. She attends an urban university and enjoys the diversity and energy of city life, but in her free time is actively involved in social activities centered around her Scottish background. Mary is preparing to start providing in-home counseling services to families who are in need of emergency intervention. She will meet several different families, all with their own backgrounds, traditions, and cultural beliefs. As she goes into client homes, it is especially important for her to be respectful and communicate effectively in order to empower them to deal with the situation at hand.

To prepare herself, Mary meets with a number of other students and faculty. They discuss a number of diversity issues, including communication, trust, and possible differences in values and beliefs.

After meeting one of the families, Mary is at a loss. When she encourages them to try different approaches, family members appear to understand but seem very subdued and give her virtually no feedback. Their cultural background appears to make them hesitant to question or even ask questions of Mary, whom they perceive to be in a position of authority. Mary is hesitant to continue with her visits until she can assess what is taking place.

Questions:

1. What might Mary do differently to prepare for her home visits?

2. If you were to evaluate Mary's ability to influence and empower her clients, what are four questions you might ask her? What are four questions you might ask her clients?

3. How might Mary encourage her clients to open up, ask questions, and give her the feedback she needs?

Case Study Three

Michael is a Black college graduate, and the divorced father of a teenage son, Aaron, who attends a private school in the well-to-do suburb where they live. Michael works as a senior manager for a small consulting firm. The job requires quite a bit of travel and a great deal of networking. Michael's performance evaluations have been excellent. He enjoys the long hours his job requires. One of Michael's subordinates, Sarah, is actively involved with her church, and she spends much of her time after work and on weekends doing volunteer work. As a Christian, she feels deeply committed to serving others whenever she can, particularly those in her community. When she can, she also participates in company-sponsored volunteer projects.

After hearing about Sarah's volunteer work, the head of the firm asked Michael to talk to Sarah. Specifically, he asked Michael to express to Sarah that she needs to channel more of her time and energy into her work.

Soon thereafter, Michael called Sarah into his office to discuss her performance since her last annual evaluation. He gave Sarah a great deal of positive feedback but needed to address the quantity of her volunteer work. He said, "You know I see you do all this volunteer stuff and that's all well and good. But if you have this much time on your hands, you really should be spending more of your time with client work and developing business proposals."

Michael feels very conflicted about this issue. He almost feels as if the underlying message from his supervisor is to stop helping people who need it, and spend more time at work.

Questions:

1. Could Michael have handled this matter more effectively? Explain.

2. Under what conditions is it appropriate for a supervisor to comment about an employee's volunteer work?

3. Which of Michael's leadership skills is being tested? Explain.

 Key Terms

Leadership	Situational leaders	Long-term orientation
Self-managed teams	Individualism	Short-term orientation
Orpheus Process	Collectivism	Indulgence
Diversity-conscious leadership	Large power distance cultures	Restraint
Mirror-imaging	Small power distance cultures	Micro-level orientation
Self-monitoring	Strong uncertainty avoidance	Macro-level orientation
Instrumental leaders	Weak uncertainty avoidance	Culture shock
Expressive leaders	Masculine cultures	
Leadership styles	Feminine cultures	

Exercises

Exercise 1

Think of a task you recently completed that involved people from diverse backgrounds. As you tried to inspire, influence, and empower people to achieve a shared objective, what leadership skills did you draw on? Based on this experience and your knowledge of diversity-conscious leadership, what skills do you need to improve? Explain.

Exercise 2

Write your own assessment tool of at least ten questions to help individuals determine their leadership style preference. Include a key to interpret results (example: if you answered "a" to questions 1, 3, 6, and 7, you prefer a certain leadership style). Distribute the assessment to at least ten people. Analyze the results.

 Notes

[1] J. M. Kouzes and B. Z. Posner, *The Leadership Challenge* (San Francisco: Jossey-Bass, 2007), xxii.

[2] André Martin, *A CCL Research Report: Everyday Leadership*, Center for Creative Leadership, 2007, 5.

[3] John Kotter, *The General Managers* (New York: Free Press, 1982).

[4] David Dotlich, Peter Cairo, and Stephen Rhinesmith, *Head, Heart, and Guts* (San Francisco, CA: Jossey-Bass, 2006), 135.

[5] T. S. Taylor, "What's in a Name? Bias, Sometimes," *Chicago Tribune*, Chicagoland Final Edition, Dec. 29, 2002, 5.

[6] Marshall Goldsmith, "The Fallacy of 'If They Understand, They Will Do,'" *Workforce Management*. Online, May 2007. Available: http://www.marshallgoldsmithlibrary.com/cim/articles_print.php?aid=407.

[7] Paul Hersey, Ken Blanchard, and Dewey Johnson, *Management of Organizational Behavior* (Upper Saddle River NJ: Prentice Hall, 2007).

[8] Geert Hofstede, *Culture's Consequences: International Differences in Work-Related Values* (Beverly Hills, CA: Sage Publications, 1980).

[9] Robert House, Paul Hanges, Mansour Javidan, Peter Dorfman, and Vipin Gupta (eds.), *Culture, Leadership, and Organizations: The GLOBE Study of 62 Societies* (Thousand Oaks, CA: Sage Publications, 2004).

[10] André Martin, *The Changing Nature of Leadership*, Center for Creative Leadership, 2007, Available: http://www.ccl.org/leadership/pdf/research/natureleadership.pdf.

[11] "Developing Successful Global Leaders," *Training*. Online, May/June 2011. Available: www.trainingmag.com.

[12] Patricia O'Connell, "How Companies Develop Great Leaders." Online, February 16, 2010. Available: http://www.businessweek.com/stories/2010-02-16/how-companies-develop-great-leadersbusinessweek-business-news-stock-market-and-financial-advice.

[13] "Developing Leaders," *Training Magazine*, March 2007, 88.

[14] William Pagonis, "Leadership in a Combat Zone," *Harvard Business Review*, Dec. 2001, 107–116.

9

Preparing for the Future

Learning Outcomes

Upon completion of this chapter, you will be able to:

- Analyze the interrelationship between diversity and inclusion.
- Explain why diversity consciousness expands opportunities.
- Discuss future challenges that will test our diversity consciousness.
- Elaborate on how diversity consciousness improves our abilities to find common ground.
- Explain how the life experiences of various generations impact their diversity consciousness.

Employees at Specialisterne, a software firm in Denmark, excel at managing data as well as testing software. Their memory skills, attention to detail, ability to follow through on directions, and work ethic make them excellent employees. They also share one other characteristic in common. The majority of employees at this company are individuals with autism spectrum disorders (ASDs). The term ASD refers to a wide range of lifelong, pervasive, developmental brain disorders.

Many organizations in the United States and abroad do not even consider interviewing or hiring job candidates with autism spectrum disorders. Oft-cited characteristics of people with ASDs, including poor social skills, hypersensitivity to noise, touch, and even light, and difficulty dealing with anything out of the ordinary, make them a job risk in the eyes of many employers. But Specialisterne is different. Its CEO, Thorkil Sonne, has a child with autism and learned to appreciate his gifts. Moreover, he understands the importance of creating an environment that brings out and values those gifts. Consequently, Specialisterne operates a little differently than most organizations. As Sonne says, "Though we expect employees to do their jobs well, we don't ask them to excel socially or to interact all the time with others. We just find them the right role. That takes tremendous stress off them."[1]

MyStudentSuccessLab

MyStudentSuccessLab is an online solution designed to help you acquire and develop (or hone) the skills you need to succeed. You will have access to peer-led video presentations and develop core skills through interactive exercises and projects.

A utism spectrum disorder is found worldwide among males and females of all ages, the well-to-do and impoverished, and all ethnic and racial groups. In the future, people with autism spectrum disorders will be an increasing percentage of the workforce in the United States. According to recent estimates, more than one percent of the children in the U.S. have ASDs. Yet, as adults, they continue to encounter difficulty finding employment, in spite of their distinctive and valuable skill set. Specialisterne has reaped the benefits of its highly skilled workforce. Its customers include Nokia, Deloitte, Microsoft, and Oracle. Sonne looks at the *"dandelion model"* to explain his company's success. The dandelion is seen as a weed, something that detracts from the beauty of a lush lawn or garden. However, the way we view this dandelion may very well change if we nourish it in a different setting. In that case, it has a multitude of uses as an ingredient in salads, beer, wine, natural medicines, and coffee. The dandelion itself does not change from situation to situation; rather, it is the way we look at the dandelion and make use of its virtues.

DIVERSITY CONSCIOUSNESS AND INCLUSION

In the twenty-first century, many of the nation's largest organizations are devoting an increasing amount of attention and resources to creating environments that are both diverse and inclusive. An inclusive workplace moves beyond numbers and demographics. **Inclusion** refers to the process of promoting a sense of belonging and empowerment by involving everyone and valuing their unique talents and contributions. This definition acknowledges that belongingness and uniqueness can coexist. For instance, an individual in an inclusive environment does not have to suppress or sacrifice his or her individuality or diversity in order to feel accepted. While diversity refers to all kinds of differences, inclusion refers to whether we value, respect, and leverage those differences. Contrary to popular opinion, diversity does not insure inclusion.

University of Southern California Professor Mor Barak defines an **inclusive workplace** as an environment that welcomes and utilizes diversity at all levels. As an example, inclusion refers to relationships among individuals and groups, employees and customers, and organizations as well as communities. Her interviews of business leaders and employees around the globe point to the benefits of such a workplace. According to Mor Barak, "employees who were more included in the organization's decision-making and information networks were more satisfied, more committed to the organization, and felt more productive that those who were not." Among the benefits were improvements in employee retention, recruitment, organizational image, and relationships with customers.[2]

Recently, I facilitated a training program for the leadership of a large metropolitan law enforcement organization. The department was under investigation by the U.S. Department of Justice, in large part because the demographics of the organization did not reflect the demographics of the population it serves. While the organization's employees were predominantly White, especially upper-level leaders, the communities it serves were much more mixed, both racially and ethnically.

Prior to one of the training sessions, the head of the organization said to me, "We don't have a diversity problem here." While that sentiment was not shared by many other participants in this program, what emerged was an organization that was dealing with the issue of inclusion. A considerable number of employees, particularly minorities, felt left out of the loop, so-to-speak. While they acknowledged systemic efforts to recruit more women, African-Americans, and Latinos, many felt that those in power did not really listen to them and their concerns. Furthermore, management did not seem to value their unique voices when making key decisions that impacted the entire organization and those they serve.

Viewing diversity and inclusion as a problem is misguided and shortsighted. This view is an outgrowth of the compliance-based model. According to this model, which is rooted in the past, diversity is all about insuring representation of certain groups in order to comply with the law. While compliance is certainly a component of a diverse, inclusive workforce, the model of the future speaks to opportunity and growth. This is made possible by the maximization of **human capital**, a concept defined by Adam Smith in *The Wealth of Nations*. In his classic inquiry into what builds a nation's wealth, Smith defines human capital as "the economic value of an employee's skill set, including knowledge and experience."

The consequences of a lack of inclusion in the twenty-first century are profound. Without it, we run the risk of not acknowledging and listening to everyone's voice. This can have catastrophic consequences. Consider the consequences when we do not cast a wide enough net to find the next great idea. Those ideas that can mean the difference between success and failure or good and great may very well come from people we are inclined to overlook because they lack credentials, seniority, or authority. Without reaching out and developing meaningful, authentic relationships with such people, we may never hear from them. Or perhaps the chilly climate of our organization or the barriers that arise because of our individual and collective biases makes open and honest sharing of ideas difficult.

Exclusive behaviors and environments serve to limit our resources, including the diversity, reach, and power of our social and informational networks. Our inability to lead inclusively limits the size and quality of our talent pool. When people find themselves "left out" and marginalized through no fault of their own, this can negatively impact recruitment, job performance, decision-making, and turnover. Additionally, communication and teamwork suffer. For too many employees and customers, there is a recurrent feeling of being underappreciated and even invisible.

In education, exclusiveness can be found in a school's resources, curriculum, classroom climate, pedagogy, and the expectations of teachers and staff. Schools can unknowingly operate on the basis of one cultural model and in the process, exclude others. When this occurs, students may experience alienation and isolation. Consequently, student retention, engagement, and achievement are likely to suffer. In his book, *Courageous Conversations*, Glenn Singleton argues that achievement gaps persist because schools are not designed to educate all students, and educators lack the commitment, knowledge and skill to affirm diversity. Singleton makes it clear that educators need to examine thoroughly their beliefs and practices in order to "re-create schools." This requires open and honest conversations about issues that are often "swept under the rug." While Singleton focuses on underserved students who experience exclusion due to their race, any discussion of this nature needs to focus on all of the ways in which diversity intersects with schooling.

Temple Grandin, a well-known author and activist who has autism, makes it clear why we need to be inclusive of people who not only look different but think differently. She says, "The world needs all kinds of minds" working together. Moreover, Grandin emphasizes that we should place more of our focus on those things that we do well. While this is easy to understand, especially in a society such as ours, it is difficult to actually value all minds in our daily personal and professional lives. As an example, Temple Grandin did not behave or think conventionally. Because of her gender, poor social skills, appearance, and inability to communicate effectively, people were inclined to dismiss her provocative and unconventional ideas. Yet those who did engage and truly listen to her uncovered a mind that was capable of reinventing the livestock handling industry. Specifically, her ability to see "in pictures," almost as if she was looking at an object from many different angles, and sense how a cow feels and thinks, made it possible for Grandin to design more humane and effective slaughterhouses. Grandin, Professor of Animal Science at Colorado State University, expounds on these ideas in her new book, *The Autistic Brain: Thinking Across the Spectrum.*

Diversity consciousness allows us to be more inclusive. When we construct realities, we become more aware of people like Temple Grandin and all of the people she represents. Awareness, however, is only one component of diversity consciousness. Tapping and harnessing intellectual and other forms of diversity require follow-though and commitment. Through diversity consciousness, we become more effective communicators. We look to continually develop and refine our ability to question ourselves and our insular thinking. We engage and seek to understand people, cultures, and histories that have been marginalized by the way we and others interact in everyday life.

One of my mentors, the late Dr. Ira Zepp, taught me the value of asking questions. To paraphrase Dr. Zepp, a good question is more inclusive than a good answer. Asking people questions and listening intently to their answers are inclusive behaviors. Whereas questions bring people together, answers tend to be more divisive. Shirley Engelmeier, a business consultant, gathered data from more than 300,000 corporate employees in the United States in an attempt to identify those behaviors that build inclusive workplaces. Her findings point to the importance of simple behaviors. When participants were asked, "When do you feel included?" their most common response was "When I'm asked my opinion" and "When they ask me how to make a change."[3] While context is all important, the act of asking pertinent and meaningful questions can serve to validate the experiences and perspectives of others. And while we might not necessarily agree with or act on responses to our questions, the questioning process encourages involvement and engagement, particularly when it is repeated over time.

> Inclusion is about representation in all forms, without prejudice and bigotry. It is about a willingness to learn and work together, not to promote one race, creed, or culture, but the human race as a whole.
>
> I have conservative parents who believe in economic or social liberalism, I have anarchist friends, socialist friends, lesbian and straight friends, friends who don't participate in politics at all, disabled friends, friends in the armed services, and friends of all socioeconomic levels. I have a variety of relationships that keep me grounded and deeply rooted in issues that affect those outside me, which has helped me to have an inclusive attitude.
>
> —Other perspectives

Expanding Opportunities

Opening our minds to the possibilities and potential of diversity and inclusion provides us with an "edge" for a number of reasons.

1. *Diversity consciousness prepares you for everyday life.* The more prepared we are for life, the greater our opportunities. The benefits of diversity consciousness extend far beyond a particular job or field of employment. By developing diversity consciousness, you have fundamental skills you need for *any* job. Furthermore, the value of these skills extends to one's relationships at home, at school, in the community, and elsewhere. As your consciousness builds within you in each of these settings, you are better able to meet the growing demands of your many roles.

The Value of Relationships

Recently, a local journalist and radio talk-show host died of cancer. After listening to his political commentary on the way to work each day, I thought we shared very little in common. Yet, during the last few days of his life, he said something that resonated with me. He talked about how politics was not that important; rather, what makes life worth living are our personal relationships with others. Clearly, we cannot avoid relationships, nor can we avoid diversity. According to a social theory known as *symbolic interactionism*, we develop meaning in everyday life through our relationships with others. As multidimensional individuals, we are constantly trying to adjust to new situations and manage different realities.

Diversity consciousness helps us modify our behaviors and think more inclusively. For example, we become more aware of how we categorize people and define diversity. At work, we become more attuned to who is and who is not included on diversity teams and councils. We are more mindful of our behavior with family, friends, and acquaintances, and what messages we are communicating to children and adults about the value of diversity. And in all of our relationships, we are more sensitive to feelings of inclusion by everyone, regardless of whether they are minorities or majorities. Each and every one of these experiences, however insignificant they might seem at the time, accelerates the growth of our diversity consciousness.

2. *Diversity consciousness empowers you and others.* It gives you skills that enable you to capitalize on your own potential and help others to realize their potential. Moreover, diversity consciousness allows you to understand interpersonal, group, and cultural diversity in your life; and equally important, your ability to make choices in the midst of this diversity. In one of my classes, a heated discussion about social inequality illustrates how diversity consciousness can point the way to action and empowerment. Samuel, a student who has served time in prison, laments the lack of opportunities "out there." "All I see is negative," he says. "I see brothers on the corner selling drugs. I see prostitutes. I go back to my old neighborhood in L.A. Some of my friends went to jail, some got shot, and some are incoherent." From his point of view, he has few if any choices.

Other students take issue with what Samuel is saying. They argue that despite all the barriers—where he was born, who his friends are, his criminal background—he does have important choices to make. One student, who describes herself as a poor single parent, feels that Samuel is confusing "insurmountable barriers" with "stumbling blocks." She elaborates: "People who tell me I cannot do it or I am crazy for going to school and raising a child are stumbling blocks. They are easy to overcome because I do not let them mentally become a barrier. If I let these same people mentally debilitate me, then they become a barrier. They make me unable to use the one thing that could help me overcome them. That is my mind." This student was clearly empowered by her ability to make sense of the relationship between her environment and her choices in life.

Each and every person, whatever their diversity, needs to accept themselves and feel proud even in the face of oppression. Change takes time. But with education and understanding, piece by piece, the world can become a better place.

—Another perspective

3. *Diversity consciousness changes the way we view differences.* Diversity consciousness gives us the awareness and understanding we need to embrace, value, integrate, and leverage differences. The Peles Castle (Photo 9.1), located in mountains of Romania, is a striking example of what can be accomplished when diverse talents and perspectives come together. Its construction in the later part of the nineteenth century was a multinational undertaking. "Italians were masons, Romanians were building terraces, the Gypsies were coolies. Albanians and Greeks worked in stone, Germans and Hungarians were carpenters. Turks were burning brick. Engineers were Polish and the stone carvers were Czech. The Frenchmen were drawing, and the Englishmen were measuring."[4]

Not too long ago, my youngest daughter shared her thoughts about people with disabilities. She observed, "People see disability as a disadvantage, as something you're stuck with. But I see it as more of a gift." To me that comment represents the promise of diversity consciousness. Because of this mindset she sees things in other people who appear different, things that others may not see. At times, the beauty of diversity is hidden from view because of our cultural lens, values, and assumptions. A disability, for example, does not hide the promise of diversity. Our culturally bound views do. When we learn to acknowledge, accept, and respect diversity, when we develop the realization that diversity is a gift, then we change who we are, our relationships with others, and our view of what is possible.

4. *Diversity consciousness prepares us for the future.* Journalist Donna Britt writes, "There have never been so many nations within our nation, linked and separate, distant and rub-up-against intimate. Never so many restaurants, markets, hair salons, doctors' offices and small businesses where English is barely spoken. So many enclaves where entire worlds exist, hidden or in plain view."[5] In the future, these trends will become even more pervasive regardless of where we live or what we do for a living. The world's religions, languages, customs, and ethics will continue to find their way into our schools, workplaces, neighborhoods, and technologies. And both local and global demographic trends, political change and legislation, economic developments, and public policy will continue to impact how we view diversity and practice inclusion.

Photo 9.1 Peles Castle, Romania.

A Profile in Diversity Consciousness

Sylvia Stultz's passion in life was teaching social skills. As a clinical psychologist, she helped children with social interaction difficulties become aware of interpersonal cues, carry on conversations, and make friends.

A few years ago, Sylvia became sick and was diagnosed with a rare malignant tumor. In the process of undergoing treatment at a number of well-known institutions, she began to notice parallels between the settings in which she worked and the clinical settings in which she received care. Care in both settings ranged from empathy and responsiveness by staff members to staff who were emotionally distant and severely lacking in diversity consciousness.

From that moment on, until the end of her life some two years later, Sylvia focused all of her energies on helping others. Specifically, she taught a variety of diversity skills to hospital staff. At one institution, she arrived at 10:15 A.M. to see a radiologist, who would be conducting a serious, delicate procedure to kill cancerous tissue. After waiting more than five hours, she finally met the medical team. After the doctor described the treatment plan, he asked Sylvia if she had any questions. In a firm but polite manner, she said, "Yes. Why do you keep your patients waiting for five hours?"

Because the doctor said he had no control over the schedule, Sylvia e-mailed someone who did, the Clinical Center's director. In her e-mail, she wrote, "As a psychologist and health-care provider myself, I wonder if there may be ways in which my experiences could alert you to the possibility that sometimes 'the system' underestimates the tremendous sense of vulnerability of your patients. We are sick, grateful, and afraid. Waiting for hours is not just inconvenient; it is frightening and disempowering— downright unhealthy. . . . If we and the other patients knew that the system was set up respectfully and if we had been given information, options, or apologies, the situation would have felt entirely different."[6] The director was so moved by Stultz's e-mail that he made reducing patient wait time a priority, abolishing "block scheduling" in which a number of patients report at the same time, and instituting individual appointments. Also, patients are now asked to keep track of how long they wait and to inform the clinic's head nurse.

Sylvia encountered similar problems at other institutions as her cancer worsened and made her weaker. Too often, staff was unresponsive to her emotional needs, and their eye contact and body language conveyed a lack of interest. Despite her condition, she made a point of discussing these issues with her caregivers.

However, one institution stood out. A nurse, whom Sylvia called "the nurse with the white hat," established a system that made patients feel more valued. When a patient rang the call button, the staff member closest to the patient's room—nurse, technician, or janitor—would respond immediately. As a result, not only did Sylvia feel much safer and calmer, she also sensed an improvement in her body's response to the cancer treatment.

Embracing diversity, now and in the future, is imperative, according to Martha Barnett, former president of the American Bar Association. "People from various ethnic, racial, and cultural backgrounds provide a wealth of talent, perspective, insight, and innovative thinking that we would not otherwise have. Our society can only become richer and healthier for the contributions that our diverse population brings."[7] Expanding opportunities by embracing diversity, however, is not a given. Nor is it linear. Rather, we will make advances, regress, and struggle with doubts about the value of diversity. We will need to remind each other that diversity is not all about race and gender. But if we develop our diversity consciousness, we will learn to adapt, grow, and hopefully come to see diversity as a gift that enriches all of our lives in a multitude of ways.

FUTURE CHALLENGES

Steve Jobs, a visionary who had an uncanny knack for peering into the future and foreseeing social and digital developments, was very fond of a quote by Wayne Gretzky, one of the greatest hockey players of all time. Gretzky said "I skate to where the puck is going to be, not where it has been."[8] By focusing on the future, Jobs positioned Apple to be on the cutting edge of technology. In a similar manner, diversity consciousness prepares us for a future in which diversity will challenge and present us with new and exciting opportunities.

> The day on which one starts out is not the time to start one's preparations.
> —A Nigerian proverb

In the future, diversity consciousness will enable each of us to empower others by creating space for other people—a space in which people can create and evaluate new ideas; a space where people can "come together and have a meaningful conversation; a space in which people can be more effective, more agile, and more prepared to respond to complex challenges."[9] Likewise, our awareness, understanding, and skills in the area of diversity will allow us to build and nourish environments in which teamwork and synergy can thrive.

A number of notable challenges lie ahead. Four in particular will test our diversity skills: demographic shifts, leveraging technology and global connections, finding common ground, and the potential for divisiveness. These challenges will have implications for each of us.

Demographic Shifts

Within the lifetime of today's teens, population changes will significantly alter how we conceptualize age, race, ethnicity, religion, and other dimensions of diversity. Four generations can now be found in the U.S. workplace, and soon there will be five. Our life expectancy continues to increase, with people over 85 the fastest growing segment of the U.S. population. America's aging Baby Boomers (those born roughly between 1946 and 1964) are staying on the job longer and seeking more flexible work options. Society is more aware of multiracial identities and more accepting of same-sex couples and marriages. Social institutions, such as the government, family, economy, education, and medicine, are finding they have to adapt.

With regard to racial and ethnic diversification, census data indicate a much greater percentage of the U.S. population will be Hispanic, Asian/Pacific American, and Native American by the year 2060 (see Fig. 9.1). The steady growth of intermarriage will continue to make the racial and cultural mix that much more blurred and complex. Census projections show that the United States will become a "majority-minority" nation in the not too distant future (2043). By the year 2060, minorities will comprise 57 percent of the U.S. population.[10] Keep in mind that social scientists refer to a **minority** as a category of people who are singled out and denied equal opportunities by those in power, or the **majority**. The term minority does *not* reflect population size. It remains to be seen whether an increase in the size of minorities translates into a significant increase in power and opportunities.

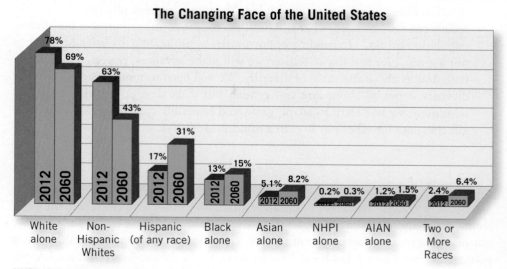

The Changing Face of the United States

NHPI: Native Hawaiian and Other Pacific Islander
AIAN: American Indian and Alaska Native

Figure 9.1 The Changing Face of the United States.
Source: U.S. Census

In all likelihood, linguistic diversity will accompany this demographic shift just as it has in the past. *Language Use in the United States*, a report by the Census Bureau, documents the magnitude of this change. Since 1980, the number of people speaking a language other than English at home has more than doubled. At the same time, a majority of these individuals reported speaking English "very well." The changing nature of linguistic diversity will continue to shape future challenges. For instance, data from the Migration Policy Institute reveals that the five languages most common among individuals with limited English proficiency (LEP) in 2010 were Spanish, Chinese, Vietnamese, Korean, and Tagalong. Just two decades earlier (1990), French, Italian, and German were among the top five.[11] As we grapple with the implications of linguistic diversity, it is imperative to keep in mind that overcoming communication barriers is a challenge for all of us. By understanding that we all need to learn other languages and cultures throughout our lifetime, we will expand our diversity consciousness and develop a deeper appreciation of the benefits of linguistic diversity.

Thinking Through Diversity

One aspect of the debate over immigration deals with the meaning and power of words. Some argue that the term "illegal immigrant" criminalizes and stigmatizes people, not their behavior. Others dismiss this concern, saying the debate is a waste of time and takes our attention away from other more important issues. How do you feel about the terms "illegal immigrants" and "illegals?"

Immigration will continue to drive population growth and diversity. Pew research projections indicate that immigrants and their descendants will account for the vast majority of population growth in the United States through mid-century. In the future, the bulk of new immigrants will not be coming from Europe but from other regions of the world, such as Asia, Latin America, and the Caribbean.[12] If trends continue, many of these individuals will not necessarily gravitate to traditional immigration-destination states such as California, Texas, New York, and Florida; rather, they will disperse nationwide. This is true of both documented and undocumented immigrants.

In the years ahead, population changes and immigration rates will continue to leave their mark on religious diversity. The Pew Landscape Survey, which deals with religious shifts in the United States, shows that Catholics significantly outnumber Protestants among foreign-born adults. Moreover, immigrants are increasingly likely to identify with a number of world religions, such as Islam, Buddhism, and Hinduism.[13]

As religious diversity continues to shift in the United States, data from Pew show the percentage of Protestants continues to decline to approximately 50 percent. Among U.S. adults, nearly 25 percent call themselves Catholic, followed by numerous other religions (almost 5 percent). These include those who identify themselves as Jewish, Muslim, Buddhist, Hindu, and people of other faiths. Interestingly, more than 40 percent change their religious affiliation at some point in their lives, and a growing number (16 percent) identify themselves as unaffiliated. Unaffiliated is a very diverse grouping, including people who call themselves atheist and agnostic, those who say they are "nothing in particular," and some who go on to say religion is "very important" to them.[14] Many of these changes are being fueled by young adults, which points to continuing change and fluidity in the religious landscape of the United States.

Developing our diversity consciousness will become even more critical as we attempt to meet the challenges posed by these radical demographic shifts. Diversity consciousness begins with an examination of our worlds and ourselves. We may, however, find it tempting to avoid self-examination by focusing on others, especially with regard to certain dimensions of diversity. For example, a nationwide poll by the *New York Times* examined people's views of themselves and their neighborhoods versus the larger community and country as a whole. Interestingly, people view race relations as generally good in their neighborhoods, where they work, and at their children's schools. They depict themselves and their neighbors as open-minded, but are less positive about the rest of the country. As their attention moved away from home, respondents saw much more room for improvement.[15]

> "My family looks like the U.N. It ranges from Jews to Buddhists. We have East Indians. We have a couple of American Indians, a couple of Europeans. My husband is from Lima, Peru. And it's great. The fights we have in our family are not about color. They're about religion."
>
> —Another perspective

Leveraging Technology and Global Connections

The indispensability of diversity consciousness becomes even more apparent when we examine the social, technological, and economic changes that are occurring all around us. In the United States, knowledge workers and service workers continue to replace laborers. Consequently, different skills are necessary. For most jobs, skills that enable us to absorb and share information are more important than mechanical or physical abilities. The frequency of interpersonal, intergroup, and cross-cultural interactions is increasing as well. These changes, along with growing global competition, make diversity consciousness a bottom-line, strategic issue.

Due to technological advances, the rest of the world will become more fused with our immediate world in the years ahead. James Becker, former senior consultant at the Social Studies Development Center at Indiana University, states: "We don't look at the world as separate pieces of real estate, but as a society in which people interact in different ways."[16] The increased flow of communications, goods, and people is making distance less important. However, cultural barriers are much more difficult to overcome than geographic barriers. With globalization a reality today, it is becoming increasingly necessary to look at the "big picture" (see Photo 9.2).

For those innovative, flexible thinkers who can adopt a multicultural perspective, global connections will open up opportunities. Conversely, ethnocentric thinking will be a liability to an even greater degree than it has been in the past. In a booklet titled *Transforming Higher Education: A Vision for Learning in the 21st Century*, Donald Norris and Michael Dolence state that tomorrow's student, teacher, and worker need to move beyond thinking "out of the box." Rather, they will need to see "around the curvature of the earth."[17] The ability of university students to deal with globalization is the subject of a recent study by IBM. Researchers surveyed 3,600 students in higher education from more than forty countries. While findings from this survey show that students are extremely concerned with issues dealing with globalization, only 40 percent indicated that their college education is adequately preparing them to deal with such issues.[18]

> It is imperative that I develop a global perspective in order to attain a more definitive and unbiased perception of who I am, and not just who they say I am. If given the choice between the fish bowl and the ocean, I for one choose the ocean.
>
> —Another perspective

Photo 9.2 Students, representing different regions of the world, work in teams to solve complex problems. This global simulation requires them to see across geographical and cultural boundaries. *Source: Courtesy of the Office of Communications, Colgate University, Hamilton, NY.*

As technology grows, global connections envelope our lives. As one business consultant points out, the global marketplace is not only the Pacific Rim or faraway places. It includes downtown Toronto, Phoenix, Spokane, and lesser known places. In short, "the global marketplace is wherever organizations do business."[19] According to experts, U.S. companies that cannot understand what is going on around the world will not be successful at home or abroad. Companies such as Microsoft understand the implications of globalization. With 90,000 employees in more than 90 countries, their future is dependent on developing regions of the world, such as India, Nigeria, Brazil, and China, which Microsoft acknowledges will make up an increasing share of the world's population by 2050. On its Web site Microsoft describes a vision that underscores the interrelationship among diversity, inclusion, globalization, and success. Their "Global Diversity and Inclusion Vision Statement" reads, "To be led by a globally diverse workforce that consistently delivers outstanding business results, understands the various cultural demands of a global marketplace, is passionate about technology and the promise it holds to tap human potential, and thrives in a corporate culture where inclusive behaviors are valued."[20]

Thinking Through Diversity

In what ways will an increasingly global environment alter the skills required by your chosen career?

In an environment becoming more globally interconnected each day, it is absolutely essential to be diversity conscious. If our thoughts and actions are too restricted, we waste precious human resources and miss opportunities. Global competition necessitates that companies view inclusiveness as a business imperative, impacting goods, products, and services, in addition to recruitment, hires, training, audits, and suppliers. Companies of all sizes can ill afford to ignore any talent or idea, from wherever it might come.

Finding Common Ground

Too often, our preoccupation with finding, understanding, and accommodating differences makes it seem like our commonalities are nonexistent or less important. Our ideas regarding various dimensions of diversity may make it difficult to identify with others and realize all that we share in common. Distinguished historian David Cannadine, in his new book *The Undivided Past: Humanity Beyond Our Differences*, explores how people throughout history have discovered ways to cross barriers and embrace our common humanity. He examines specific dimensions of diversity, including religion, nation, class, gender, and race. In his analysis, Cannadine supports his argument that these categories of human identity are usually not as divisive or salient as media commentators, politicians, or social scientists make them out to be. According to the author, binary thinking which takes the form of "us" versus "them" does not do justice to the multiple, fluid nature of our identities. As an example, Cannadine argues that human solidarity is generally much more important than class solidarity. With regard to religion, people get along quite well in spite of their religious differences, and religions share many beliefs and teachings. For many of us, our religious beliefs encourage us to be more inclusive in the way we feel and act. In his conclusion, Cannadine supports a more balanced approach. While he is not in favor of glossing over these differences, he feels that our attention should focus more on what unites us.

Through diversity consciousness, we find common ground. Our differences and similarities are not distinct entities; rather, they interrelate. To illustrate, engaging our differences helps us see our similarities. Diversity consciousness allows us to make connections and reach out to others who share so much more in common with us than we might assume. Vincente Martinez, photographer and community organizer, finds these connections in our pasts. He asks, "Where do our pasts tie in? We all come from agrarian backgrounds at some point in our past that are very rich with folklore, history, oral history, and values."[21] Whether we examine historical or contemporary human relations among individuals, groups, and societies, diversity consciousness enables us to recognize our differences and understand the fear, mistrust, and ignorance that mask our commonalities.

Discovering and valuing what we share in common requires nothing less than a lifelong commitment to expose ourselves to new and perhaps uncomfortable

Photo 9.3 The arts provide us with a basis for engaging and communicating with each other, as well as the opportunity to discover "Common Ground."
Source: Photo by Pamela Zappardino of the Ira and Mary Zepp Center for Nonviolence and Peace Education, a program of Common Ground on the Hill, Ltd.

situations and settings. This involves much more than books, webinars, workshops, and even dialogues about diversity issues. Indeed, some argue that one of the best ways to learn about each other is through life experiences that involve diversity but are not about diversity. Former U.S. Senator Bill Bradley writes, "Only through doing things together that have nothing to do with race will people break down the racial barriers . . . in a way that conversation cannot."[22]

Although Bradley focuses on the issue of race, what he says applies to all facets of diversity. One promising avenue for developing our diversity consciousness is Common Ground, a community program cited by Bradley. Held annually at McDaniel College in Maryland (see Photo 9.3), this week-long program for people of all ages from all over the world offers a wide variety of hands-on activities with master musicians, artists, and craftspeople. The thinking behind Common Ground is that the arts allow us to experience each other as artists, as human beings. Walt Michael, Director of Common Ground, expands on this idea. "You learn about yourself when you paint, play music, or engage in some other art form. In the process of self-discovery, a lot of stereotypes go out the window. As an example, our expectations about who prefers what kind of music might be reversed . . . maybe a Black student becomes fascinated by bluegrass music while a White student gets into the blues."[23]

Another promising, innovative program uses the game of basketball to help children from communities in conflict come together, play together, and find common ground. PeacePlayers International, a non-profit organization, was created in 2001 on the principle that "children who play together can learn to live together." (See Photo 9.4.) By using basketball as a tool for building understanding and leadership, both boys and girls from very diverse backgrounds learn to break down barriers. For example, Protestants and Catholics from Northern Ireland, Jews and Arabs from Israel and the West Bank, and Turkish Cypriots and Greek Cypriots from Cyprus find that they can work and play together and in the process, undo long-held prejudices and develop partnerships. Brendan Tuohey, one of the founders of PeacePlayers, observes that children form bonds in order to compete and win. He

> We all do better when we work together. Our differences do matter, but our common humanity matters more.
> —Former President Bill Clinton

Photo 9.4 Children Who Play Together Can Live Together.
Source: Courtesy of PeacePlayers International, Washington, DC.

adds, "There's a growing understanding of what sport can do to transform communities . . ."[24]

Continuing Potential for Divisiveness and Hope

Numerous surveys in recent years reveal that growing diversity in the United States is giving rise to a sense of pessimism about the future. This pessimism is fueled by what many perceive as the downside of diversity and change. People are skeptical about whether the motto *e pluribus unum* (out of many, one) can become a reality. Does the emphasis on diversity weaken our sense of oneness?

Corporate and community initiatives aimed at recognizing diversity and promoting its value can have unintended effects, especially if they stress style over substance. For example, misunderstanding and intolerance can become more of a problem if we do not handle diversity training with care. Sporadic, poorly integrated programs are apt to generate only cosmetic changes and may very well increase divisiveness and skepticism. Some well-intentioned training may actually teach people to stereotype by ignoring the diversity within groups. Also, programs that focus exclusively on human differences may reinforce ignorance of our many similarities.

In all likelihood, hatred and hostility will continue to be a major social problem as our lives inevitably become more interconnected and diverse. W. E. B. Du Bois, civil rights leader and author, as well as the first African-American to earn a doctorate from Harvard University, foresaw the potential divisiveness of diversity years ago. Du Bois stated that the problem of the twentieth century would be the problem of the color line. In the 1960s, the historic Kerner Commission provided a similar warning. The Commission warned: "Our nation is moving toward two societies, one black, one white—separate and unequal."[25] Since that time, the lines or divides have been transformed. There are more divisions and inequality is more complex. Although the race divide is still a central issue, it is one of many. A growing number of divides are economic as well as cultural.

 Thinking Through Diversity

What do you feel is the most important thing you have done in your community to promote the value of diversity and inclusion?

Recent surveys show a growing openness to change, especially among younger generations. For instance, data from Pew show **Millennials**, also known as Generation Y (born between 1981 and 2000), and to a lesser extent **Generation X** (born between 1965 and 1980), to be more open to interracial marriage, gay couples raising children, and nontraditional family arrangements (see Fig. 9.2). With regard to immigration, Millennials are significantly more likely than their elders to say that immigrants strengthen the country.[26] The openness of younger people stems in part from the **cohort effect**, which refers to the unique historical experiences that can shape and mold a generation's thinking and behaviors. The student editor of this book, a Millennial herself, describes her upbringing thus: "I think Generation Y is a lot more inclusive culture than our predecessors because of the type of culture that existed in America when we were being raised. We saw anti-bullying ads, HIV and STD ads, anti-smoking ads, moralistic and scientific cartoons, religious diversity, interracial relationships on TV; and the feminist movement and the GLBT (gay, lesbian, bisexual, transgender) community were represented in the media. We were infused with all these moral and ethical issues from an early age and that has helped us become inclusive adults."

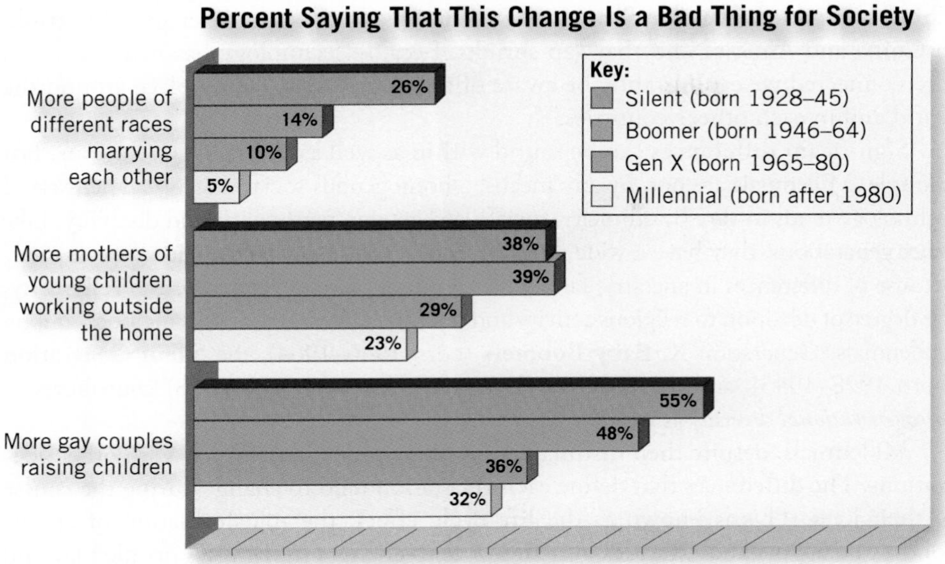

Percent Saying That This Change Is a Bad Thing for Society

More people of
different races
marrying
each other

- 26%
- 14%
- 10%
- 5%

Key:
- Silent (born 1928–45)
- Boomer (born 1946–64)
- Gen X (born 1965–80)
- Millennial (born after 1980)

More mothers of
young children
working outside
the home

- 38%
- 39%
- 29%
- 23%

More gay couples
raising children

- 55%
- 48%
- 36%
- 32%

Figure 9.2 Openness to Change Among Generations.
Source: Pew Research Report, Millennials: A Portrait of Generation Next.

Millennials, the largest generation in the history of the United States, live in a world that is unmistakably diverse. According to Pew surveys:

- They are likely to have interracial friends and neighbors of different religions and ethnicities.

- While many are religiously unaffiliated, they nevertheless believe in the importance of prayer. Furthermore, they believe that religion plays a vital role in bringing communities together and many actively reach out to those in need.[27]

- Generally, they are highly educated and respect their elders.

- Millennials embrace technology as well as diverse modes of expression.

- A sizable majority has created a profile online and a sizeable minority has a tattoo and a piercing in some place other than an ear lobe.[28]

- In comparison to prior generations, they are more likely to speak a language other than English and more apt to have a family member or close friend who is gay.

Jess Rainer, a millennial himself and co-author of *The Millennials*, remarks, "We do not feel a need to be diverse, and we do not seek out relationships for that purpose. It is just who we are."[29]

When the Pew Research Center asks Millennials what makes them distinctive, the overriding response is technology. For Millennials, new technologies represent a **period effect**, meaning major, life-altering events like wars, natural disasters, social movements, and technological advances that impact all generations, but some more than others. Often the young are greatly affected because they may be more impressionable and less "set in their ways." New technologies permeate the everyday lives of Millennials. They use technology to communicate, nurture friendships and cultivate romance, protest, brainstorm, and build community bonds. Also, technology has globalized their pop culture, music, and a wide range of other experiences. David Burstein, author of *Fast Future: How the Millennial Generation Is Shaping Our World*, elaborates; "if you look at an average 65-year-old in America and an average 65-year-old in

China you will find a significant culture barrier. Compare an average 22-year-old in China and America and that gap shrinks. Because technology has made us all so interconnected we can instantly be aware of the same events taking place around the world and in each other's countries."

Significant differences can be found within as well as between generations. For example, Millennials are not, by any means, a homogenous social category. Their use of technology tends to vary by ethnicity, social class, gender, personality, and disability. Like other generations, they have a wide range of values, goals, and political ideologies, partly because of differences in ancestry, family background, place of residence, and **religiosity**, the degree of devotion to religious activity and doctrine. The range of ages included among Millennials, Generation X, **Baby Boomers** (born 1946–1964), the **Silent Generation** (born 1928–1945), and the **Greatest Generation** (born prior to 1928) contributes to *intragenerational diversity* as well.[30]

Millennials, despite their distinctiveness, share much in common with other generations. The differences that define each generation tend to change during the course of their lives. This is known as the **life cycle effect**, the transformation of an age cohort's behaviors and attitudes over time due to changes in the roles people play and their biological maturation. As the younger generation of today ages, they will discover that they share more and more in common with today's seniors. Marriage and parenthood are priorities for Millennials. They value the opportunity to share their opinions. Lastly, they have a deep respect for older generations and admire some of their traits, such as the work ethic of Baby Boomers.

Millennials and youth worldwide provide a window into a future. However, that future hinges on the abilities of people of all ages to learn from each other, work together, and value all of our contributions regardless of the labels we create and affix to people. While the future will encompass more diverse relationships that cross geographical and cultural boundaries, individual and structural barriers will undoubtedly remain. Social and economic inequality and human rights issues in the twenty-first century will continue to influence our needs and wants as well as our dreams. Age-old and emerging religious and political divisions will alter how we perceive others, and the reach of our understanding and empathy. Geographical distance will be less of a consideration for many, but certainly not all.

In recent years, many forms of intergroup hostility and intolerance show little or no sign of abating. This is not simply the work of a select few. When we think of intolerance, how many of us visualize someone affiliated with a terrorist organization, a member of the Ku Klux Klan (KKK), or a neo-Nazi? Unfortunately, intolerance can also come dressed in a three-piece suit, a military uniform, or the more casual wear of a college student. Schools, places of worship, and job sites throughout the country have recently witnessed an upsurge in hate crimes. Hate literature, graffiti, threatening messages sent via social media, property damage, noose incidents, and physical violence point to a continuing cultural lag between the diversity we encounter and our ability to respect or at least tolerate that diversity.

As we examine the negatives associated with diversity, it is important to remember how far we have come, both individually and collectively. The late William Raspberry, a Pulitzer Prize-winning journalist, wrote: "All of us are capable of getting so caught up in the distance that remains to be run that we forget to give ourselves full credit for the distance we've come."[31] It is all too easy to focus solely on our shortcomings and the social problems that have seemingly become a permanent fixture in our communities. We tend to do this because much of the change in the area of diversity is incremental and hardly noticeable. Additionally, what we read and see in the media often emphasizes the negative.

On a broader level, it is important to remember the barriers of discrimination, segregation, and bigotry that have fallen. Alice Moy keeps her perspective by remembering her past. "It's like fifth heaven today I would say, for people who come over now. Opportunities galore. It wasn't available to us at that time, even though we were born here and we went to school here. Now I remember I had friends who attended and graduated from MIT, attended and graduated from Harvard—no one would hire them. Where did they end up? They ended up working for Chinese restaurants. No American firm would hire them."[32]

Change is one of the few things we can count on as we look to the future. Technology, globalization, shifting demographics, and the continuing potential for divisiveness will challenge our adaptability and our ability to get along with each other. If we can develop diversity consciousness in ourselves, we will be much better prepared to meet these challenges and open our minds to many more people, cultures, and opportunities.

> Change will not come if we wait for some other person or some other time. We are the ones we've been waiting for. We are the change that we seek.
> —President Barack Obama

 ## Case Studies

Case Study One

Ligua is a car salesperson who works on a commission basis, as well as a part-time student, wife, and mother. Periodically, Ligua thinks back to her childhood and wonders how much things have changed since then. In middle school, she had Anglo teachers who were surprised that she was Latina and smart. Some of them seemed to think that she could not fully grasp what was being said and should not be considered for advanced placement classes. Ligua noticed that when White teachers worked one on one with White students, it was hands on. The teachers would lean toward the students and touch their hands or shoulders. But when working with her and other minorities, there was no leaning and no touching. She wonders if this kind of thing still goes on today. And if so, is it prevalent?

Ligua's educational experiences and those of her children provide her with the motivation to go to school, be a teacher, and make a difference. In one of her education classes, the teacher asked students to outline their *"sphere of influence,"* that is, those lives that they have the power to change. Ligua thought about this long and hard. Given her future as a teacher, she sees her sphere of influence growing and extending well beyond her family.

Case Study Two

Mary is a White social work student who plans to go on for a MS degree and work in a clinical setting. She attends an urban university and enjoys the diversity and energy of city life, but in her free time is actively involved in social activities centered around her Scottish background. According to Mary, her ultimate goal in life has a spiritual foundation. By spiritual, she does not actually mean religion, like going to church or some religious ritual. Spiritual success to Mary is how connected she is with herself, how much time she spends with herself, and how at peace she is with herself.

Deep down, Mary wants to do everything she can to change people's lives for the better. She wants to start in her community, by giving something back because she has been given so much by so many. Although she is not exactly sure of her career plans, Mary knows she wants to do something to motivate others, to give others a second and a third chance. Working at a food bank helped her realize this.

Mary has never experienced what it is like to go to bed hungry. Ever since she can remember, she always had the luxury of a well-stocked refrigerator and pantry to satisfy her appetite. When she was full at dinnertime, she threw away food that she didn't want. Untouched, forgotten food in the refrigerator was discarded without a second thought. She has always taken food for granted; including the fresh fish and poultry, fresh fruits and vegetables, and other foods she buys to keep healthy.

At the food bank, she remembers standing in an assembly line of volunteers like herself. For hours at a time, Mary performed the monotonous task of combining one tablespoon minced onion, six bouillon cubes, one scoop navy beans, and one scoop kidney beans. She mixed the seasonings in a small plastic bag, taped it shut, and then repeated this process. Initially, she did not find this experience particularly fulfilling. Mary did not really stop to think about what she was doing or for whom she was doing it. But when she was through, she saw the hundreds of plastic bags of soup. She knew that even though she wouldn't be there to witness it, those children and adults who do not have enough food or enough healthy food would appreciate her efforts. Although not solving the world's hunger problem, Mary's efforts perhaps would help others in some small way. It opened up her eyes to a world that was invisible to her up to that point.

Case Study Three

Michael is a Black college graduate and the divorced father of a teenage son, Aaron, who attends a private school in the well-to-do suburb where they live. He works as a senior manager for a small consulting firm. Michael can still hear his wealthy grandfather, Grandpa Joe, refer to poor Whites as "white trash" and poor Blacks as "niggers." The forceful tone in Joe's voice when he uttered those words was something Michael always hated. Michael also remembers being scared when the two of them would drive through the "poor" part of town. Joe would go on and on about how "those people" lived and how they were too lazy to work.

Michael loves his grandfather because Joe is fundamentally a good man to his wife and his family, but Michael doesn't respect his views toward poor Whites and Blacks. It bothers Michael that certain coworkers, with whom he shares an office, may be just as biased and ignorant as his grandfather, only they are more adept at hiding it.

Even though he is ashamed to admit it, Michael sometimes feels compelled to judge people the same way. "It's really easy to judge or exclude people based on their social class," he says. "But it seems to be much more admirable to recognize what people of all social classes have to offer." How to do that, he thinks, is one of his biggest challenges.

 # Key Terms

Inclusion	Millennials (or	Religiosity
Inclusive workplace	Generation Y)	Baby Boomers
Human capital	Generation X	The Silent Generation
Minority	Cohort effect	The Greatest Generation
Majority	Period effect	Life cycle effect

Exercises

Exercise 1: **The Transformation of Barbie**

The Barbie doll is the world's best-selling toy. Three Barbies are sold every second. Sales each year exceed $2 billion. In recent years, Barbie has undergone significant changes in order to broaden her appeal. According to one toy analyst, Barbie is like Betty Crocker. Her looks get updated to keep up with the times. Answer the following questions regarding Barbie and her transformation.

1. Find someone who remembers what Barbie dolls looked like decades ago. Ask this person the following questions. How did Barbie look years ago? Describe her physical appearance. What about her occupations? Could you choose the race or ethnicity of Barbie? How was it different from today's Barbies?

2. Visit a local toy store and see what kinds of Barbie dolls are for sale. Do you think the image of Barbie has been altered? Why? Is the change driven by financial and/or social concerns? Explain. Finally, what do you think of the changes?

3. Considerable controversy has been generated by Barbie's body proportions. There are those who argue that Barbie's body measurements deviate significantly from those of real women, and this may lead to body dissatisfaction, eating disorders, and a negative self-image. Others counter that critics such as Nickolay Lamm (using Photoshop, Lamm juxtaposed two images on the Web—a more realistic body type using data from the Center for Disease Control and a model of Barbie) are making unproven assumptions about a link between toys and body image. Barbie, they maintain, is simply a toy. Which of these arguments is closer to your point of view? Why?

Exercise 2: **Classroom for All**

Situation: You have been appointed to serve on a statewide task force on higher education. Your work on the task force requires you to create an orientation course at the college level for incoming first-year students. The purpose of this course is to acquaint students with the skills they need to be successful. Your responsibility focuses on the part of the course that deals with diversity skills.

Directive: Submit an outline of the diversity skills to be taught. Briefly describe:

• Each skill.

• The connection between the skill and student success.

• Ten specific resources that students will use. These may include videos, books, journal articles, and Web sites. List the skill or skills each resource addresses.

 Notes

[1] Andres Tapia and Jonathan Kaufman, "Diversity Case in Point: A Company Where People with Autism Are the Norm." Online, April 17, 2012. Available: http://www.diversitybestpractices.com/news-articles/diversity-case-point-company-where-people-autism-are-norm.

[2] Cynthia Monticue, "Inclusion Is Key to Productive Workforce," *USC News*. Online, February 24, 2005. Available: http://www.usc.edu/uscnews/stories/11025.html.

[3] Shirley Engelmeier, *Inclusion: The New Competitive Business Advantage* (Minneapolis, MN: InclusionINC Media, 2012), 55.

[4] Peles Castle: A Jewel of the Romanian Cultural Heritage." Online, Nov. 28, 2010. Available: http://www.chain.to/?m3=23653.

[5] Donna Britt, "Relishing Region's Many Hues," *The Washington Post*, Oct. 15, 1999, B1.

[6] Susan Okie, "Teaching Hospitals How to Listen," *The Washington Post*, Dec. 12, 2006, F1.

[7] Martha Barnett, letter to the author, July 2, 2002.

[8] "Steve Jobs Used Wayne Gretzky As Inspiration," *Los Angeles Times - Sports Now*. Online, Oct. 6, 2011. Available: http://latimesblogs.latimes.com/sports_blog/2011/10/steve-jobs-used-wayne-gretzky-as-inspiration.html.

[9] André Martin, Center for Creative Leadership (CCL), *The Changing Nature of Leadership*, 2007. Available: www.ccl.org/leadership/pdf/research/natureleadership.pdf.

[10] U.S. Census Bureau, "U.S. Census Bureau Projections Show a Slower Growing, Older, More Diverse Nation a Half Century from Now." Online, Dec. 12, 2012. Available: http://www.reuters.com/article/2012/12/12/idUS200526+12-Dec-2012+PRN20121212.

[11] Migration Policy Institute, "LEP Data Brief," Dec. 2011.

[12] Paul Taylor and D'Vera Cohn, "A Milestone En Route to a Majority Minority Nation." Online, November 7, 2012. Available: http://www.pewsocialtrends.org/2012/11/07/a-milestone-en-route-to-a-majority-minority-nation/.

[13] Pew Forum on Religion and Public Life, "Religious Affiliation: Summary of Key Findings." Online, June 23, 2008. Available: http://religions.pewforum.org/reports.

[14] Michelle Boorstein and Jacqueline Salmon, "In Major Poll, U.S. Religious Identity Appears Very Slippery," *Washington Post*, Feb. 26, 2008, A1+.

[15] Kevin Sack and Janet Elder, "Poll Finds Optimistic Outlook But Enduring Racial Division," *New York Times on the Web*. Online, July 11, 2000. Available: http://www.nytimes.com/library/national/race/071100sack-poll.html.

[16] Karen Rasmussen, "Gaining Perspective on Global Education," *ASCD (Association for Supervision and Curriculum Development) Curriculum Update*, Summer 1998, 3.

[17] Donald Norris and Michael Dolence, *Transforming Higher Education: A Vision for Learning in the 21st Century* (Ann Arbor, MI: Society for College and University Planning, 1995), 3.

[18] IBM, "IBM Study: Education Lags in Preparing Students for Globalization and Sustainability." Online, June 17, 2010. Available: http://www-03.ibm.com/press/us/en/pressrelease/31937.wss.

[19] Trevor Hitner, letter to the author, March 15, 1998.

[20] Microsoft, "A Vision and Strategy for the Future." Available: http://www.microsoft.com/about/en/xm/importedcontent/about/diversity/en/us/vision.aspx (accessed April 11, 2013).

[21] Study Circles Resource Center, *Toward a More Perfect Union in an Age of Diversity*, 1997, 18.

[22] Bill Bradley, "How America Can Make Brotherhood Work," *Reader's Digest 75th Anniversary Issue*, 1997, 96–101.

[23] Walt Michael, letter to the author, Jan. 9, 1998.

[24] Jorge Castillo, "Crossover Move: PeacePlayers Allows Conflicted Groups to Team Up on Court," *The Washington Post*, July 7, 2010, D6.

[25] National Advisory Commission on Civil Disorders, *Report of the National Advisory Commission on Civil Disorders* (New York: Bantam, 1968), 1.

[26] Pew Research Report, *A Portrait of Generation Next. Confident. Connected. Open to Change*, February, 2010, Chapter One, 6.

[27] Morley Winograd and Michael Hais, "Service, Inclusion Are Paths to Salvation for Religion in the Millennial Era." Online, Oct. 25, 2012. Available: http://www.nationaljournal.com/thenextamerica/demographics/opinion-service-inclusion-are-paths-to-salvation-for-religion-in-the-millennial-era-20121025.

[28] Pew Research Center, "*Millennials: Confident. Connected. Open to Change*." Online, February 24, 2010. Available: http://www.pewsocialtrends.org/2010/02/24/millennials-confident-connected-open-to-change/.

[29] Thom Rainer and Jess Rainer, *The Millennials* (Nashville, TN: B & H Books, 2010).

[30] As defined by Pew Research Center, "*Millennials: Confident. Connected. Open to Change*," *Executive Summary*. Online, February 24, 2010. Available: http://www.pewsocialtrends.org/2010/02/24/millennials-confident-connected-open-to-change/.

[31] William Raspberry, from a lecture at Kansas State University, *Vital Speeches of the Day*, June 1, 1995, 493–496.

[32] Alice Moy, as found in Balch Institute of Ethnic Studies, "The Bachelor Society," *Perspective*, Spring/Summer 1998, 4.

Bibliography

ABC News. *The Eye of the Storm* (video) (Mount Kisco, NY: Guidance Associates, 1981).

Adler, Nancy and Allison Gundersen. *International Dimensions of Organizational Behavior* (Boston: South-Western College Pub., 2007), 140.

Aguilar-San Juan, Karen (ed.). *The State of Asian America* (Cambridge, MA: South End Press, 1994), 74.

Allen, Jodie. "Obama's Black Audience: What Surveys Show About the Attitudes and Priorities of African Americans, Pew Research Center. Online, July 14, 2008. Available: http://www.pewresearch.org/2008/07/14/obamas-black-audience/.

Allport, Gordon. *The Nature of Prejudice* (Reading, MA: Addison Wesley, 1954).

Alves, Julio. "Class Struggles," *Chronicles of Higher Education,* 53(8), 2006, Available: chronicle.com/weekly/v53/i08/08b00501.htm.

American Management Association (AMA). *AMA 2010 Critical Skills Survey.* Online, April 15, 2010. Available: http://www.amanet.org/news/AMA-2010-critcal-skills-survey.aspx.

American Management Association. "What Do Organizations Really Want?" *AMA Catalog of Seminars,* Oct. 1997.

Angelou, Maya. *I Know Why the Caged Bird Sings* (New York: Bantam Books, 1993).

Appel, Morgan, David Cartwright, Daryl Smith, and Lisa Wolf. *The Impact of Diversity on Students* (Washington, DC: Association of American Colleges and Universities, 1996), x.

Aronson, Elliot and Neal Osherow. "Cooperation, Prosocial Behavior, and Academic Performance: Experiments in the Desegregated Classroom," *Applied Social Psychology Annual,* 1, 1980, 174–175.

"Artists/Daniel Keplinger," Phyllis Kind Gallery, http://www.phylliskindgallery.com/artists/dk/bio.html (accessed June 15, 2013).

Ashe, Arthur. *Days of Grace* (New York: Ballantine Books, 1993), 186.

Associated Press. "Bicycling 'Info Ladies' Bring Internet to Remote Bangladesh Villages," FoxNews.com. Online, November 2, 2012. Available: http://www.foxnews.com/world/2012/11/01/bicycling-info-ladies-bring-internet-to-remote-bangladesh-villages-where/

Associated Press. "Dharun Ravi Sentence in Rutgers Webcam Case Renews Hate Crime Law Debate" *The Washington Post.* Online, May 22, 2012. Available: washingtonpost.com/national/.../glQAuiODiU_print.html.

Association of American Colleges and Universities. "The Educational Value of Diversity: Research from Louisville High Schools," *Diversity Digest,* Winter 2001, 10, 11.

Axtell, Roger E. *Gestures: The Do's and Taboos of Body Language Around the World* (New York: Wiley, 1991), 10.

Balch Institute of Ethnic Studies. "The Bachelor Society," *Perspective,* Spring/Summer 1998, 4.

Bandura, Albert. "Exercise of Human Agency Through Collective Efficacy," *Current Directions in Psychological Science,* 9, 2000, 75–78.

Barnett, Martha. Letter to the author, July 2, 2002.

Bates, Karen G. and Karen E. Hudson. *Basic Black: Home Training for Modern Times* (New York: Doubleday, 1996).

Beatty, Richard. *The Interview Kit* (New York: John Wiley & Sons, 2000).

Belenky, Mary, Blythe Clinchy, Nancy Goldberger, and Jill Tarule. *Women's Ways of Knowing* (New York: Basic Books, 1986).

Bell, Ella and Stella Nkomo. *Our Separate Ways: Black and White Women and the Struggle for Professional Identity* (Boston, MA: Harvard Business Review Press, 2003).

Benschop, Yvonne. "The Micro-Politics of Gendering in Networking," *Gender, Work, and Organization,* 16(2), 2009, 217–237.

Bingham, Raymond. "Leaving Prejudice Behind," *The Washington Post Health Section,* Sept. 6, 1994, 9.

Blanchard, Fletcher, Terri Lilly, and Leigh Ann Vaughn. "Reducing the Expression of Racial Prejudice," *Psychological Science,* 2, 1991, 101–105.

Block, J. Richard and Harold Yuker. *Can You Believe Your Eyes?* (New York: Brunner/Mazel, 1992).

Bogardus, Emory. "Measuring Social Distance," *Journal of Applied Sociology,* 9, Mar./Apr. 1925, 299–308.

Boorstein, Michelle. "A Mission of Understanding," *The Washington Post,* Jan. 15, 2007, AO1.

Boorstein, Michelle and Jacqueline Salmon. "In Major Poll, U.S. Religious Identity Appears Very Slippery," *The Washington Post,* Feb. 26, 2008, A1+.

Bradley, Bill. "How America Can Make Brotherhood Work," *Reader's Digest 75th Anniversary Issue,* 1997, 96–101.

Branigin, William. "Immigrants Question Idea of Assimilation," *The Washington Post,* May 25, 1998, A1.

Brenner, Joanna. "Pew Internet: Social Networking," Pew Research Center. Online, Sept. 17, 2012. Available: http://pewinternet.org/Commentary/2012/March/Pew-Internet-Social-Networking-full-detail.aspx.

Britt, Donna. "Relishing Region's Many Hues," *The Washington Post,* Oct. 15, 1999, B1.

Burstein, David. *Fast Future: How The Millennial Generation Is Shaping Our World* (Boston, MA: Beacon Press, 2013).

Burton, John. *Conflict: Resolution and Prevention* (New York: St. Martin's Press, 1990).

Cannadine, David. *The Undivided Past: Humanity Beyond Our Differences* (New York: Alfred Knopf, 2013).

Carson, Benjamin. "Carson Philosophy Is 'Think Big,'" *The Baltimore Sun,* Aug. 24, 1997, 6H.

Cart, Julie. "Irked by Mascot, Team Retaliates," *LOS ANGELES Times Online.* Online, March 15, 2002. Available: https://www.patrick.af.mil/deomi/Library/EOReadFile/Native%20Americans%20Issues/NAISpring02/lrked%20by%20Mascot.pdf

Cass, Connie and Jennifer Agiesta. "Poll: Young People See Online Slurs as Just Joking." Online, September 20, 2011. Available: http://news.yahoo.com/poll-young-people-see-online-slurs-just-joking-070620137.html.

Castillo, Jorge. "Crossover move: PeacePlayers allows conflicted groups to team up on court," *The Washington Post,* July 7, 2010, D6.

CBS News. "Steve Jobs Thought Different." Online, Oct. 5, 2011. Available: http://www.cbsnews.com/2100-205_162-20116354.html.

Center for Work-Life Policy. "Asian Americans Still Feel Like Outsiders in Corporate America." Online, July 20, 2011. Available: www.worklifepolicy.org.

Chansanchai, Athima. "She Walks the Line of Poverty, Incognito," *The Baltimore Sun,* Sept. 16, 2001, 1N+.

Chmielewski, Dawn. "YouTube Diversifies With Shaq, Russell Simmons," *Los Angeles Times.* Online, Oct. 8, 2012. Available: http://articles.latimes.com/2012/oct/08/entertainment/la-et-ct-you-tube-diversifies-with-shaq-20121008.

Chua, Roy and Michael Morris. "Innovation Communication in Multicultural Networks: Deficits in Intercultural Capability and Affect-based Trust as Barriers to New Idea Sharing in Inter-Cultural Relationships," *Working Paper 09–130,* 2009, 1–20.

CIA. *The World Factbook.* Available: https://www.cia.gov/library/publications/the-world-factbook/fields/2212.html (accessed November 9, 2012).

Clark, D. Anthony, Lisa Spanierman, Tamilia Reed, Jason Soble, and Sharon Cabana. "Documenting Weblog Expressions of Racial Microaggressions That Target American Indians," *Journal of Diversity in Higher Education,* Vol. 4(1), Mar. 2011, 39–50. Available: http://search.ebscohost.com/login.aspx?direct=true&db=pdh&AN=dhe-4-1-39&site=ehost-live, 5 of 13.

Common Sense Media. "Social Media, Social Life: How Teens View Their Digital Lives." Online, June 26, 2012. Available: http://www.commonsensemedia.org/research/social-media-social-life/key-finding-2%3A-teens-more-likely-to-report-positive-impact–.

Connolly, Ceci. "Report Says Minorities Get Lower-Quality Health Care," *The Washington Post,* March 21, 2002, A2.

Cooper, Joel. "The Digital Divide: The Special Case of Gender," *Journal of Computer Assisted Learning,* Vol. 22, No. 5, 320–334, 2006.

Cortés, C. E. "The Societal Curriculum: Implications for Multiethnic Education." In J. A. Banks (ed.), *Education in the 80's: Multiethnic Education* (Washington, DC: National Education Association), 1981.

Cose, Ellis. *Color Blind* (New York: HarperPerennial), 226.

Cose, Ellis. "Revisiting 'The Rage of a Privileged Class,'" *Newsweek.* Online, February 2, 2009. Available: http://www.thedailybeast.com/newsweek/2009/01/24/revisiting-the-rage-of-a-privileged-class.html.

Covey, Stephen. "How to Succeed in Today's Workplace," *USA Weekend,* Aug. 29–31, 1997, 5.

Covey, Stephen. *The Seven Habits of Highly Effective People* (New York: Simon & Schuster, 1989).

Critchell, Samantha. "Silent Since September and Learning a Lot," *The Washington Post,* May 15, 2001, C4.

Crozier-Hogle, Louis and Darryl Babe Wilson. *Surviving in Two Worlds: Contemporary Native American Voices* (Austin, TX: University of Texas Press, 1997), 139.

Cullen, Countee (ed.), *Caroling Dusk* (Secaucus, NJ: Carol Publishing Group, 1993), 187.

DeSantis, Andrea and Wesley Kayson. "Defendants' Characteristics of Attractiveness, Race, and Sex and Sentencing Decisions," *Psychological Reports,* 81, 1997, 679–683.

Desmond, Matthew and Mustafa Emirbayer. *Racial Domination, Racial Progress,* (New York: McGraw Hill, 2010), 534.

"Developing Leaders," *Training Magazine,* March 2007, 88.

"Developing Successful Global Leaders," *Training.* Online, May/June 2011. Available: www.trainingmag.com.

Devine, Dan. "LeBron James, Miami Heat Put Their Hoods Up to Show Support in Trayvon Martin Case," sports.yahoo.com. Online, March 23, 2012. Available: http://sports.yahoo.com/blogs/nba-ball-dont-lie/miami-heat-put-hoods-show-support-trayvon-martin-182102000.html.

Dinan, Stephen. "Immigration Growth at Highest Rate in 150 Years." Online, June 5, 2002. Available: http://www.washtimes.com/national/20020605-76931088.html.

DiversityInc. "Mentoring Case Studies–Diversity Best Practices." Available: http://diversityincbestpractices.com/mentoring/mentoring-case-studies/ (accessed September 19, 2012).

Dotlich, David, Peter Cairo, and Stephen Rhinesmith. *Head, Heart, and Guts,* San Francisco, CA: Jossey-Bass, 2006.

Du Bois, W. E. B. *The Souls of Black Folk* (New York: Fawcett, 1961).

Editor, Management at Work, "Tuckman's Team-building Model." Online, February 12, 2008. Available: http://management.atwork-network.com/2008/02/12/tuckmans-team-building-model-forming-storming-norming-performing/.

Ehrenreich, Barbara. *Nickel and Dimed: On (Not) Getting By in America* (New York: Picador, 2011).

Enayati, Amanda. "Not Black, Not White," *The Washington Post,* July 13, 1997, C1.

Engelmeier, Shirley. *Inclusion: The New Competitive Business Advantage* (Minneapolis, MN: InclusionINC Media, 2012), 55.

Feagin, Joe. "The Continuing Significance of Race: Anti-Black Discrimination in Public Places," *American Sociological Review,* 56, 1991, 101–116.

Federal Glass Ceiling Commission. *A Solid Investment: Making Full Use of the Nation's Human Capital* (Washington, DC: U.S. Department of Labor, 1995), 6.

Feistritzer, C. Emily, "Profile of Teachers in the U.S. 2011, National Center for Education Information, July, 2011; and Pew Research Center, "Hispanic Student Enrollments Reach New Highs in 2011," August 20, 2012, Available: http://www.bing.com/search?q=Pew%2C+Hispanic+Student+Enrollments+Reach+New%22&form=DLCDF8&pc=MDDC&src=IE-SearchBox

"A First-hand Account of the Dialogue Experience." Online, January 14, 2011. Available: http://thebeautyjackson.com/2011/01/14/im-black-and-therefore-i-am-diverse/

Fletcher, Michael. "Crazy Horse Again Sounds Battle Cry," *The Washington Post,* Feb. 18, 1997, A03.

Fong, Timothy and Larry Shinagawa. *Asian Americans: Experiences and Perspectives* (Upper Saddle River, NJ: Prentice Hall, 2000).

Ford, George S. and Sherry Ford. "Internet Use and Depression Among the Elderly," Phoenix Center for Advanced Legal and Economic Public Policy Paper No. 38. Online, October 15, 2009. Available: http://dx.doi.org/10.2139/ssrn.1494430.

Fox, Susannah. "Digital Divisions," Pew Research Center. Online, October 5, 2005. Available: http://www.pewinternet.org/Reports/2005/Digital-Divisions/01-Summary-of-Findings.aspx.

Frankenberg, Ruth. *White Women, Race Matters: The Social Construction of Whiteness* (Minneapolis, MN: University of Minnesota Press, 1993), 198.

Friedman, Thomas. *The World Is Flat* (New York: Farrar, Straus, and Giroux, 2006).

Fryberg, Stephanie, Hazel R. Markus, Daphna Oyserman, and Joseph Stone. "Of Warrior Chiefs and Indian Princesses: The Psychological Consequences of American Indian Mascots," *Basic and Applied Social Psychology*, 30, 208–218, 2008.

Fulbeck, Kip. *part asian 100% HAPA* (San Francisco: Chronicle Books, 2006).

Gallagher, Carol. *Going to the Top* (New York: Viking Press, 2000).

Gallagher, Charles. "White Reconstruction in the University," *Socialist Review,* 24, 1994, 165.

Garber, Megan. "The Digital (Gender) Divide: Women Are More Likely Than Men to Have a Blog (and a Facebook Profile)." Online, April 27, 2012. Available: http://www.theatlantic.com/technology/archive/2012/04/the-digital-gender-divide-women-are-more-likely-than-men-to-have-a-blog-and-a-facebook-profile/256466/.

Gardner, Chris. *The Pursuit of Happyness* (New York: Amistad Press, 2006).

Gardner, Howard. *Frames of Mind: The Theory of Multiple Intelligences* (New York: Basic Books, 1983).

Gaskins, Pearl Fuyo. *What Are You? Voices of Mixed-Race Young People* (New York: Henry Holt and Co., 1999).

Gibson, M. A. "Parental Support for Schooling," paper presented at the annual meeting of the American Anthropological Association, Dec. 1986.

Gibson, Margaret. *Accommodation Without Assimilation* (Ithaca, NY: Cornell University Press, 1988).

Gold, Barbara. "Diversifying the Curriculum: What Do Students Think?" *Diversity Digest,* Winter 2001, 12–14.

Goldsmith, Charles. "Look See! Anyone Do Read This and It Will Make You Laughable," *The Wall Street Journal,* Nov. 19, 1992, B1.

Goldsmith, Marshall. "The Fallacy of 'If They Understand, They Will Do,'" *Workforce Management,* Online, May 2007.

Goleman, Daniel. *Social Intelligence: The New Science of Human Relationships* (London: Bantam Press, 2007).

Goleman, Daniel. *Working with Emotional Intelligence* (New York: Bantam Books, 1998).

Gonzales Juan L. Jr. *The Lives of Ethnic Americans,* 2nd ed. (Dubuque, IA: Kendall/Hunt, 1994).

Grandin, Temple. *The Autistic Brain: Thinking Across the Spectrum* (Boston, MA: Houghton-Mifflin Harcourt, 2013).

Granovetter, Mark. "The Strength of Weak Ties: A Network Theory Revisited," *Sociological Theory* 1 (1983), 201–233.

Gray, Katti. "Linguists and Tribe Members Work To Restore Native Languages." Online, November 29, 2012. Available: http://diverseeducation.com/article/49809/.

Griffin, John H. *Black Like Me* (New York: NAL/Dutton, 1999).

Guerney, Bernard. *Relationship Enhancement Program*, 2nd ed. (Bethesda, MD: Ideals, 1997).

Guimera, Roger, Brian Uzzi, Jarrett Spiro, and Luis Nunes Amaral. "Team Assembly Mechanisms Determine Collaboration Network Structure and Team Peformance," *Science,* 308: 697–702.

Hacker, Andrew. *Two Nations* (New York: Ballantine Books, 1995).

Hacker, Colleen. "Team-Building Tips for Coaches." Available: http://www.active.com/mindandbody/articles/Team-Building-Tips-for-Coaches (accessed Jan. 8, 2013).

Hall, E. T. and M. R. Hall. *Hidden Differences: Doing Business with the Japanese* (Garden City, New York: Anchor Press/Doubleday, 1987).

Hampton, Keith, Lauren Sessions Goulet, Lee Rainie, and Kristen Purcell. "Social Networking Sites and Our Lives," Pew Internet. Online June 16, 2011. Available: http://pewinternet.org/Reports/2011/Technology-and-social-networks.aspx.

Hart Research Associates. *Raising The Bar* (Washington, DC, 2010).

Heath, Shirley Brice. *Ways with Words* (Cambridge: Cambridge University Press, 1983).

Heatwole, Anne-Ryan, and Katrin Verclas. "Women and Mobile: Is It Really a Global Opportunity?" Online, Mar. 8, 2010. Available: http://mobileactive.org/women-and-mobile-it-really-global-opportunity.

Heigi, Ursula. *Tearing the Silence* (New York: Simon & Schuster, 1997).

Heredia, Al. "Cultural Learning Styles," *ERIC Clearinghouse on Teaching and Teacher Education,* Dec. 1999.

Hersey, Paul, Ken Blanchard and Dewey Johnson. *Management of Organizational Behavior,* (Upper Saddle River, NJ: Prentice Hall, 2007).

Hesselbein, Frances, Marshall Goldsmith, and Richard Beckhard (eds.). *The Leader of the Future: New Visions, Strategies and Practices for the Next Era* (San Francisco, CA: Jossey-Bass, 1997).

Hilbert, Martin. "Digital Gender Divide or Technologically Empowered Women in Developing Countries?" *Women's Studies International Forum,* 34(6), 479–489.

Hitner, Trevor. Letter to the author, Mar. 15, 1998.

Hoffman, Reid, and Ben Casnocha. *The Start-up of You* (New York: Crown Business, 2012).

Hofstede, Geert. *Culture's Consequences: Comparing Values, Behaviors, Institutions, and Organizations Across Nations* (Thousand Oaks, CA: Sage, 2001).

Hofstede, Geert. *Culture's Consequences: International Differences in Work-Related Values* (Beverly Hills, CA: Sage Publications, 1980).

Horowitz, Irving Louis. *The Decomposition of Sociology* (New York: Oxford University Press, 1993).

Horrigan, John. "TIG Solutions." Available: tigsolutions.com (accessed September 11, 2012).

House, Robert et al. (eds.). *Culture, Leadership, and Organizations: The GLOBE Study of 62 Societies* (Thousand Oaks, CA: Sage Publications, 2004).

Huffman, Terry. "The Transculturation of Native American College Students," in *American Mosaic: Selected Readings on America's Multicultural Heritage,* Young I. Song and Eugene C. Kim (eds.) (Englewood Cliffs, NJ: Prentice Hall, 1993), 211–219; Sonia Nieto. *Affirming Diversity: The Sociopolitical Context of Multicultural Education* (White Plains, NY: Longman, 1996).

"*The Hunger Games* 'stomach-turning' racist tweet scandal," *The Week.* Online, March 29, 2012. Available: http://theweek.com/article/index/226225/the-hunger-games-stomach-turning-racist-tweet-scandal.

Hvitfeldt, Christina. "Traditional Culture, Perceptual Style, and Learning: The Classroom Behavior of Hmong Adults," *Adult Education Quarterly*, 36(2), Winter 1986, 70.

IBM. "Human Ability and Accessibility Center," Jim Sinocchi: Finding Common Ground. Available at http://www-03.ibm.com/able/news/sinocchi.html (accessed Jan. 14, 2008).

IBM. "IBM Study: Education Lags in Preparing Students for Globalization and Sustainability." Online, June 17, 2010. Available: http://www-03.ibm.com/press/us/en/pressrelease/31937.wss.

International Center for Media and the Public Agenda (ICMPA) and the Salzburg Academy on Media and Global Change, "Going 24 Hours Without Media." Available: oneworldunplugged.wordpress.com (accessed October 18, 2012).

"Internet World Statistics." Online, June 30, 2012. Available: http://www.internetworldstats.com/stats.htm. For up-to-date information on Internet usage throughout the world, see www.internetworldstats.com.

"Internet World Stats: Usage and Population Statistics," Available: http://www.internetworldstats.com/stats.htm (accessed June 17, 2013).

Irvine, Jacqueline and Darlene York. "Learning Styles and Culturally Diverse Students: A Literature Review," in James Banks (ed.), *Handbook of Research on Multicultural Education* (New York: Simon & Schuster, 1995), 484–497.

Jacobs, Tom. "To Boost Creativity, Study Abroad." Online, August 6., 2012. Available: http://www.psmag.com/culture-society/to-boost-creativity-study-abroad-43897/.

Janis, Irving L. *Victims of Groupthink* (Boston: Houghton Mifflin, 1972).

Jayson, Sharon. "U.S. Rate of Interracial Marriages Hits Record High" *USA Today*. Online, February 16, 2012. Available: http://usatoday30.usatoday.com/news/health/wellness/marriage/story/2012-02-16/US-rate-of-interracial-marriage-hits-record-high/53109980/1.

Jenkins, Henry, with Katie Clinton, Ravi Purushotma, Alice Robison, and Margaret Weigel. *Confronting the Challenges of Participatory Culture: Media Education of the 21st Century,* (Cambridge, MA: The MIT Press, 2009).

Jenkins, Howard, with Katie Clinton, Ravi Purushotma, Alice Robison, and Margaret Weigel. "Confronting the Challenges of Participatory Culture: Media Education for the 21st Century," 2005. Available: http://digitallearning.macfound.org/atf/cf/%7B7E45C7E0-A3E0-4B89-AC9C-E807E1B0AE4E%7D/JENKINS_WHITE_PAPER.PDF (accessed September11, 2012).

Judy, Richard W. and Carol D'Amico. *Workforce 2020: Executive Summary* (Indianapolis, IN: Hudson Institute, 1997), 3.

Kahlenberg, Rebecca. "The Pursuit of a New Career Takes Persistence" *The Washington Post*, February 25, 2007, K1.

Keller, Ed, and Brad Fay. *The Face-to-Face Book: Why Real Relationships Rule in a Digital Marketplace* (New York: Free Press, 2012).

Kelly, Sanja and Sarah Cook. *Freedom on the Internet 2011* (Washington, DC: Freedom House, 2011).

Kennedy, Randall. *Nigger: The Strange Career of a Troublesome Word* (New York: Pantheon, 2002).

Kim, Yoojung, Dongyoung Sohn, and Sejung Marina Choi. "Cultural Differences in Motivations for Using Social Network Sites: A Comparative Study of American and Korean College Students," *Computers In Human Behavior*, 27(1), 2011, 365–372.

King, Martin Luther, Jr. *Where Do We Go from Here: Chaos or Community?* (Boston: Beacon Press, 1968).

Kolsti, Nancy. "Accents Speak Louder Than Words," *North Texan Online,* Online, Winter 2000. Available: http://www.unt.edu/northtexan/archives/w00/accents.html.

Kotter, John. *The General Managers* (New York: Free Press, 1982).

Kouzes, J. M. and B. Z. Posner. *The Leadership Challenge* (San Francisco: Jossey-Bass, 1995).

Kuntz, Gabriela. "My Spanish Standoff," *Newsweek*, May 4, 1998, 22.

Lahr, John. "Speaking across the Divide," *The New Yorker*, Jan. 27, 1997, 41–42.

Lam, Shyong K., and John Riedl. "Expressing My Inner Gnome: Appearance and Behavior in Virtual Worlds," *IEEE Computer*, July 2011.

Lancaster, Hal. "Learning to Manage in a Global Workplace" *The Wall Street Journal,* June 2, 1998, B1.

Lang, Daryl. "Their City in Ruins, Times-Picayune Photographers Keep Working." Online September 20, 2005. Available: http://www.pdnonline.com/pdn/newswire/mailto:dlang@pdnonline.com.

Langer, E. J. *Mindfulness* (Reading, MA: Addison-Wesley, 1989).

Lazarsfeld, Paul, and Robert K. Merton. "Friendship as a Social Process: A Substantive and Methodological Analysis," in Morroe Berger, Theodore Abel, and Charles Page (eds.), *Freedom and Control in Modern Society* (New York: Van Nostrand, 1954), 18–66.

Lencioni, John. *The Five Dysfunctions of a Team: A Leadership Fable* (San Francisco: Jossey-Bass, 2002).

Lenhart, Amanda, Rich Ling, Scott Campbell, and Kristen Purcell. "Teens and Mobile Phones," Pew Internet and American Life Project. Online, April 20, 2010. Available: http://pewinternet.org/Reports/2010/Teens-and-Mobile-Phones/Chapter-3/Sleeping-with-the-phone-on-or-near-the-bed.aspx.

Levinson, Wendy, Debra Roter, John Mullooly, Valerie Dull, and Richard Frankel. "Physician-Patient Communication: The Relationship with Malpractice Claims Among Primary Care Physicians and Surgeons," *Journal of the American Medical Association* (February 19, 1997), 553.

Levy, Becca. "Improving Memory in Old Age Through Implicit Self-Stereotyping," *Journal of Personality and Social Psychology*, 17(6), 1996, 1092–1107.

Liebeskind, Julia Porter, Amalya Lumerman, Oliver, Lynne Zucker, and Marilynn Brewer. "Social Networks, Learning, and Flexibility: Sourcing Scientific Knowledge in New Biotechnology Firms," *Organization Science*, Vol. 7, No. 4 (July–August, 1996), 428–443,

Lin, Nan, and Bonnie Erickson (eds.). *Social Capital: An International Research Program.* (New York: Oxford, 2008).

Lipnack, Jessica and Jeffrey Stamps. *Virtual Teams* (New York: Wiley, 1997).

Livingston, Gretchen. "The Latino Digital Divide: The Native Born versus The Foreign Born," Pew Hispanic Center. Online, July 28, 2010. Available: http://www.pewhispanic.org/2010/07/28/the-latino-digital-divide-the-native-born-versus-the-foreign-born/.

Lupsa, Cristian. "Do You Need a Web Publicist?" *The Christian Science Monitor*, November 29, 2006. Available: http://www.washingtonpost.com/wp-dyn/content/article/2007/03/06/AR2007030602705.html (accessed September 11, 2012).

Maddox, Amy. "Underneath We're All the Same," *Teaching Tolerance*, Spring 1995, 65.

Martin, André. *A CCL Research Report: Everyday Leadership* (Center for Creative Leadership, 2007) 5.

Martin, André. *The Changing Nature of Leadership*, Center for Creative Leadership, 2007, Available: http://www.ccl.org/leadership/pdf/research/natureleadership.pdf. (accessed October 12, 2013).

Massey, Douglas. "Latino Poverty Research: An Agenda for the 1990s," *Social Science Research Council Newsletter*, 47, March 1993, 7–8.

McBride, James. *The Color of Water: A Black Man's Tribute to His White Mother* (New York: Riverhead Trade, 2006).

McIntosh, Peggy. *White Privilege and Male Privilege* (Wellesley, MA: Wellesley College Center for Research on Women, 1988), 7.

McLuhan, Marshall. *The Mechanical Bride: Folklore of Industrial Man* (Boston: Beacon Press, 1967).

McPherson, Miller, Lynne Smith-Lovin, and James M. Cook. "Birds of a Feather: Homophily in Social Networks," *Annual Review of Sociology,* 27, 2001, 415–44.

Merkle Inc. "View from the Digital Inbox 2011." Available: http://www.ionrognerud.com/docs/Merkle_Digital_Inbox_2011.pdf. (accessed September 11, 2012).

Merton, Robert. "Discrimination and the American Creed," in *Sociological Ambivalence and Other Essays* (New York: Free Press, 1976).

Michael, Walt. Letter to the author, Jan. 9, 1998.

Microsoft. "A Vision and Strategy for the Future." Available: http://www.microsoft.com/about/en/xm/importedcontent/about/diversity/en/us/vision.aspx (accessed 4/11/13).

Migration Policy Institute. "ELL Information Center Fact Sheet Series," No. 1, 2010.

Migration Policy Institute. "LEP Data Brief," Dec., 2011.

Milano, Philip and Larry Lane. *Why Do White People Smell Like Wet Dogs When They Come Out of the Rain?* (Orlando Park, FL: Y Forum, 1999), 2, 3.

Mitchell, Robert. "The Virtual Office," *Computerworld,* January 8, 2007.

Montagu, Ashley. *Man's Most Dangerous Myth: The Fallacy of Race* (Cleveland, OH: World Publishing, 1964).

Montaigne, Michel de. "Of the Resemblance of Children to Fathers," *The Essays,* (Simon Millanges, Bordeaux, 1580), Ch. 37.

Monticue, Cynthia. "Inclusion Is Key to Productive Workforce," *USC News.* Online, February 24, 2005. Available: http://www.usc.edu/uscnews/stories/11025.html.

Moody, Mia. "New Media, Same Stereotypes: An Analysis of Social Media Depictions of President Barack Obama and Michelle Obama," *The Journal of New Media and Culture,* Volume 8, Issue 1, Summer, 2012.

"More International Students Enroll at U.S. Campuses," *Huff Post College.* Online, November 8, 2012. Available: http://www.huffingtonpost.com/2011/11/14/more-international-studen_0_n_1092602.html.

Morello, Carol and Dan Keating. "Census Confirms Skyrocketing Hispanic, Asian Growth in U.S., *The Washington Post,* March 25, 2011, A17.

Morin, Richard. "Needed: A Hillbilly Anti-Defamation League," *The Washington Post,* May 4, 1997, C5.

Morin, Richard and Michael Cottman. "Most Black Men Profiled by Police, Poll Says," washingtonpost.com. Online, June 21, 2001. Available: http://www.washingtonpost.com/ac2/wp-dyn?pagename=article&node=&contentId=A30338-2001Jun21&notFound=true.

Morrison, Toni. *Playing in the Dark* (Cambridge, Mass.: Harvard University Press, 1992).

Murphy, Mark. "Rocker a 'Prisoner,' At Least When It Comes to Treatment." Online Jan. 11, 2000. Available: http://cbs.sportsline.com/u/ce/multi/0,1329,1878900_52,00.html.

Murphy, Michael. "Social Networking and Disability," *Quest.* Online, March 31, 2011. Available: http://quest.mda.org/article/social-networking-and-disability.

Nakamura, Lisa. *Cybertypes: Race, Ethnicity, and Identity on the Internet* (New York: Routledge, 2002).

Nakamura, Lisa. "Race In/For Cyberspace: Identity Tourism and Racial Passing on the Internet." Available: http://www.humanities.uci.edu/mposter/syllabi/readings/nakamura.html (accessed January 1, 2013).

National Advisory Commission on Civil Disorders. *Report of the National Advisory Commission on Civil Disorders* (New York: Bantam, 1968).

National Crime Prevention Council. "Teens and Cyberbullying." Online, February 28, 2007. Available: http://www.ncpc.org/resources/files/pdf/bullying/Teens%20and%20Cyberbullying%20Research%20Study.pdf.

"The Nation: Students," *The Chronicle of Higher Education Almanac,* Sept. 1, 2000, 24+.

Nauert, Rick. "Social Networking for Jobs May Add to Income Inequality." Online, July 25, 2012. Available: http://psychcentral.com/news/2012/07/25/social-networking-for-jobs-may-add-to-income-inequality/42207.html.

Nieto, Sonia. *Affirming Diversity: The Sociopolitical Context of Multicultural Education* (White Plains., NY: Longman, 1996).

Norris, Donald and Michael Dolence. *Transforming Higher Education: A Vision for Learning in the 21ˢᵗ Century* (Ann Arbor, MI: Society for College and University Planning, 1995).

O'Brien, Laurie T., Glenn Adams, and Jessica C. Nelson. "Perceptions of Racism in the Aftermath of Hurricane Katrina: A Survey of Students Living in New Orleans," Unpublished manuscript, 2006.

O'Connell, Patricia. "How Companies Develop Great Leaders." Online, February 16, 2010. Available: http://www.businessweek.com/stories/2010-02-16/how-companies-develop-great-leadersbusinessweek-business-news-stock-market-and-financial-advice.

Obama, Barack. *Dreams from My Father* (New York: Three Rivers Press, 2004), 171–172.

Office Team. "Fitting In, Standing Out, and Building Remarkable Work Teams, 2007. Available: http://officeteam.rhi.mediaroom.com/index.php?s=260&item=199.

Okie, Susan. "Teaching Hospitals How to Listen," *The Washington Post,* 12/12/06, F1.

Olson, C. B. "The Influence of Context on Gender Differences in Performance Attributions: Further Evidence of a 'Feminine Modesty' Effect," paper presented at the annual meeting of the Western Psychological Association, San Francisco, CA, 1988.

Page, Susan and Maria Puente. "Poll Shows Racial Divide on Storm Response," *USA Today.* Online, September 8, 2005. Available: http://www.usatoday.com/news/nation/2005-09-12-katrina-poll_x.htm.

Pagonis, William. "Leadership in a Combat Zone," *Harvard Business Review,* Dec. 2001, 107–116.

Parillo, Vincent N. *Diversity in America* (Thousand Oaks, CA: Pine Forge Press, 1996), 65.

Pascale, R. T. *Managing on the Edge: How the Smartest Companies Use Conflict to Stay Ahead* (New York: Simon & Schuster, 1990).

Pascarella, Ernest, Marcia Edison, Amaury Nora, Linda S. Hagedorn, and Patrick Terenzini. "Influences on Students' Openness to Diversity and Challenge in the First Year of College," *The Journal of Higher Education,* Vol. 67, No. 2; Mar.–Apr. 1, 1996.

Pascarella, Ernest, and Patrick Terenzini. "Influences on Students' Openness to Diversity and Challenge in the Second and Third Years of College," *The Journal of Higher Education*, Vol. 72, No. 2, Mar.–Apr. 2, 2001.

"Peles Castle: A Jewel of the Romanian Cultural Heritage." Online, Nov. 28, 2010. Available: http://www.chain.to/?m3=23653.

"Perceptions of Poverty: A New Report." Online, May 16, 2012. Available: http://blog.salvationarmyusa.org/2012/05/16/perceptions-of-poverty/.

Peter D. Hart Research Associates, Inc. *How Should Colleges Prepare Students to Succeed in Today's Global Economy?* (Washington, DC, December 28, 2006).

Pew Forum on Religion and Public Life. "Public Remains Conflicted Over Islam." Online, August 24, 2010. Available: http://www.pewforum.org/Muslim/Public-Remains-Conflicted-Over-Islam.aspx.

Pew Forum on Religion and Public Life. "Religious Affiliation: Summary of Key Findings." Online, June 23, 2008. Available: http://religions.pewforum.org/reports.

Pew Research Center. "Blacks Upbeat About Black Progress, Prospects." Online, January 12, 2010. Available: http://www.people-press.org/2010/01/12/blacks-upbeat-about-black-progress-prospects/.

Pew Research Center. "Do Blacks and Hispanics Get Along?", January 31, 2008, Available: http://www.pewsocialtrends.org/2008/01/31/do-blacks-and-hispanics-get-along/ (accessed June 18, 2013).

Pew Research Center. "How Young People View Their Lives, Futures, and Politics," January 9, 2007, 38.

Pew Research Center. "Millennials: Confident. Connected. Open to Change." Online, February 24, 2010. Available: http://www.pewsocialtrends.org/2010/02/24/millennials-confident-connected-open-to-change/.

Pew Research Center. "Optimism About Black Progress Declines." Online, November 13, 2007. Available: http://www.pewsocialtrends.org/2007/11/13/blacks-see-growing-values-gap-between-poor-and-middle-class/.

Pew Research Center's Internet and American Life Project. "Social Networking Sites and Our Lives: Summary of Findings." Available: http://pewinternet.org/Reports/2011/Technology-and-social-networks/Summary.aspx (accessed September 13, 2012).

Pew Research Global Attitude Project. "The American-Western European Values Gap." Online, Nov. 17, 2011. Available: http://www.pewglobal.org/2011/11/17/the-american-western-european-values-gap/.

Pew Research Report. *A Portrait of Generation Next. Confident. Connected. Open to Change*, February, 2010, Chapter One, 6.

Pinchin, Jane. "Let Them Go–Because 60 Seconds of World News Is Not Enough," *The Colgate Scene*, March 2002.

Pitino, Rick and Bill Reynolds. *Learn to Succeed* (New York: Broadway Books, 2000).

Pitts, Leonard Jr. "It's Time for Men to Act Like Men," *The Baltimore Sun,* July 16, 2001, 7A.

Pitts, Leonard Jr. "Watching Whites Struggle to Understand Their Whiteness," *The Baltimore Sun,* Apr. 21, 1997, 9A.

"Poll Reveals Generational Gap in Workplace Training Programs," *Workplace Options News.* Online, July 11, 2011. Available: http://www.workplaceoptions.com/news/press-releases/press-release.asp?id=AC3DEC48BC39412B93CF&title=%20Poll%20Reveals%20Generational%20Gap%20in%20Workplace%20Training%20Programs.

Portés, Alejandro, and Ruben Rumbaut. *Immigrant America* (Berkeley: University of California Press, 1990).

Powers, William. *Hamlet's Blackberry* (New York, Harper, 2010).

Prensky, Marc. "Digital Natives, Digital Immigrants." Online, 2001. Available: http://www.marcprensky.com/writing/Prensky%20-%20Digital%20Natives,%20Digital%20Immigrants%20-%20Part1.pdf.

"Preserving a Language and Tribal History," *AARP Bulletin,* November, 2006, 8.

Price, S. L. "The Indian Wars." *Sports Illustrated,* March 4, 2002, 67–72.

Proctor, Samuel D. and William D. Watley. *Sermons from the Black Pulpit* (Valley Forge, PA: Judson Press, 1984).

Putnam, Robert. "*E Pluribus Unum*: Diversity and Community in the Twenty-First Century," *Scandanavian Political Studies*, Vol. 30, No. 2, 2007, 137–174.

"Race–The Power of an Illusion," California Newsreel, 2003, Available: http://www.pbs.org/race/000_About/002_05-godeeper.htm.

Rainer, Thom and Jess Rainer. *The Millennials* (Nashville, TN: B & H Books, 2010).

Rasmussen, Karen. "Gaining Perspective on Global Education," *ASCD (Association for Supervision and Curriculum Development) Curriculum Update,* Summer 1998, 3.

Raspberry, William (from a lecture at Kansas State University). *Vital Speeches of the Day,* June 1, 1995, 493–496.

Reeves, Terrance and Claudette Bennett. "The Asian and Pacific Islander Population in the United States: March 2002," *Current Population Reports,* May, 2003.

Reid, Alice. "Mosque's Children Await Playground," *The Washington Post,* Nov. 22, 1998, B4.

Reuters. "Time Magazine's 'Person of the Year' Is . . . You," NBCNews.com. Online, Dec. 17, 2006. Available: http://www.nbcnews.com/id/16242528/#.UU8la0xEJcY.

Reuters. "Victims by Country." Online, Sept. 20, 2001. Available: http://www.cnn.com/SPECIALS/2001/trade.center/interactive/victims.map/mpa.exclude.htmlrlUntitled.

Rice, Faye. "How to Make Diversity Pay," *Fortune,* Aug. 8, 1994, 79.

Right Management Manpower Group, "Most Expect to Get New Job by Networking." Online, January 22, 2013. Available: http://www.right.com/news-and-events/press-releases/2013-press-releases/item24727.aspx.

Riley, Dorothy W. (ed.) *My Soul Looks Back, 'Less I Forget: A Collection of Quotations by People of Color* (New York: Harper Collins, 1995).

Ritzer, George. *The McDonaldization of Society* (Thousand Oaks, CA: Pine Forge Press, 2000).

Robert Half Management Resources. "CFOs Seek Soft Skills," *SmartPros.* Online, December 19, 2007. Available: http://accounting.smartpros.com/x60128.xml.

Roberts, Sam. "in Name Count, Garcias Are Catching Up to Joneses." Online November 17, 2007. Available: http://www.nytimes.com/2007/11/17/us/17surnames.html?ci-5088&cn-9449f09cf7ac21c.

Robins, Lynne, Joseph Fantone, Julica Hermann, Gwen Alexander, and Andrew Zweifler. "Improving Cultural Awareness and Sensitivity Training in Medical School," *Academic Medicine*, 73(10), October Supplement, 1998.

Rodriguez, Clara. "Latina America," *Latina*, July 2001, 87.

Rodriguez, Richard. "Se Habla Espanol." Online, May 9, 2000. Available: http://www.pbs.org/newshour/essays/may00/rodriguez_5-9 .htmlrl.

Rosenstein, Bruce. *Living in More Than One World: How Peter Drucker's Wisdom Can Inspire and Transform Your Life* (San Francisco, CA: Berrett-Koehler, 2009).

Rothman, Wilson. "For the Disabled, Just Getting Online Is a Struggle," NBCNews.com TECH. Available: http://www.nbcnews.com/technology/ technolog/disabled-just-getting-online-struggle-125501 (accessed September 29, 2012).

Royster, Deirdre. *Race and the Invisible Hand* (Berkeley, CA: University of California Press, 2003).

Rubinstein, Moshe. *Patterns of Problem Solving* (Englewood Cliffs, NJ: Prentice Hall, 1975).

Ryan, Michelle, Michael Schmitt, and Manuela Barreto (eds.). *The Glass Ceiling in the 21ˢᵗ Century: Understand Barriers to Gender Equality* (Washington, DC: American Psychological Association, 2009), 1.

Sack, Kevin and Janet Elder. "Poll Finds Optimistic Outlook But Enduring Racial Division," *The New York Times on the Web*. Online, July 11, 2000. Available: http://www.nytimes.com/library/national/race/071100sack-poll.html.

Sacks, Oliver. *Seeing Voices: A Journey into the World of the Deaf* (Berkeley, CA: University of California Press, 1989), 127.

Sauceda, Enedelia. "Ethnic Identity, Perceptions of Racial Microaggressions, and Perceptions of University Environment as Predictors of Coping Among Latino(a) Graduate Students." Ph.D. Dissertation, Oklahoma State University, Stillwater Oklahoma, 2009.

Schradie, Jen. "The Digital Production Gap: The Digital Divide and Web 2.0 Collide," *Poetics*, Vol. 39, Issue 2, April 2011, 145–168.

Sedgwick, John. *Rich Kids* (New York: William Morrow, 1985).

Seifter, Harry and Peter Economy. *Leadership Ensemble: Lessons in Collaborative Management from the World's Only Conductorless Orchestra* (New York: Times Books, 2001).

Shapiro, Bill. "Speakers Call for Greater Effort in Combating Racism," *American Psychological Association Monitor*, 28(10), Oct. 1997, 39.

"Shashi Bellamkonda–YouTube." Online, March 15, 2012. Available: http://www.youtube.com/watch?v=R-tLjMLIF58.

Shatel, Tom. "The Unknown Barry Switzer," *Chicago Tribune Sports*. Online, December 14, 1986. Available: http://articles.chicagotribune .com/1986-12-14/sports/8604030680_1_big-eight-coach-aren-t-many-coaches-oklahoma.

Shipler, David. *A Country of Strangers* (New York: Alfred A. Knopf, 1997).

Shipley, Amy, "A Successful Science Project," *The Washington Post*, June 29, 1999, D1+.

Shkolnikova, Svetlana. "Weight Discrimination Could Be As Common As Racial Bias," *USA Today*. Online, May 21, 2008. Available: http://usatoday30.usatoday.com/news/health/weightloss/2008-05-20-overweight-bias_N.htm.

Silver, Sherry. "Advice for Adjusting to the World of Work," *Washington Post Advertising Supplement*, Oct. 19, 1997, 60, 65.

Silver, Sheryl. "New Grads: Make the Most of Your First Job," *The Washington Post High Tech Horizons*, Aug. 3, 1997, M19.

Simpson, Ian. "U.S. Race Bias Suits on the Rise, Putting Companies on the Defensive." Online, July 14, 2000. Available: http://news.excite .com/news/r/000714/13/economy-race-suits2.

Singleton, Glenn. *Courageous Conversations About Race: A Field Guide for Achieving Equity in Schools* (Newbury Park, CA: Corwin, 2005).

Slepper, Jim. "Liberal Racism," *The New Democrat*, July/Aug. 1997, 8.

Smedley, Brian, Adrienne Stith, and Alan Nelson (eds.). *Unequal Treatment: Confronting Racial and Ethnic Disparities in Health Care* (Washington, DC: National Academies Press, 2002).

Sobel, Andrew. "The Beatles Principles," *Strategy and Business*. Online, Feb. 28, 2006. Available: http://www.strategy-business.com/ article/06104?gko=8e481.

Soukhanov, Anne. *Encarta. World English Dictionary* (New York: St. Martin's Press, 1999).

Southern Poverty Law Center. "Active U.S. Hate Groups in the United States in 2012," *Intelligence Report*, Spring, 2013."

Sproull, Lee and Sara Kiesler. *Connections: New Ways of Working in the Networked Organization* (Cambridge, MA: MIT Press, 1991).

Steele, Claude. "Twenty-First Century Program and Stereotype Vulnerability," unpublished study and program, Stanford University, Stanford, CA, 1995.

"Steve Jobs Used Wayne Gretzky As Inspiration," *Los Angeles Times - Sports Now*. Online, Oct. 6, 2011. Available: http://latimesblogs.latimes. com/sports_blog/2011/10/steve-jobs-used-wayne-gretzky-as-inspiration.html.

Strait, George. "Health Care's Racial Divide." Online, March 7, 1999. Available: http://more.abcnews.go.com/sections/living/DailyNews/racial_ healthcare990224.html

Study Circles Resource Center. *Toward a More Perfect Union in an Age of Diversity*, 1997, 18.

Sue, Derald W. *Microaggressions in Everyday Life* (Hoboken, New Jersey: John Wiley and Sons, 2010).

Sue, Derald W., Christina M. Capodilupo, Gina C. Torino, Jennifer M. Bucceri, Aisha M. B. Holder, Kevin L. Nadal, and Marta Esquilin, "Racial Microaggressions in Everyday Life: Implications for Clinical Practice," *American Psychologist*, vol. 62 no. 4, May-Jun 2007, 271–286.

Surowiecki, James. *The Wisdom of Crowds* (Harpswell, ME: Anchor Publishers, 2005).

"Survey Reveals Global Employees Not Prepared for Virtual Teamwork." Online, May 4, 2012. Available: http://rw-3.com/2012/05/survey- reveals-global-employees-not-prepared-for-virtual-teamwork/.

Takaki, Ronald. *A Different Mirror. A History of Multicultural America* (Boston: Little, Brown, 1993).

Tan, Cheryl. "For College Students, Degrees of Ethnicity," *The Washington Post*, Sept. 3, 1996, B1.

Tannen, Deborah. *The Argument Culture: Moving from Debate to Dialogue* (New York: Random House, 1998).

Tannen, Deborah. *You Just Don't Understand: Men and Women in Conversation* (New York: William Morrow, 1990); *Talking from 9 to 5: How Women's and Men's Conversational Styles Affect Who Gets Heard, Who Gets Credit, and What Gets Done at Work* (New York: William Morrow, 1994); *That's Not What I Meant* (New York: Ballantine Books, 1992).

Tapia, Andrés and Jonathan Kaufman. "Diversity Case In Point: A Company Where People With Autism Are The Norm." Online, April 17, 2012. Available: http://www.diversitybestpractices.com/news-articles/diversity-case-point-company-where-people-autism-are-norm.

Tatum, Beverly. *Why Are All the Black Kids Sitting Together in the Cafeteria?* (New York: Harper Collins, 1997).

Taylor, Paul and D'Vera Cohn. "A Milestone En Route to a Majority Minority Nation." Online, November 7. 2012. Available: http://www.pewsocialtrends.org/2012/11/07/a-milestone-en-route-to-a-majority-minority-nation/.

Taylor, T. S. "What's In A Name? Bias, Sometimes," *Chicago Tribune*, Dec. 29, 2002.

Terkel, Studs. *Race: How Blacks and Whites Feel about the American Obsession* (New York: New Press, 1992), 124.

The Color of Fear (video) (Oakland, CA: Stir Fry Productions, 1994).

The University of Georgia Terry College of Business, "News Release: Hispanic Consumer Market In The U.S. Is Larger Than The Entire Economies of All But 13 Countries In The World." Online, May 1, 2012. Available: http://www.strategy-business.com/article/06104?gko=8e481.

Thomas, Roosevelt. *Beyond Race and Gender: Unleashing the Power of Your Total Work Force by Managing Diversity* (New York: American Management Association, 1991).

Toossi, Mitra. "A New Look at Long-Term Labor Force Projections to 2050," *Monthly Labor Review*, November 2006, 19–39.

Tully, Sharon. "Why to Go for Stretch Targets," *Fortune*, Nov. 14, 1994, 145–158.

Tutu, Desmond Mpilo. *No Future Without Forgiveness* (New York: Doubleday, 1999).

U.S. Bureau of Labor Statistics. Current Population Survey Annual Averages, Projections – M. Tossi, "A New Look at Long-Term Labor Force Projections to 2050," *Monthly Labor Review*, Nov. 2006, 19–39.

U.S. Bureau of the Census. "Frequently Occurring Surnames From Census 2010." Available: https://census.socrata.com/dataset/Frequently-Occurring-Surnames-from-Census-2010/uqzf-9yai (accessed Oct. 7, 2013).

U.S. Bureau of the Census. *Historical Statistics of the United States, Part II*, Series Z 20–132 (Washington, DC: U.S. Government Printing Office, 1976).

U.S. Bureau of the Census. *Projections of the U.S. by Age, Sex, Race, and Hispanic Origin 1993–2050* (Washington, DC: U.S. Government Printing Office).

U.S. Census Bureau. "U.S. Census Bureau Projections Show a Slower Growing, Older, More Diverse Nation a Half Century from Now." Online, Dec. 12, 2012. Available: http://www.reuters.com/article/2012/12/12/idUS200526+12-Dec-2012+PRN20121212.

U. S. Department of Commerce. "Closing the Digital Divide for Native Nations and Communities." Online, April 12, 2011. Available: http://www.ntia.doc.gov/blog/2011/closing-digital-divide-focus-native-american-communities.

U.S. Department of Education–Office of English Language Acquisition. "The Growing Numbers of Limited English Proficient Students 1994/95-2004/05." Online 2008. Available: http://www.ed.gov/about/offices/list/oela/index.html.

Van Ausdale, Debra and Joe R. Feagin. *The First R: How Children Learn Race and Racism* (Lanham MD: Rowman and Littlefield, 2001).

Von Oech, Roger. *A Kick in the Seat of the Pants* (New York: Harper & Row, 1986), 5–21.

Walker, Rebecca. *Black, White, and Jewish: Autobiography of a Shifting Self* (New York: Riverhead Books, 2002).

Washington, Jesse. "For Minorities, New 'Digital Divide Seen," *USA Today*. Online, Jan. 10, 2011. Available: www.usatoday.com/tech/news/2011-01-10-minorities-online_N.htm.

Washington Post-Kaiser Family Foundation-Harvard University Poll, Cecilia Kang and Krissah Thompson, "Hispanics on Web Less Than Others," *The Washington Post*. Online Feb. 22, 2011. Available: http://www.washingtonpost.com/wpdyn/content/article/2011/02/22/AR2011022207470.html.

Wax, Emily. "The Fabric of Their Faith," *The Washington Post*, May 19, 2002, C1.

Weinstein, Margery. "Conquering Conflict," *Training*, June, 2007, 56–57.

Wenger, Etienne, Richard McDermott, and William M. Snyder. *Cultivating Communities of Practice* (Boston: Harvard Business School Press, 2003).

West, Cornel. *Race Matters* (New York: Random House, 1993).

Whiting, Robert, *You've Gotta Have Wa,* (New York: Vintage, 2009).

"Why No One Under 30 Answers Your Voicemail," *DiversityInc.*, September/October 2010, 47.

Wilson, Angus. *The Strange Ride of Rudyard Kipling: His Life and Works* (New York: Viking Press, 1978), 290.

Winograd, Morley and Michael Hais. "Service, Inclusion Are Paths to Salvation for Religion in the Millennial Era." Online, Oct. 25, 2012. Available: http://www.nationaljournal.com/thenextamerica/demographics/opinion-service-inclusion-are-paths-to-salvation-for-religion-in-the-millennial-era-20121025).

"World Map of Social Networks." Online January, 16, 2012. Available: themoscownews.com/infographics/20120116/189372325.htm/.

Wray, Richard. "Deepwater Horizon Oil Spill: BP Gaffes in Full," The Guardian. Online, July 27, 2010. Available: http://www.guardian.co.uk/business/2010/jul/27/deepwater-horizon-oil-spill-bp-gaffes

X, Malcolm. *The Autobiography of Malcolm X* (New York: Ballantine Books, 1965).

Yardley, Jonathan. "Coping with History," *The Washington Post: Book World,* July 6, 1997, 3.

"You Have To Love People: The Shashi Bellamkonda Interview." Online, December 23, 2011. Available: http://www.firebellymarketing.com/2011/12/love-people-shashi-bellamkonda-interview.html.

Young, Whitney. *To Be Equal* (New York: McGraw-Hill, 1966).

Zangwill, Israel. *The Melting Pot* (New York: The Jewish Publication Society of America, 1909).

Zickuhr, Kathryn, and Aaron Smith. "Digital Differences," Pew Internet. Available: http://www.pewinternet.org/Reports/2012/Digital-differences.aspx.

Zunikoff, Jennifer Rudick, conversation with the author, June 4, 2002.

Index

Accents, 58
Accommodation Without Assimilation (Gibson), 19
Active listening, 116, 145, 146, 208, 211
Adaptability
    as benefit of diversity consciousness, 49
    in leadership, 223
    in success at work, 45–46
Addressing people, 145
Adolph Coors, 147
Adoption, 145
Affirming Diversity (Nieto), 40
African-Americans. *See* Blacks
Age
    in digital divide, 172
    discrimination based on, 55, 110
Ageism, 110
Agriculture, U.S. Department of, 56
Airline industry, teamwork in, 198
Allport, Gordon, 22, 72
Alves, Julio, 21
AMA. *See* American Management Association
American, definition of, 18
American Management Association (AMA), 139
Angelou, Maya, 135
Anger, 87
Apologies, 128
Arbitration, 210
Argument Culture, The (Tannen), 208
Aronson, Elliot, 194
ASDs. *See* Autism spectrum disorders
Ashe, Arthur, 107
Asians
    assimilation of, 19
    conflict, view of, 207
    demographic changes among, 5
    eye contact, 134
    marketing to, 46
    prejudice against, 73
    silence among, 141
    "small talk" before business,134
    workplace biases against, 50
    "yes" answers by, 15, 134
Asians in America (Center for Work-Life Policy), 50
Assimilation, 18–20
Assuming diversity, 165
Asynchronous learning, 131
AT&T, 49
Attractiveness stereotype, 69
Authoritarian leaders, 228
Autism, 37, 177, 239–240, 241–242
Autism spectrum disorders (ASDs), 239–240
Autistic Brain, The (Grandin), 242
Avatars, 171
Avoidance
    in conflict management, 209
    uncertainty, 230–231
Axtell, Roger, 126–127

Baby Boomers, 254
Bamboo ceiling, 50
Bandura, Albert, 201
Banfe, Brett, 116
Bangladesh, digital divide in, 175
Bank of America, 56
Barak, Mor, 240
Barnett, Martha, 245
Barriers to communication, 140–141

Barriers to success, 62–83
    dealing with, 41–42, 83–89
    discrimination as, 80–83
    ethnocentrism as, 66–68
    limited perceptions as, 63–65
    personal, 62
    prejudice as, 72–76
    prejudice plus power as, 77–80
    social, 62
    stereotypes as, 68–72
Barriers to teamwork, 204–205
Baseball, 104
Basic Black (Bates and Hudson), 87
Basketball, 251–252
Bates, Karen, 87
Battles, choosing, 87, 209
Beatles, The, 46
Beatty, Richard, 138
Becker, James, 248
Beginner's mind, 64
Behavioral theories of leadership, 227
Being yourself, 42
Beliefs, perceptions influenced by, 64
Bell, Ella, 155
Bellamkonda, Shashi, 174
Beyond Race and Gender (Thomas), 21
Biases
    as barrier to communication, 140
    critical thinking and, 115
    in healthcare, 54–55
    in leadership theories, 228
    self-monitoring of, 225
    workplace, costs of, 49–50
Bilingual individuals, 129
Binary thinking, 250
Bingham, Raymond, 133
Birdwhistell, Ray, 127
Black, White, and Jewish (Walker), 5
Black Like Me (Griffin), 109
Black Muslims, 106
Blacks/African-Americans
    barriers to success of, 62
    biases regarding names of, 225
    demographic changes among, 4–5
    double consciousness of, 109
    marketing to, 46
    Muslim, 106
    prejudice against (*See* racism)
    social inequality and, 112–113
    stereotypes of, 71
    values of, 23
    YouTube and, 99
Blair, Judy, 195
Blanchard, Ken, 228
Blatant discrimination, 81–82
Blended learning, 51
Blogs
    definition of, 153
    microaggressions in, 176–177
Blue eyes and brown eyes experiment, 76
Body language, 126–127
    in conflict management, 211
    cultural specificity of, 127
Bogardus, Emory, 106
Bonding, 168–169
Born leaders, 227
Box, James, 115

BP, 56
Bradley, Bill, 251
Bridging, 168–169
British Petroleum (BP), 56
Britt, Donna, 244
Brontë, Charlotte, 120
Burstein, David, 253–254
Burton, John, 206
Bush, George W., 127

Cairo, Peter, 224
California, age discrimination in, 55
Cannadine, David, 250
Capital
    human, 241
    social, 167–168
Carnegie, Andrew, 198
Carson, Benjamin, 27
Cell phones, in social networking, 154–155
Census, U.S., 4–7, 246
Center for Creative Leadership, 220, 233, 234, 235
Center for Work-Life Policy, 50
Change
    in conflict management, 212
    constancy of, 255
    real, 28
Changing Race (Rodríguez), 7
China, guanxi in, 168
Choi, S., 164
Cho Seung-Hui, 73
Chua, Roy, 182
Churches, racial segregation in, 13
Citigroup, 134
Clans, 30
Class. *See* Social class
Classism, 113
Clementi, Tyler, 177
Clinton, Bill, 251
Cognitive flexibility, 129
Cohort effect, 252
Collaboration. *See also* Teamwork
    in conflict management, 210
    in leadership, 234
    in social networking, 180
Collective action, 183
Collective efficacy, 201
Collective intelligence, 180
Collectivism, in leadership, 229
Color of Fear, The (movie), 25
Color of Water, The (McBride), 5
Common ground, finding, 250–252
Common Ground program, 250, 251
Common sense, 26, 64
Communication, 125–150
    barriers to, 140–141
    as benefit of diversity consciousness, 49
    through body language, 126–127
    in conflict management, 208
    culture and, 126–129
    definition of, 126
    developing diversity consciousness and, 132–138
    in difficult dialogues, 143–145
    electronic, 129–131
    through gestures, 126–127, 140–141
    importance of, 138–139
    inclusiveness in, 131, 145–147, 223–224